Complete Guide To Modern Rifles

By Gene Gangarosa Jr.

Stoeger Publishing Company

Title: *Complete Guide To Modern Rifles*
Editor: *William S. Jarrett*
Cover Art Design: *Ray Wells*
Book Design And Layout: *Lesley A. Notorangelo/DSS*
Project Manager: *Dominick S. Sorrentino*
Electronic Imaging: *Lesley A. Notorangelo/DSS*

Published by Stoeger Publishing Company
5 Mansard Court
Wayne, New Jersey 07470

ISBN: 0-88317-221-6
Library of Congress Catalog Card No.: 99-072950
Manufactured in the United States of America

Distributed to the book trade and to the sporting goods trade by Stoeger Industries, 5 Mansard Court, Wayne, New Jersey 07470

In Canada, distributed to the book trade and to the sporting goods trade by Stoeger Canada, Ltd., 1801 Wentworth Street, Unit 16, Whitby, Ontario L1N 8R6.

Introduction

This book, *Complete Guide to Modern Rifles*, continues the story begun in *Complete Guide to Classic Rifles*, carrying it forward to 69 of the most important modern rifle designs, all divided into five parts: Single-Shot Rifles; Bolt-Action Rifles; Lever-Action Rifles; Pump-Action Rifles; and Self-Loading Rifles. Two appendices discuss the subject of rifle sights and how to attach telescopic sights to various rifles.

Each entry begins with information about the origin, use and manufacturing history of the rifle in question, followed by information concerning each rifle's operating features and characteristics. Test-firing results come next, with an evaluation of each rifle's strong and weak points. A specifications table ends each entry. The emphasis throughout is on the practical use of each rifle and how they perform in their intended roles.

I would like to thank the many people who helped me finish *Complete Guide to Modern Rifles.* As always, my greatest thanks go to my beloved family. An author's wife and children should be given special rewards! I also acknowledge with gratitude the many manufacturers who kindly provided me with test rifles and ammunition for inclusion in this book. Finally, Stoeger Publication's editorial team has done it again, working long and hard to make this book a reality, and to them I also give many thanks.

About The Author

Gene Gangarosa Jr., a teacher and technical writer, lives in Florida with his wife and two children. His long association with firearms of all kinds began with his service in the U.S. Navy as a helicopter rescue crewman operating in the Pacific Ocean. Since 1988, he has written more than 200 articles about firearms for such publications as *Shooter's Bible, Guns, Guns & Ammo, Gun World, Combat Handguns, Petersen's Handguns, Sportsman's Gun Annual* and *Handgun Testfire.*

Gangarosa is also the author of several books, all published by Stoeger Publishing Company: ***P38 Automatic Pistol: The First 50 Years, Modern Beretta Firearms, FN/Browning: Armorer to the World, The Walther Handgun Story, Complete Guide to Classic Handguns and Complete Guide to Service Handguns.*** His next work, ***Complete Guide to Modern Rifles*** (a companion volume to ***Complete Guide to Classic Rifles***) will be published soon by Stoeger Publishing.

TABLE OF CONTENTS

Table Of Contents (cont.)

Part III: Modern Lever-Action Rifles

Part IV: Modern Pump-Action Rifles

Part V: Modern Self-Loading Rifles

TABLE OF CONTENTS (cont.)

Part I:

Modern Single-Shot Rifles

For hundreds of years, single-shot firearms reigned almost completely unopposed, both on the battlefield and during the hunt. Not until America's Civil War did repeating rifles (lever-action types to begin with) challenge the dominance of the single-shot rifle. For two decades after our Civil War, single-shot rifles continued to arm most of the world's armed forces. Only after improved bolt-action repeating rifles came on the scene starting in the late 1880s were the days of the single-shot rifle as a front-line military arm numbered.

While the single-shot rifle may have ended as a military weapon, it remained popular for hunting and target shooting and for training purposes. The justification for this continuing popularity was obvious: if you know you have only one shot, the more you will exert every effort to make it count. By contrast, a repeating firearm, with its multiple shots, might not exert the same degree of concentration needed for that first shot to hit its mark. A corollary to this argument is that somehow the single-shot hunting rifle is more "sporting." It gives the game animal a better chance of escaping should the hunter miss that first and only shot. On the other hand, if the quarry is an aggressive species--a Cape buffalo, perhaps, or a grizzly bear--then that successful first shot become even more critical. Actually, a shooter with determination can develop good discipline with any weapon, from a single-shot rifle to a machine gun, dedicating maximum effort to make every shot count. Sloppy shooting with any repeating rifle—whether lever-action, bolt-action, slide action or self-loading—may often occur with an undisciplined or novice shooter, but experienced shooters will make sure the first shot counts, whatever type of rifle they happen to use.

One argument in favor of the superior accuracy of the single-shot rifle for hunting or target shooting is that, compared to repeating rifles in the same caliber, it tends to be lighter and better balanced. Moreover, its action or firing mechanism is usually more rigid, requiring fewer moving parts to function. Whatever the reason, the lure of the single-shot rifle for hunting and target shooting remains strong. Present-day manufacturers still offer various reproductions of famous hunting, target-shooting and military arms of the 19th century, along with single-shot rifles of current design.

The reasoning behind the single-shot rifle as a training tool for teaching novice shooters is far more straightforward and convincing than the debate over its merits as a hunting rifle. The beginner must first learn the fundamentals of safe gun handling—how to hold the rifle, how to align the sight, how to control the trigger—all of which takes time to master. Other techniques involved in developing fire discipline should wait until the inexperienced shooter has mastered these four basic skills. Cautions against excessive bullet expenditure have more merit in this training scenario than they do when offered as a reason to hunt with a single-shot rifle instead of a repeating rifle.

Another reason for the enduring popularity of single-shot rifles is the resurgent interest in black-powder and muzzleloading rifles, all of which are by definition single-shot models. While such rifles have a certain value for military re-enactors, collectors and even hunters, we will consider only the breech-loading cartridge arms, which still leaves a variety of interesting single-shot rifles to consider, beginning with...

Browning Model 1885

Browning's 1885 is a reproduction of the first design bought by Winchester from John M. Browning. It did, in fact, launch Browning on a career that brought him international fame and recognition. Mechanically, the Model 1885 is an excellent single-shot design and is available in two basic versions: the so-called *High Wall* for larger calibers (such as .30-06) and *Low Wall* for smaller calibers up to .243 Winchester (see the specifications table below for a complete listing of calibers). Within the High Wall category Browning markets three sub-variations: the *Classic Hunter* with adjustable buckhorn rear sight, the *Traditional Hunter* with tang-mounted peep (aperture) rear sight, and the *BPCR* model with vernier tang peep sight, plus three aperture adjustments and a hooded front sight with built-in spirit level. All Browning Model 1885 rifles are made in Japan for the Browning Arms Company by Miroku.

The Browning Model 1885's action is shown at rest with its rearmost (tang) sight raised.

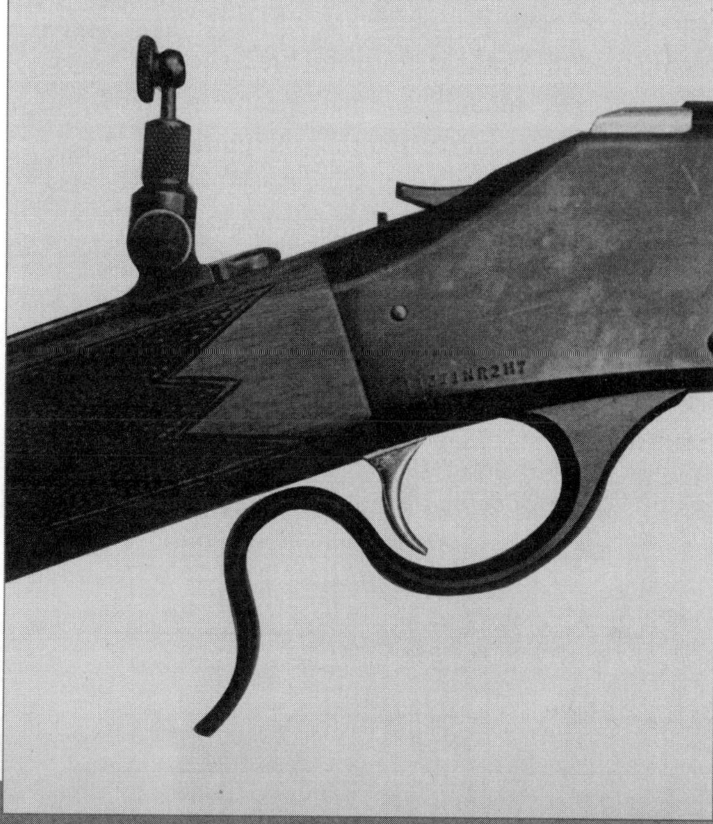

The Browning Model 1885 combines the classic lines and design features of John M. Browning's first rifle design with those emanating from modern manufacturing methods and technology.

The Model 1885 High Wall rifle features a 28-inch octagonal barrel and a select walnut stock with a straight comb. Its falling-block action is controlled by a finger lever located underneath the receiver. After firing, this lever is simply pushed forward and down, dropping the breechblock and exposing the firing chamber for unloading. It also cocks the hammer and extracts the spent cartridge casing. After loading a new cartridge, the lever is pushed back up to the receiver and the rifle is ready to fire. The action operates smoothly and with relatively little noise. Except for the Traditional Hunter and BPCR variations noted above, the High Wall rifle comes without sights, but its receiver is drilled and tapped for scope mounting.

The Model 1885 Low Wall rifle is similar to the High Wall except that its barrel is four inches shorter and its receiver is smaller and trimmer, reducing the overall length by four inches and the weight by over two pounds. This weight loss, though, comes at a price: the Low Wall cannot handle the high-intensity cartridges, whereas the High Wall can. The Low Wall variant also comes without sights. Bear in mind that an optical (telescopic) sight and its mounting hard-

With its loading lever in the down and open position, the Browning Model 1885 dropping breechblock is clearly visible.

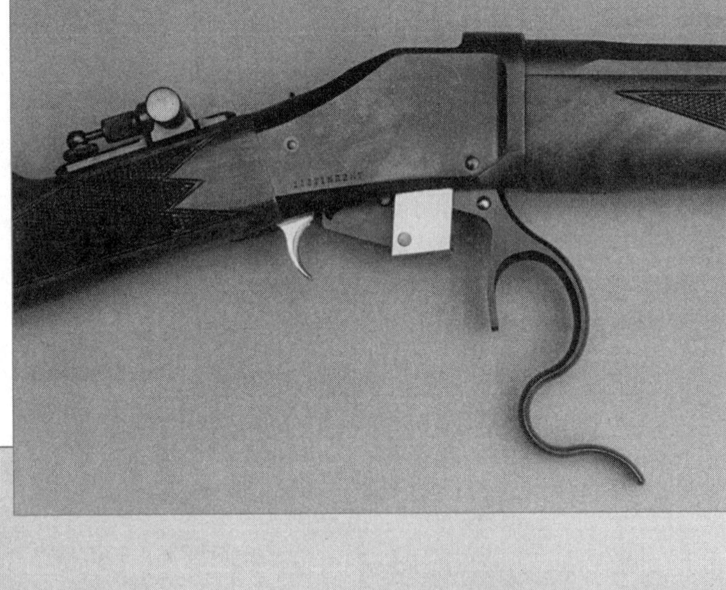

The Browning Model 1885 High Wall, while a large rifle, is graceful and well-balanced. Note the long (28-inch) octagonal barrel.

ware can add as much as several hundred dollars to the price of a rifle, so plan accordingly.

Accuracy with the High Wall rifle is excellent. Even when firing a .30-30 cartridge—a round not noted for its pinpoint accuracy beyond 50 yards or so—the High Wall delivers exceptional performance. My 3-shot, 100-yard benchrest group measured slightly over an inch, which is considerably better than one might expect with a Winchester or Marlin lever-action deer rifle more commonly associated with this cartridge. The High Wall's unusually good accuracy has to be attributed to its strong, rigid action, excellent sights and long, heavy barrel.

For those who prefer the single-shot concept, the Browning Model 1885 is a good way to go. Its trigger pull is short and crisp, adding to its accuracy potential. It's more expensive than Ruger's Number 1 rifle, but then this Browning product is extremely well

In testing for accuracy, the Browning Model 1885, using the .30-30 cartridge, fired a 1.1-inch benchrested group from 100 yards. This represents the best performance the author has ever experienced from any rifle chambered for the .30-30 cartridge.

This Browning Model 1885 High Wall fires the .30-30 cartridge ordinarily associated with lever-action rifles. This variant has integral sights, including two rear sights. A semi-buckhorn is also shown here (a peep sight is located further back, on the grip tang behind the receiver).

made. Browning rifles also tend to hold their value well, though whether a Japanese-made Browning will ever become a collector's item—as is the Belgian-made FN Browning—remains open to question. Since there are no Belgian-made Browning Model 1885-type rifles, the "Belgian Browning" versus "Japanese Browning" controversy may never be resolved. In any case, the Browning Model 1885 shoots about as well as any rifle in its price range.

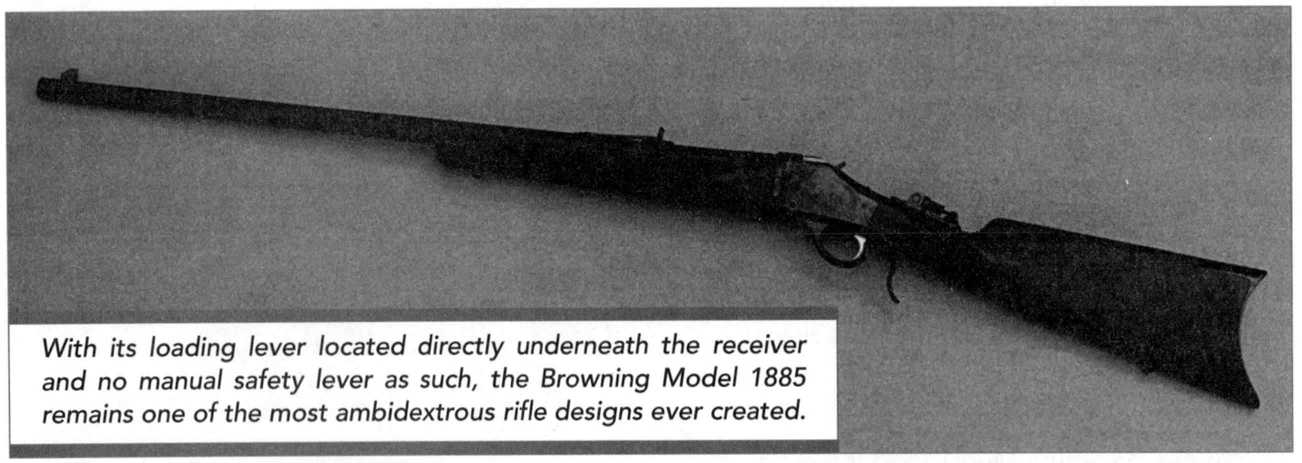

With its loading lever located directly underneath the receiver and no manual safety lever as such, the Browning Model 1885 remains one of the most ambidextrous rifle designs ever created.

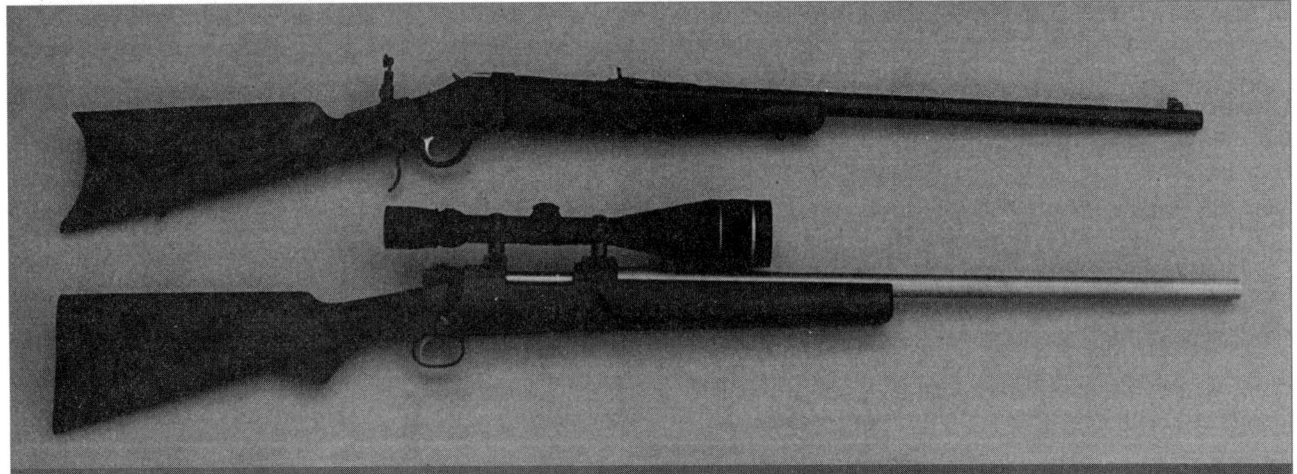

The Browning Model 1885 (top) and the Dakota Model 76 Varmint Rifle (bottom) represent two different eras in single-shot rifle design, yet both are equally suited to the task.

BROWNING MODEL 1885 SPECIFICATIONS

	HIGH WALL	LOW WALL
Overall Length	43.5 inches	39.5 inches
Barrel Length	28 inches	24 inches
Weight	8.5 pounds	6.25 pounds
Years Produced	1985-present	1995-present
Caliber Choices	.22-250, .270, 7mm Rem. Mag., .30-30, .30-06, .45-70	.22 Hornet, .223, .243 Winchester

Dakota Arms Model 76

Dakota Arms' *Model 76 Varmint Rifle* is a single-shot variant of that company's bolt-action Model 76 bolt-action repeater. Offered in a variety of fast-moving, varmint-busting calibers, this rifle made its first appearance in 1994, six years after Dakota Arms unveiled its first line of Model 76s. Important features of the Varmint Rifle include a heavy, stainless steel barrel and walnut stock. The latter has a flattened forend for more stable long-range shooting on sandbags. Total weight is just under 11 pounds, which is ideal for shooting the .223 Remington.

Operating controls are typical of most bolt-action rifles. For example, the bolt handle moves through 120 degrees, cocking the striker on the opening stroke. When the striker is cocked an indicator extending from the rear of the bolt shroud alerts the shooter that the rifle is ready to fire. The manual safety, located on the upper right rear portion of the bolt shroud, pulls back to safe and forward to fire. An intermediate setting—wherein the bolt is still moveable but the firing mechanism remains disabled—is a nice safety touch many other bolt-action rifles regrettably lack. A bolt-release lever, which is cleverly concealed on the left side of the bolt shroud, swings out from the receiver and locks open in that position. The shooter can then remove the bolt for cleaning and maintenance.

The Model 76 Varmint Rifle shares many of the same features as the classic Winchester Model 70—but controlled round feeding is not one of them. The bolt on the Varmint Rifle has two front locking lugs and a push-feed mechanism with a small claw extractor. There's also a plunger-type

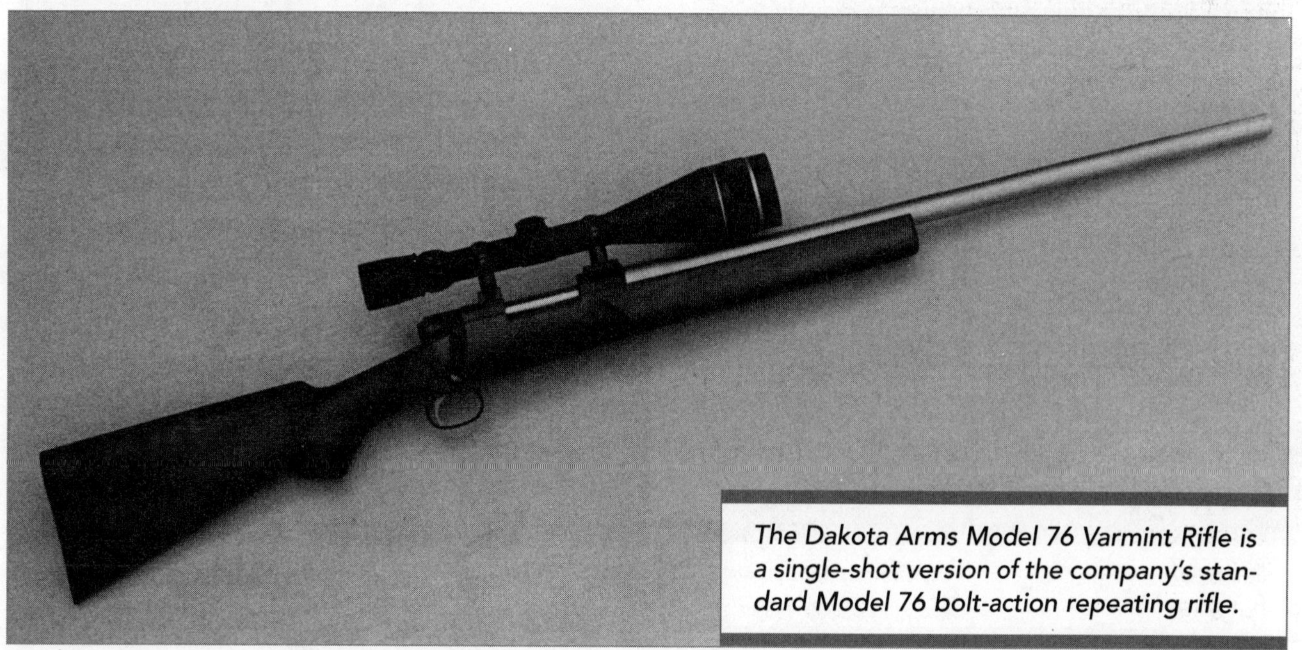

The Dakota Arms Model 76 Varmint Rifle is a single-shot version of the company's standard Model 76 bolt-action repeating rifle.

The Dakota Arms Model 76 Varmint Rifle features a three-position manual safety lever, located behind the bolt handle. When rotated forward, as shown, the safety allows the rifle to be fired.

ejector in the style popularized by Remington with its Model 700. Obviously, controlled-round feeding (CRF), while highly desirable in a military bolt-action rifle, can be a problem in situations where the rifle cannot function because of poor conditions in the field. Avoiding double-feeding cartridges and thus jamming the gun, is not going to matter much in a rifle used for potting prairie dogs from a distance of 100 yards or more. And because of the great distances at which a rifle like this one will probably be used, iron sights are not going to help much. This is, in fact, about the only smooth-barreled (sightless) rifle we tested on which iron sights were not employed. The Dakota Arms rifle we used had a huge Leupold Vari-X III Scope, adjustable from 6.5 power all the way up to 20x, plus an enormous 50mm objective lens designed for maximum light-gathering potential.

In the manual safety lever's middle position, the bolt can be moved but the firing mechanism is disabled.

In its safe setting the Varmint Rifle's manual safety lever prevents the bolt from moving and disables the firing mechanism.

This massive scope provides all the spotting power one would ever need out to several hundred yards. Testing the rifle at my usual 100-yard range seemed totally inappropriate; only on the lower magnification settings could I make any sense out of the view.

As one might expect, accuracy with the Model 76 Varmint Rifle was very good. The rifle came with three test targets shot by the Dakota Arms staff at 100 yards. Target #1 consisted of 5 shots of 55-grain Winchester PSP, creating a pattern only 7/10ths of an inch across. Target #2 fired 5 shots of 40-grain Winchester Ballistic Silvertip, making an even smaller pattern about 6/10ths of an inch across. Target #3 placed 4 shots of 55-grain Cor-Bon hollowpoint into a pattern measuring 8/10ths-inch.

The Dakota Arms Model 76 Varmint Rifle sports a Leupold Vari-X III 6.5-20x scope with massive objective lens suitable for sighting in on small, elusive targets at 300-500 yards.

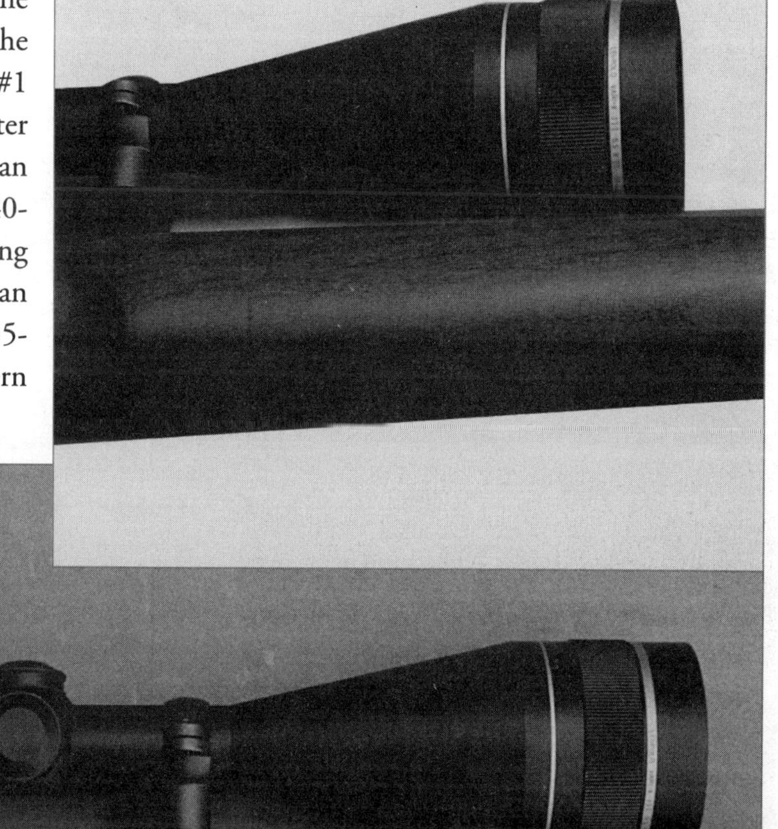

A close-up view of the Dakota Arms Model 76 Varmint Rifle action reveals the rifle's broad stock forearm and large scope.

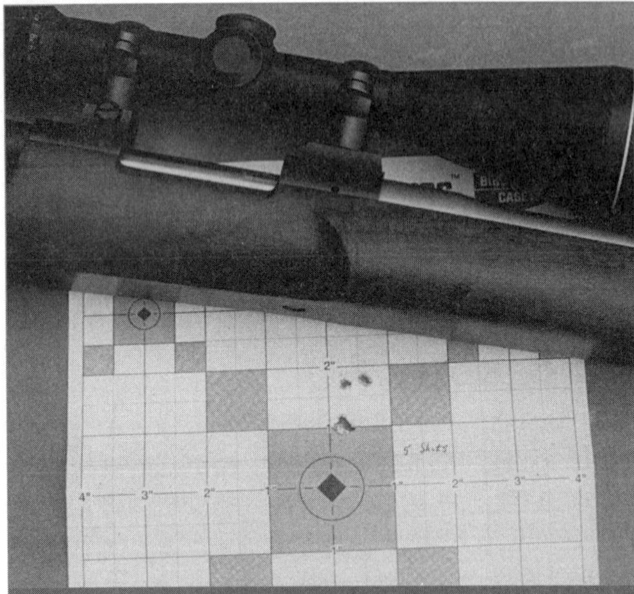

A Test Target #1 was fired at the factory with Winchester PSP (pointed softpoint) ammunition, which in .223 caliber uses a 55-grain bullet. The group measures only 7/10ths of an inch across.

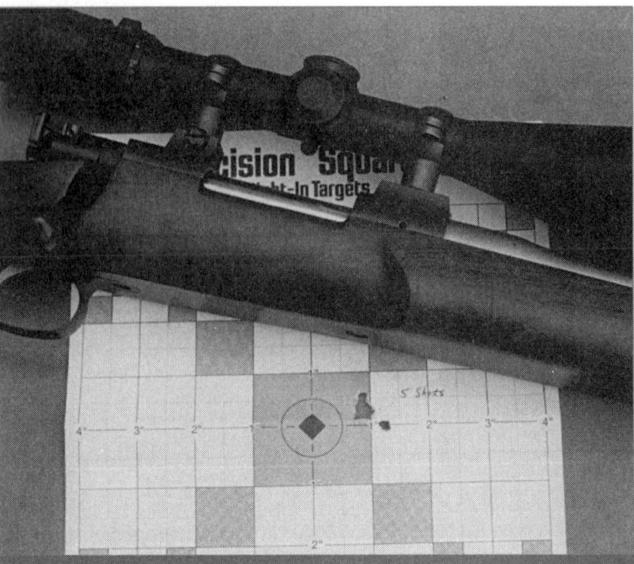

Factory Test Target #2 was fired with Winchester Ballistic Silvertip ammunition, which in .223 caliber uses a 40-grain bullet. The five-shot group placed four shots into one hole and a fifth shot "opened up" the group to a mere 6/10ths of an inch!

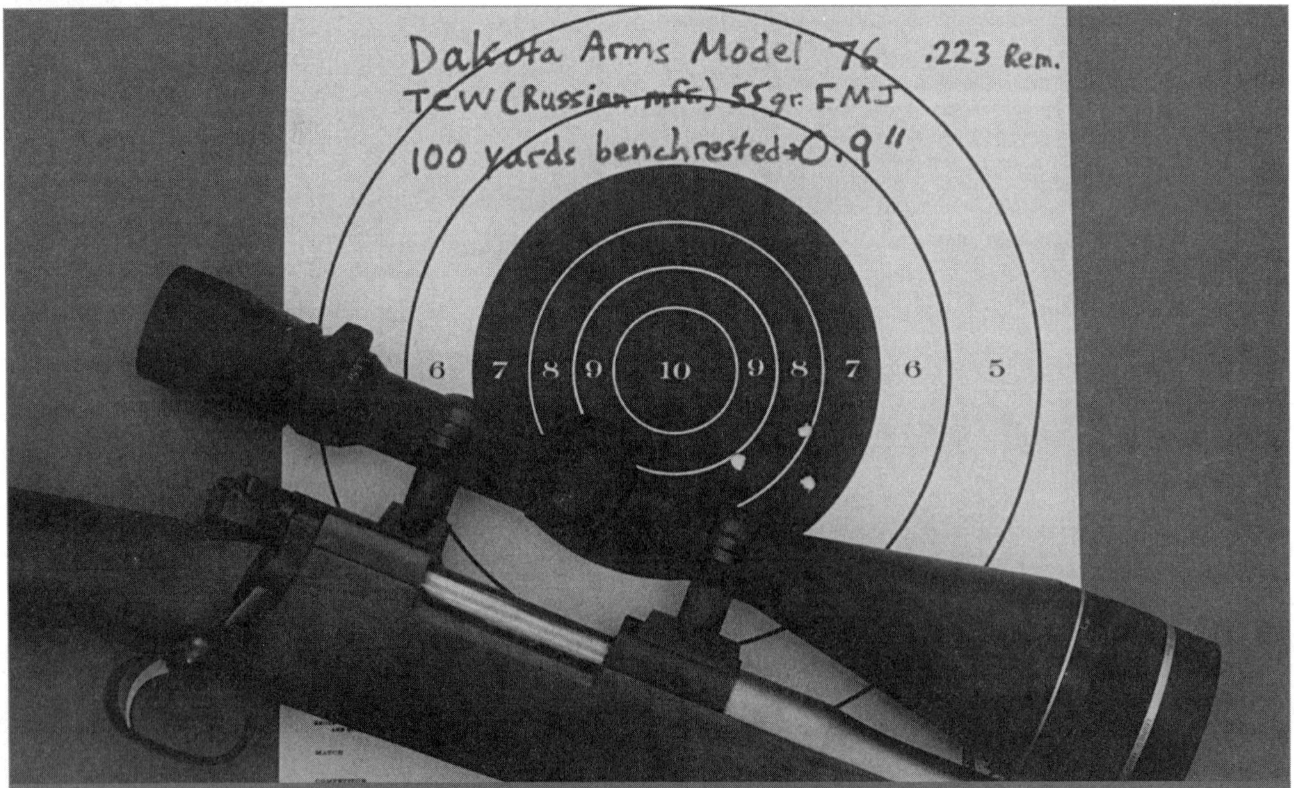

With .223 ammunition of indifferent quality, the author produced groups of less than one minute of angle (e.g., one inch at 100 yards) with Dakota Arms highly accurate Model 76 Varmint Rifle.

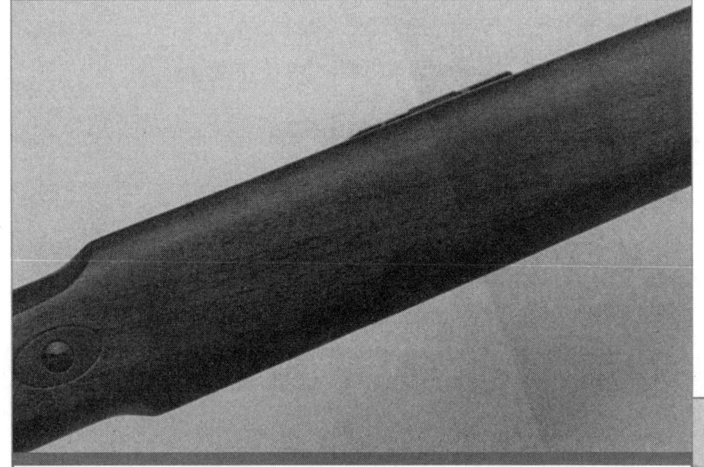

The Varmint Rifle's widened forearm is flattened on the bottom for use on a bench or sandbags.

To discriminating and well-heeled shooters, the Dakota Model 76 Varmint Rifle offers high performance indeed. It's a well-designed, well-built rifle. For the most avid collectors of single-shot rifles, Dakota Arms also makes one based on a falling-block action that opens up with an underlever and has a top tang safety. The trigger unit is removable and a single set trigger can be substituted for even greater precision.

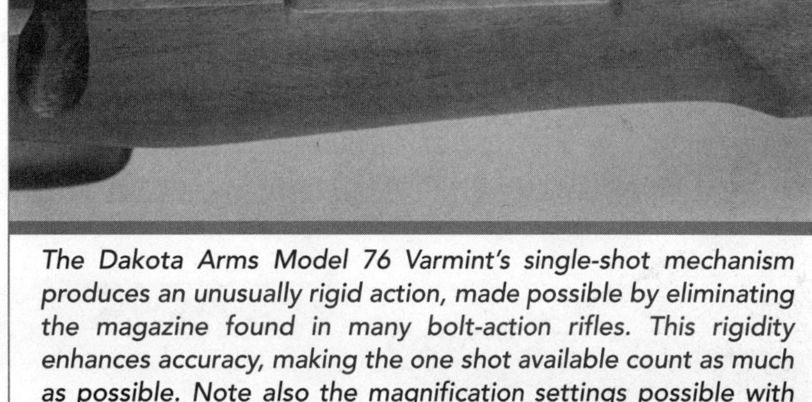

The Dakota Arms Model 76 Varmint's single-shot mechanism produces an unusually rigid action, made possible by eliminating the magazine found in many bolt-action rifles. This rigidity enhances accuracy, making the one shot available count as much as possible. Note also the magnification settings possible with the Leupold Vari-X scope.

Faced with these stellar results, which approached 1/2 MOA in one bullet type, I tried to replicate, or at least approach, these results. My best 3-shot, 100-yard group occurred with low-cost, steel-cased .223 caliber ammunition of Russian manufacture registering a 9/10ths-inch group. In my experience with shooting rifles, anything under one minute of angle (that translates into 1 inch at 100 yards) is a good result. As one might expect, the hefty Model 76 exhibited mild recoil characteristics, while the trigger pull was extraordinarily smooth and light.

DAKOTA ARMS MODEL 76 VARMINT RIFLE

	MODEL 76
Overall Length	44.0 inches
Barrel Length	24.0 inches
Weight	11.0 pounds
Years Produced	1994-present
Caliber Options	.17 Remington, .22BR, .222, .22-250, 220 Swift, .223, 6mm BR, 6mm PPC

Harrington & Richardson (H&R 1871, Inc.) Ultra

Harrington & Richardson's Ultra is essentially similar to the New England Firearms (NEF) Handi-Rifle. Based on the company's highly successful line of inexpensive break-open shotguns, the Ultra's ancestor originally appeared as the Model 158 Topper rifle in .30-30 and .45-70 calibers. To load and reload, the shooter presses down on a latch located next to the external hammer. This unhinges the frame and allows it to extract the empty cartridge casing automatically and expose the breech, enabling the shooter to load a new round. When Harrington & Richardson went out of business in 1986, production stopped until the company was reorganized as H&R 1871, Inc. several years later. Its decision to reintroduce this model in 1993 proved a wise move, for the Ultra has become highly successful.

Two main versions of the Ultra single-shot rifle are now available. The Ultra Varmint, introduced in 1993, comes in three popular rifle chamberings: .223, .270 and .30-06 (the latter two calibers include a compensator to make firing more pleasant). The Ultra Varmint has no iron sights, but it comes with a scope mount. The Ultra Hunter, which made its debut in 1995, is basically similar to the Varmint model but is chambered only for the 7mm Mauser and 7x64mm rounds. It features a cinnamon-colored, hand-checkered laminated stock and forend.

The H&R Ultra single-shot rifle offers great appeal to collectors while retaining good shooting capabilities. Among several commemorative editions released by H&R, this Whitetails Unlimited Commemorative Rifle (1997) chambers the .45-70 cartridge. Another Whitetails Unlimited Commemorative Edition, released in 1998, chambered the .30-30 caliber.

The basic H&R Ultra action can also be fitted with shotgun barrels. Shown here is a 12 gauge Ultra Slug Hunter Deluxe. Note the laminated wood stock.

HARRINGTON & RICHARDSON ULTRA

	ULTRA
Overall Length	35.5 inches with 22-inch barrel
Barrel Length	22, 24 or 26 inches, depending on caliber
Weight	7.5 pounds
Years Produced	1993-present
Caliber Choices	*Varmint:* 25-06, .308, .357 Rem. Max. • *Hunter:* .223, .270, .30-06

New England Firearms (NEF) Handi-Rifle

As part of the corporate entity that evolved from the original Harrington & Richardson empire, New England Firearms was responsible for reviving the classic H&R Topper single-shot rifle design. Known as the Handi-Rifle, this model was announced in 1989, just three years after the original H&R firm had closed its doors. Similar to the Ultra (covered above), the Handi-rifle is a versatile, low-cost rifle suitable for both beginning and advanced shooters. Whereas the Ultra is available with only a scope mount option, the NEF Handi-Rifles offer integral iron sights or scope mounts depending on their cartridge chamberings. There is no manual safety. When the hammer

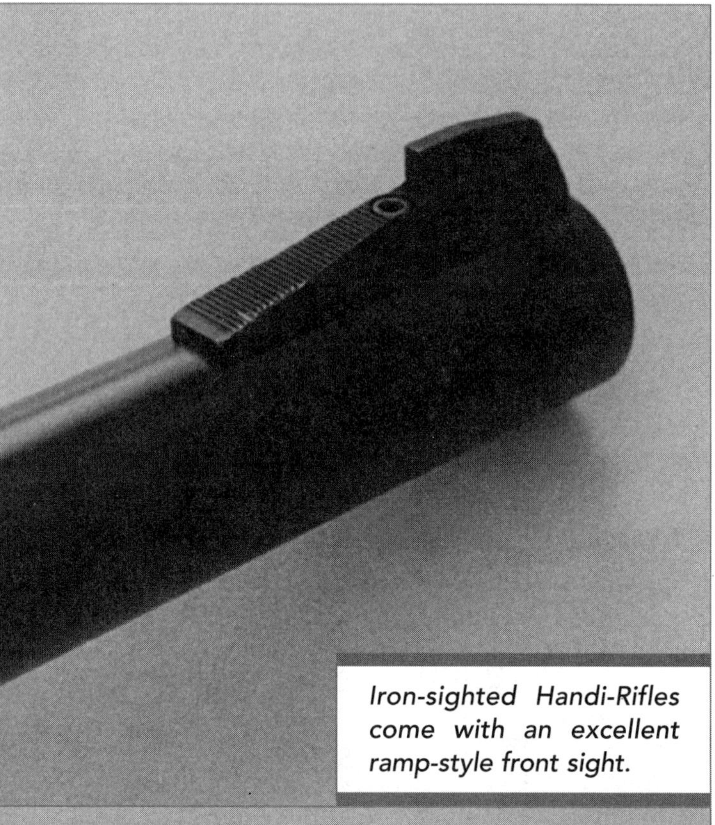

Iron-sighted Handi-Rifles come with an excellent ramp-style front sight.

The H&R 1871/New England Firearms Handi-Rifle boasts an excellent design. The Weaver-compatible scope rail on the barrel of this .270 Winchester variant indicates rapid scope mounting capability.

The Handi-Rifle's optional rear sight is both rugged and fully adjustable.

is uncocked, the rifle will not fire (a transfer bar safety system prevents the hammer from making contact with the firing pin until the trigger is pressed, raising the transfer bar). Shooters who use this type of single-action rifle are urged *not* to lower the hammer onto a chambered cartridge and leave it there; instead, they should load only immediately before firing. Otherwise, the firing chamber must be kept unloaded at all times to prevent accidents.

The rifle sent to me by New England Firearms for testing typified the flexibility of the Handi-Rifle system. It arrived with a barrel chambered and rifled for the .270 Winchester cartridge and with no iron sights (but a Weaver-style scope mount was

This Handi-Rifle is shown with hammer uncocked. The control to the right of the hammer is the release lever, which opens the breech end of the barrel for reloading.

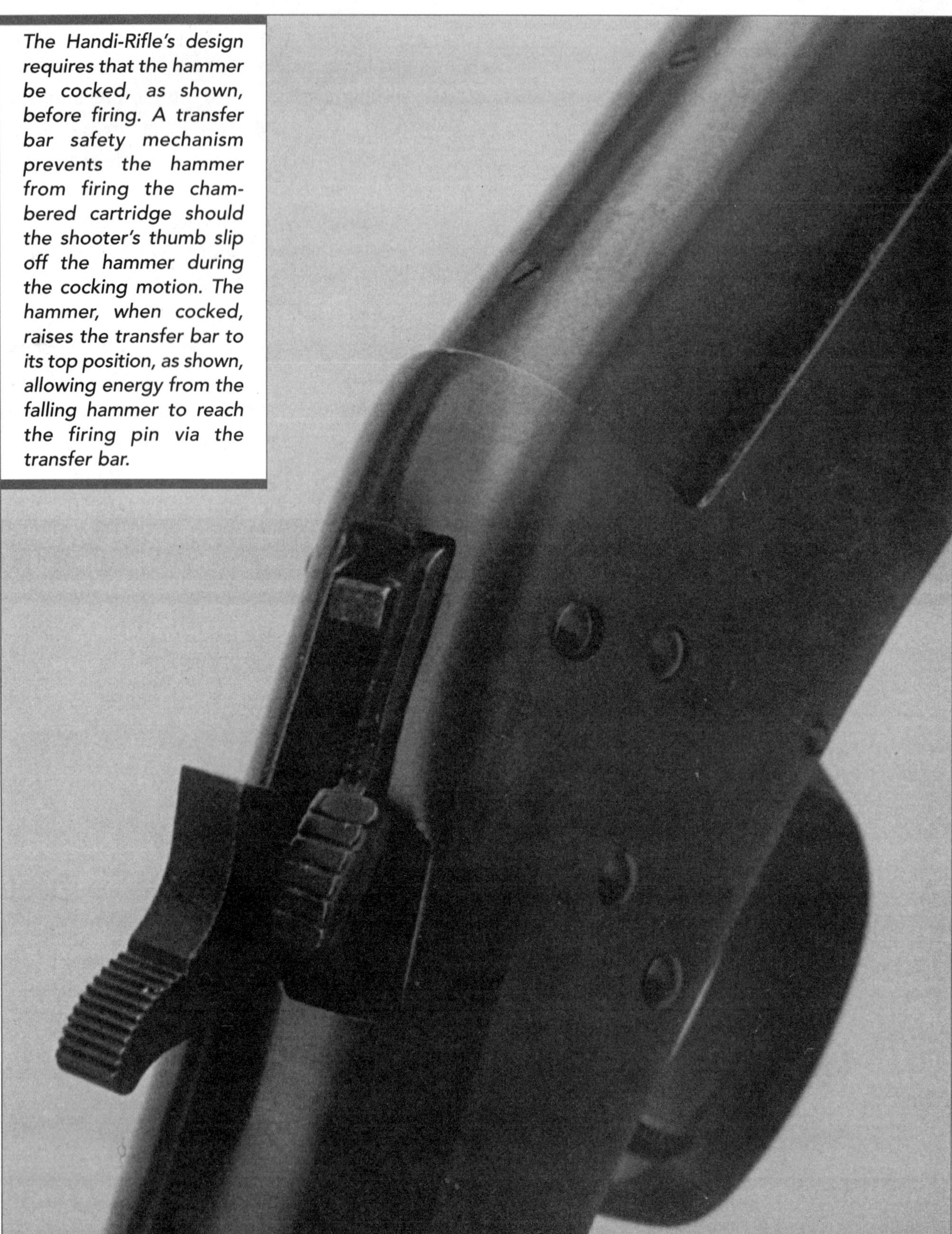

The Handi-Rifle's design requires that the hammer be cocked, as shown, before firing. A transfer bar safety mechanism prevents the hammer from firing the chambered cartridge should the shooter's thumb slip off the hammer during the cocking motion. The hammer, when cocked, raises the transfer bar to its top position, as shown, allowing energy from the falling hammer to reach the firing pin via the transfer bar.

This three-shot benchrested group fired from 100 yards with a .44 Magnum measures just 1.3 inches across.

A Handi-Rifle tested by the author produced a 3-shot benchrested group fired from 100 yards with a .223 caliber barrel that measured exactly two inches across. A scope was used because the .223 barrel came without integral sights.

The Handi-Rifle's most accurate group was produced with the powerful .270 Winchester caliber barrel. This 3-shot benchrested group fired from 100 yards measures 9/10ths of an inch across. Recoil was considerable, however, in this relatively small, light rifle.

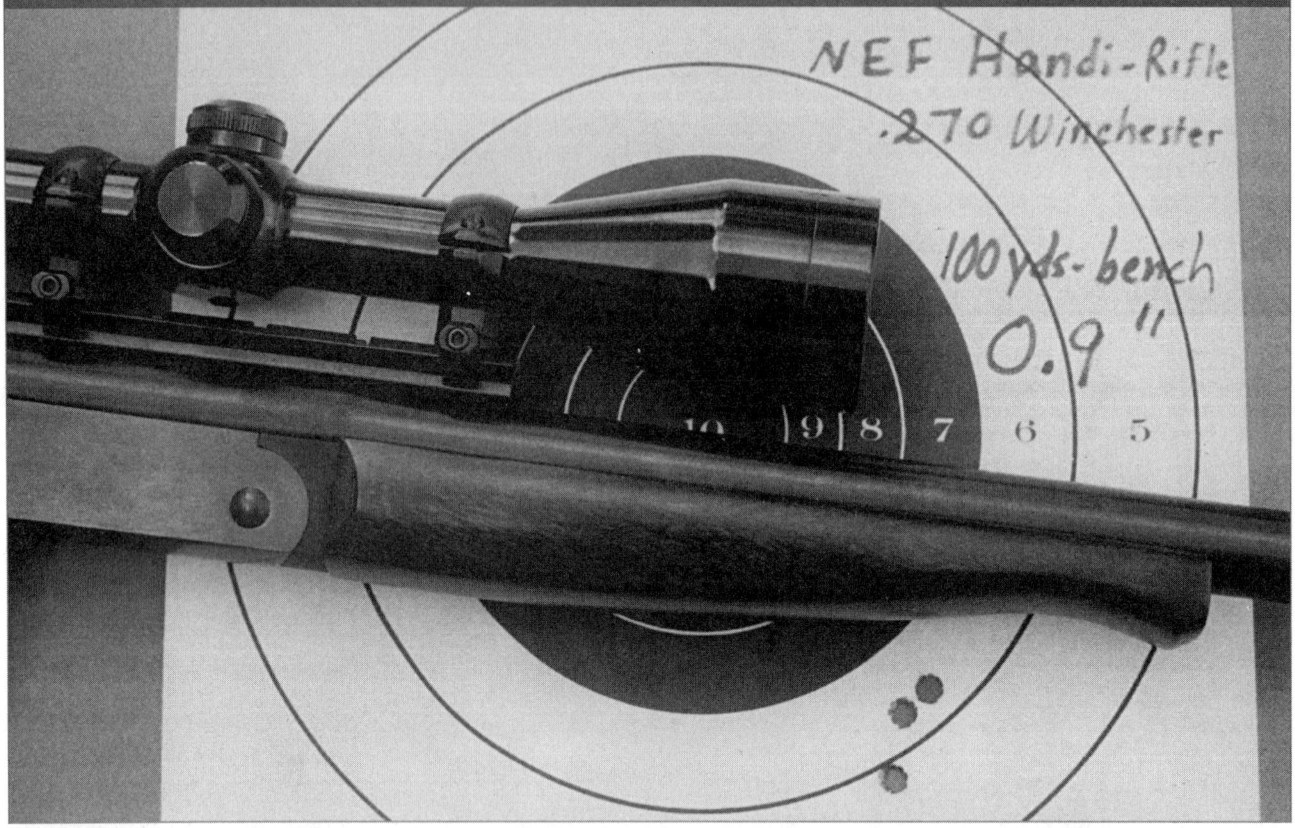

The Handi-Rifle's ability to change calibers quickly—simply by removing and exchanging barrels—remains one of this gun's most popular features. Note that the .44 Magnum caliber barrel (top) has both front and rear iron sights, while the .223 Remington caliber barrel (shown in place) and the .270 Winchester caliber barrel (below) both have rails for mounting telescopic sights instead of integral front and rear sights.

attached). Accessories included a barrel chambered for the .44 Magnum cartridge (iron sights attached) and a .223 Remington caliber heavy-contour barrel (without sights but with a Weaver scope base). This versatile combination offered three guns for the price of one modestly-priced rifle. The .270 Winchester, despite its punishing recoil, proved the most accurate, delivering a group measuring 9/10ths of an inch from a benchrest set up 100 yards from the target. While such accuracy was expected from the .270 Winchester, the .44 Magnum surprised us with its fine accuracy, delivering a group slightly over one inch at 100 yards. With the .223 barrel in place, though, the Handi-Rifle was less accurate but still not too shabby—with a 2-inch 100-yard group. [In my experience .223 caliber rifles tend to be particular about what ammunition they use; a different brand would probably have worked better.]

In general, the New England Firearms' Handi-Rifle is a highly recommended, versatile and flexible low-cost rifle system. Shooters of single-shot rifles cannot possibly match this model within a similar price range; indeed, one would be hard-pressed to improve on the Handi-Rifle at any cost.

The Handi-Rifle comes with a thick rubber buttpad, a desirable feature when using heavy calibers fired from this relatively short, lightweight gun.

NEW ENGLAND FIREARMS HANDI-RIFLE

	HANDI-RIFLE
Overall Length	36 inches with 22-inch barrel
Barrel Length	22, 24 or 26 inches, depending on caliber
Weight	7-8 pounds, depending on caliber
Years Produced	1989-present
Caliber Choices	.223, .22 Hornet, .30-30, .243, .308, .270, .280, .30-06, 7x57mm, 7x64mm, .44 Magnum

New England Firearms (NEF) Youth Handi-Rifle

Harrington & Richardson (now known as H&R 1871, Inc.) and New England Firearms (NEF) are related corporations working out of the same facilities at Gardner, Massachusetts. One of the most appealing products in their line is the "Youth Model" Handi-Rifle, which is based on the highly successful—and inexpensive—line of break-open rifles (see also Handi-Rifle and Ultra specifications above). The Youth Model Handi-Rifle differs only in length (it's slightly shorter) and is chambered in milder calibers. It also has a slightly redesigned stock featuring a shorter length of pull and a thick, soft rubber recoil pad.

The Youth Model Handi-Rifle comes in .223 Remington (5.56mm) and .243 Winchester chamberings, which offer beginning shooters a soft recoil coupled with relatively authoritative and widely available cartridges. As with any Handi-Rifle, shooters may update their Youth Models later on with full-sized adult stocks and alternative barrels chambered for other cartridges. As with other rifles in the Handi-Rifle line, the Youth Model has no integral (iron) sight but does include a Weaver-type scope rail ready for easy installation of a telescopic sight.

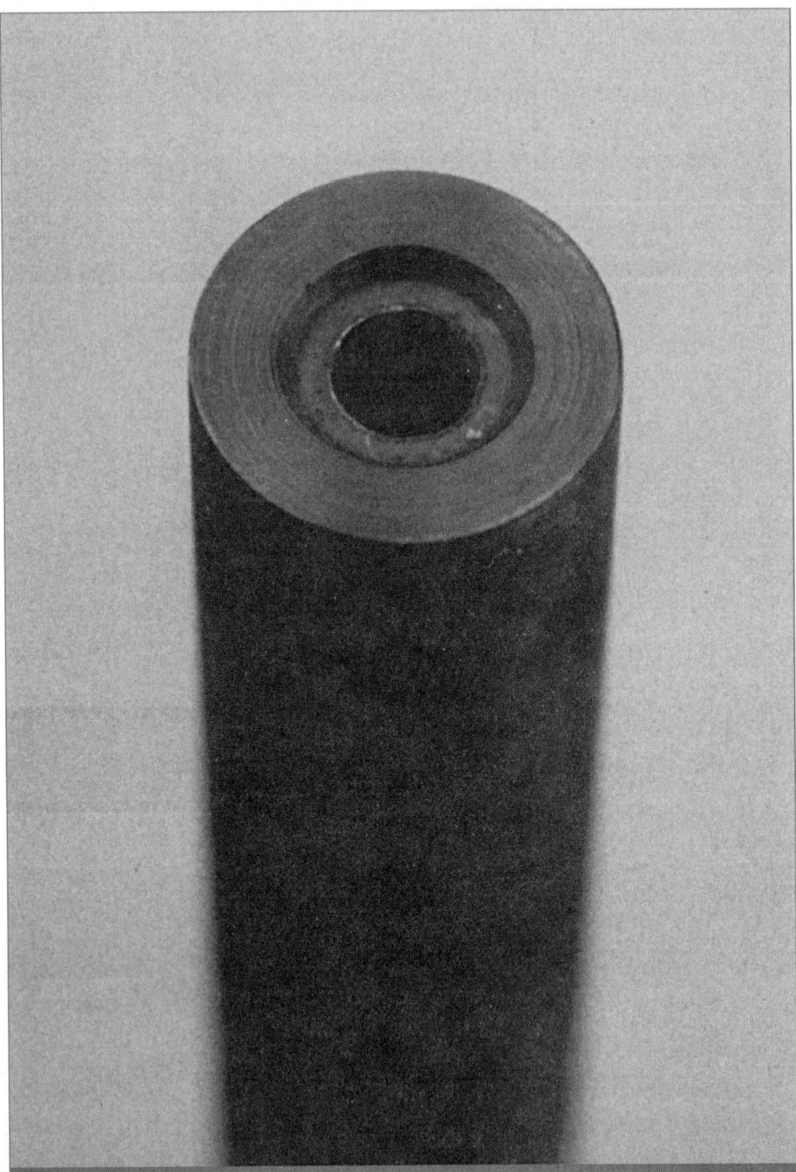

The heavy barrel on the NEF Youth Handi-Rifle contributes to the rifle's weight problem. There's more steel wrapped around the bore than is needed. Thus, in December 1998 New England Firearms announced a Super Light Youth rifle with synthetic stock and a noticeably thinner barrel contour chambered for the larger .243 Winchester cartridge.

The best 3-shot, 50-yard benchrested group fired by the author with the Youth Handi-Rifle measures 8/10ths of an inch across.

The best 3-shot, 100-yard benchrested group fired by the .223 caliber Youth Handi-Rifle spanned 1.8 inches using Remington/UMC 55-grain FMJ.

Not all .223 caliber ammunition is created equal. Using Russian-made TCW ammunition, the Youth Handi-Rifle only produced a 3-shot, 100-yard benchrested group measuring a disappointingly large 2.6 inches across. Extraction with this steel-cased ammunition was next to impossible. Careful ammunition selection in .223 caliber is important (TCW ammunition worked fine in other .223-caliber rifles tested for this book).

The Youth Model Handi-Rifle tested for this book chambered the .223 cartridge. As with other rifles in this often controversial caliber, accuracy and reliability varied widely depending largely upon the brand of ammunition used. For example, the rifle did not respond well to steel-cased ammunition made by Russian Manufacturers, sometimes even refusing to eject fired cases (the company advises against using ammunition with soft primers, which can cause ejection problems). With ammunition it liked, notably Remington's economy-priced UMC brand with a 55-grain FMJ bullet, the Youth Handi-Rifle performed superbly, firing a 50-yard benchrested group measuring 1.8 inches across.

While I was impressed overall with the Youth Model Handi-Rifle, some areas need improvement. First, a lighter, thinner barrel would help reduce its weight, making the rifle more manageable for young shooters. The Youth Model Handi-Rifle's commitment to a telescopic sight adds further to the weight, cost and complexity of this rifle. Nevertheless, I applaud New England Firearms' commitment to make the shooting sports accessible to young and/or beginning shooters. And, like other H&R/NEF products, the Youth Model Handi-Rifle offers good value for the money.

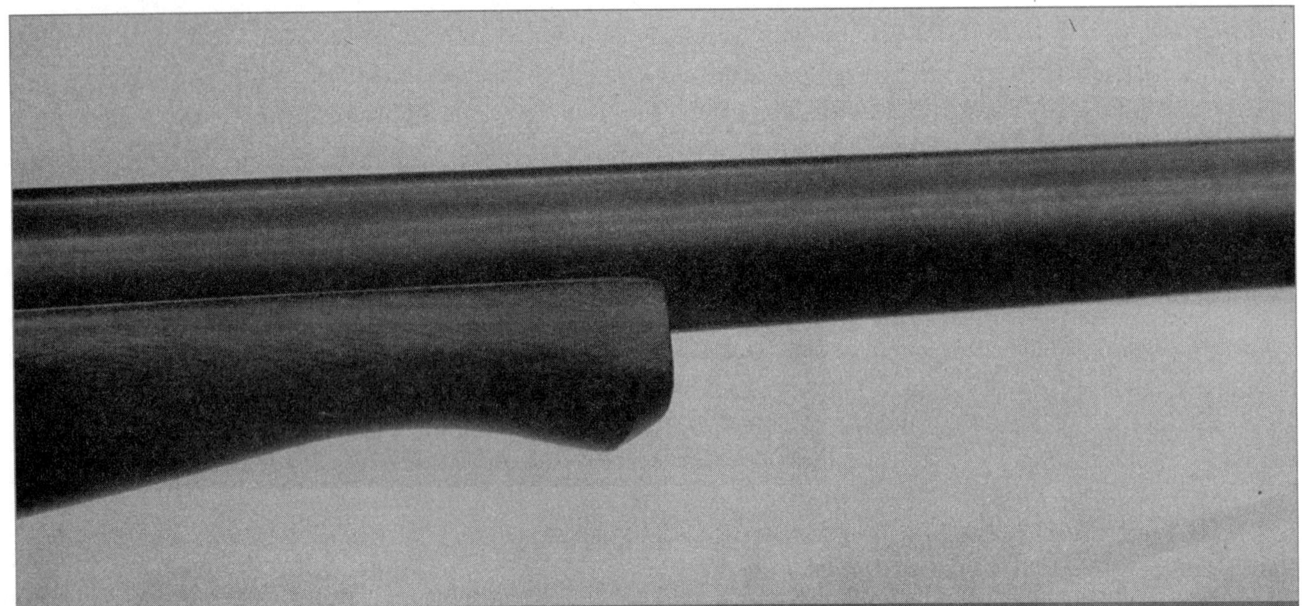

The heavy barrel contour on the Youth Handi-Rifle shows clearly in this view. While a heavy barrel makes for improved accuracy, it also adds weight. Note the elegant schnabel tip, a touch of class unusual for such an inexpensive rifle.

NEF YOUTH HANDI-RIFLE

	YOUTH HANDI-RIFLE
Overall Length	35.9 inches
Barrel Length	22 inches
Weight	7.0 pounds
Years Produced	1998-present
Caliber Choices	.223 Remington, .243 Winchester

Ruger Number I

Ruger's Number 1 single-shot rifle first appeared in 1967. Inspired by the graceful lines of the 19th-century Farquharson single-shot rifle made in England, and mechanically by the 19th-century Fraser single-shot rifle (also made in the UK), the Number 1 represents an improvement on both. Ruger's design objectives were to combine the element of strength, ease of handling and manufacture, all of which the company has succeeded in doing.

Variations of the Number 1 include the Model 1B, 1S, 1A, 1H and 1V, plus the .45-70 caliber Number 1 Government Model, all dating from 1967. All variations remain in production with the exception of the Government Model, whose manufacturing history is covered in more detail below. The 1B has a 26-inch barrel with a tapered quarter rib on its top rear portion. It weights about 8 pounds. Original chamberings included .220 Swift, .22-250, 6mm Remington, .243, .25-06, .270, 7mm Remington Magnum, .30-06 and .300 Magnum, to which Ruger has since added .218 Bee, .22 Hornet, .257 Roberts, .280 Remington (1979), .338 Winchester Magnum (1973), .270 Weatherby and .300 Weatherby (both added in 1987). Intended strictly for scope mounting, the 1B has no fixed sights. Its front sling swivel is located near the tip of the rounded forend.

The Model 1A lightweight model (7_ pounds) offers the following caliber choices--.243, 7x57mm, .270 and .30-06—of which the 7x57mm (7mm Mauser) is the least common. Nevertheless, it is versatile and well suited to this version of the Number 1 rifle, offering good power

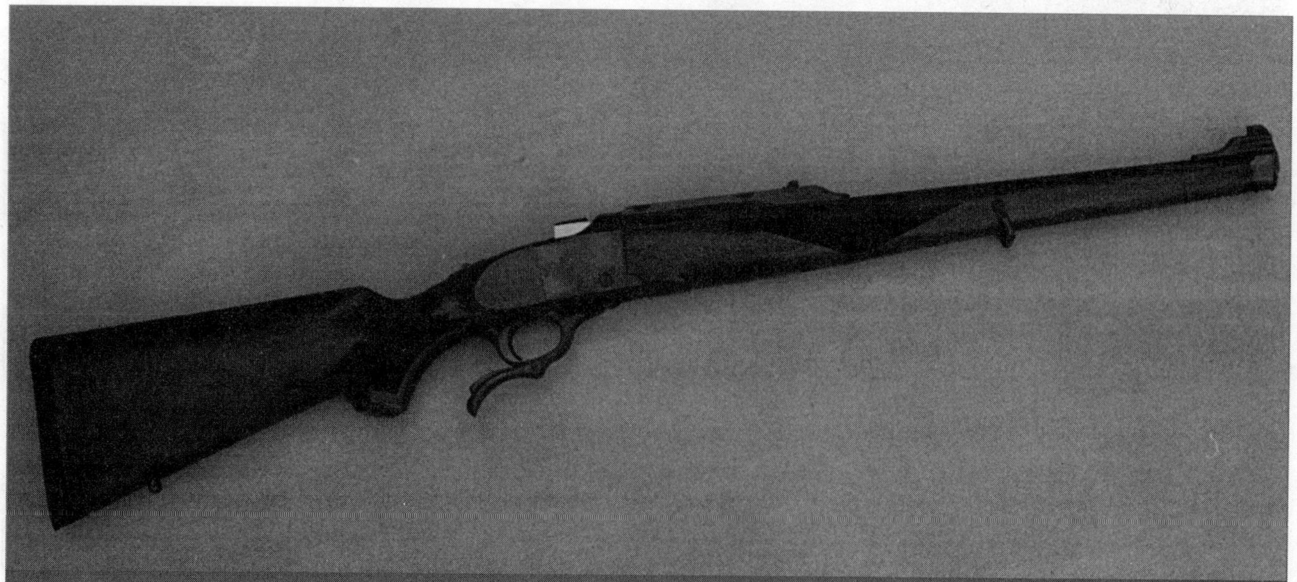

The graceful lines on the Ruger Number 1 remind single-action fans of the Farquharson rifles popular during Great Britain's reign in the late 19th Century.

with relatively mild recoil for such a comparatively lightweight rifle (see the caliber section for more information on specific rifle cartridges). The 1A also features fixed front and folding rear sights, while retaining the scope-mounting capabilities of the Model 1B.

The 1V (Special Varminter) variation sports a 24-inch heavy barrel. It's intended specifically for taking small, elusive quarry, such as prairie dogs or woodchucks, at extended ranges. Flat-shooting long-range calibers and high-powered scopes are therefore the order of the day. No fixed sights are available on the Number 1V, and indeed they would be useless against small targets several hundred yards away. Caliber options available in this variant include .22-250, .220 Swift, .223 and .25-06 (earlier, Ruger offered .222 and 6mm Remington chamberings as well). Thanks to its unusually thick barrel, the 1V, at nine pounds, remains one of the heaviest Number 1 rifles.

The Model 1H (Tropical Rifle) is a heavy-caliber model intended for those brave souls who insist on doing battle with dangerous game armed with a single-shot rifle. The 1H is available in large, powerful chamberings only. These include the .375 Holland & Holland Magnum and .458 Winchester Magnum, to which Ruger has subsequently added the .404 Jeffery, .416 Rigby and .416 Remington Magnum. The

The Ruger Number 1 comes quickly to the shoulder and balances there quite well.

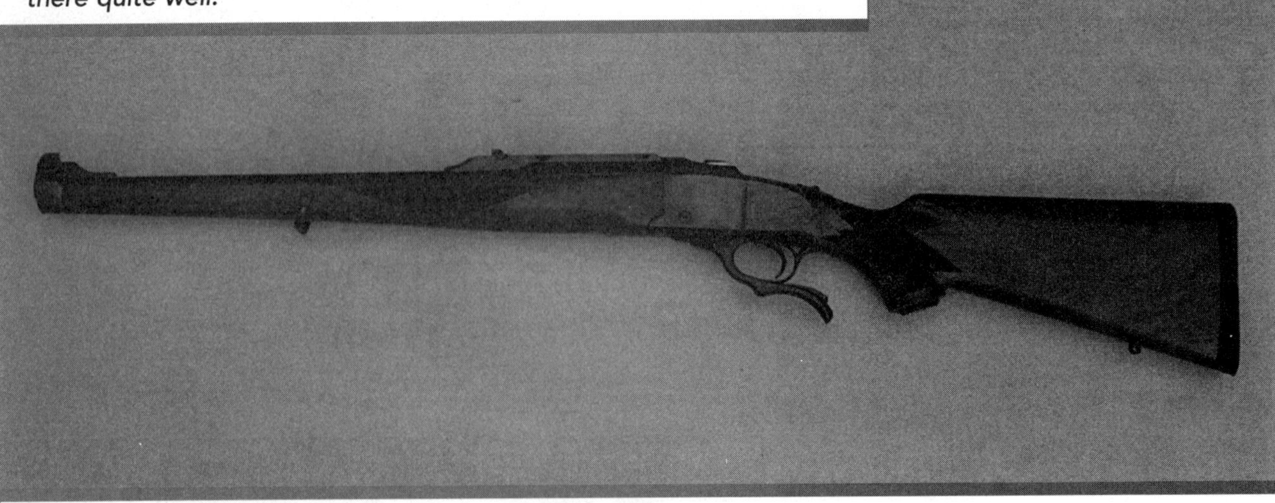

The Ruger Number 1 is one of the most ambidextrous firearms designs available.

1H, along with the Special Varminter, is the heaviest Number 1 rifle, weighting nine pounds unloaded in the .416 Rigby and .458 Winchester Magnum variants. These extremely powerful calibers, intended for the largest and most dangerous game, require the hefty weight of a solid, well-built rifle in order to make the recoil as tolerable as possible. Because of the close range at which most large game is taken, the Number 1H rifle uses iron sights, a front ramp with gold bead, and an adjustable folding rear sight. A standard front swivel is affixed to a band on the barrel several inches ahead of the forend.

As with the Tropical model, the 1S Medium Sporter has a sling swivel located several inches closer to the barrel (instead of the forend) plus a fixed front sight, a folding rear sight, and the capability for mounting a Model 1B scope. Its barrel, which is thinner and contains less steel, is about half a pound lighter than the 1B. Caliber choices include .218 Bee, 7mm Remington Magnum, .300 Winchester Magnum, .338 Winchester Magnum and the .45-70. Interestingly, the .45-70 caliber has gone through a history of its own. After Ruger introduced the .45-70 version in 1967 as the "Number 1 Government Model," the company dropped this model in 1974 following the introduction of a .45-70 caliber version of the Number 3 rifle. Basically a Number 1 design, the Number 3 differed slightly in appearance, most notably by eliminating the

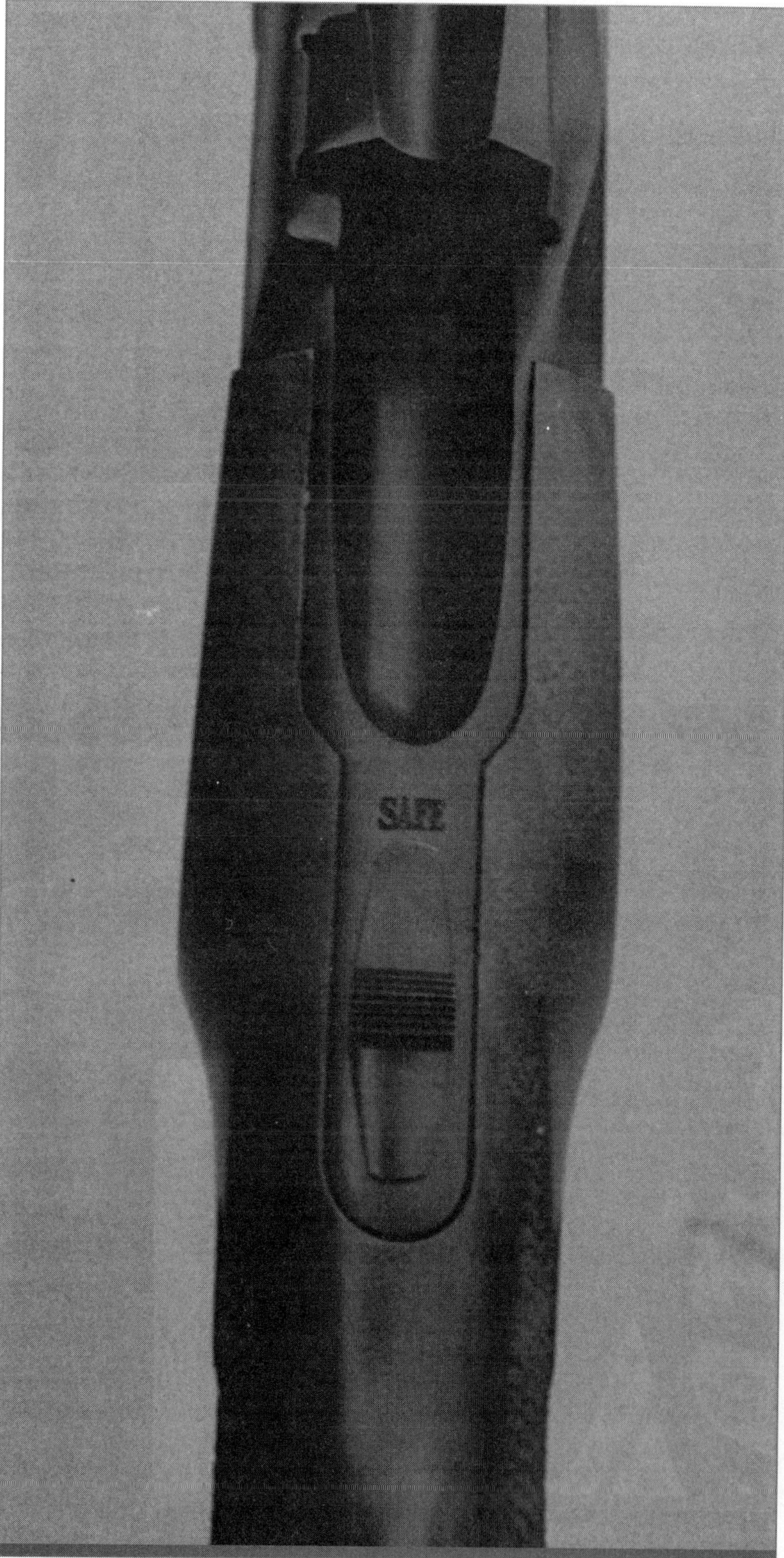

The tang safety on the Ruger Number 1 pushes forward to fire and to the rear for its safe setting.

The Ruger Number 1 is available with a choice of sights or sightless and ready for scope mounting. This RSI variant uses a beaded front sight.

pistol grip in favor of a stock with a straight wrist. Other changes included a curbed butt plate, a slimmer loading lever, and a barrel band that secured the stock forend around the barrel. Ruger produced the Number 3 rifle in the following calibers: .30-40 Krag (1972-1978); .45-70 (1974-1987); .223 (1980-1987); .375 Winchester (1980-1984); and .44 Magnum (1985-1987). Since 1973 Ruger has marketed its Number 1S Medium Sporter variant chambered for the .45-70 cartridge.

The Number 1 RSI International made its first appearance in 1983. Its name comes from the elegant full-length stock popularized by the Austrian Mannlicher sporting rifles. The RSI has a lightweight barrel only 20 inches long, making it an exceedingly handy package for the

The .270 caliber Ruger Number 1 tested for this book produced a 2.5-inch 3-shot group from the bench at a distance of 100 yards. Using a scope would shrink the group size somewhat.

single-shot rifle enthusiast. Caliber choices include .243 Winchester, 7x57mm Mauser, .270 Winchester (tested for this book) and the .30-06.

With all Number 1 rifles, one loads or unloads the firing chamber by pushing the loading lever down and forward. This action drops the breechblock far enough to expose the firing chamber—ejecting along the way whatever cartridge casings or live rounds exist in the chamber—before cocking the striker. The manual safety consists of a sliding tang located behind the action. One pushes forward to fire and to the rear (exposing the word SAFE) to the safe setting (but only when the action is cocked).

As for sighting arrangements, I prefer the choice offered on a variant similar to the RSI, where one can

This Ruger Number 1 is shown ready to fire. Note that the loading lever is pushed up against the triggerguard, while the breechblock has risen into the space behind the barrel.

Pushing the loading lever down and forward drops the breechblock out of the way. The spent cartridge casing is extracted and the firing chamber exposed.

A side view of the Ruger Number 1 exposes the loading lever in the down position, with the triggerguard shown as a separate piece from the loading lever.

use the iron sights (furnished) or attach a scope with the handy mounting system that comes with the rifle. For added convenience, the rear sight folds out of the way should you choose to attach an optical sight. Ruger has carried this desirable feature over into several of its other designs.

The wooden furniture used in the Number 1 rifle is both beautiful and elegant, yet supremely practical and functional. The stock features a straight comb along with a pronounced pistol grip that is comfortably checkered. Considering the quality and finish of this wood, it would make a fine addition to a gun cabinet filled with top-quality firearms. The trigger pull is light and crisp. Extraction of spent cartridge casings is a problem in some types of single-shot rifles, particularly among those firing black-powder cartridges which, after extended use, require cleaning. But the Number 1 vigorously extracts spent cartridge casings, or even complete rounds, flawlessly. Unlike New England Firearms' Handi-Rifle, however, the Number 1 does not eject them far enough, even when the loading lever is operated with authority. Sometimes the empty casing will simply lie in the open action. What counts, though, is that it has been extracted from the firing chamber, where it can be easily plucked or shaken from the feedway, thus clearing a path for a reload.

Accuracy with the Number 1 RSI merits high praise. In our tests, it delivered a well-centered, three-shot benchrested group from 100 yards measuring 2.5 inches. Due mostly to its light weight, recoil in the powerful and versatile .270 Winchester round was pronounced. But the excellent stock design helped minimize damage to the shoulder. All in all, the rifle was not at all unpleasant to fire. Considering that many single-shot rifles sell for well over twice the current price of a Number 1, this model is an outstanding buy.

Even the Number 1 variants with iron sights are easily adapted to operation with a telescopic sight. Note the clearance slot cut in the sight rib to accommodate a telescopic mount.

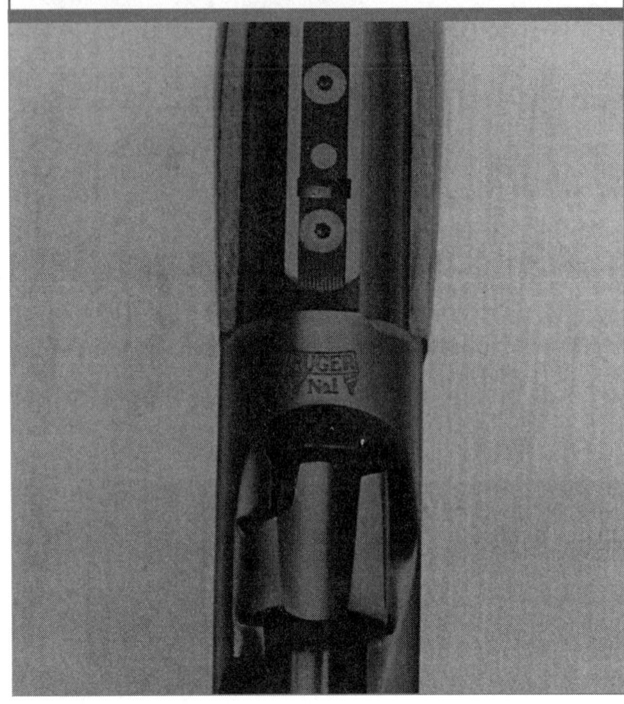

RUGER NUMBER 1 (RSI INTERNATIONAL VARIATION)

	RUGER NUMBER 1
Overall Length	36.5 inches
Barrel Length	20.0 inches
Weight	7.2 pounds
Years Produced	1967-present (1983-present for RSI variant)
Manufacturer	Sturm, Ruger and Company, Prescott, AZ
Caliber Choices	.243, 7x57mm, .270, .30-06 (see text for other variants)

Springfield Cavalry Carbine Model 1873 (Navy Arms)

The Model 1873 Springfield Cavalry Carbine ranks high among the many high-quality replica arms for which Navy Arms has become famous over the years. Val Forgett, Jr., president of the company, is a long-time enthusiast of classic black powder firearms. Originally, he created the company to make replicas of famous old guns available to shooters and collectors of average means. He reasoned that selling replicas would especially benefit those who were unwilling to risk life, limb and gun by pushing old guns to their limits when an authentic replica was available. Old guns, moreover, would not be destroyed in the firing process. In this endeavor, Navy Arms has succeeded admirably. The replica arms offered by the company are of superb quality, with performance and handling rivaling their illustrious originals. Since its beginnings Navy Arms has diversified into various surplus and modern smokeless powder firearms designs as well (see Index).

The Navy Arms Model 1873 Springfield Cavalry Carbine covered here is a replica of one of the most interesting firearms ever created. Upon its first appearance in carbine form in 1876, it was actually a shortened version of the single-shot "trapdoor" infantry rifle dating from the Civil War. Such weapons served with the ill-fated Seventh Cavalry in its disastrous defeat at the Little Big Horn in June 1876. Other rifles of this type also served throughout the Indian Wars of the late 19th century. Despite complaints of poor cartridge extraction and ejection, and the continuing demand for a magazine-fed repeating

The Springfield Model 1873 replica made by Pedersoli and imported by Navy Arms recreates the classic 19th-century U.S. Cavalry arm. General Custer's ill-fated Seventh Cavalry carried weapons similar to this at the Battle of the Little Big Horn. Note the distinctive half-stock, a style widely used on sporting rifles but shown here recreating the look of cavalry carbines.

rifle, the "Trapdoor Springfield" remained the U.S. Army's official service rifle until 1894.

The heart of the "trapdoor" mechanism is a breechblock that hinges forward. The U.S. Patent Office attributed the design to Erskine S. Allin, Master Armorer at the government's National Armory in Springfield, Massachusetts. It even awarded Allin a patent (number 49,959, dated September 19, 1865). Evidence suggests, however, that Allin actually took ideas from other inventors who had submitted designs to the Armory. In any event, the government spent a considerable amount--more than $124,00--in settling infringement suits brought by spurned inventors. This unanticipated outlay of funds undoubtedly paved the way for the "Trapdoor Springfield's" eventual adoption by the U.S. Army in May 1873, even though better designs for a single-shot

The Navy Arms replica Springfield Model 1873, like the original service rifle/carbine, employs a four-position hammer. The hammer is shown all the way down.

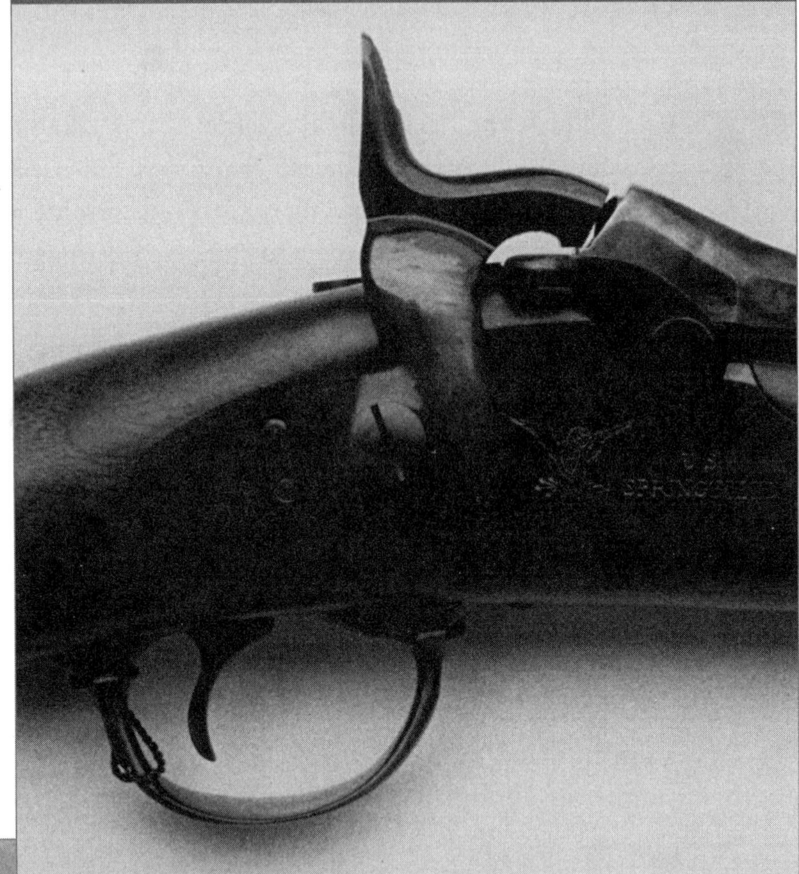

This left-side view of Navy Arms' replica Springfield Model 1873 reveals a saddle ring, indicating the carbine's origins as a weapon with which to arm horse cavalry.

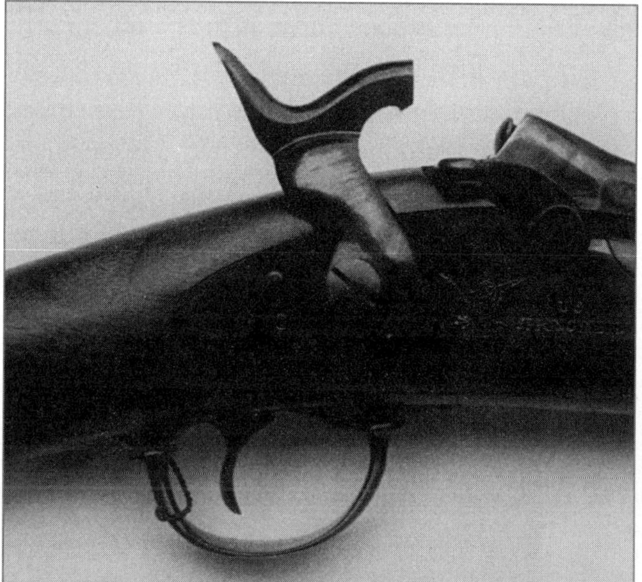

In its half-cock setting, the Navy Arms replica Springfield Model 1873's breechblock is opened by pushing down on the thumb lever to the right of the breechblock, slightly ahead of the hammer.

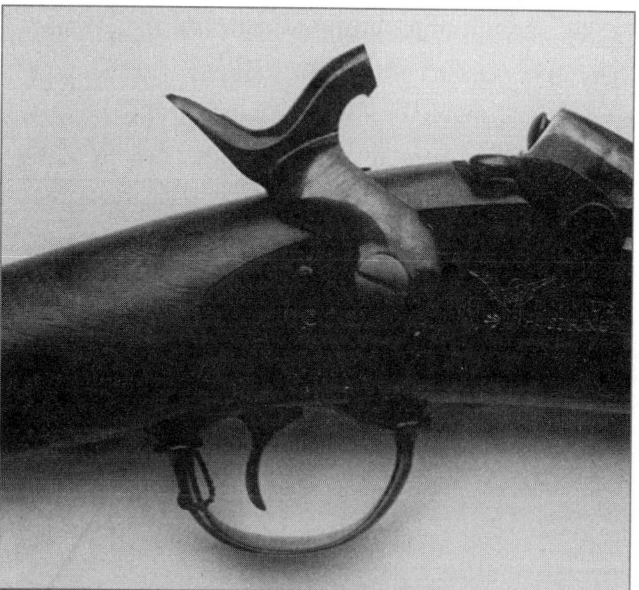

Drawing back the hammer to full cock, the Pedersoli/Navy Arms replica Springfield Model 1873 can now be fired, much as a 19th-century cavalryman would have fired the original.

The Navy Arms Springfield Model 1873 also contains a "safe position," in which the shooter sets the hammer after loading the firing chamber. Note that in this position the hammer covers the breechblock release lever. The shooter then brings the hammer from this position to full cock before shooting.

breechloading military rifle were available by then. Whatever its origins, the trapdoor mechanism worked reasonably well by the standards of the day and provided more than adequate service. It also offered a huge increase in rate of fire over the aging paper-cartridge muzzleloaders used by the Army up to that time; in fact, in early battles against Indian warriors it proved a formidable "secret weapon."

To operate the trapdoor rifle, the large spur hammer was first thumbed to a half-cock setting. A lever located at the rear of the action was then pushed down, opening the breechblock. After a single cartridge was placed into the breech, the breechblock was lowered until it snapped shut. The shooter then drew the hammer back to full cock, took aim and fired. This simple system allowed the U.S. government to upgrade and recycle hundreds of thousands of obsolete muzzleloading rifles left over from the recently concluded Civil War.

Other features of the Navy Arms Model 1873 Springfield Cavalry Carbine include a sporter-style half stock that exposes most of the barrel, a fairly short overall length, and a saddle ring on the left side of the action. As a military gun—or, more correctly, a reproduction of what was once an armed forces rifle—the Navy Arms replica has a military-style ladder rear sight, adjustable out to 2000 yards (actually, the odds of hitting something at that distance with this heavy, slow-moving .45-70 round are slim at best). With the standard 405-grain military bullet, the .45-70 develops a muzzle velocity of just over 1,300 feet per second, which was acceptable by the standards of the time but not by those of modern rifle cartridges. Considering its great bullet weight, the .45-70 is not a round to contemn; indeed, virtually all North American game animals have at one time or another fallen to it. In its more modern loading, though, a 300-grain bullet with a muzzle velocity of 1,880 feet per second improves ballistics considerably.

The Navy Arms Springfield Model 1873's ladder-type rear sight is theoretically adjustable out to 2000 yards, though a hit at that distance on anything smaller than a moose is unlikely at best.

Like many other Navy Arms replicas, its Springfield Cavalry Carbines are made in Italy--in

A left-side view of the Navy Arms Springfield Model 1873 indicates no attempt has been made to pass this replica off as an original Model 1873 cavalry carbine.

Given the slow speed and looping trajectory of the .45-70 cartridge, a well-centered 2.4-inch benchrest-ed group--fired from a Navy Arms Springfield Model 1873, as shown, with one bullet lying directly on the point of aim at the target's center--is cause for celebration.

this case the Davide Pedersoli firm, which is located in the northern Italian region of Gardone Valtrompia, near the Beretta factory. The quality of these rifles—from the walnut stock to the high-polish blued barrel and lockplate to the color case-hardened breech mechanism and buttplate—is breathtakingly superb. This is truly a beautiful gun.

Accuracy with 3-shot benchrested groups fired from 100 yards measured less than 2 1/2 inches across. Recoil with this relatively lightweight gun when firing a heavy, powerful cartridge is considerable, but nothing a determined shooter can't handle with ease. It's not a gun one would want to use to teach a beginning shooter, however, despite the advantages of a single-shot rifle for training purposes. Modern ammunition loaded with smokeless powder virtually eliminates the powder fouling that contributed so greatly to the extraction and ejection difficulties noted in those early battles fought with the Model 1873. By contrast, the reproduction carbine we tested performed trouble-free. Overall, this single-shot rifle was impressive with its delightful handling qualities and its historical significance.

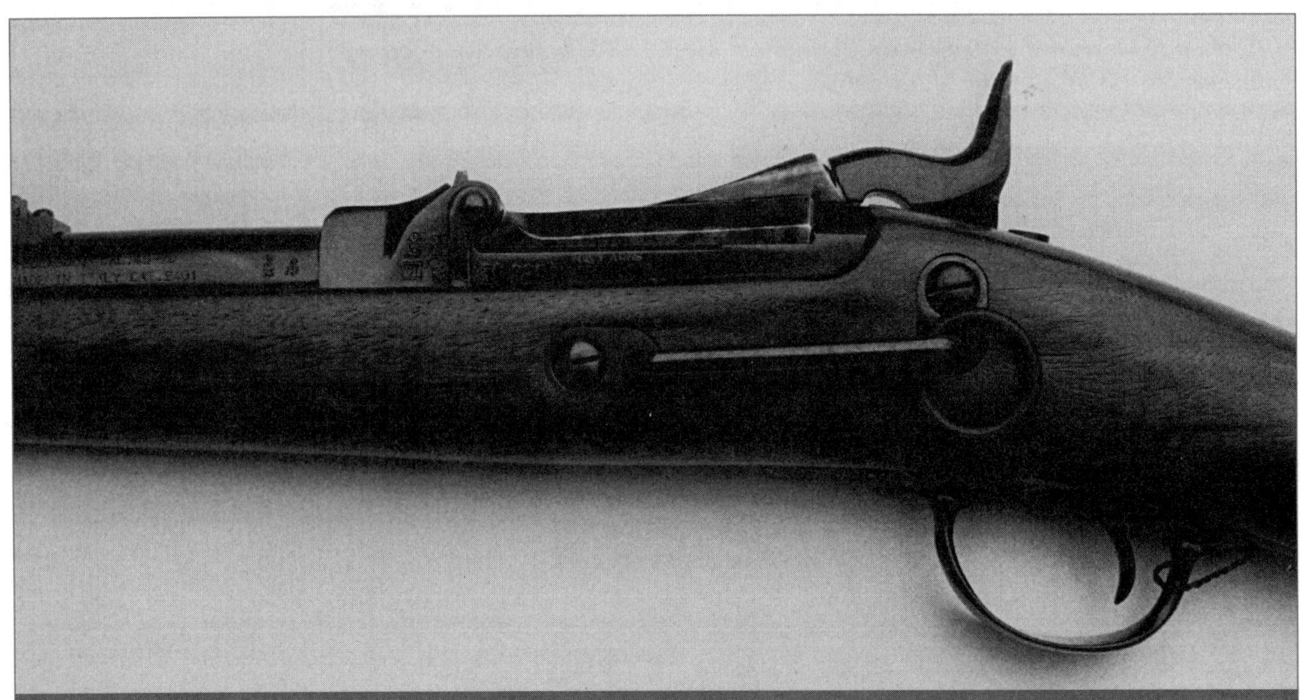

A close-up view of the Navy Arms Springfield Model 1873's receiver reveals the carbine's distinctive saddle ring.

NAVY ARMS 1873 SPRINGFIELD CAVALRY CARBINE

	1873 SPRINGFIELD
Overall Length	40.5 inches
Barrel Length	22.0 inches
Weight	7.0 pounds
Years Produced	1991-present
Caliber	.45-70

PART II:

MODERN BOLT-ACTION RIFLES

For slightly more than a century, the bolt-action rifle has served as an important armed forces weapon as well as a major component of civilian collections. From the 1890s to the 1940s, bolt-action rifles armed virtually all the world's armed forces; even today, they continue to serve the military for such specialized duties as sniping. Many civilian shooters still favor bolt-action rifles for their accuracy and ability to handle extremely powerful cartridges. Despite the development of several new and promising self-loading rifle designs, not to mention strong competition from other traditional rifle types, such as the lever action rifle, more rifle manufacturers now produce a wider variety of bolt-actions than any other type of rifle.

Military surplus bolt-action rifles are extremely popular today, mainly because they tend to be well-made guns. Often a half-century or more in age, these guns are still in no danger of wearing out. The main reason why they are replaced is generally the desire among the armed forces to keep up with their real or potential enemies who have armed themselves with the latest fancy weapons.

Many of these old guns frequently end up in the United States, which supports a lucrative market in military surplus firearms. These rifles offer good value to the beginning shooter or as "sporters" (the latter are often modified, however, in such a way as to destroy their historical and collector's value). For these and other reasons, the serious bolt-action rifle enthusiast may start off with a military surplus rifle but almost certainly will move eventually to one made in the modern era. These often exist in a variety of price ranges and with features sought after by bolt-action enthusiasts. Even the least expensive of these models generally offer good quality and design. Most, though, still use the same type of non-detachable or "blind magazine;" i.e., having loaded the rifle, the shooter may unload live rounds only by cycling rounds through the action and into the firing chamber prior to ejection. This type can be both dangerous and rough on the cartridges themselves; hence, rifles in the higher price ranges generally add either a detachable magazine or a quick-release floorplate to their list of options.

Another factor to be aware of in bolt-action rifles involves the sights. Many a shooter will buy a bolt-action rifle intending to fit an optical (telescopic) sight to the receiver. However, unless the rifle comes with its receiver already tapped and drilled for a sight, its owner will have to hire a gunsmith to do it. Depending on its manufacturer and special features, adding a scope can raise the rifle's price, in some cases by as much as, or even more than, the rifle itself costs. Finally, most bolt-action rifles that are already drilled and tapped for scope mounting come without fixed (iron) sights, which can be an annoying omission.

Mountain Eagle

Another feature affecting the price of a bolt-action rifle is corrosion-resistant stainless steel. Less expensive rifles generally offer a blued finish that is attractive but not especially durable. Combined with synthetic or laminated wood stocks, a stainless steel or corrosion-resistant coating can make a major difference in how well a rifle holds up. Many of the rifles tested for this book, for example, quickly began to rust in the high humidity of Florida where I live. Even without such arduous exposure to the elements, rusting would likely occur on, say, an extended hunting trip.

Fluted barrels may also add to the cost of a rifle while offering certain advantages, such as lowering its weight significantly and improving accuracy. By reducing the weight, however, fluting the barrel also increases recoil. One way to counter-act this is by adding a muzzle brake. Browning and Winchester offer the so-called B.O.S.S. system on some of their rifles, thus combining the features of a muzzle brake and a barrel vibration damper. Because a muzzle brake greatly amplifies noise levels as well, Browning offers a B.O.S.S. unit whose sole function is to dampen barrel vibrations, thereby enhancing accuracy. Savage offers a muzzle brake, too, which shooters can turn to strictly as an option.

As with any type of firearm, embellishments tend to separate the least expensive from the expensive. Browning, for example, can offer virtually any amount of engraving one desires—but at a price! In more expensive models, smoothness of movement by the bolt leads, theoretically, to improved accuracy, more reliable loading and ejecting, and the speed at which the action operates. Another major selling point with bolt-action rifle shooters is controlled-round feeding. In this process, an extractor claw holds each cartridge firmly by the rim from the time the round leaves the magazine until it passes into the firing chamber. With rifles lacking controlled-round feeding , the bolt simply pushes the round into the firing chamber. Both systems have their admirers and detractors. Some shooters prefer the large Mauser-type claw extractor and fixed ejector--a system which by necessity leaves the cartridge case partially unsupported--on the grounds that this system makes ejection far more certain. In other designs, the cartridge case head is supported all the way around as protection against catastrophic failure.

Following a century or more of exhaustive testing, both on the world's battlefields and in numerous hunts, the bolt-action rifle has emerged with a mature and perfected design. As a result, the shooter has a greater variety of features from which to choose than can be found in any other type of rifle.

Ruger Model 77

Browning A-Bolt

The A-Bolt first appeared in 1985. Unlike other Browning products, which have at some point been manufactured by Fabrique Nationale (FN) in Belgium, the A-Bolt has been made solely by Miroku in Japan from the beginning. Still, the A-Bolt line has passed through numerous variations in its relatively short but illustrious history. It all began with the *Hunter Grade,* the basic rifle of the A-Bolt line, which first appeared in 1985. At first, it had no frills whatsoever, with only a matte blue finish on its action and barrel and a satin-finished hardwood stock. True to form, Browning couldn't leave it at that, sensing the need to embellish the rifle. As a result, beginning in 1987, the A-Bolt Hunter was given a gold-plated trigger and a glossy finish on its stock, among other improvements. Because the A-Bolt Hunter usually comes without iron sights—it's drilled and tapped for telescopic sight mounting—Browning offers fixed sights on this model. Its optional iron sights, which are fully adjustable for windage and elevation, also feature a high-visibility gold bead on the front sight protected by a hood. Regrettably, all other A-Bolt variants come without iron sights, requiring owners to mount their own scopes.

The next step up from the Hunter grade is the *A-Bolt Medallion model.* Introduced in 1985, it has a high-polish blued finish on the barrel and receiver, a gold-plated trigger, and a rosewood forend and grip cap. Because the A-Bolt's flat action surfaces practically invite engraving, Miroku began engraving the Medallion grade rifle's receiver in 1987 with a photo-etching process. The *Gold Medallion,* introduced in 1988, includes this engraving process with the name "Gold Medallion" appearing in gold leaf on the right side of the receiver. The stock is made of top-quality walnut and the pistol grip, which is slightly larger than that found on the Hunter and standard Medallion models, has a grip cap made out of

The Browning A-Bolt is a mature, well-seasoned rifle that is still gathering admirers after almost two decades in production.

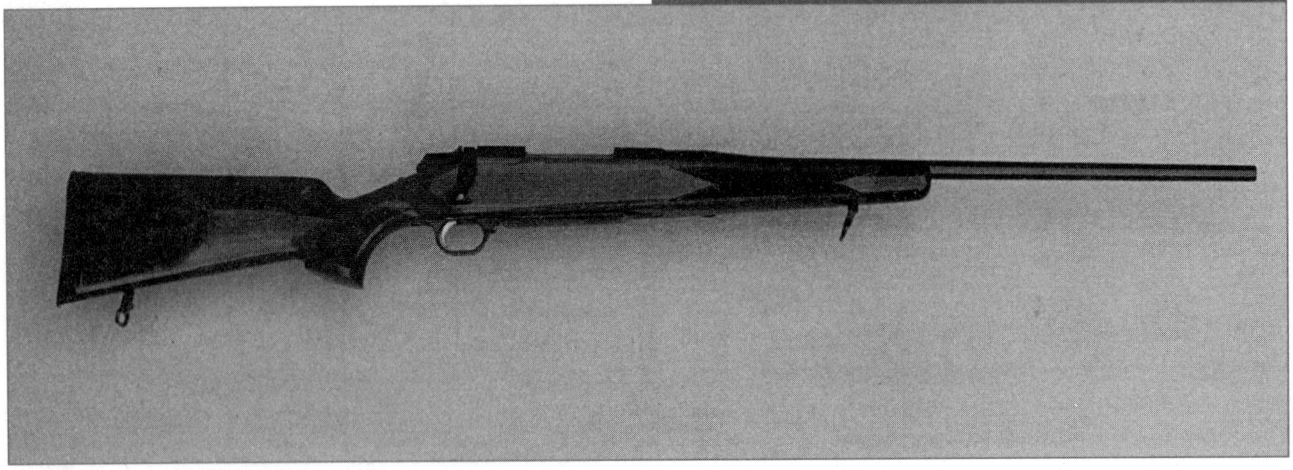

One advantage of the A-Bolt's configuration is its breech face, which completely supports the end of the cartridge casing. In the event of a pierced primer, for instance, a protective ring of steel lies between the shooter and the expanding gases.

The A-Bolt's distinctive fluted bolt retains strength while lowering weight and eliminating excess bulk.

rosewood, with a thin brass spacer between the rosewood cap and walnut stock. The stock forearm, also fashioned from rosewood, has a brass spacer separating it and the walnut. A rubber recoil pad also features a brass spacer between it and the walnut stock.

For smaller or younger shooters, Browning announced in 1988 the *Micro Medallion A-Bolt* variation, which weighs a little over six pounds (a saving of 11 ounces compared to the standard rifle). To achieve this weight reduction, the Micro Medallion's barrel was shortened two inches. Because the smaller rounds allowed only a short-action bolt to be fitted, magazine capacity was reduced. To create an easier length of pull for smaller shooters, the Micro Medallion stock was shortened 5/16th of an inch. By limiting the Micro Medallion to a short action, it could fire only the .223 Remington, .22 Hornet, .22-250 Remington, .243 Winchester, .257 Roberts and 7mm-08 rounds. This also reduced muzzle blast and recoil.

Browning has been making left-handed A-Bolt rifles since the Medallion model first appeared in 1987. At first, the only caliber choices available for left-handers were .270 Winchester, .30-'06 and 7mm Remington Magnum. But over the years Browning has made the left-handed A-Bolt in the following additional calibers: .25-'06 Remington, .280 Remington, .338 Winchester Magnum and .375 Holland & Holland Magnum.

The *A-Bolt Stainless Stalker* variant made it first appearance in 1987. Its receiver, barrel and bolt handle are all made from matte-finished stainless steel for resistance against foul weather. Early Stainless Stalkers had wood stocks painted black with rough, stippled surfaces. Browning changed the stock in 1988 to a

Because the A-Bolt generally comes without integral iron sights, the receiver must be drilled and tapped for mounting a scope.

black-colored, graphite-fiberglass composite material offering corrosion resistance that was far more effective than wood. The graphite stock also offered superior recoil absorption. A left-handed version of this model appeared in 1990.

The *Camo Stalker* featured a laminated stock finished in shades of black and green to blend with woodland foliage. Like the A-Bolt Hunter, this model wore a matte (non-glare) blued finish on its barrel and action. Caliber offerings were limited to .270, .30-'06 and 7mm Remington Magnum. Browning produced the Camo Stalker with its interesting laminated stock only from 1987 to 1990, with some 1500 made in all.

The *A-Bolt Composite Stalker*, with its matte blued finish on receiver and barrel, was introduced in 1988. The stock was made of graphite for strength, light weight and weather resistance. The *Euro-Bolt* version, by contrast, offered a more European look than did the rest of the A-Bolt series. It features a schnabel forearm, a rounded bolt shroud at the rear of the receiver, a dull blued finish on all metal parts, a satin-finished stock, and a Mannlicher-inspired "butterknife" bolt handle.

In addition to the centerfire caliber choices (see above), Browning once made a .22 Long Rifle or .22 Magnum rimfire A-Bolt called the *A-Bolt 22*. Introduced in 1986, this full-sized bolt action rifle—as big as the standard A-Bolt—actually cost about $150 less than the least expensive centerfire A-Bolt. Browning offered it both in Grade I and, beginning in 1988, Gold Medallion grades before discontinuing the model in 1997. As part of its *Browning Big Game Animals of North America* series, the company has also offered the A-Bolt in limited editions. The *Big Horn Sheep* issue (1986-1987) was available in .270 caliber and came with a 22-inch barrel only. It featured a walnut stock made of the choicest grade wood, all embellished with elegant skipline checkering and extensive

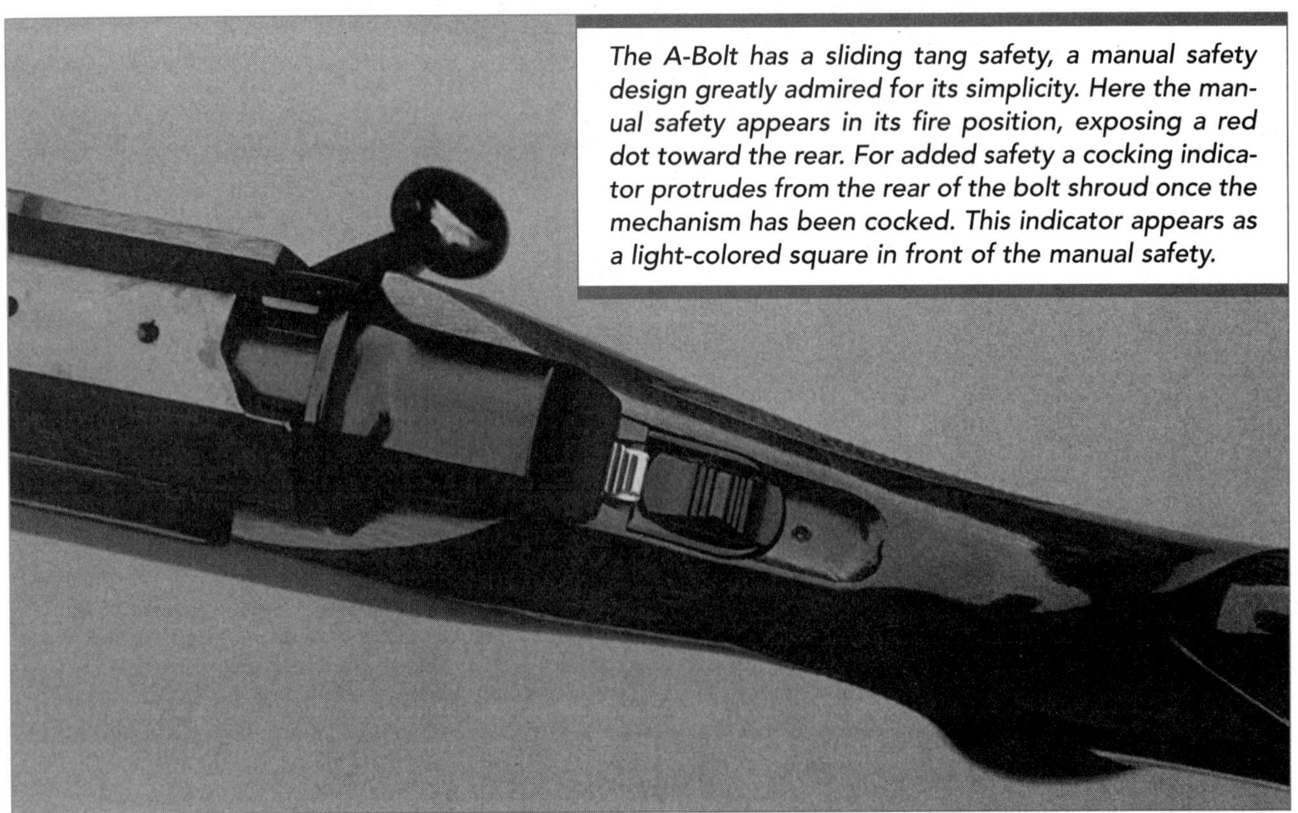

The A-Bolt has a sliding tang safety, a manual safety design greatly admired for its simplicity. Here the manual safety appears in its fire position, exposing a red dot toward the rear. For added safety a cocking indicator protrudes from the rear of the bolt shroud once the mechanism has been cocked. This indicator appears as a light-colored square in front of the manual safety.

engraving. The receiver, barrel triggerguard and magazine floorplate bore engravings, too, including an engraved bighorn sheep inlaid in 24-karat gold.

The *Pronghorn* limited edition issue appeared in 1987, after only 500 were produced. Its only caliber choice was .243. Extensive engraving covered the receiver, barrel, triggerguard and magazine floorplate, and on each side of the receiver appeared an engraving of a pronghorn antelope plated with 24-karat gold. The floorplate also depicted a family of pronghorn antelope, engraved and plated with 24-karat gold. Rosewood caps appeared at the front of the stock forearm and pistol grip cap, set off from a walnut stock by brass spacers. Then, in 1993, Browning announced an improved A-Bolt line: A-Bolt II. These rifles are much the same as the originals except that the bolt on the new model is less likely to bind or stick, thanks to the addition of a non-rotating bolt sleeve to the action. This model also features an improved trigger mechanism. As of 2000, Browning offers the *A-Bolt II* series in Hunter, Medallion, Micro Medallion, Gold Medallion, Varmint, Eclipse, Eclipse Varmint, Stainless Stalker and Composite Stalker styles. All are as described (except for the Eclipse and Varmint models, which did not exist prior to the A-Bolt II). The Eclipse has a thumbhole stock made of laminated wood and the standard A-Bolt barrel; the Eclipse Varmint model, meanwhile, carries a heavy bull barrel. It also features a heavier barrel, a flattened forend, a palm swell on the pistol grip, and a laminated wood stock.

In 1994 Browning added the B.O.S.S. (Ballistic Optimizing Shooting System) option to the

When reloading, the A-Bolt's clever dual-loading magazine can either be unhinged (as shown) or detached completely.

In this view the manual safety is in the fire position, but the cocking indicator is not visible. That means the striker is uncocked and the rifle is not ready.

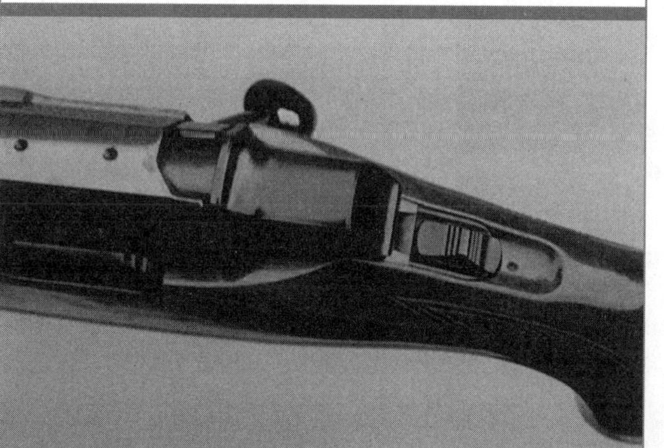

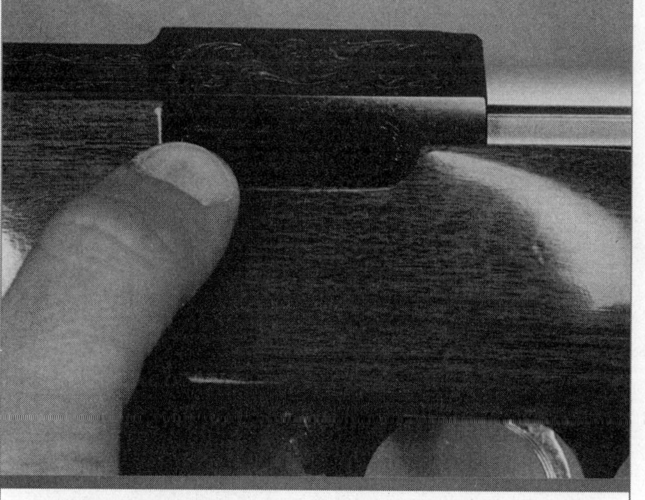

A bolt release, located on the left side of the A-Bolt's receiver, pushes in so the bolt can be removed.

A-Bolt line. This muzzle device adjusts the barrel vibrations generated upon firing as a way to increase accuracy. The B.O.S.S. is available as an option on any A-Bolts which do *not* have iron sights (but it is standard on the Eclipse and Varmint models). As for calibers, a wide range of choices is available (see specifications table). To accommodate these caliber options, Miroku makes the A-Bolt in three bolt styles: short action, long action standard and long action magnum. The bolt head contains three locking lugs and has a short 60-degree bolt throw for fast bolt manipulation. Like many modern bolt-action rifles, the A-Bolt employs a plunger-type ejector in the bolt face. The bolt handle itself has a flattened knob; it looks odd but makes for quick and easy manipulation.

The A-Bolt's controls feature a tang-mounted safety that moves back to safe and forward to fire. When the striker is cocked, a red cocking indicator protrudes from the rear of the bolt shroud. This allows the shooter to observe (or feel) whether or not the rifle is cocked. The grooved gold-plated trigger adds another touch of class typical of FN/Browning products. Other extras include a rosewood-tipped pistol grip cap and forend. The extremely versatile magazine design is wonderfully clever. Browning offers a choice of either detaching the magazine altogether for loading or, if one prefers, hinging the magazine down from the front and reloading without detaching it from the rifle. In the short-action calibers, magazine capacity is four rounds. Exceptions include the .223 caliber, which holds up to five rounds, and the Micro-Medallion variant in .284 caliber, with its maximum of only three rounds. The long-action standard calibers hold up to four rounds, while the magazine capacity in the long-action magnum calibers is three rounds.

The rifle tested for this book—an A-Bolt II "Medallion" model in .270 Winchester caliber—shot wonderfully. Because it included no iron

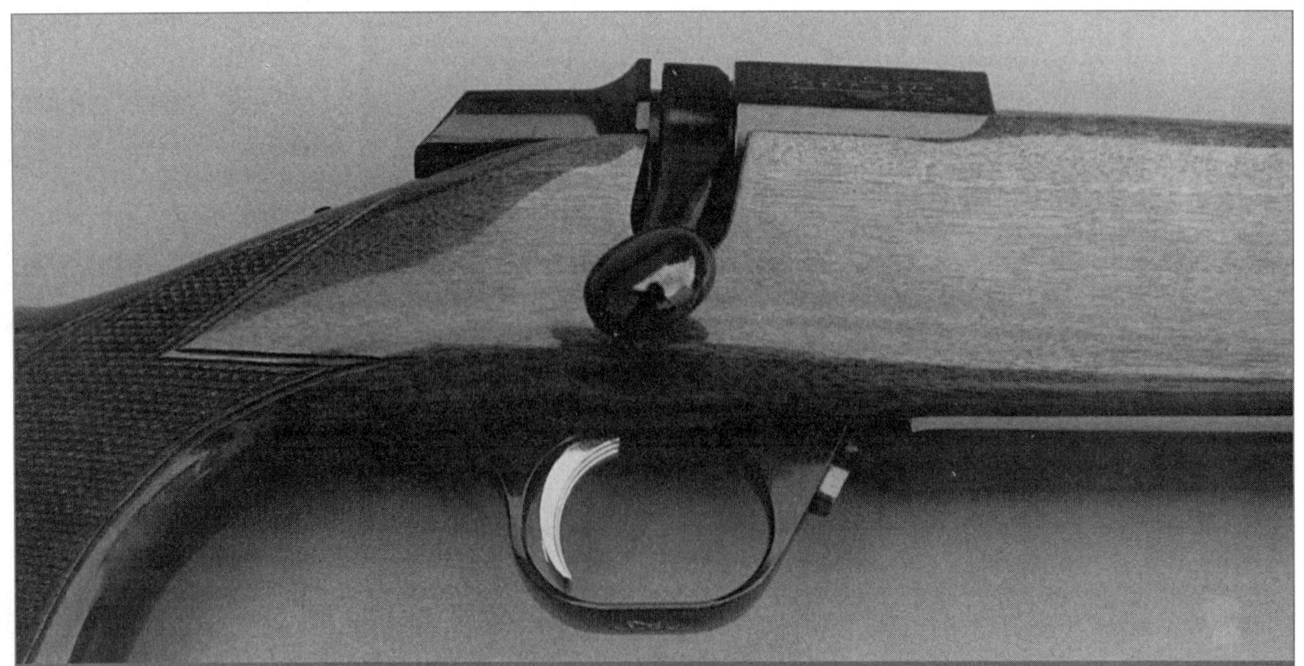

The A-Bolt has a distinctive bolt handle with a flattened knob at the end. Its purpose is to speed up bolt manipulation between shots.

sights on its barrel (which most A-Bolt rifles do not), a "Buck" variable 3-9x telescopic sight by Millett was added. Three-shot groups from the 100-yard bench scarcely less than an inch apart proved the norm, placing this rifle slightly below the magic "one minute of angle" accuracy mark sought by hunters. Recoil in the .270 Winchester caliber could certainly be felt but was not excessive. The stock is well designed to help ease recoil, along with a buttplate that sports a generously-sized recoil pad to soften the blow still further.

The A-Bolt remains one of the best bolt-action systems ever offered. It also offers a price structure flexible enough to suit almost any checkbook. With calibers ranging from .22 Long Rifle to .375 H&H Magnum (left- and right-handed actions) and a choice of matte blue, bright blue and stainless finishes, the A-Bolt offers something good for virtually every shooter.

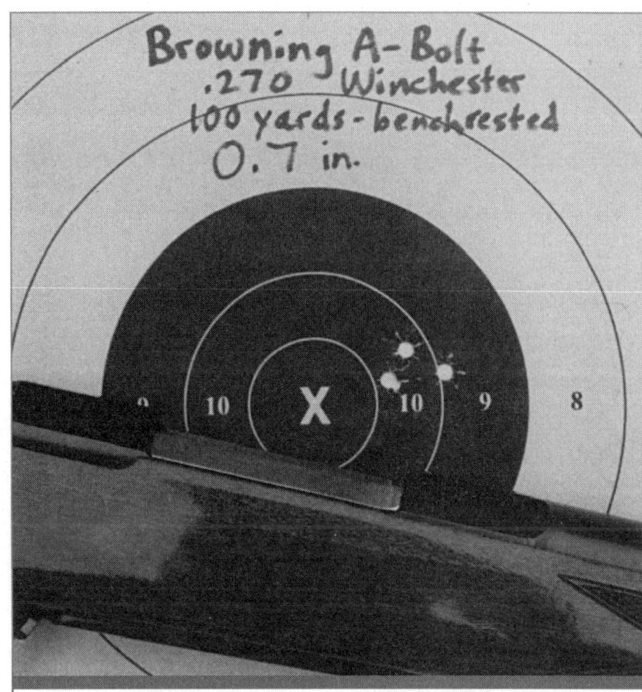

When tested with the .270 Winchester caliber, the A-bolt delivered 3-shot groups of less than 1 minute of angle (1 inch at 100 yards). This group, measuring 7/10ths-inch, was fired with Winchester's 140-grain Fail Safe bullets.

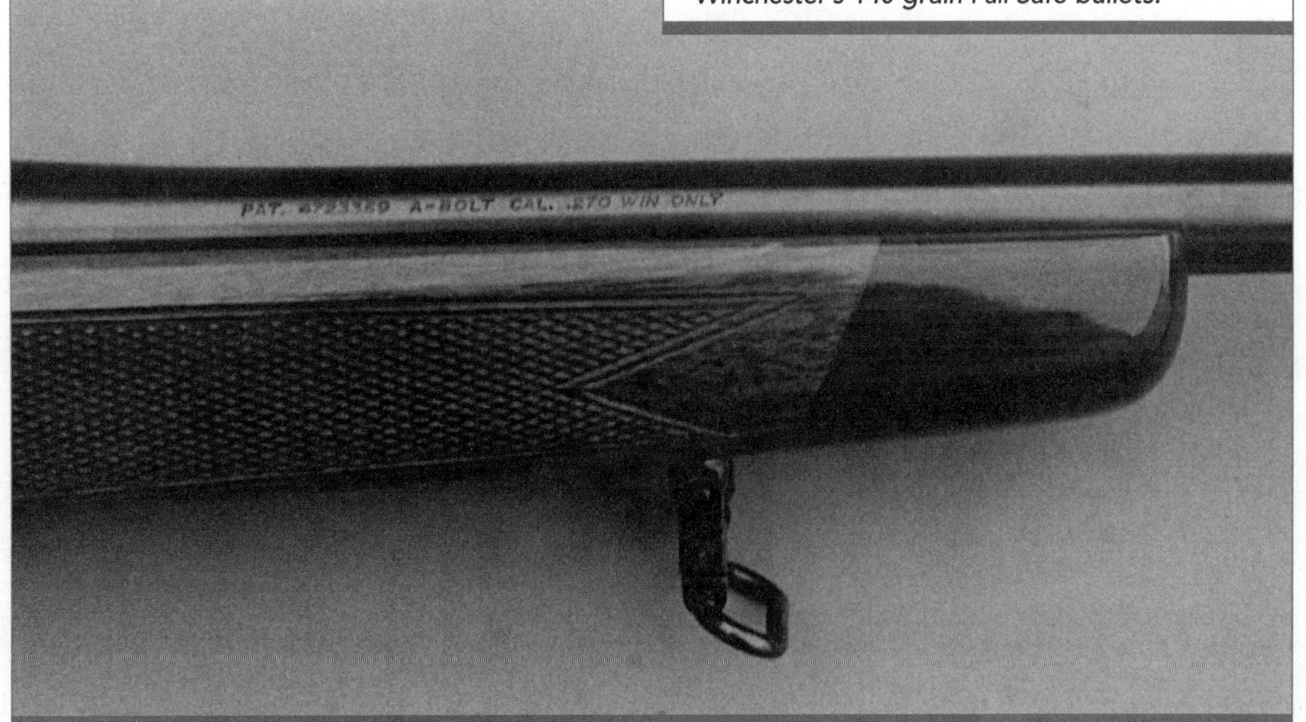

The A-Bolt comes from the factory with numerous extra touches, such as sling swivels. Note also the rosewood endcap.

BROWNING A-BOLT

	A-BOLT
Overall Length	41.75 inches (short action) 44.75 inches (standard and magnum action)
Barrel Length	22 inches standard; 26 inches on magnums
Weight	6.5-7.5 pounds
Manufacturer	Miroku Firearms Manufacturing Company, Japan
Importer	Browning Arms Company, Morgan, Utah
Years Produced	1985-present. See text for dates of specific variants.
Caliber/Capacity	See chart below for chamberings/text for capacities

CHAMBERING CAPACITIES FOR BROWNING A-BOLT

	Ec	C/S	E/B	G/M	Htr	Med	Mic	Stls	V
Short Action									
.22 Hornet							X		
.223 Remington		X			X	X	X	X	X
.22-250 Remington	X	X	X		X	X	X	X	X
.257 Roberts							X		
7mm-08 Remington		X			X	X	X	X	
.243 Winchester	X	X	X		X	X	X	X	
.284 Winchester							X		
.308 Winchester	X	X	X		X	X	X	X	X
Long Action Standard									
.25-'06		X			X	X	X	X	
.270 Winchester	X	X	X	X	X	X	X	X	
.280 Remington		X			X	X	X	X	
.30-'06	X	X	X	X	X	X	X	X	
Long Action Magnum									
7mm Remington Magnum	X	X	X	X	X	X	X	X	
.300 Winchester Magnum		X		X	X	X	X	X	
.338 Winchester Magnum		X			X	X		X	
.375 H&H Magnum						X		X	

KEY: *Ec=Eclipse* *C/S=Composite Stalker* *E/B=Euro-Bolt* *G/M=Gold Medallion* *Htr=Hunter* *Med=Medallion* *Mic= Micro Medallion* *Stls=Stainless Stalker* *V=Varmint*

Century Sporters

All Century Sporters are military surplus bolt-action rifles that have been modified to sporter configurations. Examples include the Swedish Mauser Models 96/38, the Mauser Model 98, the Enfield Pattern 14 and the Lee-Enfield. While the original action remains the same, Century has added a new barrel and a weatherproof, synthetic Bell & Carlson stock (the bayonet mounting lugs and cleaning rods have been dropped, of course). Also deleted are the original military-type iron sights, which means scope mounting is mandatory, along with (in the modified Mausers) a longer, turned-down bolt handle and low-mounted safety (to clear the scope; a typical military Mauser three-position safety won't clear the eyepiece on low-mounted telescopic sights). Oddly enough, the ex-military Mausers sporterized by Century have kept their stripper-clip guides even though, with the typical mounted scope, stripper clips can't be used. Evidently the guides were retained since milling them off would involve considerable extra machine time, raising the cost of what is intended to be a low-cost rifle.

The Century 98 Sporter may not look much like its progenitor, the classic Mauser Model 98 military rifle, but its rugged and reliable mechanism remains the same.

The rifle tested for this book was an ex-Mauser Model 98. Rechambered to .30-'06 caliber from its original 8mm

Mauser, it proved an effective conversion. The stock was pleasant to hold and the rifle proved comfortable to shoot, too, thanks to its thick rubber recoil pad. As for accuracy, 3-shot benchrested groups from 100 yards measured in the 2.5- to 3-inch range, which is at least adequate for an ex-military rifle in this price range. Because this was one of my early efforts in swapping telescopic sights on several unsighted rifles, these results might have been better. In general, though, I am not in favor of converting military surplus rifles into sporters, because they lose most of their historical identity in the process. It must be admitted, though, that Century does a good job of it. Their conversions are functional, attractive and reasonably priced, especially when one takes into account the high performance they offer.

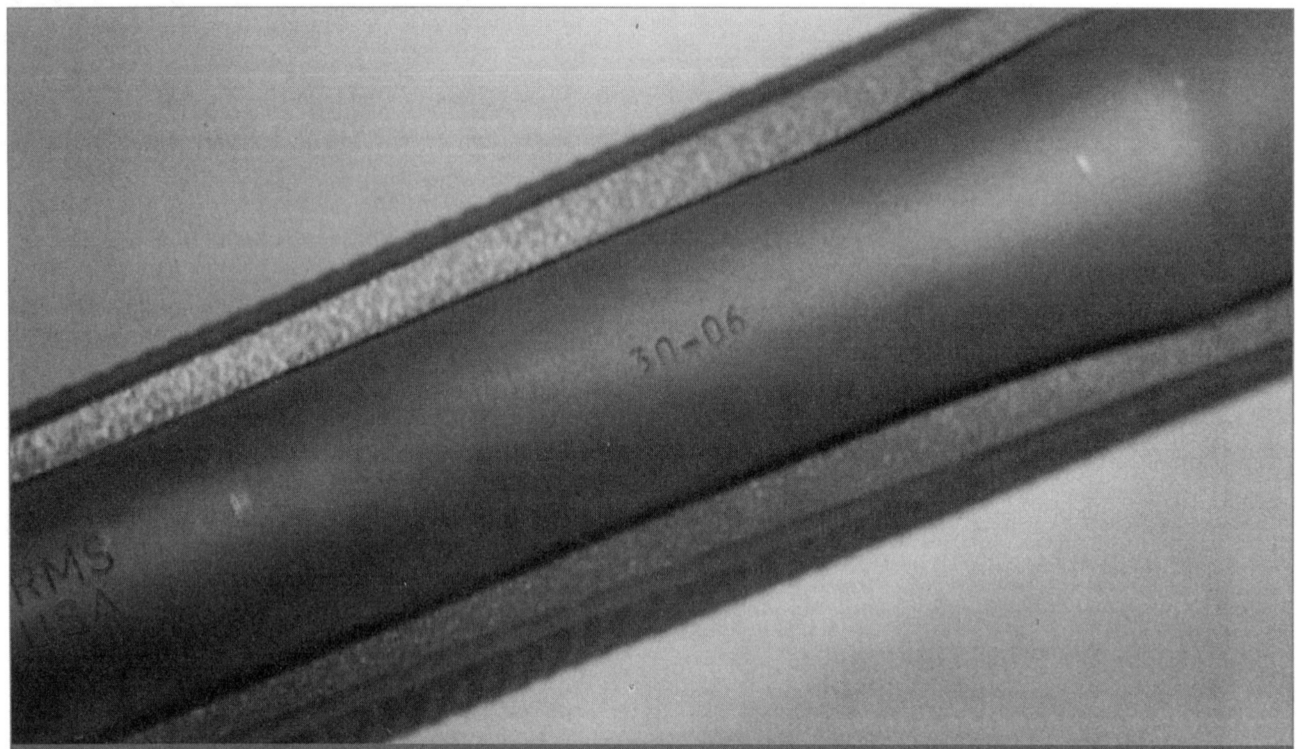

The Century 98 Sporter's caliber marking—in this case .30-06—appears on the barrel. Despite its age, the .30-06 remains an excellent all-around hunting cartridge, effective against all but the most dangerous game animals.

CENTURY SPORTER 98 (FORMERLY MAUSER MODEL 98)

	SPORTER 98
Overall Length	44.0 inches
Barrel Length	24.0 inches
Weight	7.0 pounds
Importer	Century International Arms, St. Albans, VT
Years Produced	1991-present
Caliber/Capacity	.243, .270, .308 and .30-06/5 rounds

Howa Lightning (Howa Model 1500)

Browning's A-Bolt is not the only excellent rifle made by the Japanese. The Howa Lightning (imported by Interarms) is an equally fine bolt-action model. Howa, having created its first SAKO-type bolt-action rifle in 1973, and having made barreled actions for Weatherby's Vanguard model until 1995, is no newcomer when it comes to making top-quality bolt-action rifles. The company's Lightning model (introduced in 1973) was originally imported by Smith & Wesson as the Model 1500 during the late 1970s and early 1980s. Mossberg bought up Smith & Wesson's entire stock in 1985 and for the next three years marketed these rifles as the

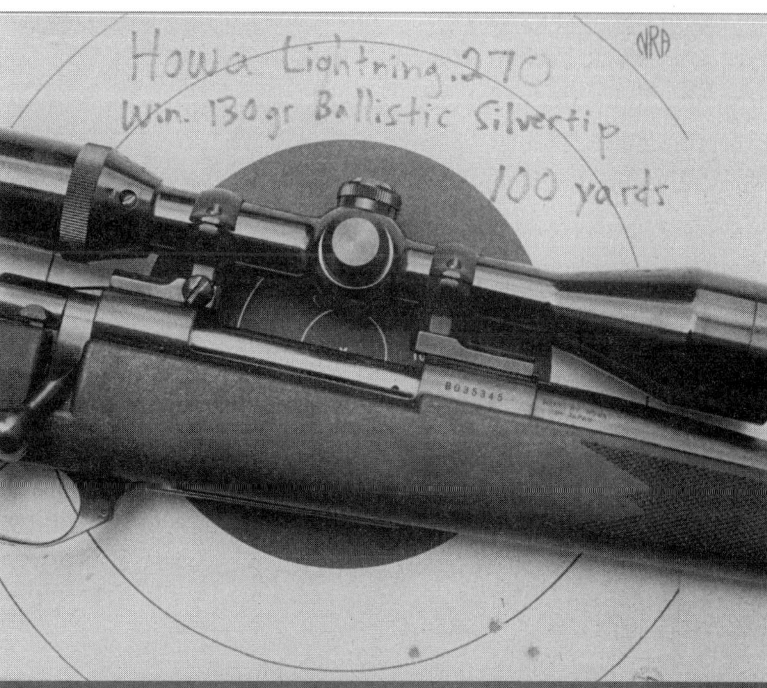

The Howa Lightning, while not the most accurate rifle tested, performed quite well as this 1.5-inch, 100-yard benchrested group attests.

The Howa Lightning combines elements of other successful bolt-action rifles, notably SAKO and Remington's Model 700.

"Mossberg Model 1500" (Weatherby's Vanguard during that period was still another example of the Model 1500). Smith & Wesson's Model 1500 came with a wooden stock (as did the Weatherby variants) either plain or embellished with skipline checkering. When Interarms began importing the Model 1500 from Smith & Wesson in 1988, a synthetic stock became standard. Gun styles do, after all, fall in and out of fashion like clothing and everything else.

While the Lightning's bolt mechanism owes much to SAKO, other influences, notably the Mauser Model 98 and the Remington Model 700, are also evident. It's a strong yet simple unit, with one especially notable feature. Unlike most bolt-action rifle bolts, the Howa bolt features "compound cocking," which occurs when the shooter first lifts the bolt handle to open the bolt. The rest of the cocking motion takes place at the end of the reloading stroke, when the shooter pushes the bolt handle down to seat it prior to the next shot. Compound cocking is a useful feature because it makes the initial bolt lift less arduous than with other designs deemed fashionable since shortly before World War I. Another rifle using compound cocking is the Accuracy International PM (L96A1), which has been used by the British army and a number of other military and police forces as a sniper rifle. Slightly more than three-fourths of the Howa's cocking energy is transferred to the initial bolt lift, with the rest occurring when the shooter pushes the bolt back down into its seat.

Other than the magazine floorplate release latch, which is located in the forward portion of the triggerguard, controls on the Howa Lightning are pretty straightforward. The safety is the sliding type that goes forward to fire and back to safe. It is easy to operate with the shooter's right thumb and is

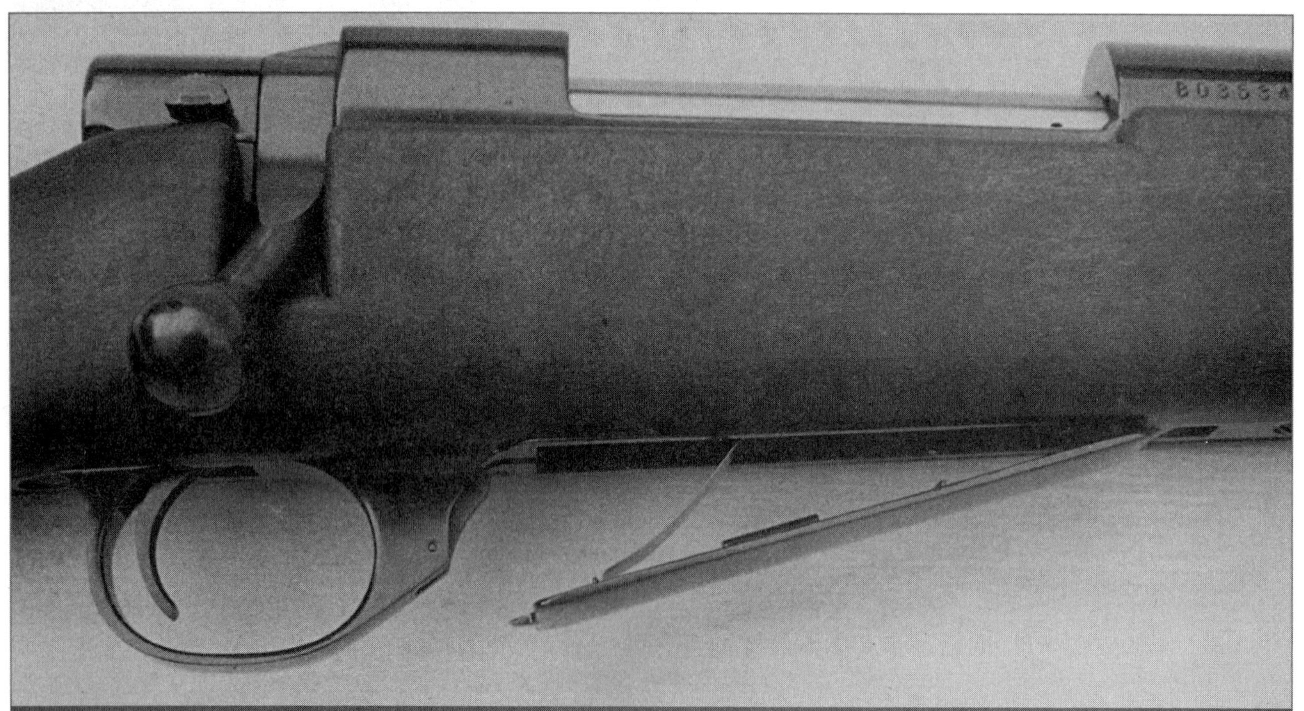

The Howa Lightning features a detachable magazine floorplate for fast, safe unloading. Note the floorplate latch in the extended web at the leading edge of the triggerguard. The sliding manual safety, located behind the bolt handle, also appears in this view.

silent in operation, a characteristic all hunters appreciate. Other desirable features of this rifle include a weather-resistant polymer stock, a wide choice of both standard and magnum calibers, a hinged magazine floorplate for fast, safe unloading, and a receiver tapped and drilled for an optical (telescopic) sight. Like most modern rifles set up for telescopic sights, the Lightning regrettably comes without any provision for fixed (iron) sights, a fault shared with many current rifles. In my opinion, any high-quality rifle should include simple, sturdy iron sights along with easy scope-mounting provisions. Unfortunately, the rifle manufacturers don't seem to be getting this sort of feedback from their customers. It's important to remember that a good scope and its mounting hardware can easily cost as much as, or even more than, the gun itself.

In testing the Lightning for accuracy (using a .270 Winchester-chambered variant), results were good. Although no iron sights came with the rifle, the Lightning accepts the same kind of telescopic sight mounts as the ever popular Remington Model 700, making the purchase of a suitable scope and scope mounts relatively easy. All things considered, the Howa Lightning, with its fine SAKO features, is an excellent rifle for the money. While perhaps not the best-performing rifle available, it is a competent performer and worthy of serious consideration to those rifle shooters who need a quality gun on a tight budget.

Like many other rifles, the Howa Lightning comes without integral (iron) sights. The scope mounted here is Millett's "Buck," a rugged and reliable 3-9x variable-power unit with outstanding optical qualities at a reasonable price.

HOWA LIGHTNING

	LIGHTNING
Overall Length	42 inches (standard calibers)
Barrel Length	22 inches (standard calibers); 24 inches (magnum calibers)
Weight	7.5 pounds
Manufacturer	Howa Machinery, Ltd., Nagoya, Japan
Importer	Interarms
Years Produced	1993-present
Caliber/Capacity	.223, .22-250, .243, .270, .308, .30-06, 7mm Remington Magnum, .300 Winchester Magnum, .338 Winchester Magnum/5 rounds

Mountain Eagle (Magnum Research)

The Mountain Eagle rifle, introduced in 1996 and sold by Magnum Research, comes with a synthetic stock and features a SAKO-built action. Integral Leupold scope rings are also standard. The company's goal is to create an out-of-the-box rifle with all the features needed for serious target work or hunting included in the price.

The Mountain Eagle is offered in a variety of chamberings, all of the high-performance, high-accuracy variety. Some are a bit on the exotic side, but I requested for our tests a rifle chambered for the .270 Winchester cartridge (first introduced in 1925 with Winchester's famous Model 52 rifle). Despite its age, this cartridge remains an excellent

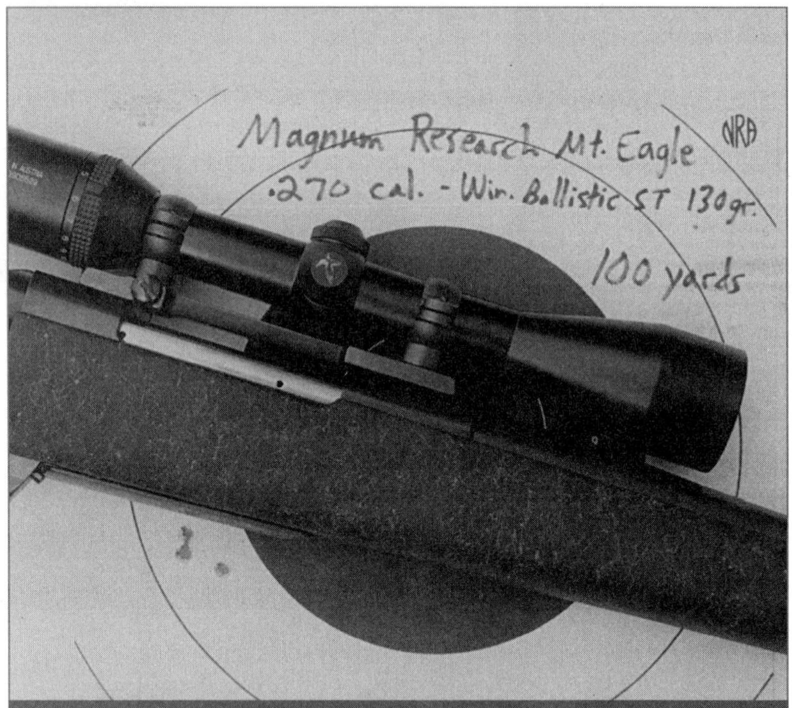

A Mountain Eagle rifle chambered in .270 Winchester caliber with a 130-grain bullet produced this 8/10ths-inch group. This combination offers reduced recoil and high velocities, making it an excellent varmint round at extended ranges.

The Mountain Eagle offers top performance right out of the box (photograph courtesy of Magnum Research).

The safety on this Mountain Eagle is located on the right side of the receiver, behind the bolt handle. As shown, it has been rocked forward to its fire position, exposing a red dot. Note the protruding cocked-striker indicator, which appears as a small pin extending behind the bolt shroud.

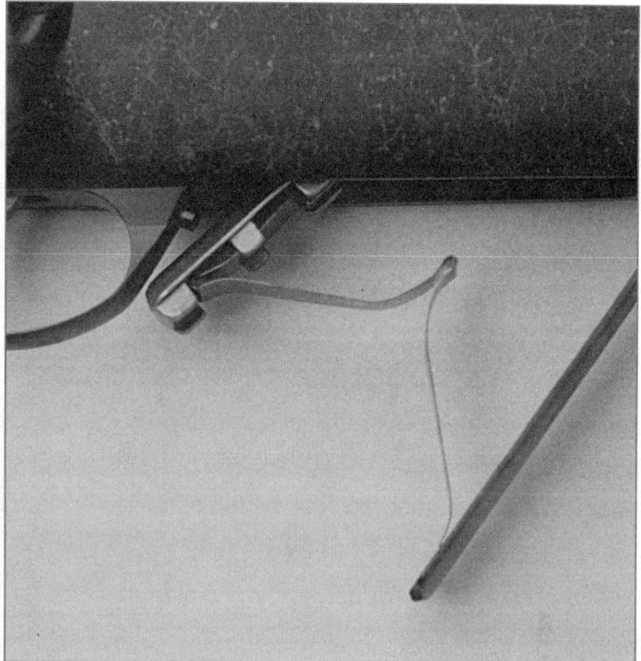

When the magazine floorplate springs open, the Mountain Eagle's magazine can be easily and safely unloaded. The detachable-floorplate option is safer than a blind magazine and offers fewer parts to keep up with than does a detachable box magazine.

The leading edge of the Mountain Eagle's triggerguard reveals a small button that serves as a release for the detachable magazine floorplate.

The Mountain Eagle comes straight from the factory box with a scope mount and scope rings, saving new owners considerable expense.

The Mountain Eagle's bolt mechanism comes from SAKO in Finland. The bolt release is the checkered steel button located on the receiver just below the adjustment ring on the telescopic sight.

The Mountain Eagle is set up for telescopic sight mounting all the way, including a raised cheekpiece on the left side of the stock.

medium-caliber round with good accuracy potential out to 500 yards. Created from a .30-06 cartridge casing (necked down at the case mouth to accept a 7mm diameter bullet), the .270 Winchester proved a good test cartridge in many of the rifles we tested, offering adequate killing power for all but the largest African or North American game. Its impressive accuracy and widespread availability make it a favorite with many shooters.

Chambering the Mountain Eagle for the .270 Winchester cartridge proved a wise choice, for test results demonstrated sensational accuracy. A typical 3-shot benchrested group fired from 100 yards measured a mere 8/10ths of an inch across. Moreover, the rifle is easy to shoot, its SAKO-type bolt cycling with smooth precision and efficiency.

While the Mountain Eagle's price may seem high, bear in mind that scope rings come with it. Add a scope, sight it in, and the Mountain Eagle will shoot as well as any rifle on the market short of a custom gun costing several times as much. In short, this is a top choice among modern bolt-action rifles.

The author tested the Mountain Eagle with a Swarovski Optik 3-10x variable-power scope—an excellent combination.

MOUNTAIN EAGLE

	MOUNTAIN EAGLE
Overall Length	44 inches (standard)
Barrel Length	24 inches (standard) or 26 inches (Varmint)
Weight	7.8 pounds
Manufacturer	Magnum Research, Inc. Minneapolis, MN
Years Produced	1996-present
Caliber & Capacity	.22, .223, .270, .280, .30-06, 7mm Remington Magnum, .300 Winchester Magnum, .300 Weatherby Magnum, .338 Winchester Magnum, .340 Weatherby Magnum, .375 H&H, .416 Remington Magnum/5 rounds

Remington Model Seven

The Model Seven, Remington's diminutive carbine version of the Model 700, first appeared in 1983. Basically a Model 700 with a shortened action, barrel and buttstock, the Model Seven has become extremely popular with deer hunters and others who seek a lightweight bolt-action carbine of modern design in chamberings that appeal to modern hunters. A handsome and well-designed rifle, the Model Seven has replaced Remington's efficient but homelier Model 600 and 660 series of short sporting rifles.

Like the Model 700, the Model Seven design combines a two-lug bolt with a cartridge case-head support around the bolt face, a small claw extractor and plunger-type ejector. In the event of a catastrophic cartridge case failure, a hole drilled between the two bolt locking lugs directs the expanding powder gases downward into the magazine well, destroying the magazine spring and follower rather than squirting hot gas and metal into the shooter's face and eyes.

The Model Seven's controls include a two-position manual safety located on the right rear portion of the receiver. The fire setting lies toward the front and the safe setting is to the rear. When applied, either on its rearward or safe setting, the manual safety locks the bolt and fire-control mechanism. When pushed forward carefully with the thumb and forefinger, the safety control operates silently, a positive feature for hunters not wishing to startle game animals at a critical moment in the hunt. Another safety feature is the cocking indicator, which can be seen in the shroud at the back end of the receiver. When the striker is cocked, it indicates that the firing pin spring is under tension and ready to release when the trigger is pulled. The indicator now appears level with the shroud. When the rifle is uncocked, the indicator sinks into the shroud about an eight of an inch. The magazine, which is a fixed type,

Remington's Model Seven is a handy little carbine variant of the company's world-famous Model 700 bolt-action rifle.

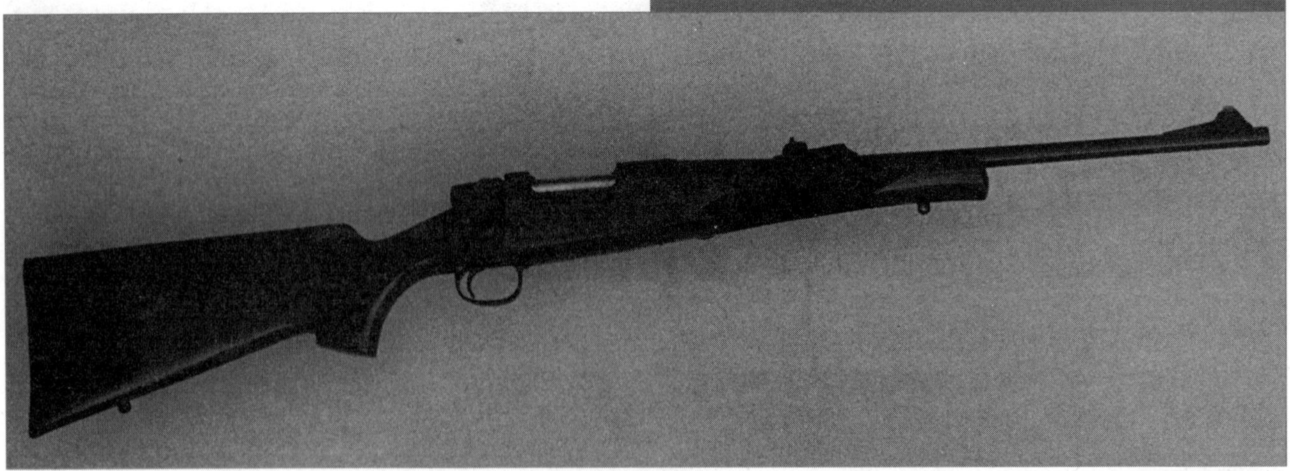

includes a pushbutton release in front of the triggerguard. This enables the shooter to open the magazine floorplate from below and unload without having to cycle live ammunition through the action. As with the model 700, the Model Seven features a smoothly operating bolt handle; in fact, it operates easier than the Model 700, thanks to its shorter action body and much shorter cartridges.

In Remington's attempts to create a design suitable to as many shooters as possible, the Model Seven has appeared in several different versions. The standard Model Seven, introduced in 1983, features a walnut stock with schnabel forend and iron sights (the rear sight is adjustable). Caliber choices include .223, 243, .260 Remington, 7mm-08 and .308. Between 1993 and 1996, the company also offered standard Model Sevens in a .17 Remington caliber version, in .222 Remington caliber, and,

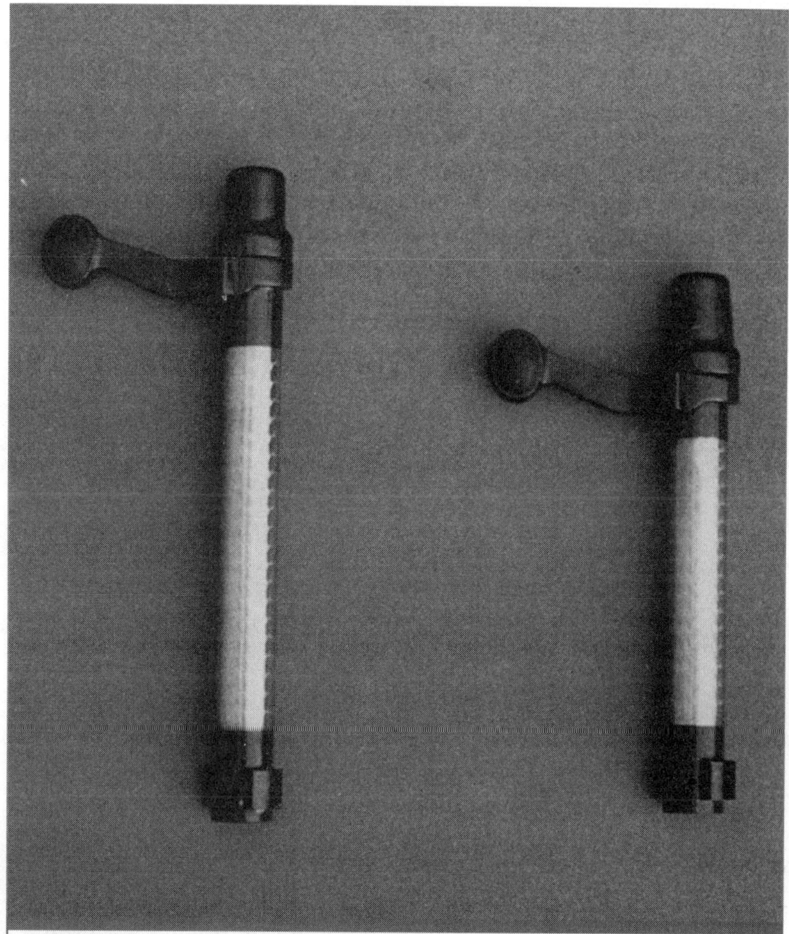

The Model Seven bolt (right) is appreciably smaller than that found on the Model 700 (left), making it possible for Remington to build the Model Seven with more compact dimensions.

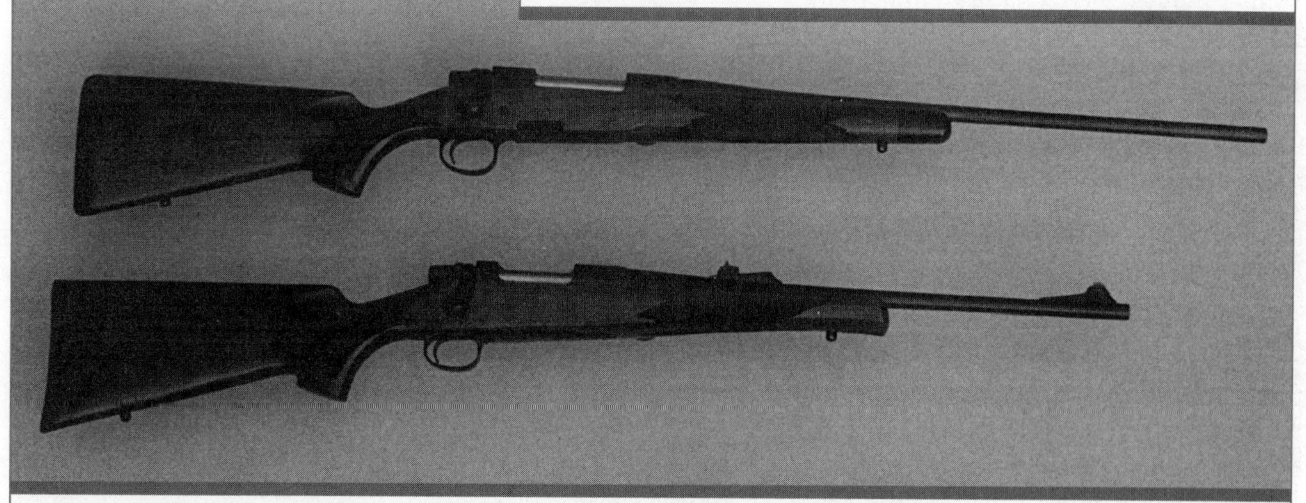

The Model Seven (bottom) is noticeably smaller and lighter than the Model 700 (top), but it handles in the same way, making these two rifles logical companions.

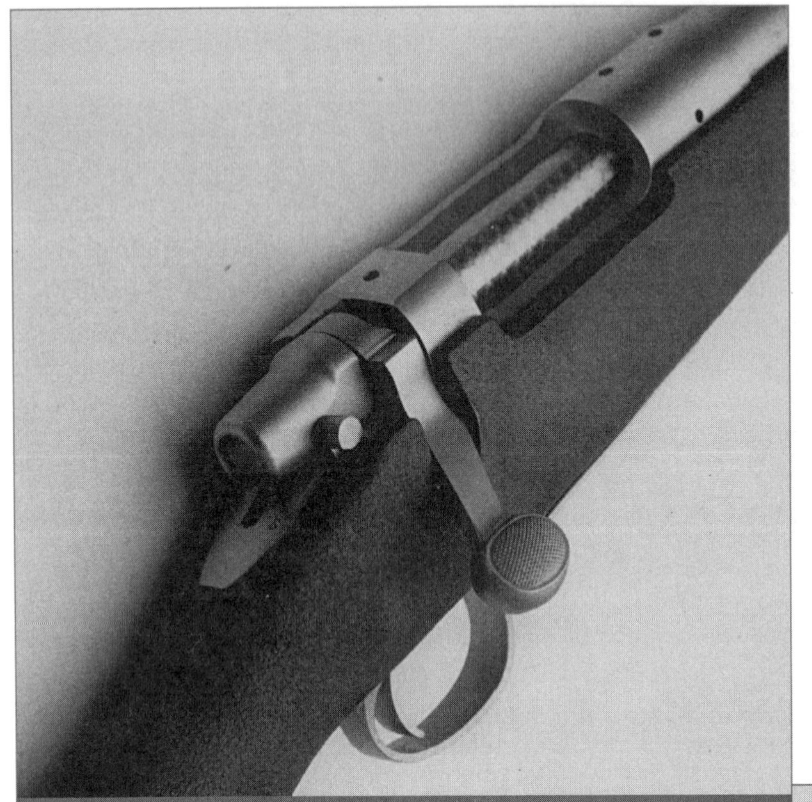

The Model Seven includes a cocking indicator that protrudes into the hollow bolt shroud at the rear of the receiver. The indicator shown indicates the striker is cocked and the rifle can be fired. Note also that the manual safety on the right side of the receiver, slightly behind the bolt handle, has been pushed forward to its fire setting.

make the FS stock more durable than an all-fiberglass stock would have been. The stock on the Model Seven Custom KS was made entirely out of Kevlar for even greater durability. Introduced in 1987, this variant was available on special order only from Remington's Custom Shop. In 1993, when the standard Model sold for only $519, the Custom KS was priced at $949.00.

Beginning in 1993, Remington revamped the Model Seven line, keeping the standard Model Seven Youth rifle in production, dropping the Kevlar-stocked model, and introducing several variants, including the Model Seven Youth rifle, which is essentially the same as the standard Model Seven from 1983 to 1992, a 6mm Remington caliber version. Magazine capacity runs up to 5 rounds in .223 and up to 4 rounds in all other chamberings.

The Model Seven FS Rifle, produced from 1987 to 1989, had a gray fiberglass stock and was available in .243, 7mm-08 and .308 calibers. The stock material, plus the parkerized finish on all metal parts, made the FA variant more weather-resistant than the standard blued steel and wooden Model Sevens. Reinforcements made of Kevlar at the points where barrel and action made contact with the stock helped

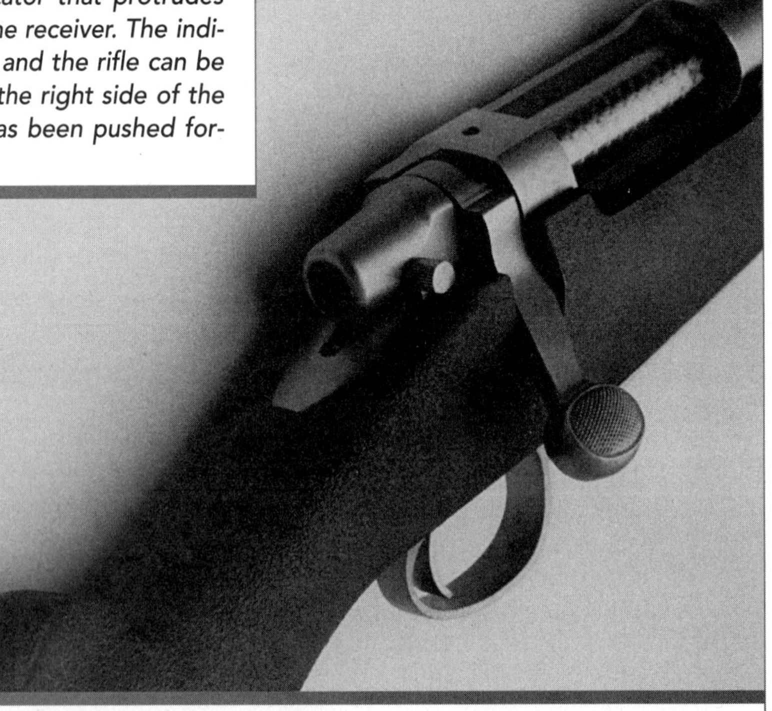

Here the Model Seven striker is uncocked, which means the indicator lies well forward in the bolt shroud and is no longer visible through the small hole at the rear of the receiver

but an inch shorter in the stock, thus reducing the length of pull to 12 3/16 inches. The only caliber choices on the Youth Model are .243 and 7mm-08 (for less recoil).

The Model Seven Custom MS Rifle, which also dates from 1993, employs a full-length, laminated Mannlicher-style wood stock, adding half a pound to the overall weight. Metal parts have a high-polish, blued finish. Remington makes this model available in a wide variety of chamberings, including .222, .223, .22-250, .243, .150 Savage, .257 Roberts, 6mm Remington, 7mm-08, .308, .35 Remington and .350 Remington Magnum calibers. Because of its limited production and many custom features, the Model Seven Custom MS Rifle costs more than twice as much as the standard Model Seven.

The Model Seven SS, which was introduced in 1994, has a slightly

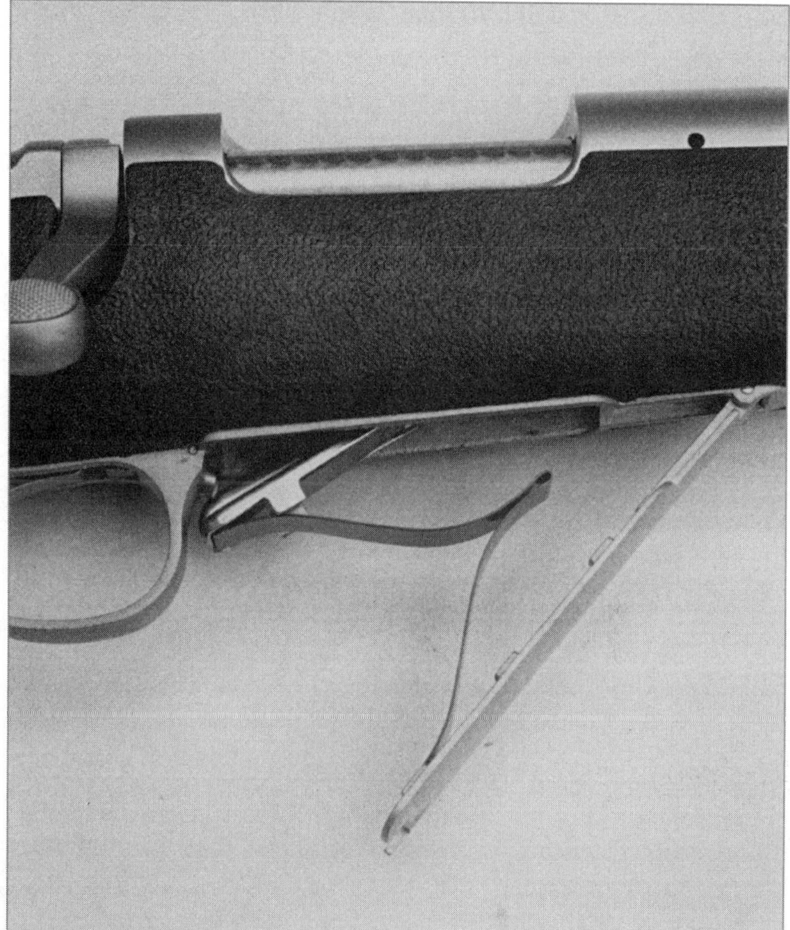

The Model Seven has a detachable floorplate, combining convenience with low cost.

The Remington Model Seven (bottom) is chambered for the .223 caliber cartridge, as is the Ruger Mini-14 (top).

longer (20-inch) stainless steel barrel than the other variants. A stainless steel action and grayish-black synthetic stock round out this model's improved weather resistance over the standard Model Seven. Caliber choices are .223, 243, .260, 7mm-08 and .308. And finally, Remington now markets two additional Model Sevens: the Mannlicher and Model KS (available only from the Remington Custom Shop).

In common with the Model 700, the Model Seven offers a crisp, light trigger pull. This, combined with a free-floated barrel (except for one pressure point at the tip of the forend), contributed to

The Model Seven's short bolt throw makes it a pleasure to shoot and one of the fastest-firing commercial bolt-action rifles available.

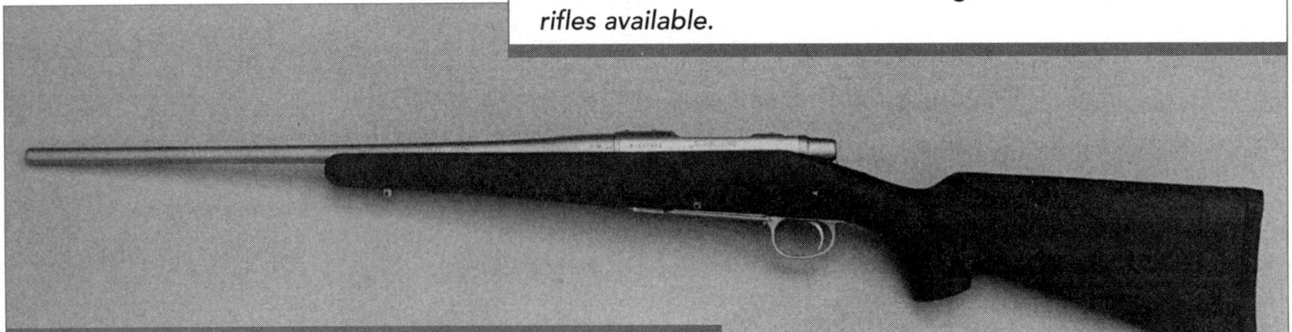

The Remington Model Seven SS features a stainless-steel barrel and action. The barrel is slightly longer than the standard Model Seven's. Note also that no sights have been fitted.

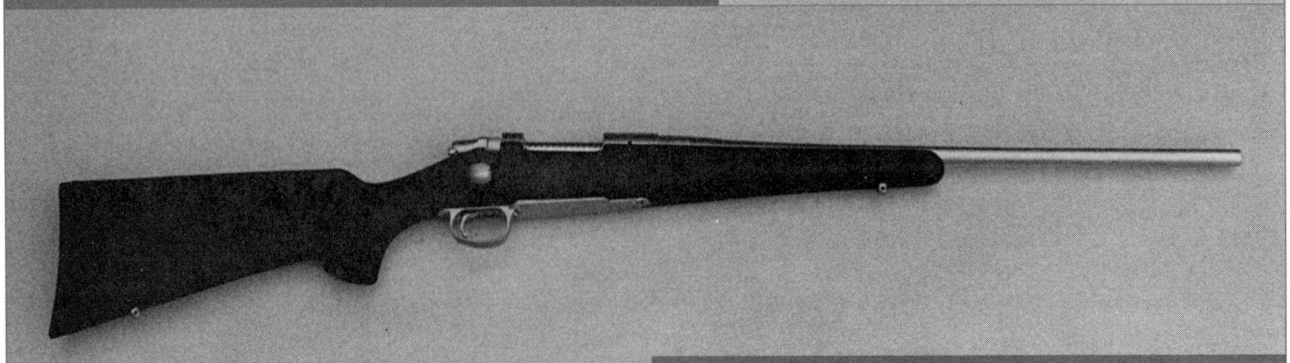

This stainless steel "SS" model is identical to the one above except it has a synthetic stock.

the pleasing accuracy I noted when testing this rifle. With an open-sighted Model Seven in .223 caliber, 3-shot groups fired from the 100-yard bench typically went into less than two inches. A .243 caliber version with scope did even better, delivering a tight 1.3-inch 3-shot group from 100 yards.

Recoil in these relatively mild chamberings is no problem. This short, light gun is a delight to handle, especially for those small in stature. As for the Model Seven's more vigorous chamberings, notably the 7mm-08 and .308 Winchester, recoil is much more noticeable. A Model Seven chambered for one of the larger rounds is the kind of gun a shooter would want to spend an afternoon with. Both the 7mm-08 and .308 Winchester are cartridges of medium intensity and quite mild-mannered in most rifles made to fire them. The Model Seven, however, is a bit on the light side for such rounds. My advice to novice shooters is to choose a Model Seven in .223 or .243 instead. Its handiness, though, makes this rifle an excellent choice as a brush gun for close-quarters hunting of small to medium-sized game.

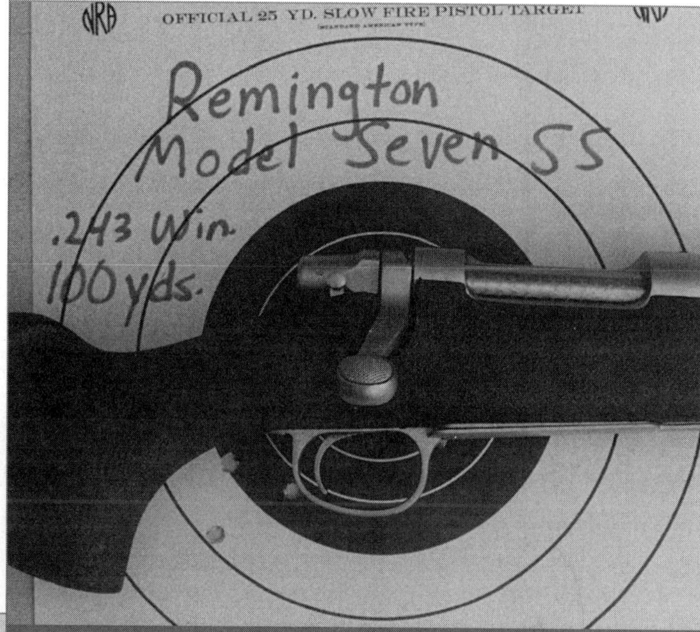

The Remington Model Seven SS proved highly accurate, putting three shots into a 1.3-inch group from a benchrest set up 100 yards from the target.

The standard Model Seven with integral sights in .223 Remington caliber produced this 3-shot group measuring 1.8 inches. Point of aim was the target's center.

REMINGTON MODEL SEVEN

	MODEL SEVEN
Overall Length	37.5 inches (standard); 36.5 inches (youth); 39 inches (SS)
Barrel Length	18.5 inches (standard and youth); 20 inches (SS and Custom)
Weight	6.25 pounds (standard); 6.0 (youth); 6.75 (custom)
Years Produced	1983-present
Chamberings	see text

Ruger Model 77

Ruger's Model 77 is a modified and modernized rifle of the Mauser Model 98 type that dates from 1968. Like its arch-rival, the Remington Model 700, it pioneered cost-cutting manufacturing techniques, specifically the use of investment casting to make receivers. As is its custom, Ruger began early on to introduce numerous variations, beginning in 1971 with a modified shape for the bolt handle.

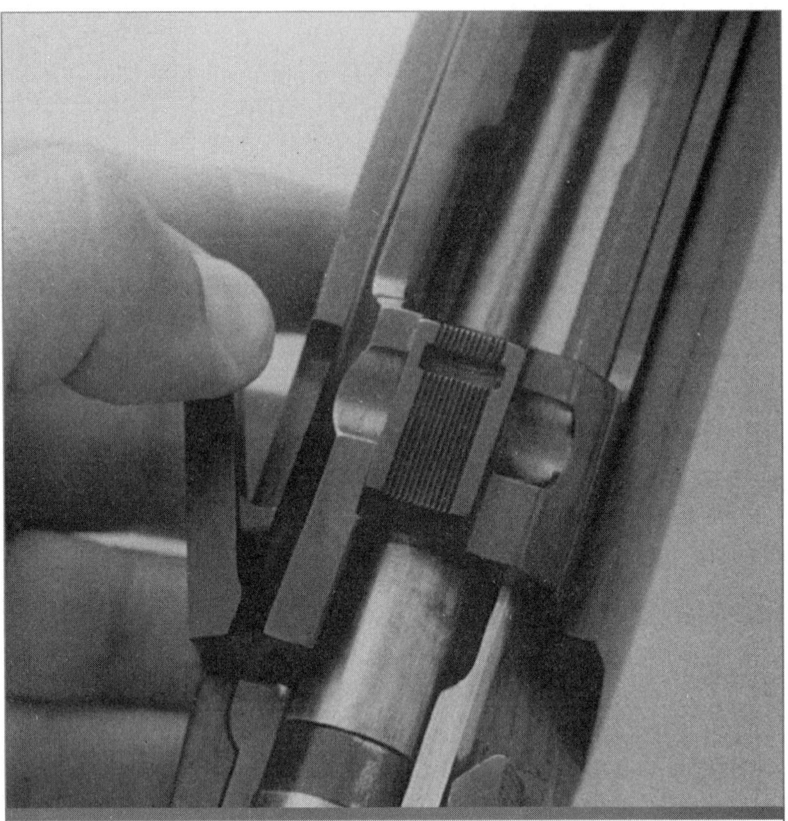

The bolt on the Model 77 can be removed in the time-honored Mauser fashion. Once the rifle is unloaded, the release latch is pulled out (as shown) while the bolt is withdrawn from the back of the receiver.

The current Mark II configuration, which dates from 1989, represents a return to controlled-round feeding made famous by the classic military Mauser rifle. The Model 77's controls include a three-position manual safety, which allows loading and unloading with the safety on (another feature of the early Mauser military rifles that got

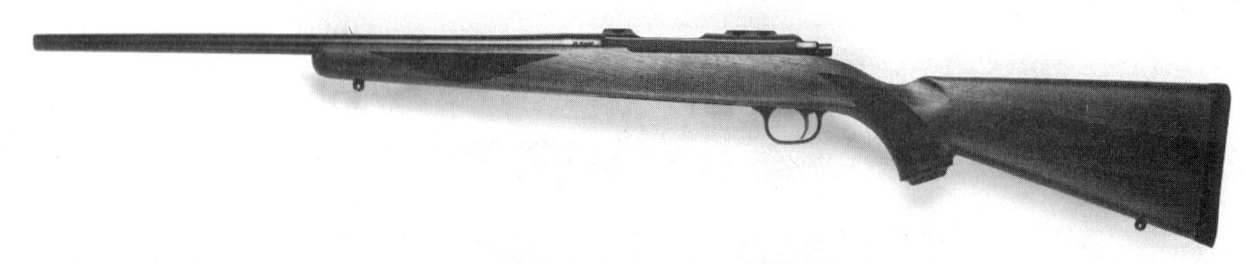

Ruger's Model 77 bolt-action rifle comes in a wide variety of receiver and stock configurations, as well as several cartridge chamberings (photo courtesy of Sturm, Ruger and Company)

The Model 77 RSI shows off its detachable magazine floorplate.

lost). As a modern refinement of the Mauser type safety, that used by the Model 77 is better suited to operating with a scope. It's mounted low on the right rear of the receiver and moves back horizontally, rather than vertically, to its safe setting, then forward to fire. This system neatly avoids the problems of adapting an early Mauser rifle, with its vertically-moving safety, to a low-mounted scope. Even the Model 77 rifles with their attached iron sights can mount a telescopic sight with ease. The rear sight simply folds down to accommodate mounting a scope low to the receiver. Ruger includes, at no extra charge, scope mounts on the receiver and matching rings.

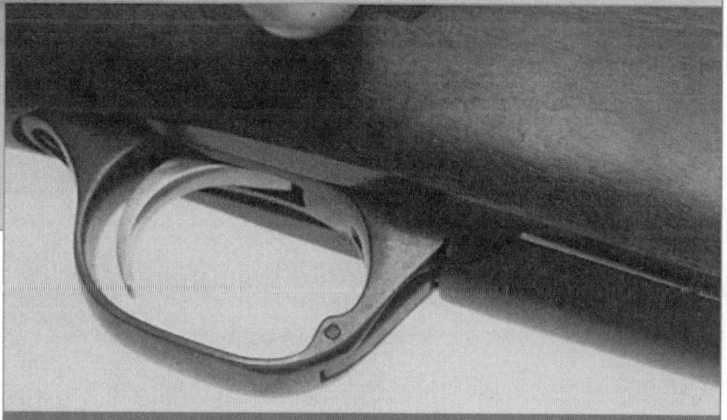

The latch for the Model 77 RSI's detachable magazine floorplate is located in the leading edge of the triggerguard.

The Ruger Model 77 includes a cocked-striker indicator, shown protruding from the rear of the bolt shroud. This indicates the rifle is ready to fire. Note the hemispherical cutouts in the receiver for scope-mounting (ahead of the bolt handle).

My tests with a Model 77 in the Mark II RSI configuration in .243 caliber revealed excellent handling for this carbine-sized variant; but considering the small cartridge, recoil proved surprisingly sharp. As noted, even cartridges known for their comparatively gentle recoil can get feisty in a gun that has a shorter barrel or is significantly lighter than rifles normally chambered for the cartridge in question. The trick to handling recoil in this instance is to seat the buttplate firmly into the shoulder pocket so it can't be punched back. By contrast, holding the rifle loosely against the shoulder will enable the rifle to push back hard with a jolt powerful enough to bruise the shoulder.

The Mark II RSI rifle's combination of folding-down iron sights and scope mountings indicate Ruger's careful attention to detail—as does the rifle's beautifully

The Ruger Model 77 RSI produced this 1.8-inch group from a benchrest at 100 yards, which is good for a short-barreled, iron-sighted .243 caliber rifle at this distance.

This short, lightweight Ruger Model 77 RSI is a pleasure to carry, thanks to its compact length and light weight.

The Ruger Model 77 RSI (second from left) is one of a variety of small carbines popular with today's shooters. Also shown are a Rossi Model 92 lever-action carbine (far left), a U.S. M1 Carbine (second from right), and a Colt .223 caliber carbine (far right).

fitted and finished wooden stock. In general, the excellent workmanship, the wide range of calibers, the choice of wooden or polymer stocks, plus the option of blued or stainless steel metal parts, all contribute to the tremendous appeal and popularity of the Ruger Model 77 series.

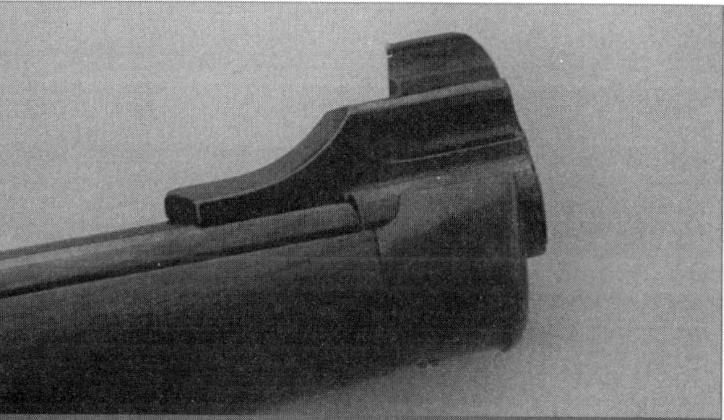

The Ruger Model 77 RSI has a distinctive endcap, and its wooden stock extends almost to the muzzle. This style was popularized in the early 1900s by Steyr/Mannlicher.

In addition to its provision for scope mounting, the Ruger Model 77 RSI includes a rear sight which can be raised (as shown) when a scope is not in use.

Like many other Ruger rifles, the Model 77 RSI is prepared for quick and convenient scope mounting via hemispherical cutouts in the receiver.

RUGER MODEL 77

	MODEL 77
Overall Length	39.75 inches (with 18.5 inch barrel)
Barrel Length	18.5 inches (RSI); 20; 22; 24 (magnum calibers)
Weight	6 pounds (Ultra Light); 7 pounds; 9.25 (Magnum)
Manufacturer	Sturm, Ruger and Company, Prescott, AZ
Years Produced	1989-present (Mark II variants)
Caliber Options	See chart below

	Mark II	Ultra Lt.	RSI	Magnum	All-Weather	Express	VT Target
.223	X	X			X		X
.22-250						X	
.220 Swift							X
.243	X	X	X		X		X
6mm Rem	X						
.257 Roberts	X	X					
.25-06	X					X	
6/5x55mm	X						
.260 Rem							
.270	X	X	X		X	X	
.280	X						
7mm-08							
.308	X	X	X		X		X
.30-06	X	X	X		X	X	X
7mm Rem Mag	X				X	X	
.300 Win Mag	X				X	X	
.336 Win Mag	X				X		
.375 H&H				X			
.416 Rigby				X			

Current Ruger Model 77 Calber Options not shown above: .22 LR, .22 WMR, .44 Magnum, .22 Hornet
Ruger Model 77 Discontinued Caliber Options: .250-3000 Savage, .358 Winchester, .458 Winchester

Sako TRG-S

Since its formation in 1924, SAKO of Finland has established an enviable reputation for excellence in design and manufacture of world-class rifles. SAKO (pronounced SOCK-o) is an acronym for *Suojeluskuntain Ase-ja Konepaja Osakeyhtiö*, which translates into "Arms and Machine Factory for the Defense Corps." Finland formed the *Suojeluskuntajärjestö*, or "Finnish Defense (literally, "Protective") Corps" in late 1917, immediately after the Bolshevik revolution in Russia. The chief mission of Finland's Defense Corps was to oppose a takeover of the country by pro-communist Finns (Finland had been a part of Russia under the czars). From January 1918 to May 1918, a fierce civil war led to victory (with some help from Sweden and Germany) for Finland's anti-communist White Army over pro-communist Red Finnish forces. As a result, Finland signed a declaration of independence from Russia on July 20, 1919.

The Defense Corps remained in existence after the war for independence and became closely associated with Finland's armed forces. It did not, however, attempt to compete with the country's military forces for the limited output generated at the government-owned rifle, submachine-gun and pistol factory, called the *Valtion Kivääritehdas*, or VKT (State Rifle Factory). Instead, the Defense Corps set up SAKO as its own facility. From 1924 to 1927 SAKO operated from a converted brewery in Helsinki before moving to a new factory in the city of Riihimäki. There SAKO quickly established a reputation for excellence. The company's first 38,000 rifles, called Model 24s, served both the Finnish Defense Corps and armed forces for the next 20 years. SAKO'S second rifle, the Model 28, appeared in 1928. This was the first rifle of the Mosin-Nagant type to use a stock with a pistol grip instead of the straight-wristed stock used by the Russians on their own Mosin-Nagants. SAKO

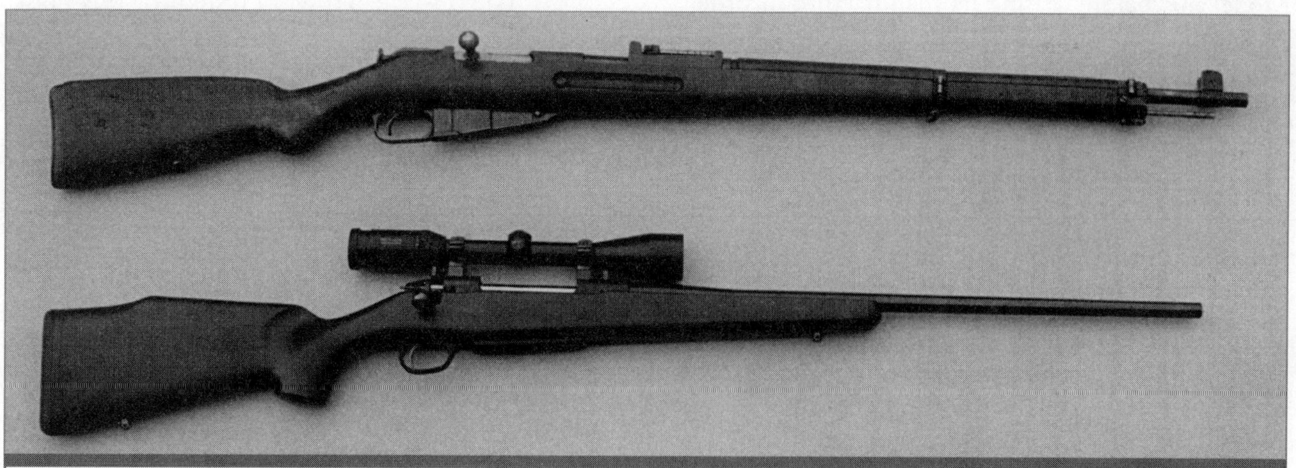

SAKO's TRG-S rifle (bottom) carries on the tradition of stellar accuracy established during World War II by SAKO's highly regarded M39 (top).

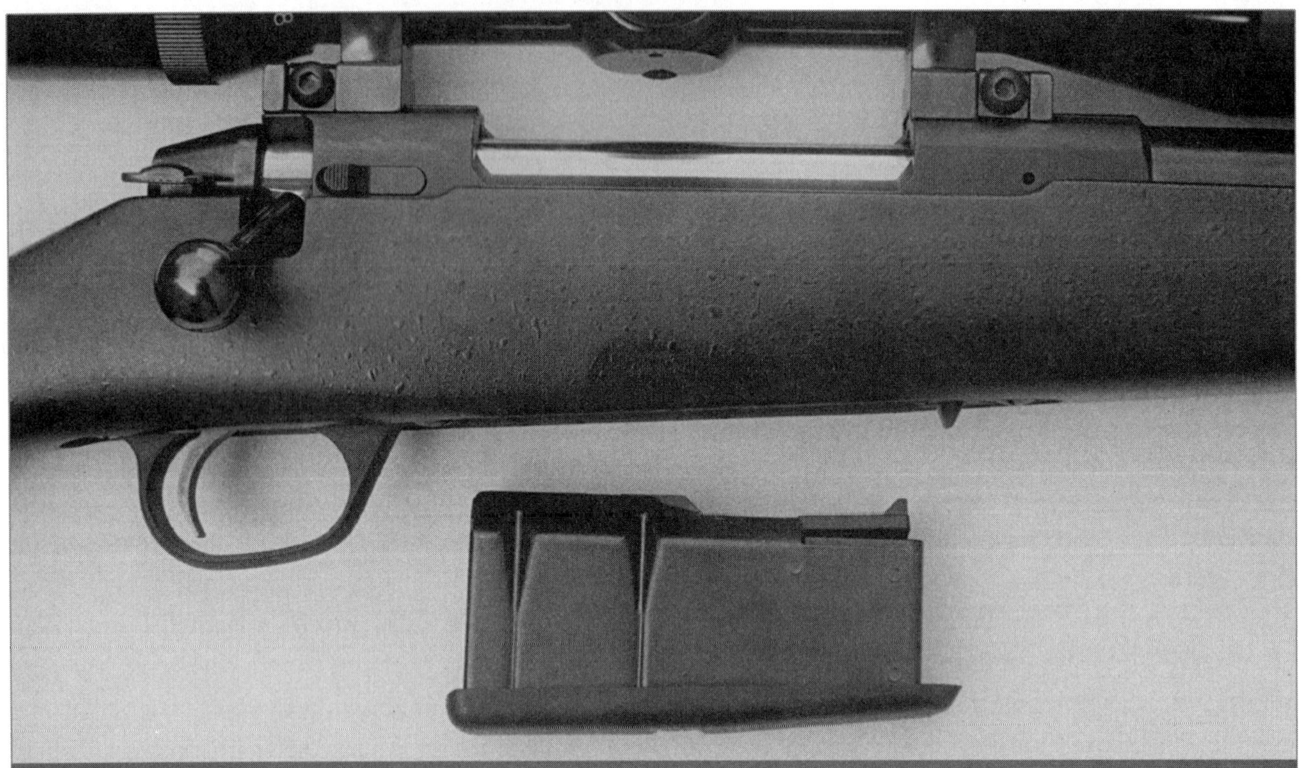

Like many modern bolt-action rifles, the TRG-S comes with a detachable box magazine, eliminating the problems that arise from combining telescopic sights with Mauser-style magazine.

built about 30,000 Model 28s before switching to the Model 30, which added an improved Mauser-style rear sight and a modified magazine. Series production of the Model 30 began in 1931, and by 1940 the company had made some 60,000 Model 30s before ceasing its manufacture in order to concentrate on an even better rifle: the Model 39.

Many shooters (including the author) rank SAKO'S Model 39 among the finest rifles of the Mosin-Nagant type ever made. It combined the expertise of the Finnish Defense Corps and Finland's armed forces to produce a rugged and reliable rifle of superb quality and performance. With its relatively short 27-inch barrel and pistol-grip stock, the Model 39 handled much better than the typical Mosin-Nagant rifle made during the czarist or communist eras. Its heavy barrel, moreover, made it possible to shoot this rifle more effectively than virtually any standard Mosin-Nagant made anywhere. Finland's acceptance test for the Model 39 required each rifle to shoot a 3-shot group measuring 33mm (1.3-inch) or smaller at 100 meters (109 yards). Any rifle not meeting this high standard was summarily rejected for service. The 55-year old M39 tested for this book did even better, delivering a 3-shot, 1-inch group from a 100-yard benchrested position, which is a perfect 1 minute-of-angle (1 MOA) group. Many modern rifles cannot do as well—and few can do any better.

The Model 39 appeared just in time to help Finnish forces oppose the Soviet invasion of their country in November of 1939. In the "Winter War" that followed, the outnumbered Finns inflicted enormous losses against the Red Army. Finally, in February 1940, the exhausted Finns were forced to sue for peace. Between 1939 and 1940, SAKO produced approximately 71,000

Model 39s. These rifles saw more service against the Soviets during the so-called "Continuation War," during which Finland joined the German invasion of the USSR in June 1941. That war ended in late 1944, when the Soviets, after repelling the German forces, offered the Finns a choice: either switch sides and kick the Germans out of Finland, or risk invasion and occupation by the Soviets. Understandably, the overmatched Finns threw in their lot with the Soviets and turned their Mosin-Nagant rifles against their former German allies.

For the next 18 months or so, SAKO ceased to exist as a rifle manufacturer, its factory having been occupied by the Finnish Red Cross to avoid being dismantled and shipped back to the USSR. Finally, in 1946, the company returned to making sporting rifles. The Finnish Defense Corps no longer existed as an outlet for paramilitary rifles and Finland's armed forces had switched to using self-loading Soviet-type weapons. SAKO seized the opportunity to switch from the aging Mosin-Nagant bolt action in favor of the more popular Mauser bolt mechanism (slightly modified to suit SAKO'S concept of the ideal bolt-action sporting rifle). Earlier, during the Continuation War, SAKO had begun development of the so-called Model 1942.

SAKO's initial postwar design efforts led to the L-46 or A-Series, which went into production in 1946. The L-461, or Vixen, action handled smaller centerfire calibers, including .218 Bee, .22 Hornet and .222. The slightly larger L-579, or Forester, action appeared in 1957 and was intended for such intermediate-sized cartridges as the .243 Winchester, 7.62x39mm Soviet and .308 Winchester (7.62x51mm NATO). The longest action—the L-61 or Finnbear—appeared in 1961, firing magnum cartridges like the .30-06, .300 H&H Magnum and .338 Winchester Magnum. All rifles built on these three A-Series actions looked much the same. Two locking lugs were built into the L-46 and L-59 actions and three in the L-61 action. A recessed or plunger-style ejector was used rather than the classic Mauser blade ejector, providing almost complete support of the cartridge-case head. SAKO's A-Series receivers also had a wide, matted rib on top, complete with integral scope-mounting dovetails. This system provided exceptionally strong and secure optical scope mounting, a system which the company has continued to this day.

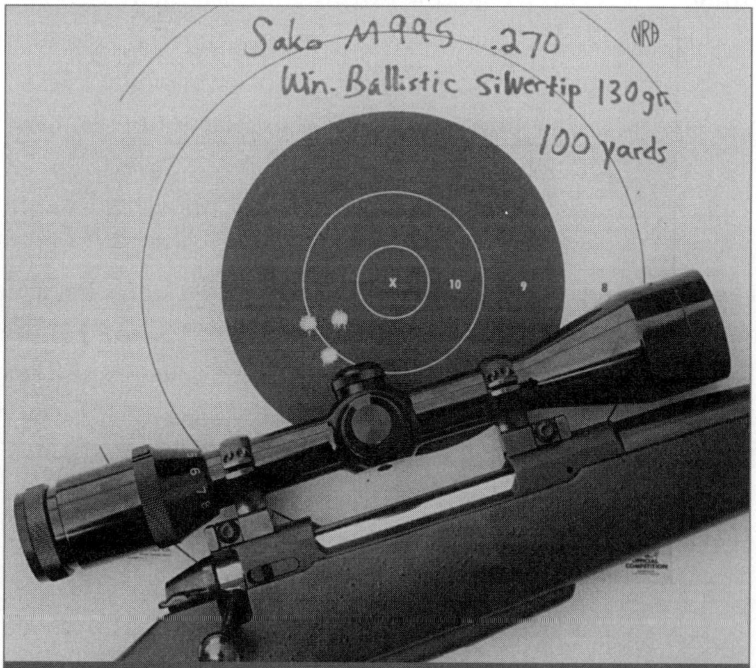

In addition to its own product line, SAKO has also sold large numbers of rifles to other rifle companies for sale under their own brand names. One of these—Marlin's Model 322—combined SAKO's L-46 action with a barrel featuring

The .270 caliber TRG-S tested for this book by the author produced superb 3-shot benchrested groups measuring a mere 7/10ths of an inch from a distance of 100 yards.

This close-up view of the rear scope mount area on the TRG-S shows the bolt release button just ahead of the bolt handle. The safety is located right behind it and is in its fire setting.

Marlin's well-known Micro-Groove rifling. Regrettably, the rifling wore out too quickly in the high-intensity calibers for which Marlin had made this gun. Despite building a more durable Model 422 fitted with a stainless steel barrel, Marlin stopped selling SAKO bolt-action rifles in 1959. Browning, Colt and Harrington & Richardson have over time sold complete SAKO rifles made to their specifications (or built on SAKO actions). SAKO has also sold its actions to gunsmiths for developing rifles to their own specifications. Several prominent modern rifles have also reflected considerable SAKO influence. These include such stellar products as the Howa Lightning, the Weatherby Vanguard and the Mountain Eagle (which also has an action made by SAKO).

In 1984 SAKO announced its "Fiberclass" model, an L-61 action in a synthetic stock with a black crinkle finish. Its success has been due largely to the proven SAKO firing mechanism in a more rugged, weather-resistant configuration than usual. Then, in 1989, SAKO and Valmet, Finland's state-owned arms factory, sought to interest the Finnish armed forces in a new sniper rifle: the TRG-21. Among its many advanced features this new model sported the following: a 10-round magazine, adjustable trigger, an exceptionally strong integral bipod, adjustable stock, cocked-striker indicator, an almost noiseless manual safety, and a threaded muzzle for affixing such accessories as a suppressor. It even offers the capability of upgrading from the standard 7.61mm (.308) round to the high-powered .300 Winchester Magnum. In addition, the Finnish armed forces have bought SAKO's TRG-41, which is a TRG-21 rechambered to the even more powerful .338 Lapua Magnum cartridge, for sniper use.

To recoup the expenses involved in developing the TRG-21, SAKO has offered the rifle to various military and police forces. Not surprisingly, sales of this highly specialized and expensive rifle has been limited. In an ongoing effort to make a profit on the design, SAKO has now produced a more conventional sporting rifle, the TRG-S, which incorporates many of the TRG-21 features but at a much lower cost. Introduced in 1993, the TRG-S offers several features. For example, instead of SAKO's Mauser-inspired bolt system with its two forward locking lugs, the TRG-S has three locking lugs located on the front of the bolt. This extra lug gives the TRG-S a faster 60-degree lift on the bolt handle, as opposed to the 90-degree rotation required on the early Mauser and Mosin-Nagant bolt actions. The box magazine is detachable by means of a release catch in the front. The Monte Carlo stock is made of reinforced polyurethane with a black crinkle finish and comes complete

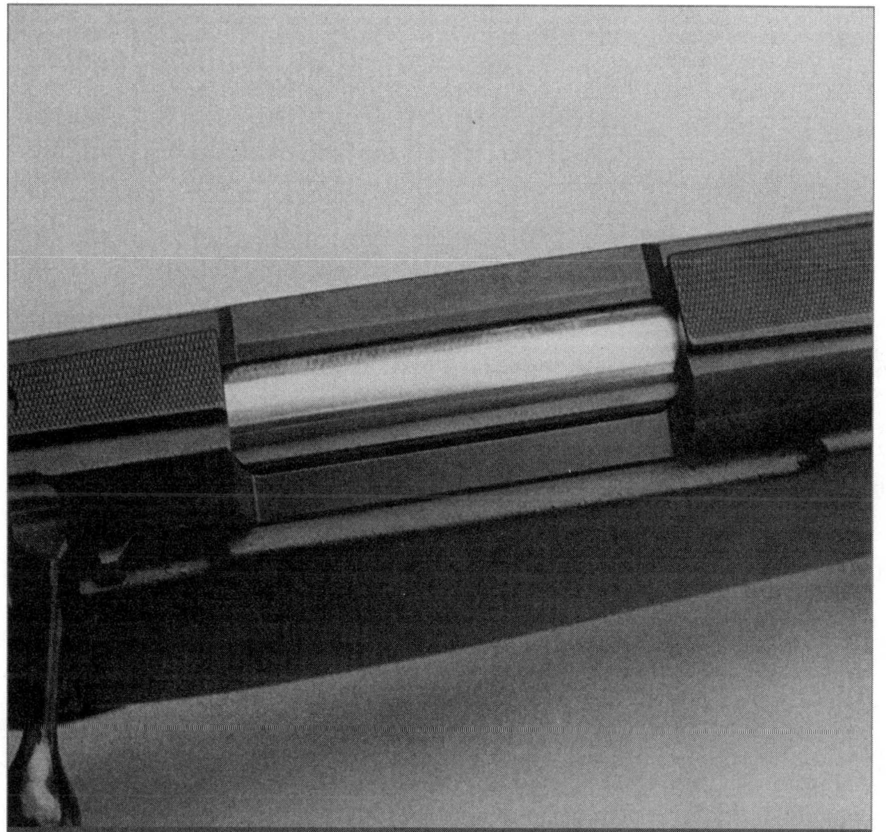

For many years SAKO has used a clever dovetailed, matted receiver top to accommodate its own distinctive brand of scope mounts.

with integral sling swivels. It also surrounds a strong metal chassis containing the working parts, including a device for adjusting trigger pull.

The manual safety catch on the TRG-S, which is located on the right rear portion of the receiver, when pushed forward to fire, exposes a red dot. The firing pin cocks on opening the bolt, causing the rear end of the striker mechanism to protrude slightly from the rear of the bolt. This exposes a raised red ring, which is easily visible from the side or rear of the gun and indicates its ready status. Regrettably, the manual safety can be operated only with the striker cocked. This deficiency has since been corrected in SAKO's latest rifle: the Model 75.

No iron sights are fitted on the TRG-S, but SAKO's traditional matted receiver rib with integral scope-mounting dovetails is standard. This creates an exceptionally solid mounting system for a quality telescopic sight. I fitted the test rifle with, first, a Swarovski 3-10x variable-power scope with 42mm objective, and later with a Millett "Buck" 3-9x variable power. The rifle worked well with both scopes. Shooters who lack iron sights on their rifles should bear in mind that the cost of a telescopic sight can easily double the purchase price.

Here, a TRG-S is shown with its scope mounts fitted.

Aside from its three locking-lug arrangement, bolt construction of the TRG-S is typically SAKO. Instead of welding the handle onto the bolt body, as so many other rifles have, the bolt body and handle of the TRG-S are made of a single piece of steel. SAKO has also made the TRG-S with its bolt face recessed all the way around, except for the point where the thin blade extractor is visible. A plunger- or button-style ejector protrudes through the bolt face opposite the extractor Should a cartridge case fail, the shooter is protected by two holes drilled into the bolt for gas to escape. In the event of a ruptured case head or pierced primer, the hole near the tip of the firing pin will vent most of the gas through a matching hole drilled in the receiver, away from the shooter's face. The second hole, positioned well back on the bolt body, vents the remaining gases. Those that did not vent through the front hole will now escape straight down into the magazine well, rather than blowing directly into the shooter's face. *[These precautions for handling catastrophic cartridge failures, however, do not mean shooters can discard their safety glasses and hearing protection.]*

Accuracy with the TRG-S proved sensational in our tests. Using a .270 Winchester caliber model, I recorded 3-shot benchrested 100-yards groups as small as 7/10ths of an inch. Recoil, which can be quite stiff in some rifles, was mild in the TRG-S, due mostly to its substantial weight and excellent stock design. The factory-adjusted trigger—a SAKO specialty over the years—proved exceptionally light and crisp. Moreover, the bolt and stock design of the TRG-S make it easy to keep the rifle on your shoulder while operating the bolt between shots. Regrettably, the bolt's opening stroke is quite stiff. The stock's un-traditional crinkle finish may also feel strange to some shooters. As I worked with the gun, though, I found it handled fine even with sweaty hands. Nevertheless, I still prefer a hand-checkered wooden stock.

In summary, the TRG-S is a strong, reliable and accurate rifle. It is also the least expensive SAKO centerfire rifle currently available, offering the company's legendary quality and performance at a price comparable to that of a typical Browning A-Bolt or a higher-end Remington Model 700. Shortcomings of the SAKO design are the inability to apply the safety while operating the bolt, a stiff bolt handle, and relatively poor rust resistance of the gun's blued metal surfaces. However, SAKO has addressed all these concerns elegantly in the stainless steel version of its latest rifle: the Model 75 (see below).

SAKO TRG-S

	TRG-S
Overall Length	45.5 inches
Barrel Length	22 inches (standard calibers)/24 inches (magnum calibers)
Weight	7.75 pounds
Years Produced	1993-present
Manufacturer	SAKO, Riihimäki, Finland
Importer	Stoeger Industries, Wayne, NJ
Caliber & Capacity	*Standard Models:* .143 Winchester, 7mm-08, .270 Winchester, 6.5x55mm, .30-06/all caliber 5-shot magazine • ***Magnum Models:*** 7mm Remington Magnum, .270 Weatherby Magnum, 7mm Weatherby Magnum, .340 Weatherby Magnum, .375 H&H, .416 Remington Magnum/all calibers 5-shot magazine, except .375 H&H, with a 4-shot magazine

SAKO Model 75

When SAKO announced its latest rifle series, called the Model 75, in 1997, it offered some traditional features along with some changes. Those that remain the same include SAKO's strong commitment to high manufacturing quality, including the use of cold-hammer forged barrels and integral scope-mounting dovetails on the receiver.

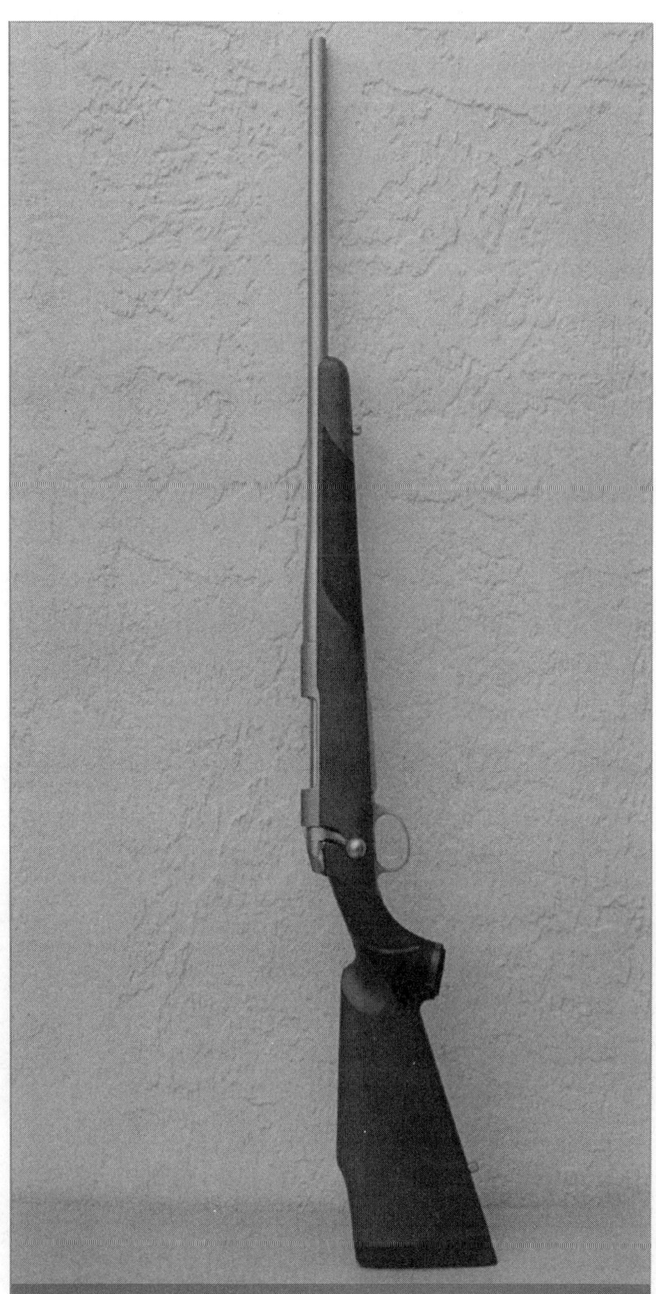
The SAKO Model 75 continues the company's tradition of high quality. Shown here is a stainless steel barrel and action combined with a synthetic stock.

As for the changes from the A-Series to the Model 75, note the following action lengths (two more than before):

- **Roman Numeral I:** *calibers .17, .222 and .223*
- **Roman Numeral II:** *calibers .22 PPC, 6 PPC and 7.62x39mm*
- **Roman Numeral III:** *calibers .22-250, .243, 7mm-08 and .308*
- **Roman Numeral IV:** *calibers .26-06, 6.5x55mm, .270, 7x64mm, .280, .30-06 and 9.3x62mm*
- **Roman Numeral V:** *calibers .270 Weatherby Magnum, 7mm Magnum, 7mm Weatherby Magnum, 7mm STW, .300 Winchester Magnum, .300 Weatherby Magnum, .338 Winchester Magnum, .340 Weatherby Magnum, .375 H&H Magnum and .416 Remington Magnum*

In addition, the bolt configuration on the Model 75 reduces the bolt handle lift from 90 to only 70 degrees. A two-position safety, together with a bolt-release lever, keep the rifle on the "safe" setting when removing the bolt. There's also the option of a fixed or detachable box magazine; and even the latter type can, in the traditional manner, be reloaded one round at a time from the top of the open action. And, with a simple substitution of a few parts, one loading device can be converted to the other, if desired. Shooters also have the choice of a European walnut or composite stock and of blued or stainless steel metal parts.

Eleven model types in all are planned for the Model 75 framework, as follows: Hunter, Deluxe, Super Deluxe, Safari (in long Type V action only), Euro, Carbine

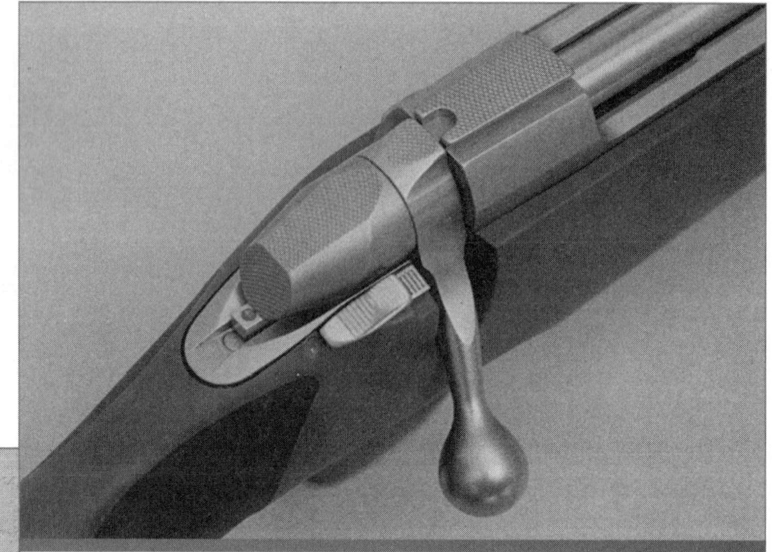

The SAKO Model 75 has a cocked-striker indicator in the form of a pin, highlighted by a red dot that protrudes from the back of the bolt shroud when the firing mechanism is cocked. In this view, note also the rear scope mount and the unique manual safety, which allows operation and/or removal of the bolt with the safety in its safe setting.

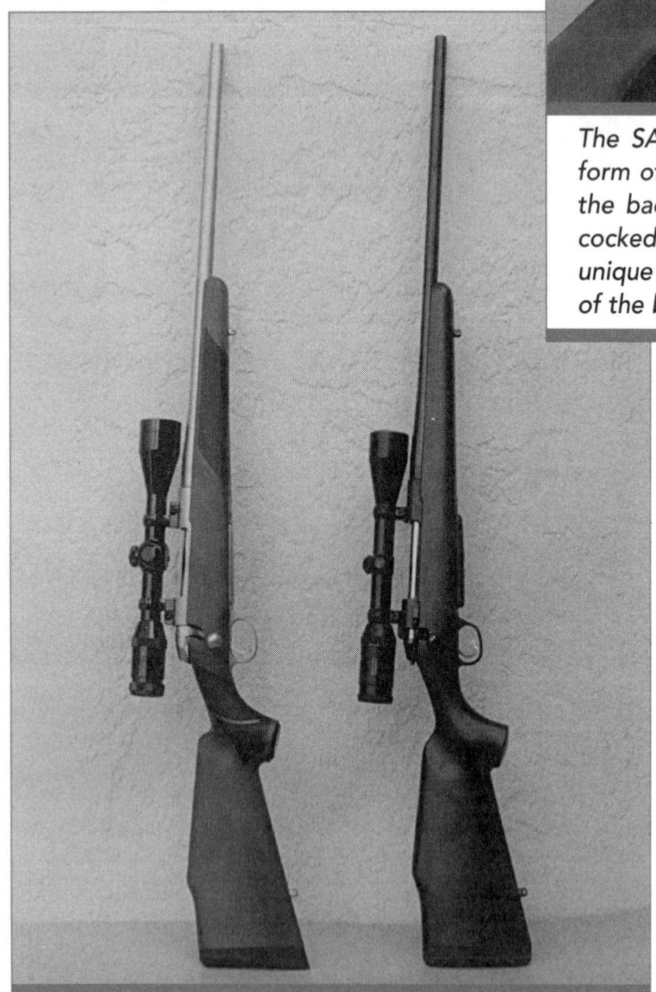

The SAKO Model 75 (left) is shown alongside the older TRG-S. While the Model 75 has replaced several of SAKO's earlier models, the TRG-S will probably remain in production, if only because it costs several hundred dollars less than the least expensive Model 75.

(in action lengths III-V only), Battue (in action lengths III-V only), Varmint, Stainless, Synthetic (in action lengths III-V only) and Stainless Synthetic (in action lengths III-V only). That represents a tremendous number of caliber choices available, enough to meet virtually every shooting need.

The Model 75 tested for this book provided excellent handling, with good recoil control and superb accuracy. In test-firing the .270 Winchester caliber, the SAKO rifle ranked high among the most comfortable in recoil among all rifles tested for this book in .270. The most accurate round—the 140 grain Fail-Safe from Winchester—delivered an outstanding 1/2-inch, 3-shot group from the 100-yard bench. That's only 1/2 MOA, which is incredibly accurate. Even Federal's Premium 130-grain offering produced a 1-inch, 3-shot group at 100 yards for 1 MOA. The 130-grain bullet, by the way, is a good choice for shooters who prefer a .270 Winchester rifle for varmint shooting. Bullet weight in that instance is not critical compared to shooting heavy, thick-skinned game, or for shooters who find the recoil from the .270 excessive in heavier bullet weights.

The Model 75's composite stock felt comfortable to hold and its stainless steel barrel and action offered exceptional rust resistance. The bolt was also easier to operate compared to the bolt used in the TRG-S. In fact, as good as the TRG-S tested, the Model 75 made significant improvements.

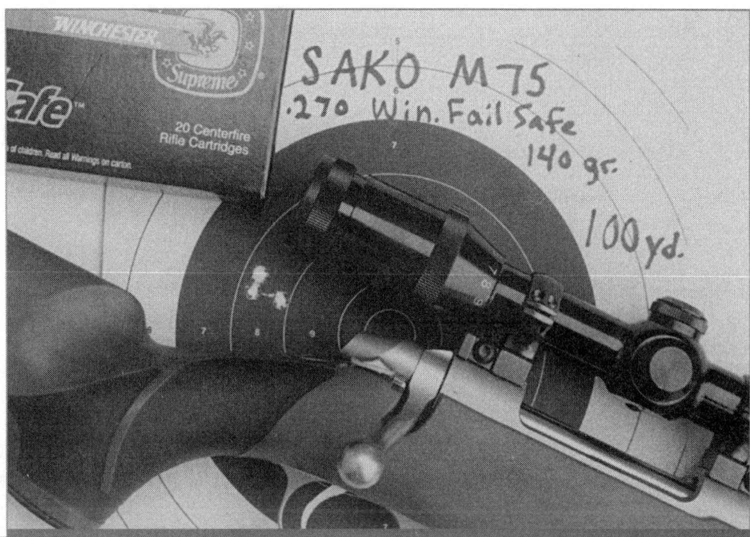

The SAKO Model 75 provides stunning accuracy. This 1/2-inch group fired at 100 yards was the author's best result with any rifle tested for this book. Even the Model 75's worst group measured only 1 inch across at 100 yards, for one minute of angle (1 MOA), the traditional standard of excellence in accuracy.

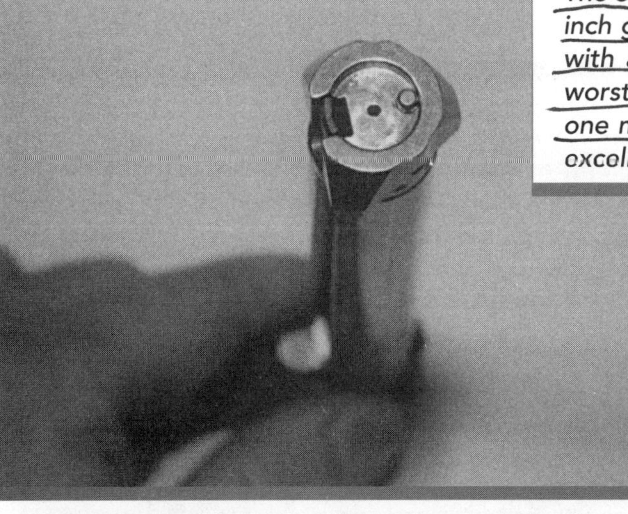

The SAKO Model 75 bolt offers full support for the cartridge case head at the expense of eliminating the controlled-round feeding (preferred by fans of the Mauser Model 98).

It will undoubtedly maintain SAKO's enviable position as one of the world's finest manufacturers of top-quality bolt-action rifles. While on the expensive side, the SAKO Model 75 offers high performance and a wide range of options. Its sturdy construction and precise accuracy also make it more than acceptable as a military sniper or police tactical response team rifle.

SAKO MODEL 75

	MODEL 75
Overall Length	43.5 inches (with 22-inch barrel)
Barrel Length	22, 24 or 26 inches
Weight	6.1 pounds
Manufacturer	SAKO Ltd., Riihimaki, Finland
Importer	Stoeger Industries, Wayne, NJ
Years Produced	1997-present
Caliber/Capacity	see text

Sauer Model 202

When J.P. Sauer (Eckenförde, Germany) introduced its Model 202 in 1994, it included several interesting features. Among them was a bolt that locked directly into the back end of the barrel by means of six locking lugs on the bolt head. This design provided the option of easy barrel replacement and, to a degree, caliber interchangeability as well. Since one feature of this system greatly reduced the strain of firing on the receiver, it also offered a lighter receiver than that found on most bolt-action rifles. In fact, Sauer now makes an aluminum-alloy receiver option available for this model.

The controls of the Sauer Model 202 (an improved version of Sauer's Model 200) include a pushbutton manual safety located slightly in front of the trigger, which the shooter releases before firing. Another pushbutton at the top of the tang protrudes slightly, revealing a red warning band painted around its base. This feature alerts the shooter to the fact that the safety has been removed. To ensure that the rifle is safe, the tang-mounted button must be pushed inwards. This two-button system may seem complicated, but it is actually easy to learn. While I still prefer a two-position tang safety, this method is not all that bad.

A firing-pin cocking indicator, which protrudes from the rear of the bolt, reveals a red mark. This indicates that the firing mechanism is cocked for an added safety check. *[One should never rely solely on such mechanical contrivances, however; the best safety equipment lies between a shooter's ears.]* On the left side of the receiver, next to the leading edge of the triggerguard, is a small lever that, when pushed in, releases the bolt for removal. While most classic bolt-action rifles—such as the Mauser Models 93, 95 and 98, the Mosin-Nagant and the Lee-Enfield—have a 90 degree angle, the Sauer bolt is limited to a 60-degree range of motion. The less motion involved in working the bolt, the faster the rifle can be fired, at least in theory. In practice,

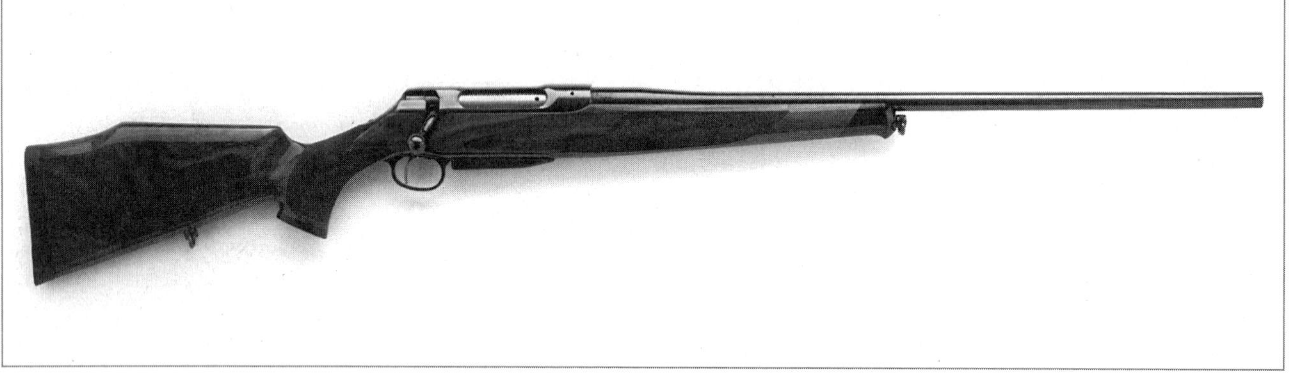

The Sauer Model 202 offers exotic European styling and top performance at a reasonable price (photo courtesy of Sigarms).

The lower safety button on the Model 202, located just ahead of the trigger, is pushed upwards to place the manual safety in its fire setting The square control located next to the leading edge of the triggerguard is pushed in so the bolt can be removed.

almost any good bolt-action rifle in the hands of an experienced shooter is capable of an awesome rate of fire. It's just easier to fire quickly with some bolt-action rifles than with others. In line with many modern bolt-action rifles, the Sauer Model 202 has a detachable magazine, whose pushbutton release is located in front of the magazine.

The Sauer Model 202 has a racy European styling which many American shooters dislike. Certainly no one will ever mistake this model for the staid and conservative Remington Model 700 or Winchester Model 70! The Sauer rifle looks far too outlandish for that. Its stock, made of beautifully figured American Claro walnut, has a pronounced pistol grip and Monte Carlo comb. A rosewood tip on the forend and fine hand checkering on the pistol grip and forend are a testament to the rifle's deluxe accommodations, as are the integral sling swivels. Unlike most modern rifles that are set up for a scope and have no fixed sights, the Sauer Model 202 has holes already drilled and tapped for mounting a scope on the receiver and for mounting fixed sights on the barrel as well. Shooters who opt for a scope mount use the same Weaver-type system as the popular Browning A-Bolt and equally exotic Steyr Pro-Hunter.

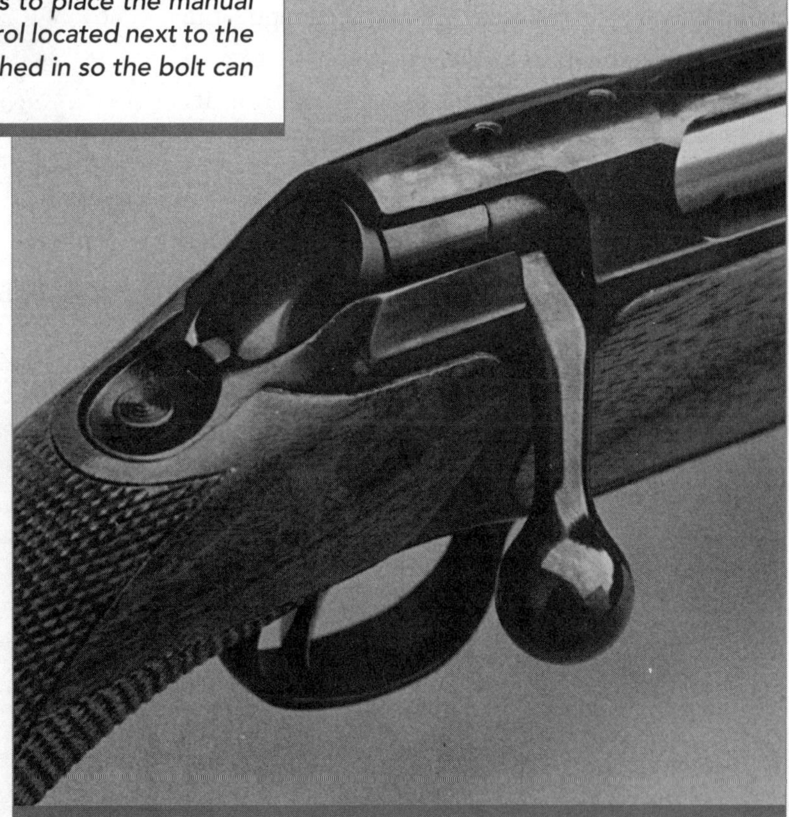

The Sauer Model 202 utilizes an unusual two-position manual safety. When the button on the tang is pushed down, it places the manual safety control into its safe setting.

The Model 202's magazine release is in the form of yet another pushbutton, only this one is located in front of the magazine, well ahead of the manual safety

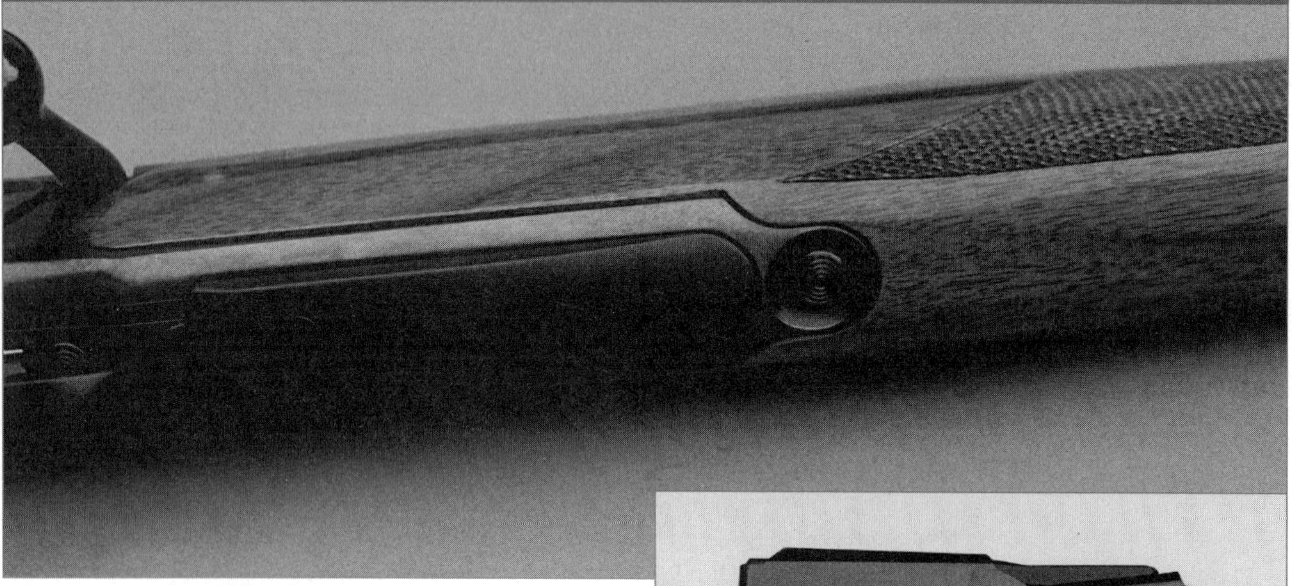

Unlike the classic early Mauser design, the Sauer Model 202 has a fully-recessed bolt face to ensure maximum support for the cartridge rim. Its plunger- or button-style ejector, similar to the modern SAKO rifles, protrudes through the bolt face opposite the extractor. In the event of cartridge case failure or a pierced primer, the Sauer Model 202 design utilizes three gas-escape holes. Two are in the bolt body itself—one well forward and the other well to the rear—opposite the firing-pin spring. The third gas relief hole is in the receiver. Again, readers are advised to wear shooting glasses whenever possible in the field, and certainly whenever they are on the

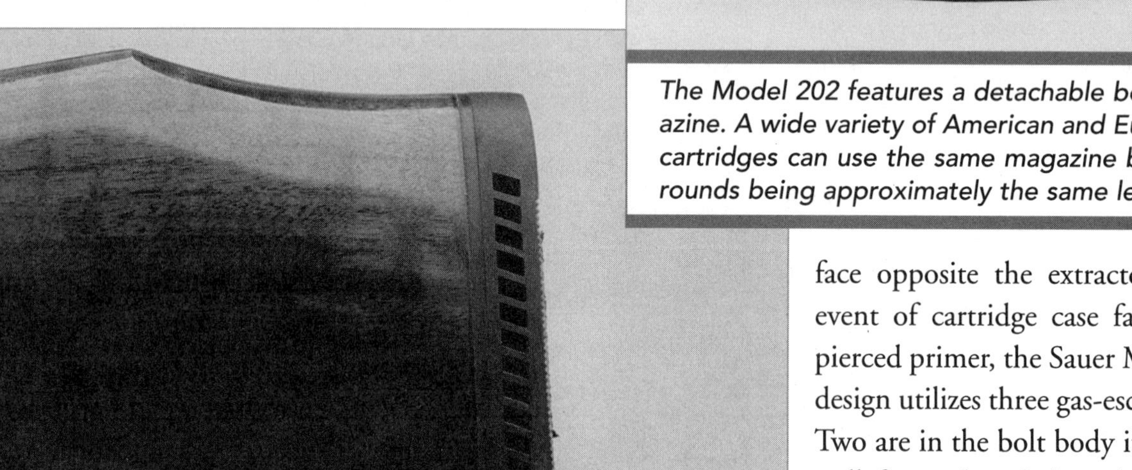

The Model 202 features a detachable box magazine. A wide variety of American and European cartridges can use the same magazine body, all rounds being approximately the same length.

The thick rubber buttpad on the Model 202 comes in handy when firing the more powerful cartridges.

The Sauer Model 202 utilizes the same type of scope mounts as the Browning A-Bolt and Steyr SBS.

Its well-designed stock, weight and substantial ventilated rubber recoil pad combine to make shooting the Model 202 a pleasure—even for shooters who are sensitive to recoil. As one might expect from a well-made gun from a top-notch European manufacturer, accuracy with the Model 202 was outstanding: the best 3-shot benchrested

Note the slight schnabel forend, sling swivel, beautifully figured wood and finely-executed checkering on this Model 202.

firing range, should a catastrophic failure of gun or cartridge occur.

Shooting the Model 202 in .270 Winchester caliber revealed quite pleasant handling. This sleek rifle is indeed fast on target despite its large size. The light, crisp factory trigger and free-floating barrel are definitely helpful in assuring accuracy.

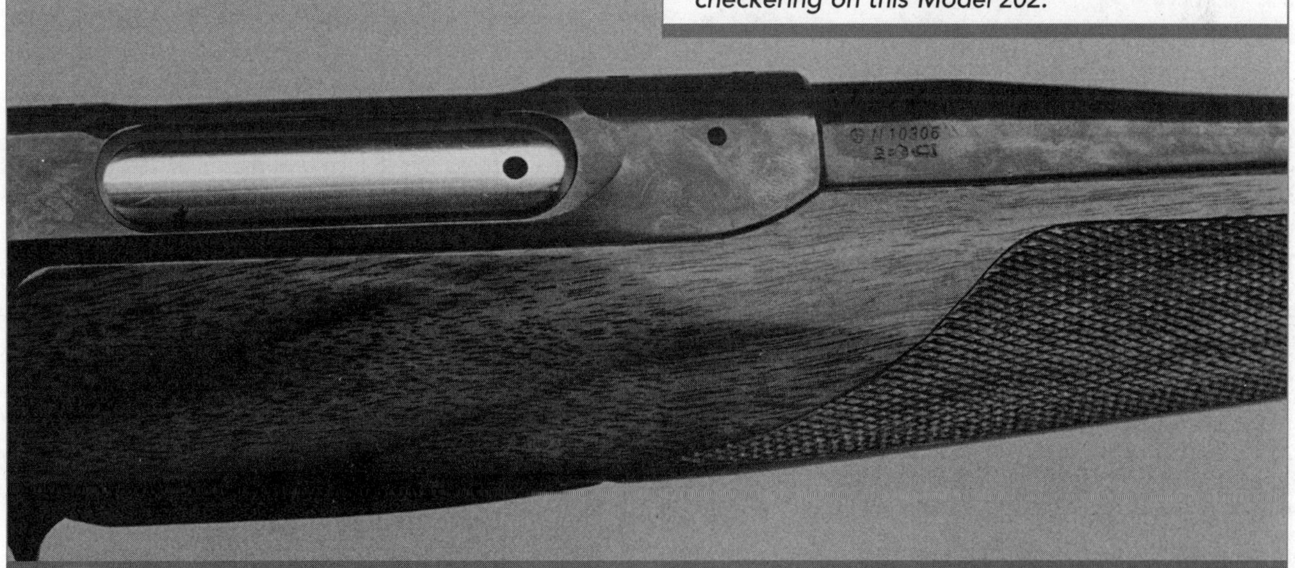
The safety features on Sauer's Model 202 include gas-escape holes in the receiver ring and bolt body. Their purpose is to vent escaping powder gases away from the shooter in the event of cartridge case failure or a pierced primer.

group from 100 yards measured just 8/10ths of an inch across.

The Sauer Model 202 is an extraordinarily well-designed rifle, too. Exotic by American standards, its appearance might easily put off potential buyers. It's not inexpensive, either, but it's a fine-shooting gun—one in which most owners would take tremendous pride. Certainly the Sauer Model 202 has a bright future ahead of it. Sauer also offers it in a left-handed version.

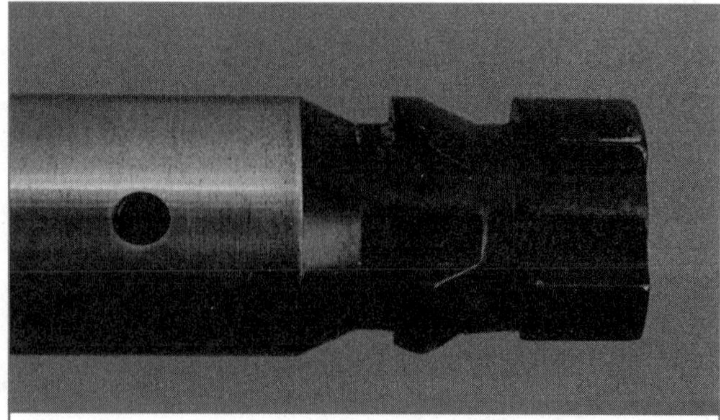

Sauer's unique bolt locks directly into the rear portion of the barrel via six locking lugs (shown). This system helps reduce the stress placed on the receiver.

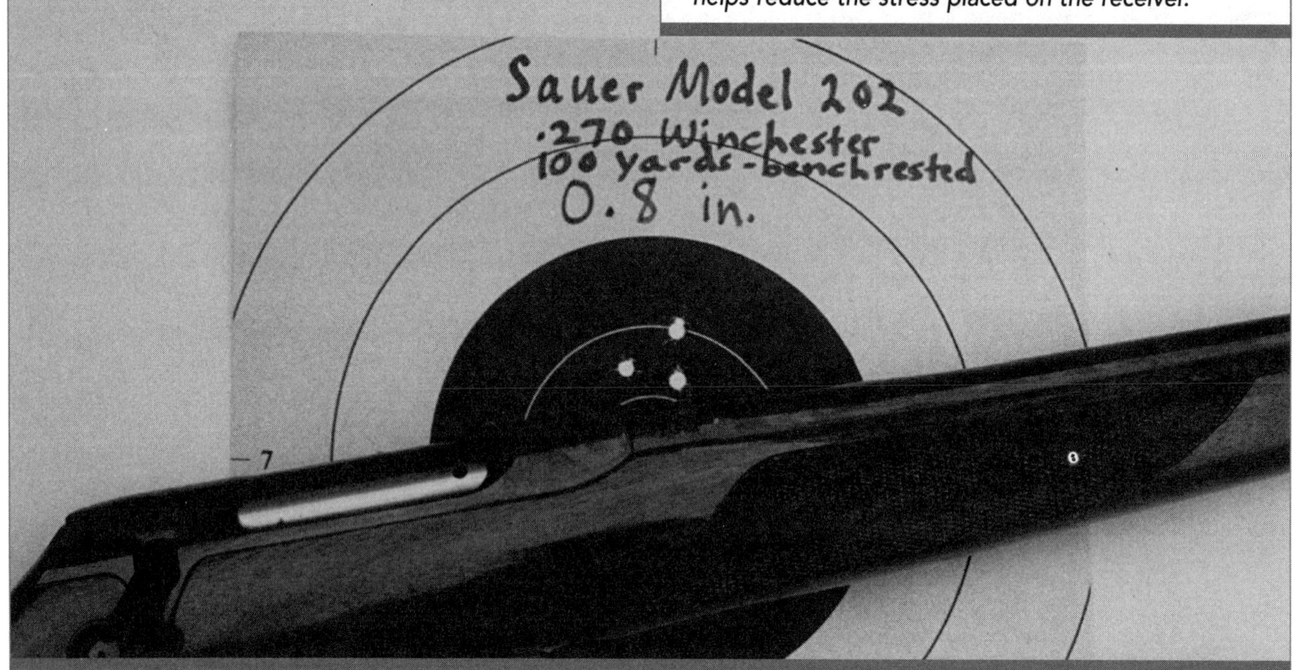

The Sauer Model 202 tested for this book proved superbly accurate, witness this .8-inch group fired at 100 yards.

SAUER MODEL 202

	MODEL 202
Overall Length	44.3 inches (with standard barrel; see below)
Barrel Length	23 inches (standard); 26 inches (magnum calibers)
Weight	7.7 pounds (standard)
Manufacturer	J.P. Sauer & Sohn, Eckenförde, Germany
Importer	SIGARMS, Exeter, New Hampshire
Years Produced	1994-present
Caliber & Capacity	*Standard:* .243, 25-06, 6.5x55mm, .270 Winchester, .308, .30-06/3 rounds *Magnum:* 7mm Remington Magnum, .300 Winchester/Weatherby Magnum, .375 H&H/2 rounds

Savage Model 93G

While rifles made for the .22 Magnum cartridge are not as common as they once were, this useful and versatile round is better represented in bolt-action rifles than in any other action type. Back in 1959, Winchester introduced the .22 Magnum cartridge as the .22 Winchester Magnum Rimfire (.22 WMR), offering shooters a significant step up from .22 Long Rifle ballistics while retaining some of its desirable characteristics compared to heftier centerfire rounds. I refer specifically to reduced cost, recoil and noise levels. By all counts, Winchester succeeded. To those in the know, the .22 Magnum is now a highly useful round for pest control and other uses where cartridges of intermediate power—between .22 Long Rifle and, say .222/.223 Remington or .243 Winchester—are indicated.

A fine example of the .22 WMR caliber rifle is Savage's Model 93G, which dates from 1994. A sturdy, utilitarian design with good performance at a reasonable price, the Model 93G combines a blued barrel and action with a walnut-finished hardwood stock. A Monte Carlo comb on the stock aids shooters who desire optical sights; the rifle's receiver is already grooved for such mounting. A modified version—the Model 93FSS—has a straight-comb stock made of black plastic and a stainless steel barrel and action for improved weather resistance. The 5-shot magazine fits almost

The .22 Magnum cartridge (center) used by the Savage Model 93G represents a significant step up from the .22 Long Rifle (left). It produces high performance with considerably less cost, noise or recoil than even smaller centerfire rounds like the .243 Winchester (right).

The Savage Model 93G offers the versatile .22 WMR (.22 Magnum) cartridge in a well-made but inexpensive rifle.

The Savage Model 93G features a wooden stock that is quite attractive considering the rifle's relatively low cost. Note the stained hardwood and impressed checkering on the pistol grip.

The manual safety control on Savage's Model 93G is located just behind the bolt handle. It pushes forward to fire, exposing a red dot.

flush with the bottom of the stock, with only the release latch protruding enough to operate by either hand. The rotary thumb safety, which comes easily to hand for a right-handed shooter, must be pushed forward to fire.

The Model 93G I tested proved highly accurate for a low-cost .22 Magnum rifle. My best 3-shot benchrested group from 100 yards measured only 2.25 inches across. Like other Savage rifles tested for this book, the magazine release seemed rather flimsy at first glance, but it held up well and the test rifle indicated no malfunctions.

The Savage Model 93G produced good accuracy results, including this 2.25-inch 100-yard benchrested group. Point of aim was the bottom of the target's black portion.

The Savage Model 93G (center) ranks among the best of the current breed of high-performance, reasonably-priced .22 Magnum rifles, including the lever-action Ruger Model 96 (top) and the pump-action Rossi Model 59 (bottom).

SAVAGE MODEL 93G

	MODEL 93G
Overall Length	39.5 inches
Barrel Length	20.75 inches
Weight	5.75 pounds
Manufacturer	Lakefield Arms, Ltd., Ontario, Canada
Importer	Savage Arms, Inc., Westfield, MA
Years Produced	1994-present
Caliber/Capacity	.22 Winchester Magnum Rimfire (AKA .22 WMR or .22 Magnum)/5 rounds

Savage Model III Classic Hunter

The Model 111 made by Savage represents an updated and slightly modified version of the company's Model 110, which was introduced in 1958. Thus the 110 became the basis for the entire bolt-action, centerfire-caliber Savage line, which also includes a lineup of Models 111, 112 and 116 in their various forms. Strong and cleverly constructed, using many stamped steel parts to save on manufacturing expenses, this well-engineered rifle is surprisingly efficient and durable, especially considering its low cost.

The Model 111 Classic Hunter tested for this book features a rugged synthetic stock and iron sights along with a receiver already drilled and tapped for scope mounts. Savage also offers wooden stocks and the choice of a detachable magazine or quick-release hinged floorplate. The three-position safety location on the tang is best

Like most modern Savage rifles, the Model 111 handles well and shoots accurately.

The Savage Model 111 Classic Hunter includes integral ("iron") sights and a synthetic stock.

for left-handed shooters but works fine for right-handers as well.

The Savage Model 111 shoots accurately, with a good factory trigger pull and excellent recoil control. A typical 3-shot 100 yard group, using Remington 150-grain Core-Lokt softpoint bullets, formed a perfectly acceptable 1.7-inch group. While it may be one of the homeliest bolt-action rifles around, the Savage Model 110 line offers real value for hunters and police forces in a powerful rifle that performs well with a variety of cartridge chamberings.

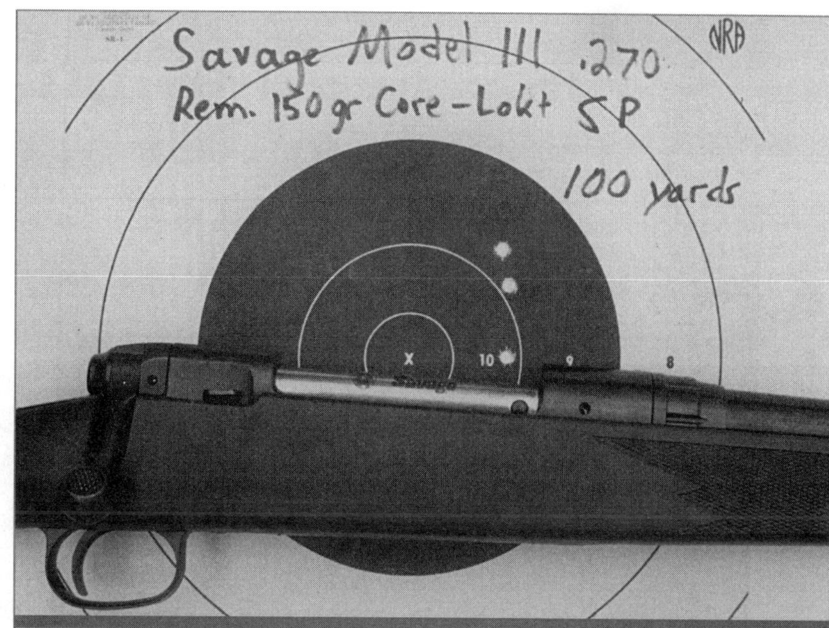

The author fired this 1.7-inch group from the 100-yard bench—a good result with iron sights.

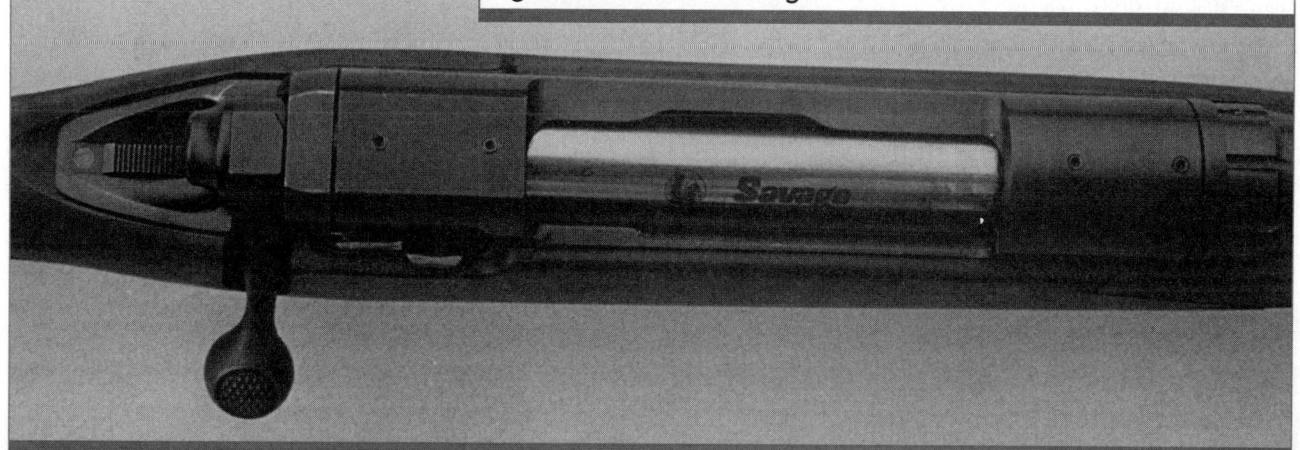

In addition to its integral front and rear sights, the Savage Model 111 comes with the receiver drilled and tapped for easy installation of a telescopic sight.

SAVAGE MODEL 111 CLASSIC HUNTER

	MODEL 111
Overall Length	43.5 inches (22-inch barrel)
Barrel Length	22 and 24 inches
Weight	6.3 to 7.0 pounds, depending on caliber
Manufacturer	Savage Arms, Incorporated
Years Produced	1994-present
Caliber & Capacity	.223, .22-250, .243, .270, .308, .30-06, 7mm Remington Magnum, .300 Winchester Magnum, .338 Winchester Magnum/5 rounds

Savage Model 116SE Safari Express

Savage Arms introduced the Model 116SE rifle in 1944 with one purpose in mind: to give sports shooters a powerful rifle at a reasonable cost. Because of the potent magnum cartridges used in this big rifle, Savage included a muzzle brake in its design. When it is turned to open, the muzzle brake is on; when the holes are covered, it's off. One of the great advantages of this system is less recoil. With the muzzle brake in operation, Savage claims a 30% reduction in felt recoil. The rifle is definitely more pleasant to fire with the muzzle brake in use. The downside, though, is that the muzzle brake contributes significantly to the tremendous noise generated by the firing of this rifle. This may not be a problem at the firing range, where ear protection is mandatory, but shooters are forewarned to put on their hearing protection devices when shooting game.

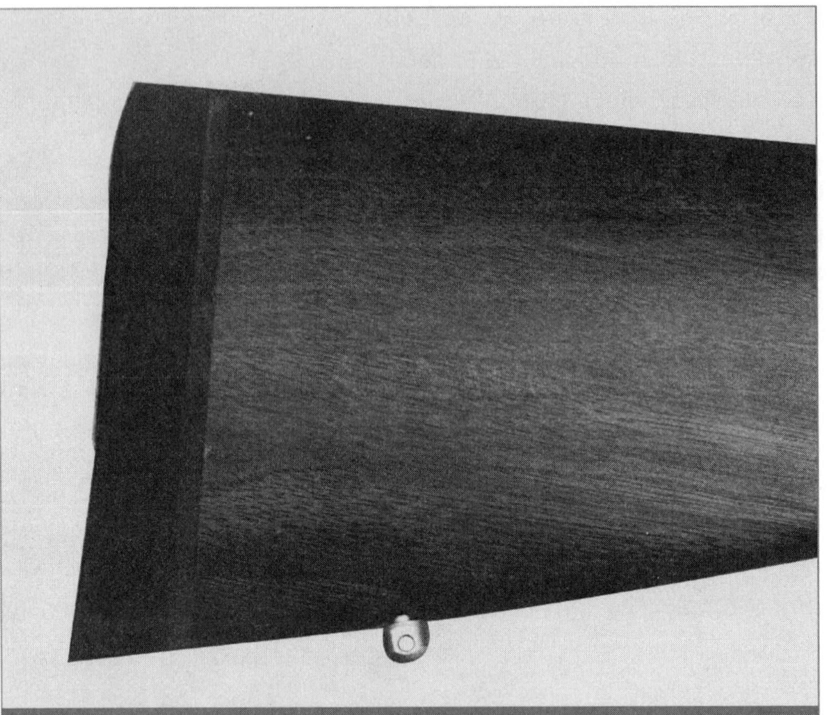

A thick rubber buttpad enables shooters to fire the Model 116SE Safari Express in relative comfort.

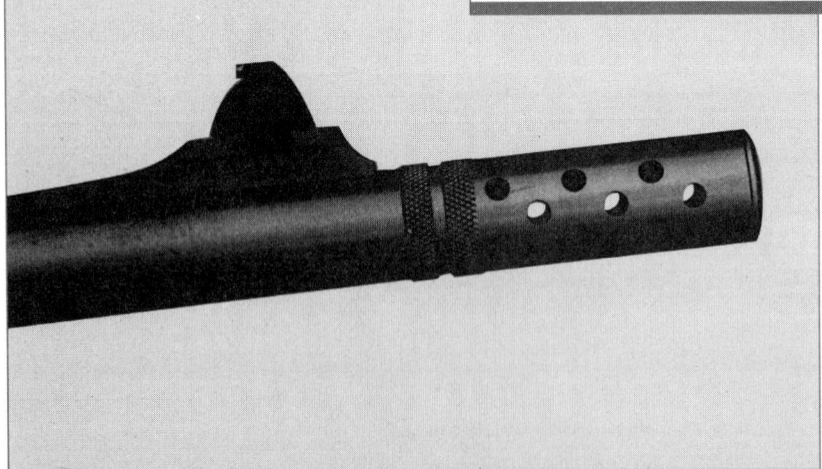

The Savage Model 116SE Safari Express has made several concessions to heavy recoil generated by the powerful cartridges for which it is chambered. The muzzle brake shown is in its "on" setting.

Among other measures Savage has taken to make the Model 116SE more resistant to the powerful cartridges it fires are the addition of a thick, vented recoil pad and dual

The manual safety on the Model 116SE Safari Express is the two-position type. It pushes forward to fire (exposing a red dot to alert the shooter) and back (covering the dot) to the safe setting.

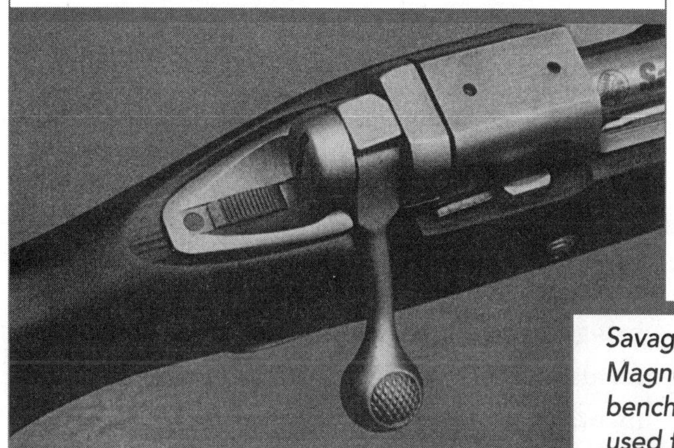

In light of the dangerous game this rifle will probably be used against, Savage also opted for controlled-round cartridge feeding and a "blind" magazine to increase the stock's rigidity and strength. Two massive frontal locking lugs and a gas-escape hole are drilled into the bolt between them. To fire, the manual safety—a sliding ambidextrous tang type—is pushed forward, exposing a red dot. To lock the bolt and firing mechanism, the safety is pulled back. The cocked-recoil bolts in the stock to prevent splitting. There's nothing delicate about the sighting arrangements, either; these include a brass bead front sight and a three-leaf express rear sight. The receiver top also comes drilled and tapped for a scope--still another option with which to enjoy the best of both worlds.

Savage's Model 116SE Safari Express in .300 Winchester Magnum caliber fired a 2.9-inch group from the 100-yard bench without heavy recoil despite the powerful cartridge used for our test.

The stock on Savage's Model 116SE Safari Express has two massive steel recoil lugs which allow it to contain recoil forces without splintering.

striker indicator is a simple lever located on the right side of the action, just ahead of the bolt handle. When the striker is cocked, the indicator rises, then lies flat once the rifle has been fired.

I tested the Savage Model 116SE in .300 Winchester Magnum caliber (most other .30 caliber cartridges run low 500 yards from the muzzle) because it offers better accuracy and power over other .30s as the target stretches out to 500 yards or more. When it was first introduced in 1963 in the Winchester Model 70 bolt-action rifle, the .300 Winchester Magnum's lightest commercial load was a 150-grain bullet that developed muzzle velocities of some 3,275 feet per second and was still going strong at 2,988 feet per second at 100 yards. The .300 Winchester Magnum's muzzle energy of 3,573 foot/pounds and residual energy of 2,974 foot/pounds at 100 yards make this a formidable cartridge indeed. It also adapted well to using heavier bullets of 165, 180 and 190 grains. In short, the .300 Winchester Magnum cartridge was, and remains, a significant step up in power, even from the .30-06. This added power translates into flatter trajectories for improved accuracy and striking power, both highly useful traits as the range increases. The price one pays for these improved ballistics is, of course, more recoil. Various .40 caliber rounds also available in this model kick even harder, which explains why Savage added a muzzle brake to its Model 116SE.

Despite all that size and weight, the Savage Model 116SE handles easily. The sights, despite being designed more for rapid shooting up close on dangerous game than for precise sight alignment, fired a 2.9-inch group at 100 yards. The rifle shot equally well with the muzzle brake turned on or off. The bolt handle is fairly stiff and the bolt stroke is longer and more awkward than on smaller, handier rifles (part of the price one pays for using a more powerful cartridge).

For those who desire a relatively soft recoil in a

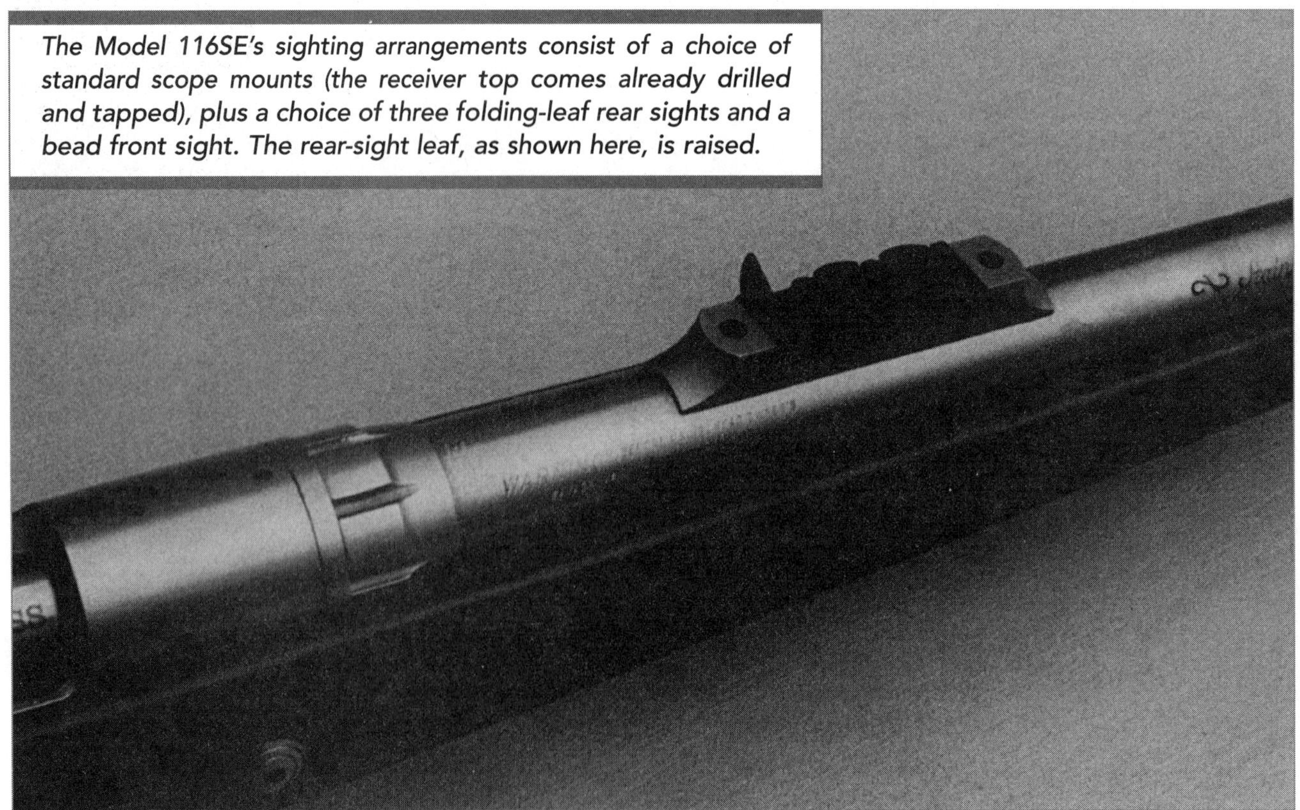

The Model 116SE's sighting arrangements consist of a choice of standard scope mounts (the receiver top comes already drilled and tapped), plus a choice of three folding-leaf rear sights and a bead front sight. The rear-sight leaf, as shown here, is raised.

powerful magnum caliber and at a reasonable price, the Savage Model 116SE has little competition. About the only other rifle that competes in what is admittedly a highly specialized category is Browning's BAR semiautomatic sporting rifle. Its self-loading mechanism helps soften the recoil, and its optional BOSS (Ballistic Optimizing Shooting System) muzzle attachment tames recoil even more. However, the BAR is limited to .338 Winchester Magnum at the maximum, whereas the Savage chambers the Model 116SE in several more powerful rounds—all the way up to .458 Winchester Magnum!

With its ebony forend and quality hardwood stock, the Savage Model 116SE is a handsome rifle that rises several cuts above the usual Savage models. Nevertheless, it's still reasonably priced compared to other high-powered rifles with these same features. Those who desire a powerful weapon suitable for large and dangerous game should note that the Model 116SE is well worth looking into.

The Model 116SE includes a cocked-striker indicator located just ahead of the bolt handle. This indicator rises (as shown) when the mechanism is cocked, then lowers to reveal its uncocked status.

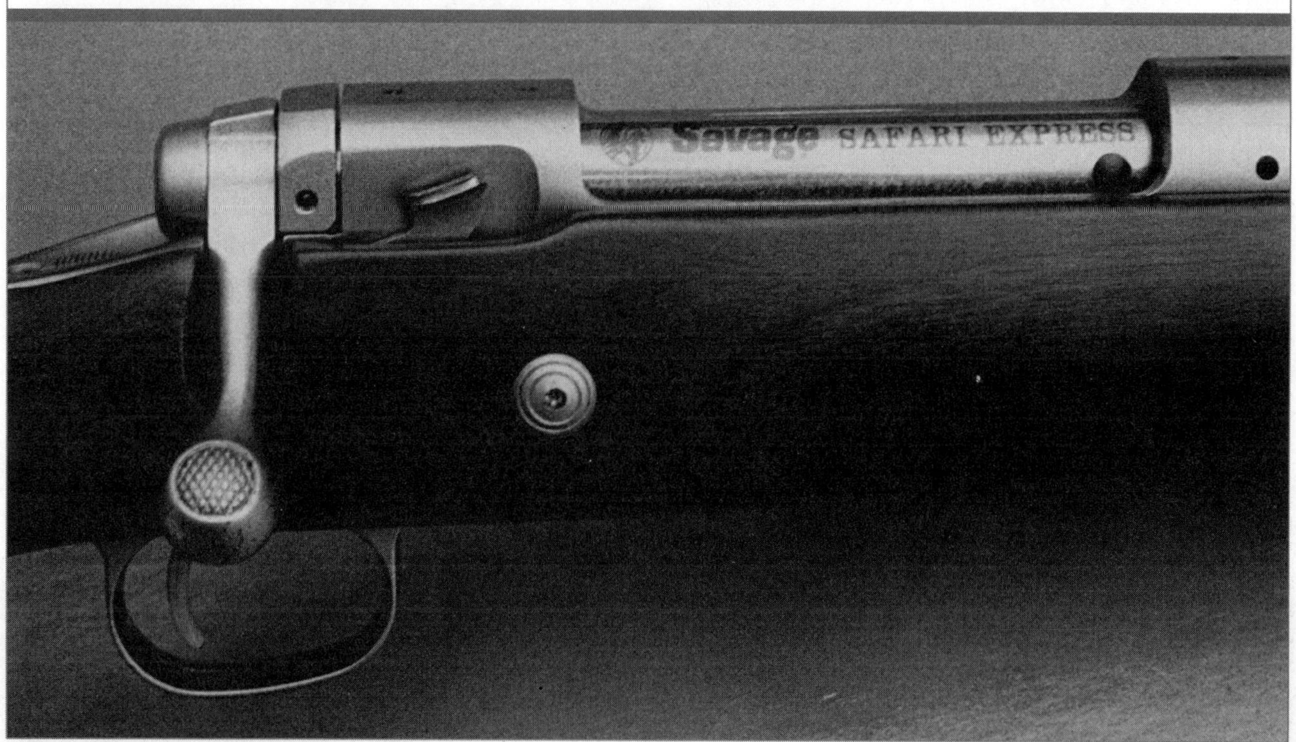

SAVAGE MODEL 116SE SAFARI EXPRESS

	MODEL 116SE
Overall Length	45.5 inches
Barrel Length	24.0 inches
Weight	8.5 pounds
Caliber Choices	.300 Win. Mag., 338 Win. Mag., .425 Express, .458 Win. Mag.
Capacity	3 rounds
Production	1994-

Steyr SBS

Soon after Steyr announced its new Model SBS in 1997, it began appearing in several different versions. The standard SBS sported a hand-checkered European walnut stock that was either Mannlicher-style (i.e., stocked to the muzzle) or half-stocked with a schnabel tip. A ramp front and V-notch rear sight were standard, along with integral scope mounts. An SBS variant, the *Forester*, has a less elaborate straight-combed walnut stock and Monte Carlo cheekpiece styled more to American tastes. This model has no sights of its own, but it will accept scope mounts made for the popular Browning A-Bolt rifle. The model tested for this book is the SBS *Pro-Hunter*, featuring a synthetic stock with adjustable butt spacers, a straight comb (without cheekpiece), and a full pistol grip with a slight palm swell. The barrel rifling is formed by the cold-hammering process, in which a smoothbore barrel is placed over a hard mandrel bearing a reverse rifling pattern. Giant mechanical hammers then literally pound the rifling pattern into the bore. The distinctive ripples, or flutes, along the outside of the barrel bear mute testimony to the tremendous force involved in this process.

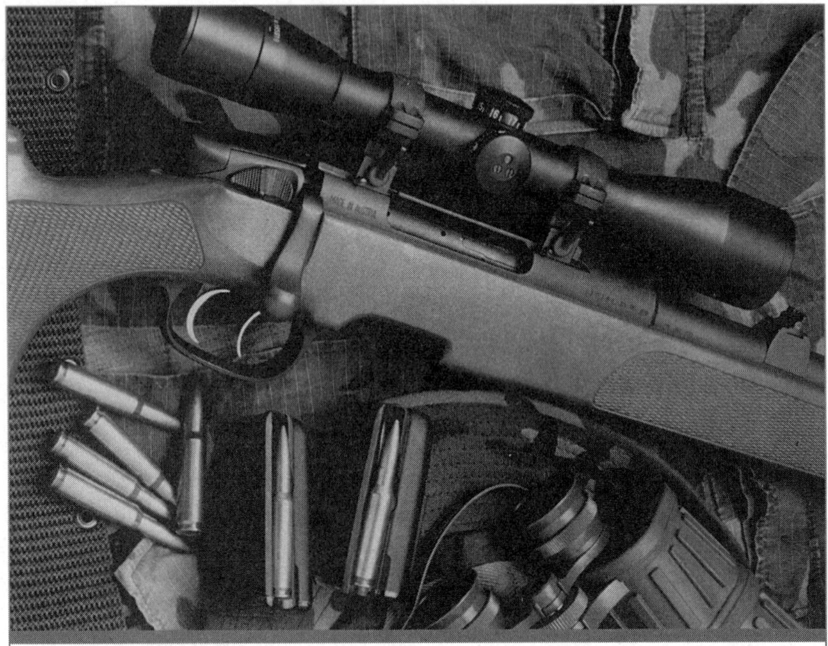

The Steyr company has been making precision bolt-action rifles since the turn of the century. The company's legendary SSG has seen widespread use as a tactical rifle for armies and police forces worldwide since its introduction in 1969 (photo courtesy of Steyr GmbH).

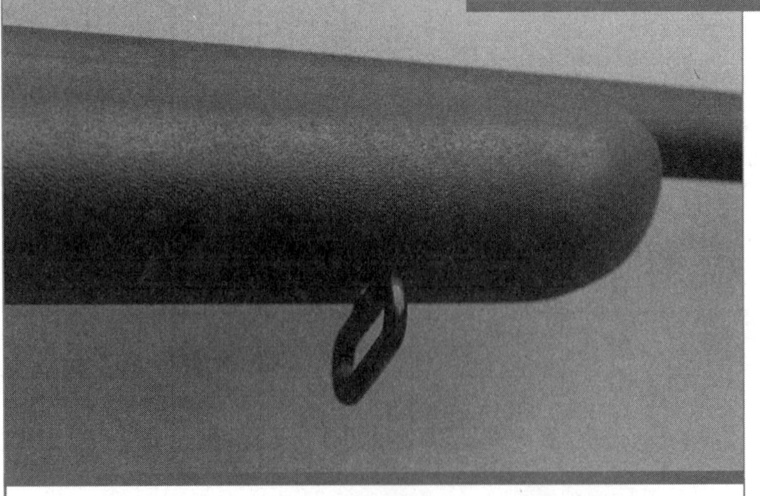

The Steyr SBS Pro-Hunter features integral sling mounts on its stock, a great convenience all too often overlooked by less conscientious manufacturers.

Rolling the Steyr SBS's manual safety control fully forward (two clicks) exposes a red dot and indicates the rifle's readiness to fire.

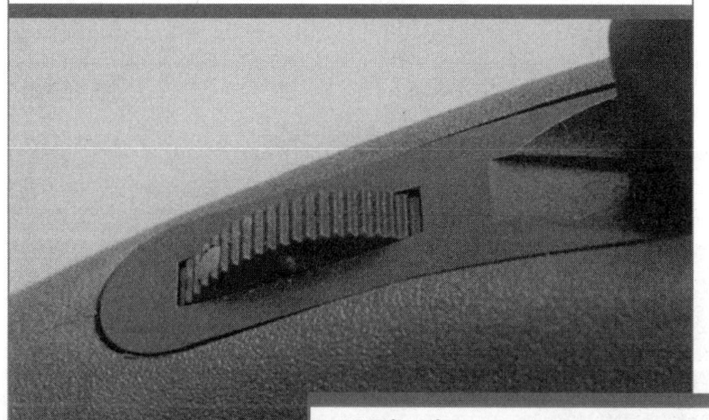

With the rotary tang-mounted manual safety brought fully to the rear, its safe setting, a gray plastic tab rises to lock the safety control into position. In this setting the bolt cannot be moved and the firing mechanism is locked. The shooter must depress this tab before the safety can be rotated forward to fire.

The distinctive polymer stock of the SBS Pro-Hunter looks odd but handles well. Its thick buttpad helps ease the recoil from these powerful cartridges (spacers may be added or deleted as desired). The Pro-Hunter's magazine is also made of polymer and features two positions. Fully in place, it automatically reloads as the shooter operates the bolt. And in its intermediate position, the magazine drops slightly and cannot feed rounds. This enables the shooter to hold the magazine contents in reserve while loading one round at a time through the firing chamber. This "magazine cutoff" style used in holding the magazine in reserve was all the rage in bolt-action military rifles at the turn of the 20th century before it went out of style. Steyr has revived it, however, for this rifle and the similar "Steyr Scout" model. The Pro-Hunter magazine is easily removed by pressing down on two long release buttons located on either side of the magazine. SBS rifles come with a standard magazine capacity of only four rounds, but the Pro-Hunter, along with the Scout Rifle, offers an optional 10-round extended unit as well.

The manual safety on the Pro-Hunter is located on the grip tang. It's an ambidextrous rotary type with three operating positions. When rolled back, the manual safety locks into position. A small spring-loaded gray plastic tab then rises, preventing forward movement of the rotary safety until the tab is depressed (a white circle also appears in the middle of the wheel, just behind the locking tab). In this safe position, the manual safety mechanism locks the bolt and trigger. After depressing the safety tab and rolling the rotary safety control forward one click, the white button appears at the top of the circle. In this

Starting from its rearmost, on-safe position, rolling the Steyr SBS's manual safety wheel forward one click, exposing a white dot, allows the bolt to be operated but keeps the firing mechanism locked.

The Pro-Hunter has a cocking indicator located at the rear of the bolt shroud. When cocked, the indicator knob protrudes far enough to become visible in the bolt shroud (as shown).

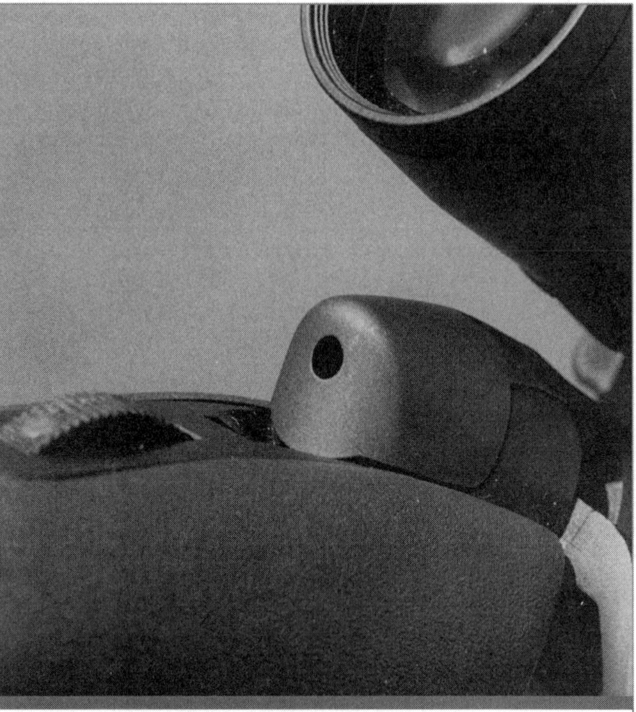

With the striker uncocked, the cocking indicator is not visible in the bolt shroud.

With the Pro-Hunter's manual safety applied, the shooter needs only to press the bolt handle until it lies almost flush against the stock. This makes the bolt less likely to catch on branches or other obstacles.

When the manual safety is rotated forward to its fire position, the bolt handle automatically springs to its normal position.

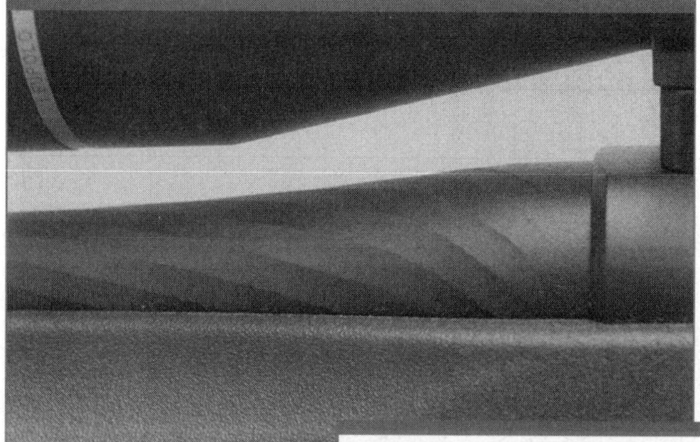

The Pro-Hunter's hammer-forged barrel retains the distinctive ripples on its surface.

position, the firing mechanism remains locked but the bolt can move.

Part of the reason for the Pre-Hunter's SBS ("Safe Bolt System") designation relates to the ability of the safety control to stay in the "on" position while the shooter is operating the bolt. Once the safety control has rolled forward one more time, exposing a red button, the rifle will fire. This system may seem complicated, but it's actually quite smooth and fast-moving. In my opinion, locating the safety on the tang, as this one is, offers the best of all worlds. It's fast, reliable, easy to operate under stress and suitable for both right-handed and left-handed shooters. My second choice (after the tang-mounted safety) is the Garand style, located in the leading edge of the triggerguard.

It's interesting to note that whenever the manual safety on the Pro-Hunter is rotated into its on-safe position, the shooter can then press the bolt handle closer to the stock, where it's less likely to catch on brush or undergrowth. When the shooter rotates the safety out of its safe setting, the bolt handle automatically springs to its normal position, where the shooter can reach it. The downside to this clever system is the bolt handle, which makes a lot of noise as it returns to its normal position. You don't want to try this maneuver when you're close to a game animal with good hearing!

The Pro-Hunter boasts one of the best scope mounting systems ever developed for a rifle. Mounting a Leupold Vari-X III 3-10 power scope to a rifle is really quite simple. Once the two locking tabs on the left side of the scope mounts have been pushed down and forward, the scope rings can be positioned on the mounts with ease. Next, push the locking tabs up and back, exposing the word "LOCK" on both mounts. The scope is now positioned properly. If this rifle only came with integral iron sights, it would be close to perfect.

The Steyr SBS features one of the best scope-mounting systems ever devised for a sporting rifle made for sale to private citizens. With the locking tabs, located on the left side of the scope mounts, pushed down as shown the telescopic sight may be inserted or removed from the scope mounts.

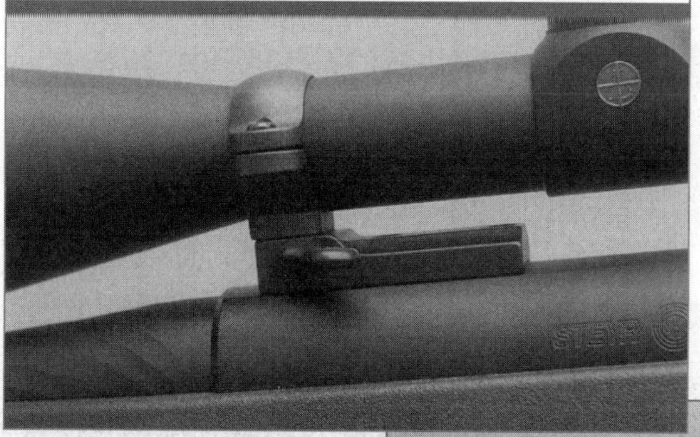

With the locking tabs (located on the left side of the scope mounts) pushed up, the telescopic sight is locked in position.

When tested in 30-'06 caliber, the Steyr SBS Pro-Hunter proved quite accurate and a joy to shoot. The best 3-shot group fired from the bench at 100 yards (using Winchester's excellent 168-grain Ballistic Silvertip bullets) spanned 1.1 inches. Another group, using Hornady's Match 168-grain boattail hollow-point (BTHP) bullets, spanned 1.3 inches. The bolt operated smoothly and rapidly, allowing easy manipulation while keeping the rifle butt against the shoulder, where it belongs. The trigger pull is short, crisp and smooth, especially so for a factory-stock rifle, and the smooth face on the trigger felt comfortable against my trigger finger. It all boils down to the fact that the Steyr SBS, especially the Pro-Hunter variant, has a great future ahead of it. It's priced competitively and comes equipped with numerous features likely to attract U.S. shooters. It truly is one of the best bolt-action sporting rifles available.

The best group fired with the Steyr SBS Pro-Hunter was this triangular-shaped three-shot pattern measuring 1.1 inches. Ammunition used was the Winchester 168-grain Ballistic Silvertip, a good hunting round.

The author's second-best group fired with the Steyr SBS Pro-Hunter was this 1.3-inch three-shot effort, for which he used the Hornady Match round with 168-grain Boattail Hollowpoint (BTHP) bullets. Even without formal scope adjustments, the rifle shot very close to point of aim, which was the exact center of the target.

STEYR SBS

	SBS
Overall Length	44.5 inches
Barrel Length	23.6 inches
Weight	7.5 pounds
Manufacturer	Steyr-Mannlicher GmbH, Steyr, Austria
Importer	GSI, Trussville, Alabama
Years Produced	1997-present
Caliber & Capacity	.243, .25-06, 6.5x55mm, 6.5x68mm, .270, 7mm-08, 7x64 Brenneke, 7.5x55mm, .308, .30-06, 7mm Remington Magnum, .300 Winchester Magnum/4 rounds standard, with a 10-round extended unit available on SBS Pro-Hunter

Tikka Rifles

The firearms company known as Oy Tikkakoski of Finland is almost as old as independent Finland itself. During the mid-1920s the Tikkakoski factory was making replacement barrels for the Finnish army's 7.65mm (.30 Luger caliber) Model 1923 Luger pistols. By 1932 production had begun on Finland's standard submachine gun, the 9mm Parabellum caliber m/31 "Suomi." In 1944, after building over 80,000 of this outstanding weapon, widely regarded as one of the best submachine guns ever built, Tikkakoski ceased military weapons production in accordance with the armistice arranged with the Soviet Union. After 20 years of producing various non-firearms products, Tikkakoski unveiled its first sporting rifle, the "Tikka Model 55." Based on the ever-popular Mauser Model 98, this new rifle eliminated the third (rear) safety lug and relied instead on the two opposed front locking lugs. Also, in order to contain the ignition from the chambered cartridge, the bolt handle had to be locked down at the moment of firing. Because it was made of good materials and was limited to fairly low-

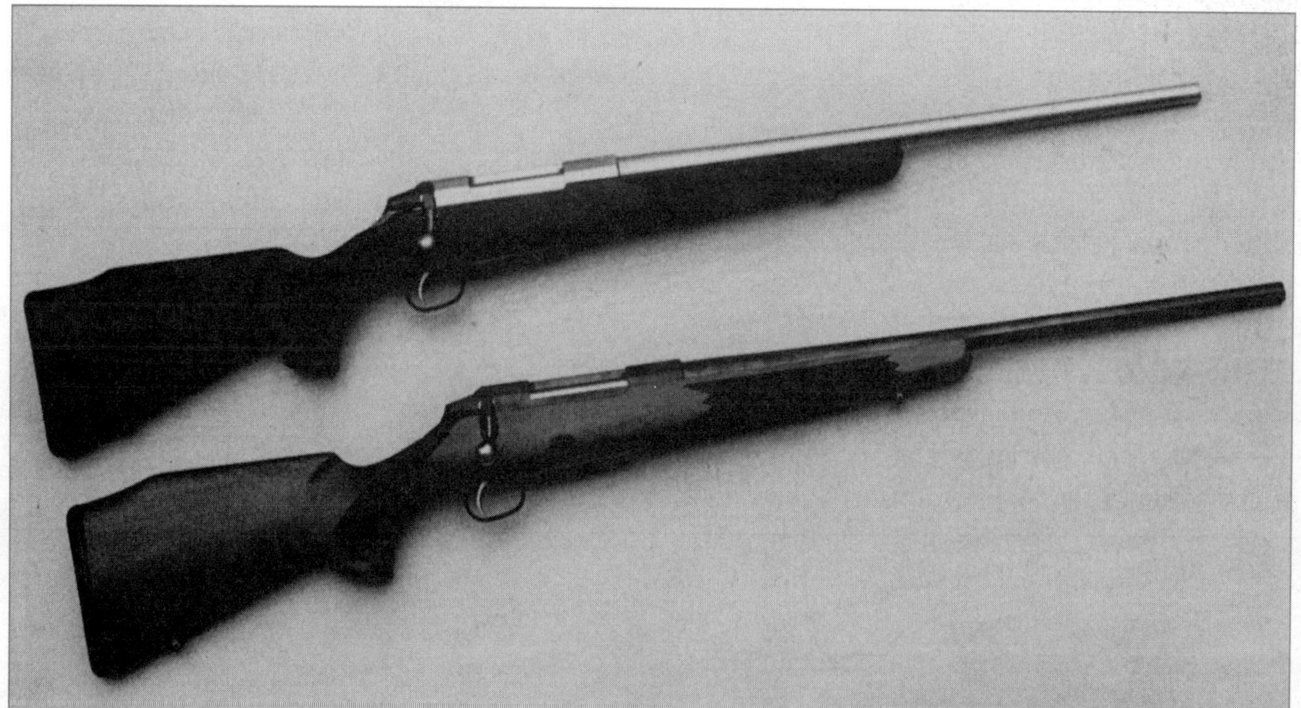

The top Tikka Model 695 rifle, with stainless steel metal parts and a synthetic stock, chambers the .30-06. The blued steel, hardwood-stocked Model 695 shown at bottom chambers the .270 Winchester cartridge. Stoeger offers .25-06, .270, .30-06 and Magnum variants for U.S. sales. Tikka also makes the 695 in 6.5mm Mauser, 7x64mm and 9.3x62mm chamberings for foreign sales.

The magazine release on the Model 695 is located at the bottom of the magazine on the right side of the stock. When the release is pressed in, the shooter can withdraw the magazine by hand.

powered cartridges, the Model 55 proved highly successful under this system. It subsequently appeared in .17 Remington, .222 Remington, .22-250, 6mm Remington, .243 Winchester and .308 Winchester chamberings. Perhaps the most remarkable feature of the Model 55 was the oversized knob at the end of the bolt handle. This sensible feature was made in recognition of Finland's harsh winters, where shooters invariably wear heavy gloves.

Since the Tikka receiver top comes already drilled and tapped, shooters have a choice of standard scope mounts or Tikka's own Optilock scope mounts (which fit in grooves machined in the receiver). Tikka's receiver grooving also allows shooters to use standard Weaver mounting hardware.

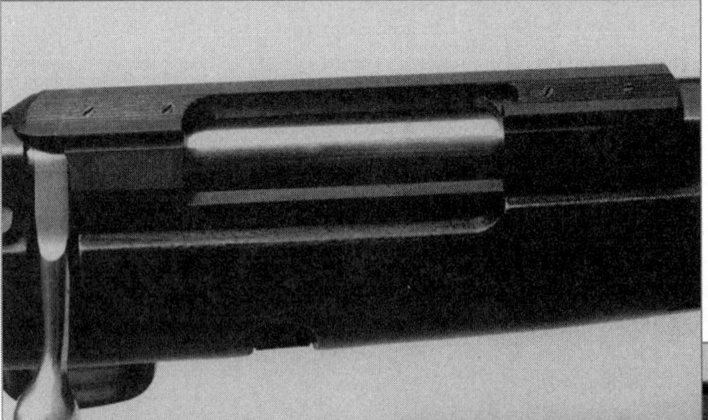

Tikka offered the Model 55 in five variants—Standard, Deluxe, Sporter, Super Sporter and SSP—each gaining a solid reputation for reliable performance at a reasonable price. The Model 65, introduced in 1972, was similar mechanically to the Model 55, the main exception being a lengthened receiver designed to accommodate magnum cartridges and the full-length, Mauser-system 6.5mm cartridge then popular in Sweden. Tikka kept the Model 55/65 series in production until 1989, at which point the company was incorporated as a branch of the SAKO/Valmet concern. Tikka then replaced the Model 55 with an improved Model 558/Model 568 series. The first digits indicated these were improved models compared to the original standard "55" or "65." The second digit indicated action length—with "5" standing for short cartridges and "6" indicating long cartridges. The final digit—"8"—indicated these were the first prototypes made in the year 1988. When production began in 1990, these designations were advanced to "590" and "690," respectively. The current models—595 (short action) and 695 (long action)—appeared in 1996. Today, Tikka uses other monikers, including "Master/Whitetail Hunter," "Master Synthetic," "Master All-Weather," "Master Sporter" and "Master Semi-Sporter." The rifles tested for this

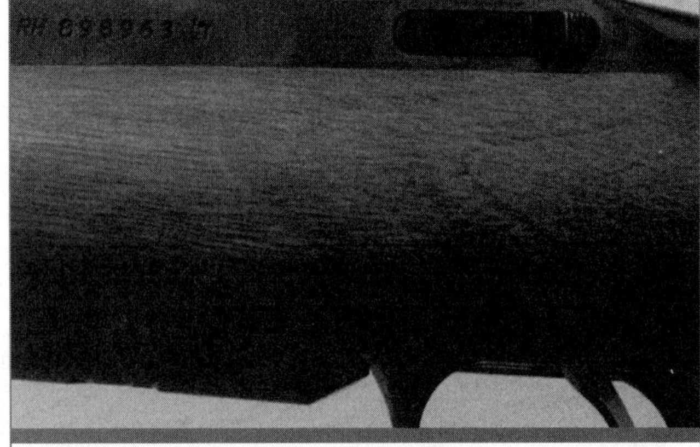

To remove the bolt on a Model 695, the gun must first be unloaded. The shooter then presses in the bolt release lever at the left rear portion of the receiver. The bolt handle is simultaneously lifted up and to the rear.

book were the "Master/ Whitetail Hunter" and "Master All-Weather."

Tikka makes the Model 595 in the following calibers: .223, .22-250, .243, 25-06, 270, .30-06, 7mm Mag. .300 Win. Mag., .308 and 338 Win. Mag. The 595 Sporter variant, made for the .223, .22-250 and .308 cartridges, features a fully-adjustable hardwood stock with an enlarged belly to completely enclose the sides of the 5-shot magazine. The Model 695 is made in .25-06, 6.5mm Mauser, .270 Winchester, 7x64mm, .30-06 and 9.3x62mm; and there's a Model 695 Magnum available in 7mm Remington Magnum, .300 Winchester and .338 Winchester Magnum. Stoeger, the U.S. importer, offers the .25-06, .270, .30-06, 7mm Rem. Mag. And 300 Win. Mag.

The Model 695's safety, a two-position type located on the right side of the bolt shroud (just behind the bolt handle), pushes forward to fire (exposing a red dot) and back (covering the dot) to its safe setting. A cocked-striker indicator protruding from the rear of the bolt shroud exposes still another red dot.

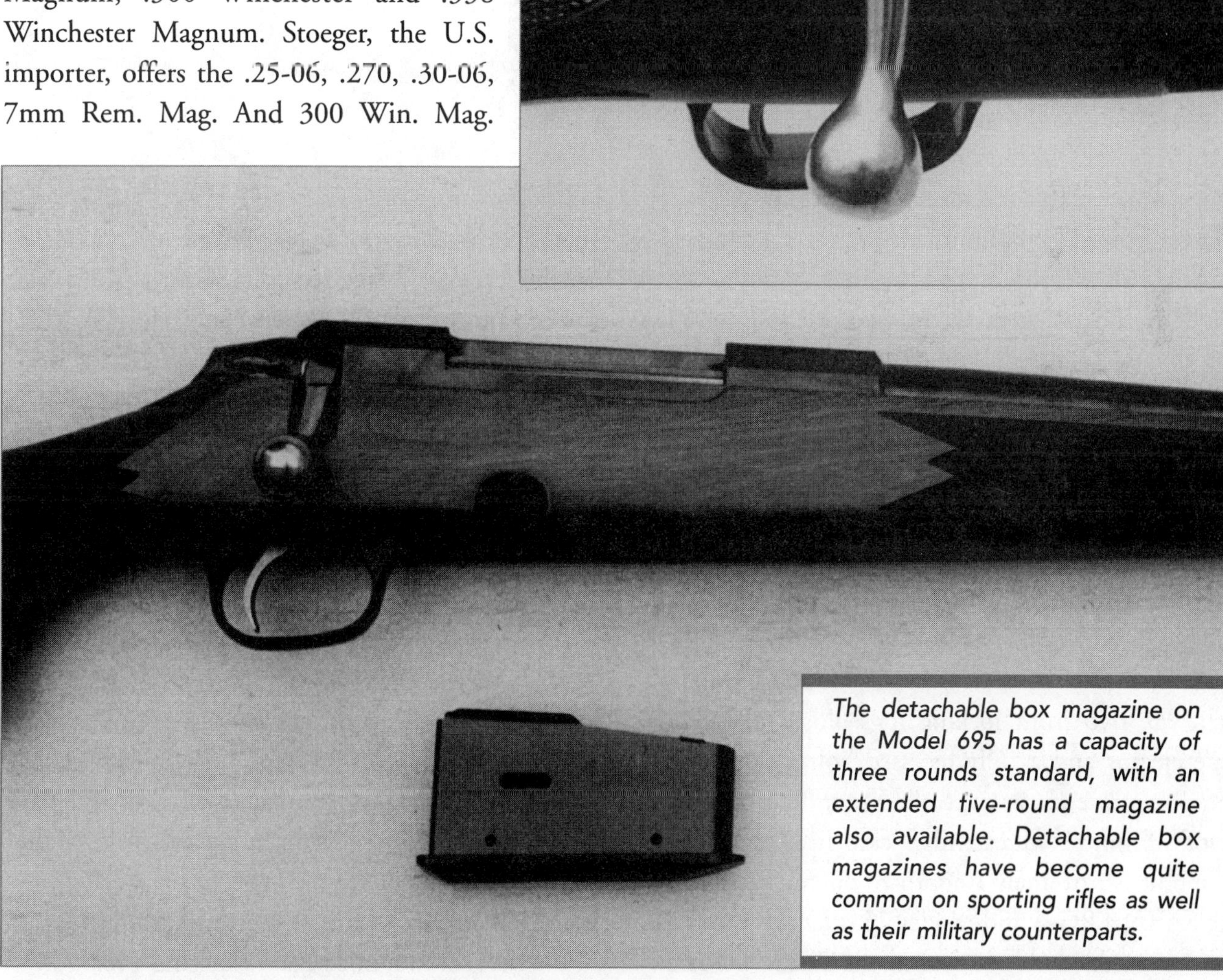

The detachable box magazine on the Model 695 has a capacity of three rounds standard, with an extended five-round magazine also available. Detachable box magazines have become quite common on sporting rifles as well as their military counterparts.

Magazine capacity is three rounds standard with an extended five-round magazine as an option. The magazine release, located on the bottom of the magazine on the right side of the stock, must first be pressed in before the shooter can withdraw the magazine by hand.

None of the Tikka rifles presently imported to the U.S. by Stoeger includes iron sights; they are instead set up solely for scope mounting. Fortunately, the scope-mounting arrangements are unusually versatile. Shooters have a choice of standard scope mounts (the receiver top comes already drilled and tapped) or Tikka's own Optilock scope mounts, which fit in grooves machined in the receiver. Both Models 595 and 695 offer cold hammer-forged barrels free-floated in the stock for maximum accuracy. They also come with a factory guarantee of 10,000 rounds minimum. Adjustable triggers, with a pull weight of two to four pounds, are standard. The triggers on the two rifles we tested felt fine as adjusted. Pull weight was light and crisp, with no initial slack. All in all, this is a superb factory trigger by any standard. Tikka also offers a set trigger as an option. There's also an adjustable spacer system. The recoil pad/buttplate is removable, allowing spacers, each 2/10ths of an inch, to be inserted between them and the recoil pad at the end of the stock.

The best group encountered when firing in .30-06 caliber measured 1.2 inches from 100 yards.

Bolt construction is Mauser-influenced; i.e., there are two front locking lugs plus a plunger-type ejector and a fully recessed bolt face. These components eschew controlled-round feeding in favor of improved cartridge case head support. The bolt is extremely smooth to operate. As with the SAKO TRG-S and Model 75 rifles (also tested for this book), bolt removal in the Tikka rifle is a snap. Simply press in the bolt release lever (located on the left side of the receiver) while at the same time pulling the bolt back and clear of the rifle. This exposes the rear end of the barrel and firing chamber for cleaning. A useful concession to cold-weather operation, by the way, is a trigger guard that extends slightly forward to accommodate a gloved trigger finger without binding. This extension is tastefully done and in no way detracts from the rifle's appearance.

The manual safety—a two-position type—is located on the right side of the bolt shroud, just behind the handle. It pushes forward to fire (exposing a red dot), then back (covering the dot) to its safe setting. There the manual safety locks the bolt handle in its closed position. A cocked-striker indicator is also standard; with the firing mechanism cocked and ready to fire, it protrudes from the rear of the bolt shroud, once again exposing a red dot.

In my tests, I fired both a traditional Model 695 with walnut stock and blued steel finish and a Model 695 with synthetic stock and stainless steel metal parts. Cartridge chamberings were .270 Winchester and .30-06, respectively. Accuracy was outstanding, registering slightly more than minute-of-angle in both chamberings using several different brands of ammunition. Both rifles were heavy enough to make them reasonably comfortable to shoot, despite the relatively hefty cartridges involved. The stocks feature a slight Monte Carlo comb to ensure good control with a telescopic sight in place.

As for prices, Tikka Models 595 and 695 fall in the same range as most top-quality American-made bolt-action rifles. Even the Model 595 Sporter, with its fully adjustable stock and other expensive custom features, costs under $1,000. This combination of unequaled workmanship, fine features and value makes Tikka's centerfire rifles excellent bolt-action choices.

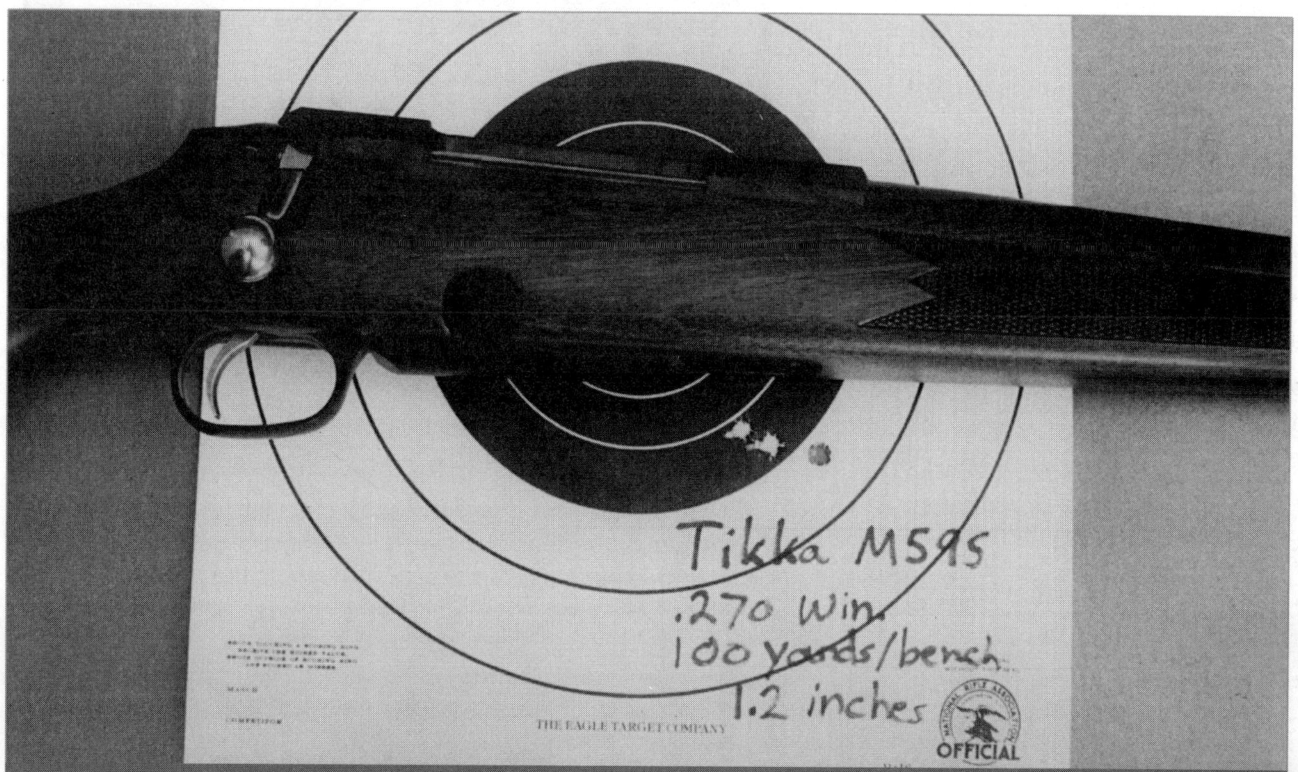

Firing the Tikka Model 695 in .270 Winchester caliber produced this impressive 1.2-inch group from the 100-yard bench.

TIKKA CENTERFIRE RIFLES

	MODEL 595	MODEL 595 SPORTER	MODEL 695M
Overall Length	42.0 inches	44.0 inches	44.5 inches
Barrel Length	22.5 inches	23.75 inches	24.5 inches
Weight	7.1 pounds	9.0-9.5 pounds	7.5 pounds
Capacity	3 rounds	5 rounds	3 rounds

TU-KKW (Norinco/Navy Arms)

The TU-KKW is similar to the German KKW, or Kleine Kaliber Wehrsport, which served as Germany's military training rifle between World Wars I and II. According to the Treaty of Versailles (1919), which officially ended World War I, military activity in Germany was severely restricted. Thus it made sense for the Germans to create a legally acceptable rimfire training rifle based on the service Model 98 Mauser rifle. Hence the creation of the KKW. Most major German firearms manufacturers, including Walther, had made KKWs for the German armed forces during WWI. Years later, Navy Arms President Val Forgett, Jr., a great enthusiast of replica firearms, saw some potential in a KKW

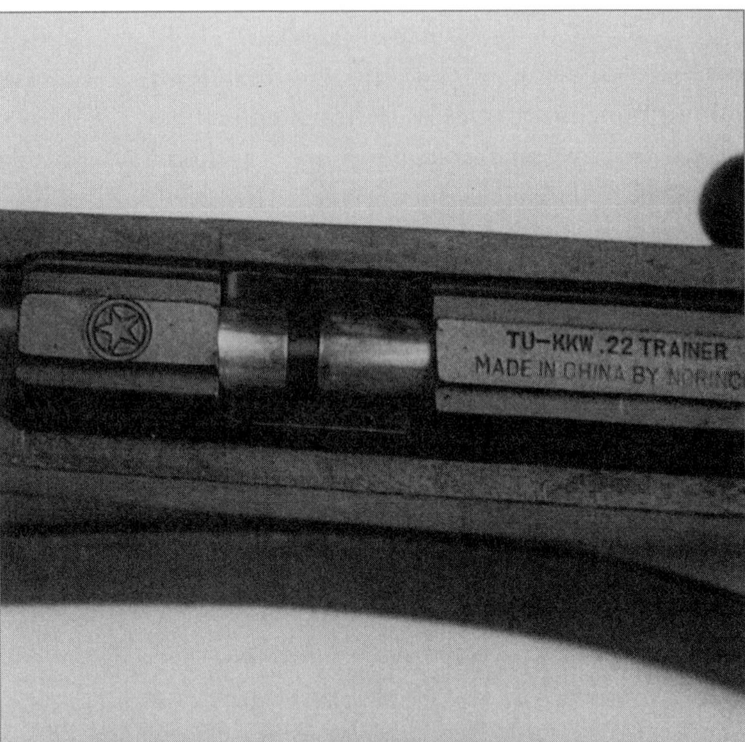

Markings on the top of the TU-KKW's receiver indicate its Chinese origin. Note the star forward of the action.

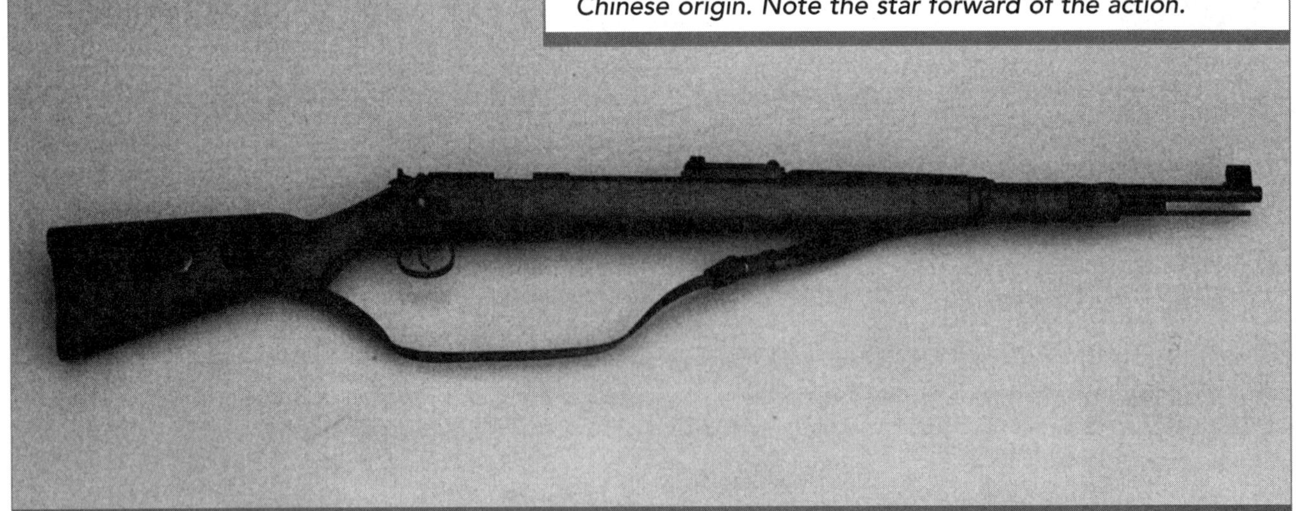

The Norinco TU-KKW is a .22LR caliber bolt-action rifle styled to resemble the famous German Mauser Kar. 98k rifle.

reissue. He persuaded Norinco of China to model one of its bolt-action .22 caliber rifles after the legendary German trainer. Thus was born the TU-KKW in 1991. The replica is actually quite remarkable. It has a German-style stock complete with sling slot, takedown bushing, and indentations in the wood beneath the bolt to facilitate manipulation of the bolt by right-handed shooters. The TU-KKW's sights closely approximate those of the service Mauser Model 98; it even includes a bayonet lug that accepts the German bayonet.

Because Norinco adapted the TU-KKW design from an existing bolt-action .22 caliber sporting rifle, it is not an exact replica of the original KKW. It differs from the original KKW primarily in its loading arrangements. The German-made KKW between the wars was a single-shot rifle, whereas the TU-KKW employed a detachable 5-shot box magazine. Another difference lay in the manual safety. Departing from Mauser practice, wherein a three-position rotary safety sits at the

The Norinco TU-KKW (right) bears a close resemblance to the centerfire-caliber military Mauser Kar. 98k (left).

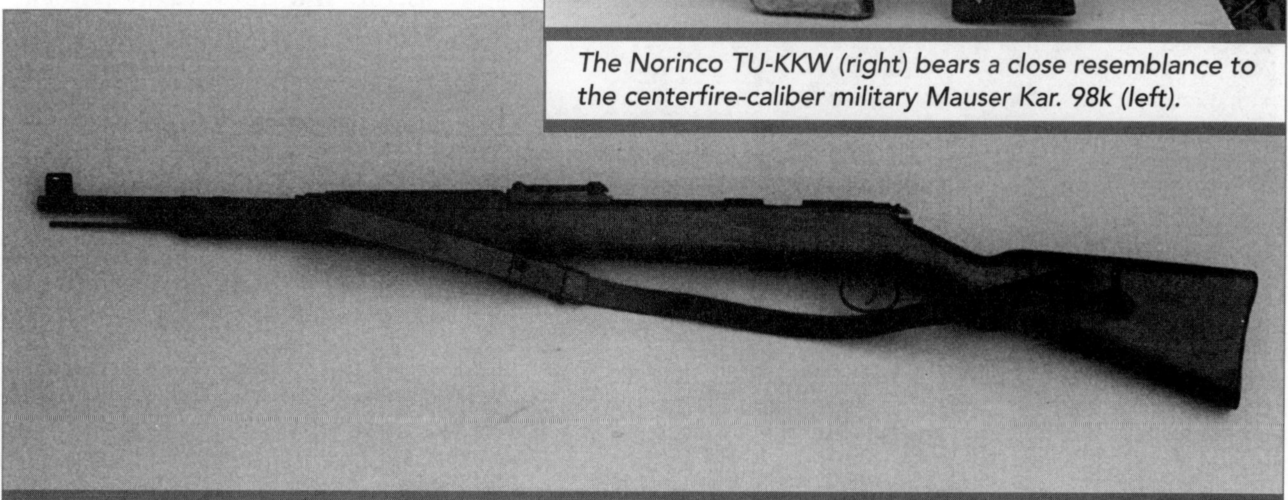

A left-side view of the Norinco TU-KWW shows off the rifle's clean, uncluttered lines. Note the sling mounts placed against the side of the stock instead of being suspended below it.

extreme end of the bolt shroud and moves straight up to its safe position, the manual safety on the TU-KKW is a two-position type. It's still located right behind the bolt, but the TU-KKW's manual safety moves back to fire, exposing a red dot, and forward to the safe setting. The shape of the TU-KKW is a remarkably accurate replica which, from a distance, is extremely hard to distinguish from the notorious German military Mauser rifle.

In this photo, the two-position manual safety has been pushed forward to its safe setting.

Beginning in 1992, Navy Arms also imported a TU-KKW variant called the TU-KKW Sniper Trainer, which added a 2.75 power scope with a quick-detachable mount. Navy Arms also announced a centerfire variant called the TU-33/40, styled after a Czech-made, short-barreled Mauser carbine used extensively in World War II by German mountain troops and airborne units. Lightweight and handy, it made a useful arm for heavily-burdened troops operating in tight spaces. Because the original Gew. 33/40 used the service 7.92x57mm (8mm Mauser) cartridge, it recoiled heavily. Navy Arms intended to make this replica in 7.62x39mm caliber with a four-shot magazine. Regrettably, the company encountered difficulties with Norinco and this rifle was never produced.

The TU-KKW's two-position manual safety moves back to fire, exposing a red dot just behind the base of the bolt handle.

As for the original .22LR caliber TU-KKW, it boasted excellent shooting characteristics of its own. My best results yielded a 1.5-inch group from 50 yards, making it competitive with virtually any other .22 Long Rifle rimfire rifle. It was fun to shoot, too, and attracted lots of attention at the test range. The TU-KKW story ended in 1995, when the U.S. Government ended all further imports of firearms manufactured in Communist China, including the TU-KKW. Nevertheless, it remains an interesting gun capable of superior performance.

The TU-KKW accepts a bayonet mount similar to Germany's. The hood over the front sight and the cleaning rod underneath the barrel are also reminders of German practice.

This rifle has a much shorter bolt travel path than the 8mm Mauser Kar 98k. Its 5-shot detachable box magazine is also a departure from Mauser practice.

TU-KKW

	TU-KKW
Overall Length	44.0 inches
Barrel Length	26.0 inches
Weight	8.0 pounds
Manufacturer	Norinco
Former Importer	Navy Arms (no longer imported)
Years Produced	1991-1995
Caliber/Capacity	.22 Long Rifle (.22LR)

Weatherby Mark V Lightweight

The Weatherby company got its start in the early 1940s, when founder Roy Weatherby decided that medium-sized cartridges, driven to high velocities, could become formidable hunting rounds. To prove his point, Weatherby created several high-performance rifle cartridges by necking down belted Holland & Holland magnum cartridge cases. He began producing his rifles in 1949. After briefly experimenting with various actions, Weatherby decided in 1954 to create his own bolt-action rifle. The result was the Mark V, which first appeared in 1958 and quickly became the mainstay of the Weatherby line. Its bolt system, to begin with, is quite unusual but highly efficient. There are nine locking lugs arranged in three groups, each containing three lugs, creating as a result an unusually short bolt throw of 54 degrees. The lugs are the same diameter as the fluted bolt body and the breech is counterbored to simplify manufacture.

Weatherby struggled for a long time to secure a reliable source of actions for his Mark V rifle. When he could not persuade the conservative gun-buying public to accept the gun as originally offered, Weatherby switched his construction contract to J.P. Sauer & Sohn in West Germany. There the Mark V rifle acquired its distinctive fluting on the bolt. Weatherby continued to acquire Mark V actions from Sauer for several years, but in 1969, bowing to rapidly rising costs, he switched suppliers and arranged for Howa Industries (Nagoya, Japan) to produce the Mark V bolt. Production began in 1971 and continued until 1997, when Weatherby began making rifles in the United States. Finally, the Mark V story had come full circle.

Since then, Weatherby has made numerous variants of the Mark V, including the Varmintmaster, which appeared in 1963. In celebration of the Mark V's 35th anniversary, a

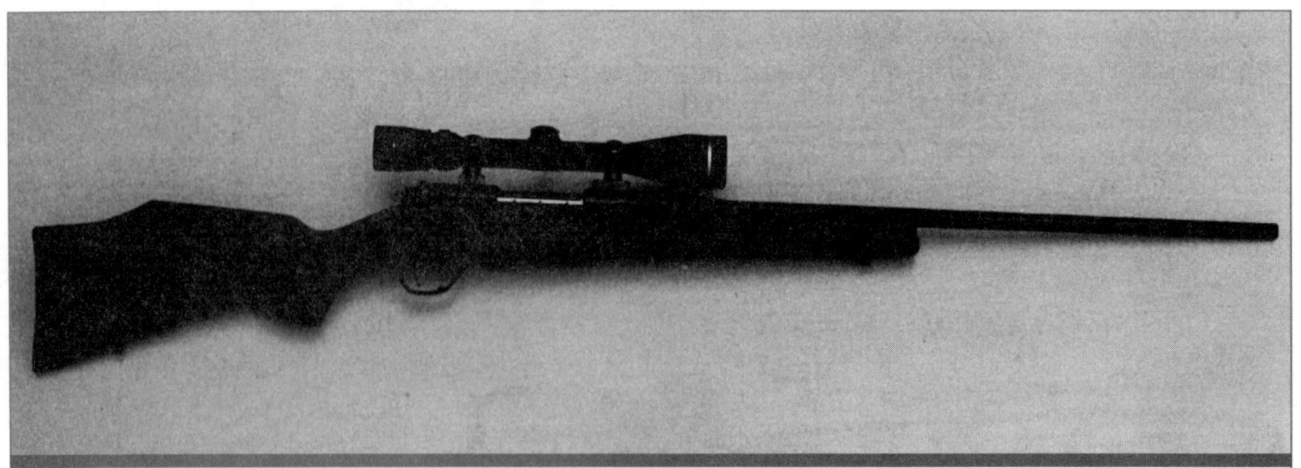

The Weatherby Mark V Lightweight has a graceful shape without the flamboyant decorative motifs typical of Weatherby rifles.

limited-production run of 1,000 Mark V commemoratives appeared. Most Weatherby rifles then featured exotic wood stocks and such extravagant features as skipline checkering, ebony forend, white spacers and a high Monte Carlo comb; indeed, this distinctive stock design, copied by other manufacturers in the 1960s and 1970s, became known as the "California Look." Several Weatherby rifles—the Lazermark and Crown Custom Series—even included fancy stock engravings and inlays. Weatherby has since departed from Mark V's extravagant wooden stocks on several occasions, witness the Mark V Fibermark rifle (1983 to 1991), the Mark V Synthetic (1995), the Mark V Stainless (1995) and the Mark V Lightweight (1997). All offer superior weather resistance while retaining the distinctive Weatherby outline. Mark V variants with wood stocks still in production include the Lazermark, Deluxe, Sporter, Eurosport and Euromark models. Fluted barrel options are available on the Stainless and Synthetic variants, plus a laminated stock option on the Mark V Stainless (Weatherby's Custom Shop continues to offer Safari Grade, Custom and Crown Custom Mark Vs on special order).

The Mark V Lightweight test-fired for this book features six locking lugs rather than the original nine, but its operating system remains the same. Weatherby also offers a Mark V Lightweight variant with a stock made of high-quality Claro walnut. Like most Weatherby rifles, this model has

Weatherby's logo appears on the bottom of the trigger-guard, much like the "Buck Mark" found on Browning rifles.

This left-side view of the Weatherby Mark V Lightweight illustrates how the rifle makes a total commitment to scoped shooting. Not only are there no iron sights on this rifle, but the stock has a Monte Carlo comb and a raised cheekpiece on the synthetic buttstock.

no iron sights; instead, it is drilled and tapped for mounting telescopic sights. Operating controls include an adjustable trigger, cocking indicator and a hinged magazine floorplate for fast unloading. The magazine floorplate is released by pushing down and forward on the button (located on the inside front surface of the triggerguard). Like most modern bolt-action rifles, Weatherby's action is cocked with the first motion of the bolt handle. The manual safety operates only when the action is cocked. When applied, the safety locks the bolt and firing mechanism, swinging back to safe and forward (exposing a red dot) to fire. When operated slowly, the manual safety is almost completely silent.

The Mark V Lightweight employs only six locking lugs, rather than the nine locking lugs found in the standard Mark V.

Weatherby offers a 1 1/2 minute of angle accuracy, which translates to a 1.5-inch target group at 100 yards. The Lightweight rifle tested by the author produced this benchrested 1.2-inch group from 100 yards away.

The trigger on the Mark V Lightweight is adjustable by means of a small screw located immediately in front of the trigger. With its factory-made crispness and light pull, only a very fussy rifle shooter would want to toy with this fine rifle. Like other Mark V rifles, the Lightweight model employs a push-feed bolt mechanism that is quite different from the classic military Mausers and more like the Remington Model 700 in its execution.

Unlike most other Weatherby rifles, the Mark V Lightweight has only one proprietary cartridge: the .240 Weatherby Magnum. Because of its scaled-down mechanism, the six locking lugs on this rifle would

The manual safety on Weatherby's Mark V Lightweight rifle is located on the right side of the bolt shroud near the rear end of the receiver. It swings back to its safe setting as shown.

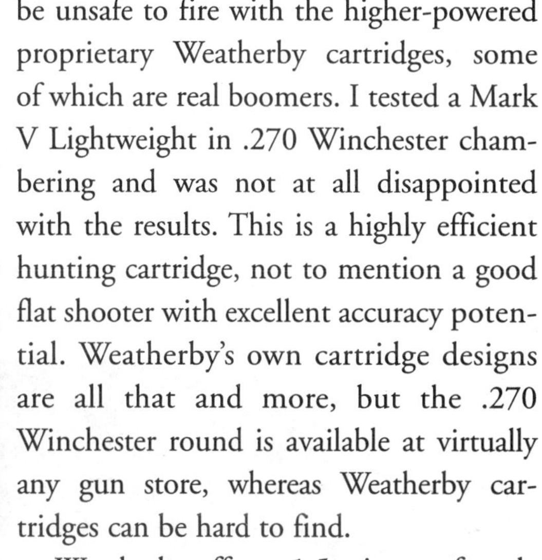

be unsafe to fire with the higher-powered proprietary Weatherby cartridges, some of which are real boomers. I tested a Mark V Lightweight in .270 Winchester chambering and was not at all disappointed with the results. This is a highly efficient hunting cartridge, not to mention a good flat shooter with excellent accuracy potential. Weatherby's own cartridge designs are all that and more, but the .270 Winchester round is available at virtually any gun store, whereas Weatherby cartridges can be hard to find.

Weatherby offers a 1.5 minute-of-angle accuracy guarantee on its centerfire rifles, but the Mark V Lightweight tested for this book did a little better. Our best 3-shot 100-yard benchrested groups measured slightly more than an inch using

In this view, the manual safety has swung forward to its fire position.

several different ammunition brands. The rifle's light weight, mostly by virtue of its thin barrel, produces a stiff recoil in .270 caliber, but it's certainly nothing unbearable. The Monte Carlo stock design, moreover, accommodates scope mounting. That, coupled with a thick rubber recoil pad on the butt, helps tame recoil further.

The only major shortcomings of the Weatherby Mark V Lightweight involve relatively poor corrosion resistance on the metal parts, which is especially disappointing considering the rifle's extremely durable synthetic stock. I also prefer a manual safety that can be left on while the bolt is being operated, but then the Weatherby Mark V is hardly the only rifle whose safety locks the bolt.

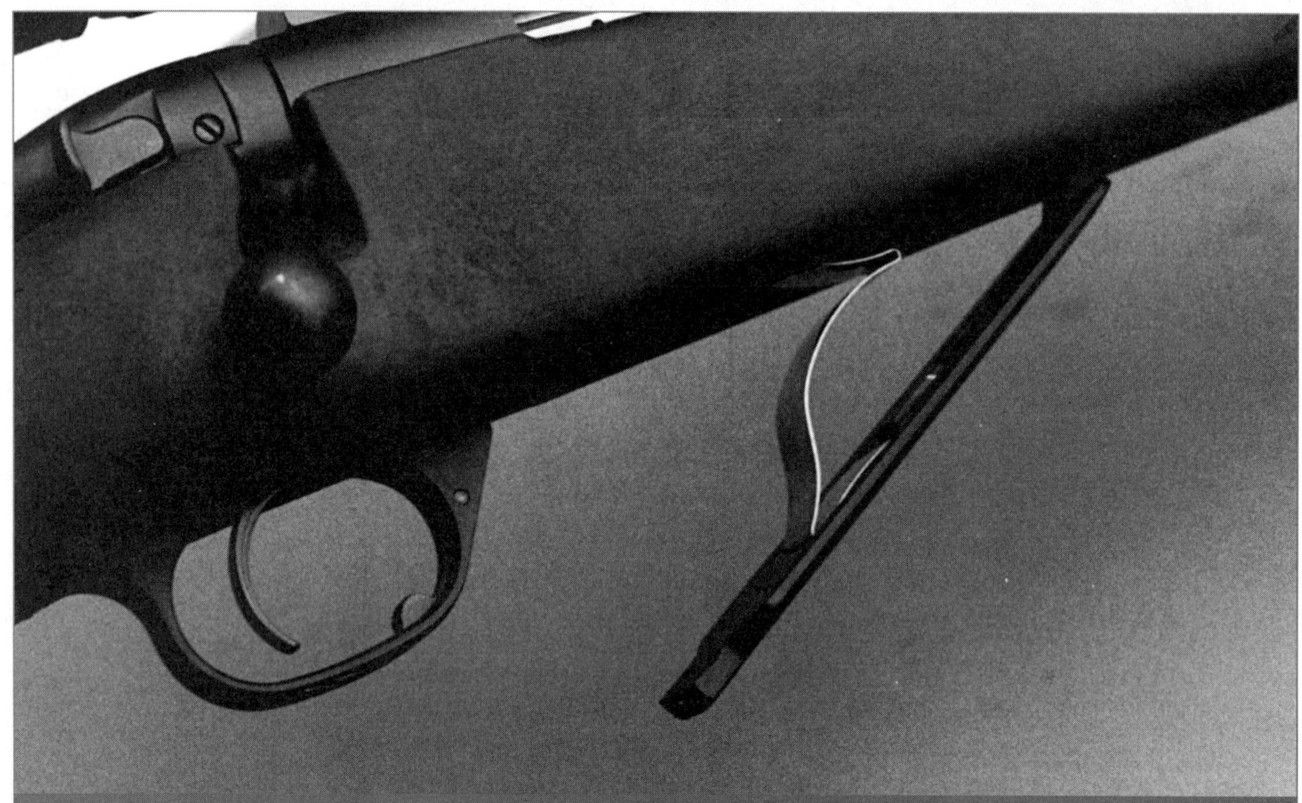

By pushing the small catch inside the triggerguard, the rear end of the magazine floorplate is released as shown. The detachable magazine floorplate makes unloading much safer than the so-called "blind magazine" design. Note also that the manual safety has rotated all the way to the rear.

WEATHERBY MARK V LIGHTWEIGHT

	MARK V
Overall Length	44 inches
Barrel Length	24 inches
Weight	6.75 pounds
Manufacturer	Weatherby, Inc., Atascadero, CA
Years Produced	1997-present
Caliber/Capacity	.30-06, .240 Weatherby Magnum/5 rounds

Part III:

Modern Lever-Action Rifles

The story behind the lever-action rifle begins in the mid-1800s, when Christian Sharps developed a single-shot rifle whose breech opened with a lever mechanism. Patented in 1848, the Sharps rifle was used extensively during the Civil War and in the settlement of the West following that conflict. The versatile Sharps rifle, which entered the metallic-cased cartridge ammunition era about the same time, appeared in a variety of chamberings, some powerful enough to kill buffalo.

In 1860, the lever-action Spencer carbine appeared. This metallic-cartridge rifle was quite advanced for its day, including a new tubular ammunition magazine mounted in its buttstock. The combination of lever action and high-capacity internal magazine gave the Spencer an exceedingly high rate of fire for its day. It also saw wide use in the Civil War and was considered well ahead of its time.

Still another advanced lever-action rifle appeared in 1860, this one designed by Tyler Henry and produced by Oliver Winchester's burgeoning firearms company. This so-called Henry rifle fired .44 caliber rimfire ammunition and held a large supply of ammo in a tubular magazine mounted below the barrel. In 1866 Winchester's company brought out an improved version of the Henry rifle (called the Model 1866) and seven years later followed up with the classic Model 1873, the first lever-action rifle to use the improved centerfire ammunition. The Model 1873 remained in production for many years, during which time the Winchester company sold more than 720,000 before production stopped in the early 1920s. Even while the Model 1873 was in its heyday, other improved lever-action designs arrived on the scene.

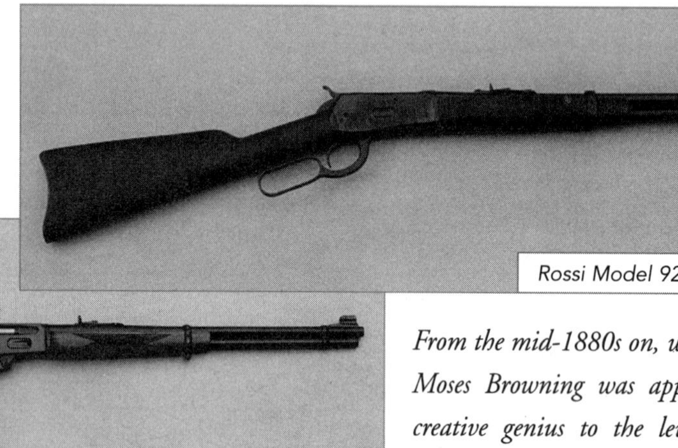

Rossi Model 92 "Puma"

Marlin Model 336CS

From the mid-1880s on, when John Moses Browning was applying his creative genius to the lever-action rifle, this type of firearm approached its current level of perfection. Working in those early years exclusively for Winchester, Browning's first lever-action rifle design featured a locking system consisting of two sturdy steel bars that slid into slots on either side of the action. Meanwhile, Winchester's own design genius, William Mason, came up with an improved tubular magazine. The result—Winchester Model 1886—could handle the most powerful cartridges of the day and became a fantastic success. Nearly 160,000 were built during a 50-year production run that did not finally end until 1936. As with many of John Browning's landmark designs, the Model 1886 outlived its inventor, who died in November 1926.

Browning followed his success with the Model 1886 by scaling down its mechanism to create for Winchester the Model 1892 lever-action rifle. It enabled the company to sell a less expensive gun, but still with the most advanced design of its time. What's more, the Model 1892, along with other caliber choices, used the same .38-40 and .44-40 cartridges as the Model 1873, whose growing obsolescence had encouraged such rivals as Marlin and others to create lever-action designs that competed directly for Winchester's large share of the market. Now, with the Model 1892 in hand, Winchester's competitive position was assured.

The introduction of smokeless-powder cartridges, which offered considerably higher power levels than the traditional black powder rounds, caused Browning to create the Model 1894 lever-action rifle for Winchester. Originally chambered for .32-40, .38-55 and .44-40 cartridges, this rifle introduced in 1895 the famous .30-30 cartridge, creating one of the best-known and most effective rifle-cartridge combinations—the Model 1894/.30-30—of all time. Doubtless it has taken more deer-sized animals on the American continent (and perhaps beyond) than any other gun/ammunition duo. It remains extremely popular both in the U.S. and Mexico, with more than three million Model 1894s built since its arrival in 1894.

Browning next created the Model 1895 lever-action rifle, once again for Winchester. Among his many innovations, Browning removed the tubular magazine beneath the barrel (which had precluded the use of high-velocity pointed bullets) and replaced it with a box magazine. The rifle was now able to use powerful centerfire cartridges with efficient pointed-nose bullets, thereby creating a safe and formidable rifle suitable for military service as well as big-game hunting. The Model 1895, which Winchester offered in both military-style carbine and rifle ("musket") forms, slowed down the growing trend toward bolt-action rifles early in the 20th century and received in turn considerable military orders. Nevertheless, the days of the lever-action gun were on their way out as military weapons, even though some American militia units carried Model 1895s in .30-40 Krag caliber during the Spanish-American War. And in 1915 the Russians placed an order for 30,000 Model 1895s in their 7.62x54mm chambering for use in World War I.

In the meantime, John Marlin began making lever-action rifles to compete with the Winchesters. The first Marlin rifle appeared in 1881 and remained in production for ten years. The next Marlin, the Model 1888, remained in production for only a year; and the third Marlin lever-action rifle—the Model 1889—introduced sideways ejection of spent cartridge casings (previously empty casings had ejected straight upward). A stronger gun than its previous versions, this model was more successful even though only 55,000 or more were built before production stopped in 1903. A smaller version, the Model 1891, sold in smaller numbers, but an improved version, the Model 1892, became the company's best-selling lever-action rifle to date, with 60,000 or so manufactured between 1895 and 1915. Production was stopped only so Marlin could devote its attention to foreign orders for Marlin machine guns used in World War I.

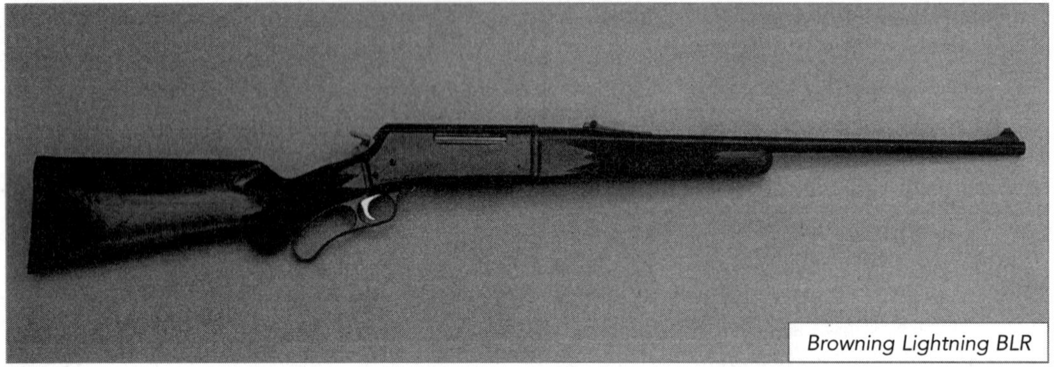

Browning Lightning BLR

Marlin's next rifle, the Model 1893, proved hugely successful. Developed specifically to compete with Winchester's excellent Model 1892, this new competitor went on to become far more successful than the Winchester Model 1892 and was, in fact, Marlin's equivalent of the Winchester Model 1894. Produced from 1893 to 1904 as the Model 1893 (and renamed the Model 93 in 1905), this model remained in production until 1936, at which time Marlin replaced it with a slightly modified and improved version, the Model 36, which Marlin kept in production until 1948. It was then improved further along Model 336 lines, in which form it remains in production to this day. This Marlin series has, over the years, competed gamely with the Winchester Model 1894 and even offers one of the same calibers—the .30-30—as a standard chambering. In 1979 the Marlin company announced that total production of the Model 1893 series had exceeded three million rifles. One unusual but recognizable feature of this series, from the Model 36 to the present day, is its pistol-grip stock as opposed to Winchester's, generally a straight comb type.

Another Marlin lever-action rifle of importance is the Model 444. Based on the proven Model 336 mechanism, it fires a .444 Marlin cartridge (developed from the .44 Magnum but longer and more powerful). Popular as a "brush gun" for hunting small to medium-sized game in dense cover, the Model 444 remains in production as well. Other lever-action rifle series produced by Marlin are the Glenfield, Western Field, Ranger and J.C. Higgins, all offered by Sears, Roebuck and other large retail distributors.

*Savage produced its own lever-action design of importance—the Model 99—which first appeared in 1899 (see also **Complete Guide to Classic Rifles**). Untraditional in appearance because of its concealed-hammer design and box magazine, this sleek and powerful rifle remained in production for many years in a wide variety of calibers. Because it employed rotary and, later, box magazines, the Savage Model 99 could fire pointed spitzer bullets. The company took full advantage of this capability to chamber the Model 99 for a variety of impressive cartridges.*

The lever-action rifle is indisputably the fastest manually-operated repeating rifle design. In fact, a skilled lever-action rifle shooter can fire rounds nearly as rapidly as he can with a semiautomatic rifle; and, because the tubular magazine found on most lever-action rifles holds more rounds than the typical sporting semi-

automatic rifle, there are more rounds to shoot before reloading.

Because the lever-action rifle is one of the most ambidextrous firearms ever conceived, left-handed shooters are strongly attracted to it. While the manual safety and cartridge casing ejection may still favor a right-handed shooter, the operating lever on a lever-action rifle comes closest of any other firearm to being complete ambidextrous. The typical lever-action rifle also looks far less menacing than other modern firearms. With it traditional wooden stock and its adoption by farmers, cowboys, ranchers and the early settlers, a lever-action rifle is less likely to attract negative attention from those who advocate the banning of guns than are more modern types of rifle.

Among the few disadvantages of the lever-action rifle is, in many cases, its tubular magazine. This limits a shooter to bullets with blunt tips, because the bullet nose must rest against the primer of the preceding cartridge. A sharp-nosed "spitzer"-type bullet could cause ignition of the cartridge immediately ahead of it in the magazine. Tubular magazines are also slow to reload; and some designs suffer from caliber limitations, depending on the strength of the breech-locking mechanism. But then, lever-action rifles and carbines that are limited to pistol calibers—the .357 Magnum, .44 Magnum or .45 Colt—develop a lot more velocity, hence more power, from their 16-inch (or longer) barrels than is possible from a shorter pistol-length barrel. Also, depending on the ejection pattern for spent cartridge casings, some lever-action rifles are unsuitable for mounting optical sights. There's also a major problem concerning the difficulty of operating a lever-action rifle from the prone position. Considerable ground clearance is needed for an unobstructed operating throw. This difficulty —of firing while prone—explains why so many lever-action rifles have only seen limited use in the military. Some military experts also criticize lever-action rifles for their lack of durability under rough operating conditions, especially when compared to bolt-action rifles.

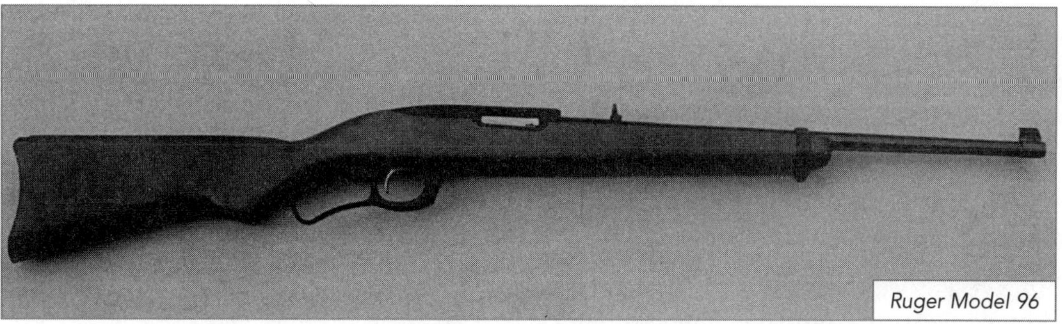

Ruger Model 96

Nevertheless, the lever-action rifle remains an important part of the firearms scene, particularly in the U.S. As evidence of this firearm's continuing popularity, Navy Arms imports several replicas of classic Henry and Winchester lever-action designs of the 19th century (made by Uberti of Italy). In general these rifles are extremely useful for hunting and self-defense purposes. As such, the lever-action rifle is likely to remain popular for many years to come.

Browning Lightning BLR

This important lever-action rifle, built by Browning, offers an innovative design with a mechanism suitable for a wide variety of rifle calibers. These include the .223, .243, .308 and even long-action cartridges like the .30-06 and on up to the powerful and versatile .300 Winchester Magnum. Browning's goal was to offer lever-action shooters a rifle of modern design capable of handling the same powerful cartridges as the most popular bolt-action sporting rifles.

Designed by Valentine (Val) Browning (John M. Browning's oldest son) and Carl Lewis, a talented Browning employee, the BLR was first manufactured in the U.S. between 1966 and 1968 by Thompson-Ramo-Woodridge (TRW) of Cleveland, Ohio, which was then under contract for the Browning Arms Company. This arrangement with TRW stood in sharp contrast to usual Browning practice, which was (and remains) to build its guns in its own assembly plant in Utah or, more frequently, to have them made by Fabrique Nationale Herstal in Belgium or by Miroku in Japan. Actually, TRW was a logical choice for the BLR. The company got its start in the lucrative automotive parts industry, and its first foray in arms production was making M14 rifles for the U.S. military. When that contract was terminated, TRW sought another outlet for its new and expensive armsmaking branch. BLR looked like the ideal solution. And so, for the next two years, TRW made BLRs in both .243 and .308 calibers. Unfortunately, technical and legal difficulties stopped the assembly lines after only enough parts for about 750 complete guns had been made. From this inventory TRW was able to assemble about 250 complete guns, only 50 of which were eventually sold (another 25 or so were "lost" in 1988, having presumably been smuggled out by

The Browning BLR has evolved only slightly in the three decades since its introduction. The current version, introduced in 1996, has a lightweight aluminum receiver and a pistol-grip stock (the barrel band of earlier BLR models has been eliminated).

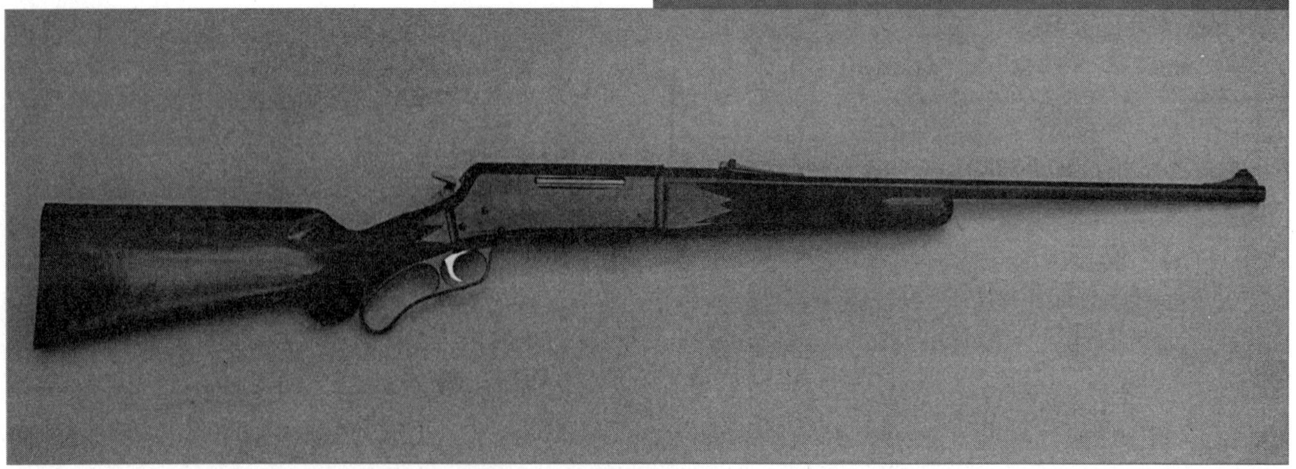

This view of Browning's Lightning BLR in operation displays its bolt fluting. Viewed at this oblique angle, the bolt appears closer to the shooter's face than it really is.

sions, not metric. FN ended up using only the barrels from TRW's production, and these lasted only a few months into 1970, the first year of FN's production of BLRs. After two years, production was passed on to the Miroku factory in Japan, which began producing BLRs in 1972 and has been doing so ever since.

The BLR is now available in both standard-action (or "short-action") and long-action receiver lengths. Caliber

When in operation, the Lightning BLR bolt protrudes well back, but without distracting the shooter. Note the 90-degree lever throw required to operate the bolt.

TRW employees). Three other BLRs were sent to Belgium to help FN set up its own production facilities for the rifle, whereupon TRW sold its remaining unassembled parts inventory to Browning, who forwarded them to FN's home factory in Herstal. The parts turned out to be mostly worthless to FN, however, since TRW had naturally made the parts according to inch dimen-

The styling of the Lightning BLR is unlike that of any other lever-action rifle. Oddly enough, the flat-sided receiver has never been embellished with factory engraving as have the other big Browning rifles.

choices in the standard-length action are .22-250, .222 Remington (discontinued in 1989), .223 Remington, .243 Winchester, .257 Roberts (discontinued in 1992), 7mm-08 Remington, .284 (discontinued in 1992), .308 Winchester and .358 Winchester (discontinued in 1992). Calibers available in the long-action model (introduced in 1991) are .270, .30-'06, 7mm Remington Magnum and .300 Winchester Magnum.

As with many rifles that enjoy long, successful production runs, the BLR has passed through several design changes. The first of these dates from 1981, when the BLR receiver was first made with flat sides. The idea was to make the rifle more like the classic lever-action rifle designs—and, perhaps more importantly, to simplify its production. In the 1981 redesign, Miroku began making the magazine shorter and almost flush with the receiver bottom. Still another change made at Miroku occurred in 1981, when the bolt was changed from eight locking lugs to a six-lug, gear-shaped bolt. Among the BLR's best features had always been its smooth action and relatively short lever throw. The rifle's strong rack-and-pinion mechanism also made it possible to handle modern rifle cartridges ordinarily unavailable to the lever-action type. These changes, made in 1981, served only to make an already good design even better.

The second series of changes occurred in 1996, when Miroku switched the receiver from steel to aluminum alloy, thereby reducing the BLR's weight by half a pound, enough to create the new Lightning BLR, which weighed only 6 1/2 pounds. This new model was also given a pistol-grip stock, while the front barrel band was eliminated. The result was a rifle that combined elegance and style in appearance—definitely not the typical lever-action rifle. The BLR has always been made only in a Grade I configuration, with no engraving or

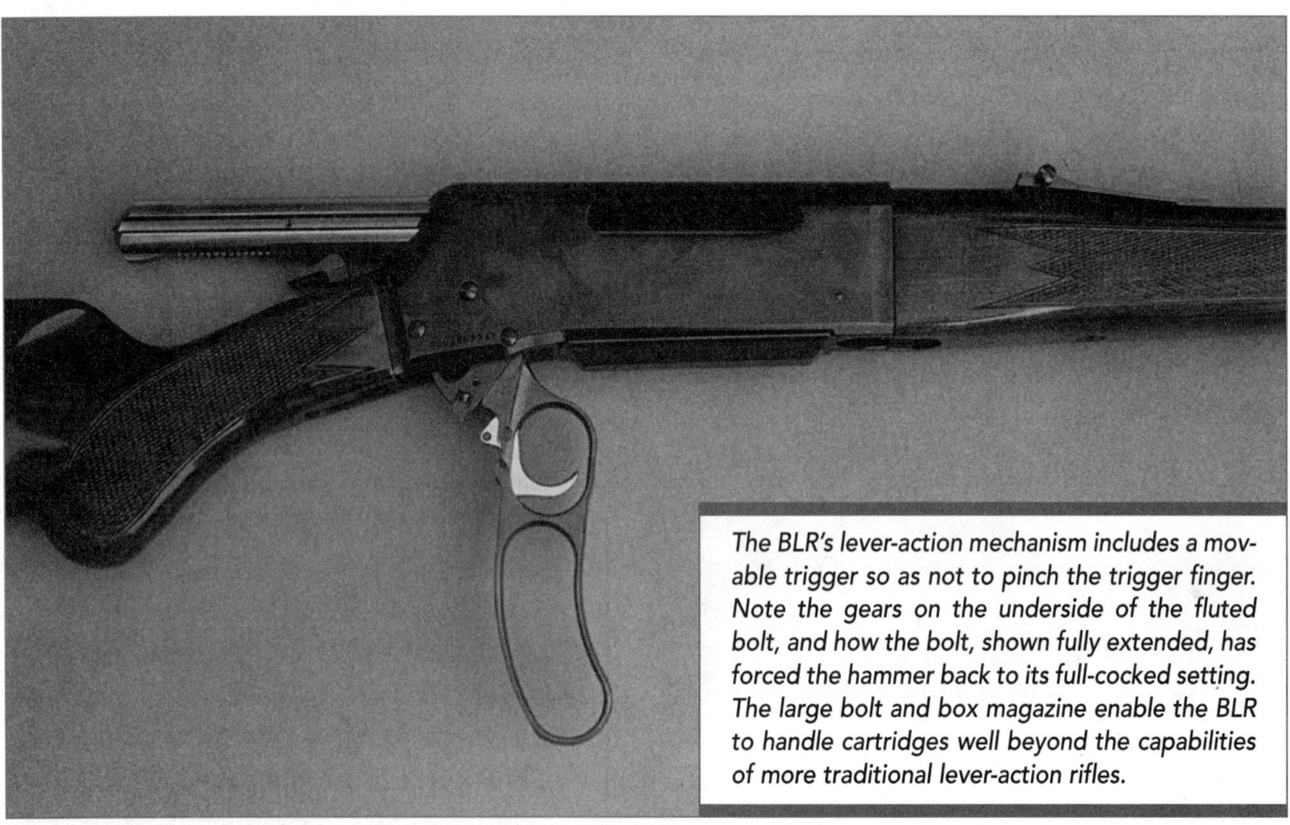

The BLR's lever-action mechanism includes a movable trigger so as not to pinch the trigger finger. Note the gears on the underside of the fluted bolt, and how the bolt, shown fully extended, has forced the hammer back to its full-cocked setting. The large bolt and box magazine enable the BLR to handle cartridges well beyond the capabilities of more traditional lever-action rifles.

other fancy embellishments aside from high polish on its blued parts and a gold-plated trigger.

The BLR's operating features include a four-position hammer: fired position, folded position, half-cocked and fully-cocked. Like most lever-action rifles with exposed hammers, the BLR does not include a manual safety device. To attain the folder-hammer position, the hammer must first be lowered to the half-cocked setting. The upper portion of the hammer is then rotated forward

The rear sight on the BLR may look small but is highly efficient with accurate shots out to 100 yards and beyond.

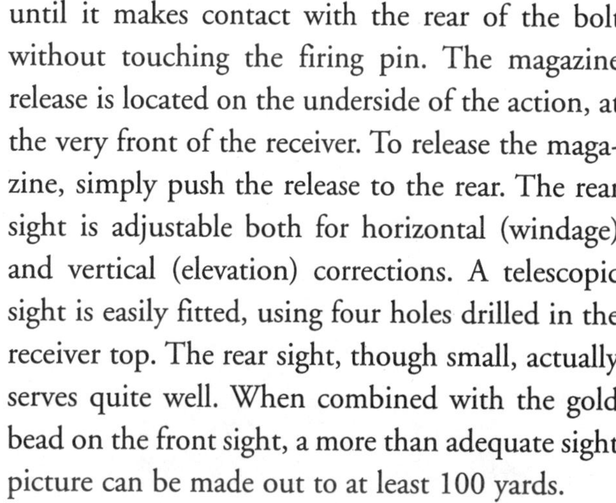

until it makes contact with the rear of the bolt without touching the firing pin. The magazine release is located on the underside of the action, at the very front of the receiver. To release the magazine, simply push the release to the rear. The rear sight is adjustable both for horizontal (windage) and vertical (elevation) corrections. A telescopic sight is easily fitted, using four holes drilled in the receiver top. The rear sight, though small, actually serves quite well. When combined with the gold bead on the front sight, a more than adequate sight picture can be made out to at least 100 yards.

Test results at the range demonstrate convincingly the BLR's impressive pedigree. Its crisp trigger and good sights translate into fine accuracy. Using a .30-06 caliber BLR, the author fired 3-shot 100-yard groups that ran as small as 1.5 inches. While I've fired other rifles that produced slightly tighter groups, the BLR's were especially well-centered, hitting almost exactly at point of aim. Despite the thick rubber recoil pad on the back of the buttstock, recoil with the BLR is fairly

For those who find the BLR's integral sights inadequate for any good reason, the rifle comes from the factory with its receiver top already drilled for easy scope mounting.

The Browning Lightning BLR's sensational accuracy has produced 1 1/2 minute of angle accuracy, almost perfectly centered at point of aim. Few lever-action rifles offer this kind of shooting, nor do most bolt-action rifles.

strong, certainly more than a military Model 1917 bolt-action or M1 Garand semiautomatic rifle in the same caliber. Shooters sensitive to recoil are definitely better off with a BLR in a smaller, milder cartridge. Shooters who insist on .30-06 performance but who shy away from recoil should probably revert to the older BLR with its steel receiver and correspondingly greater weight—or even a different rifle design, such as Browning's own BAR, with its self-loading, gas-operated mechanism soaking up the recoil impulse. The Lightning BLR's recoil is not brutal—it's simply not the type one would want to shoot all day for fun, especially in the larger calibers. Despite the recoil, the stock design of the BLR allows rapid lever manipulation for quick follow-up shots when needed. Whatever is said here does not mean to suggest that the rifle lacks appeal as a collector's item. Indeed, with three major variations—four, if a complete BLR can be found from the early TRW days—and a dozen or more existing caliber choices, there appears to be considerable scope for BLR collectors.

The Browning Lightning BLR balances well and, despite stout recoil in the larger caliber choices, is quite pleasant to shoot.

BROWNING MODEL BLR

	SHORT ACTION	LONG ACTION
Overall Length	39.5 inches	42.9 inches
Barrel Length	20.0 inches	22.0 or 24.0 inches
Weight	6.5 pounds	7.1 pounds
Caliber/Capacity	.223, .22-250, .243, 7mm-08, 308/4 rounds	.270, .20-06, 7mm Rem. Mag., .300 Win. Mag.

Marlin Model 336CS

Among the more interesting examples of the .30-30 lever-action rifle we tested was the Marlin Model 336CS. Although it first appeared in 1984 in its present form, its ancestry can be traced all the way back to Marlin's legendary Model 1893. This rifle—and the similar but smaller-caliber Model 1894 which followed—had a bolt that moved vertically and was considered an improvement over Marlin's earlier Model 1889. Unlike the competing Winchester Model 1894, which came on the scene within a few months of the Marlin gun, the Model 1894 featured sideways ejection of spent cartridge casing, enabling shooters to install low-mounted telescopic sights. By contrast, Winchester failed to add this useful feature to its lever-action rifle until the "Angle-Eject" variant was introduced in 1983-1984.

As shown, the Marlin Model 336CS's smooth and rapid lever action works by lowering away from the fixed hammer and withdrawing the bolt to cock the hammer.

The Marlin Model 336CS rifle is obviously an attractive rifle, employing a tasteful blend of traditional and modern styling. Note the hardwood stock with cut checkering. The tubular magazine below the barrel holds up to six rounds in either .30-30 or .35 Remington.

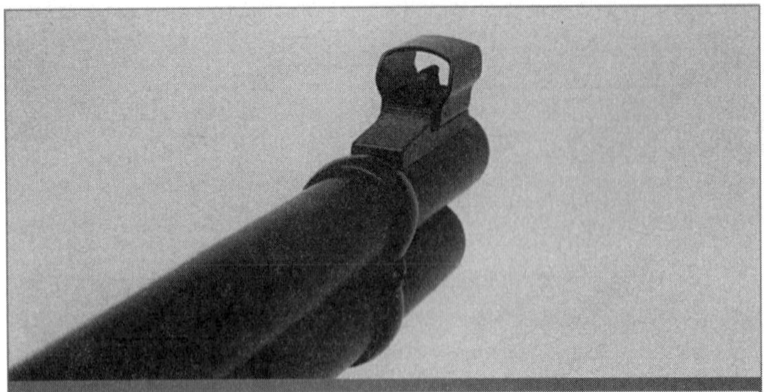
The front sight on the Model 336CS features a protective hood found on Marlin rifles, whatever the action type may be.

The direct ancestor of the Model 336CS—the Model 1936—appeared in 1936 but was re-named the Model 36 a year later. Production was halted in early 1942 so the company could devote itself to war production. A few years after World War II ended, Marlin created the Model 336, whose conventional ejection port was replaced by the Model 36's "slide-ejection" system, which it inherited from the original Model 1893. Under this system, the entire upper right portion of the receiver slides open to eject the empty cartridge casings. At the same time, Marlin also improved the extractor and rounded the bolt to simplify manufacture of the Model 336.

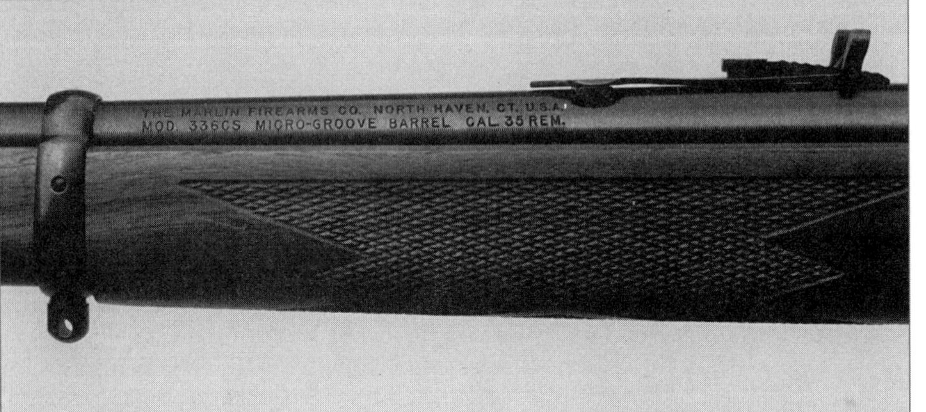

The rear sight on Marlin's Model 336CS is a typical semi-buckhorn type adjustable for windage and elevation.

First introduced in 1984, the 336CS was given a cross-bolt safety button, a feature recently added by rival Winchester to some of its

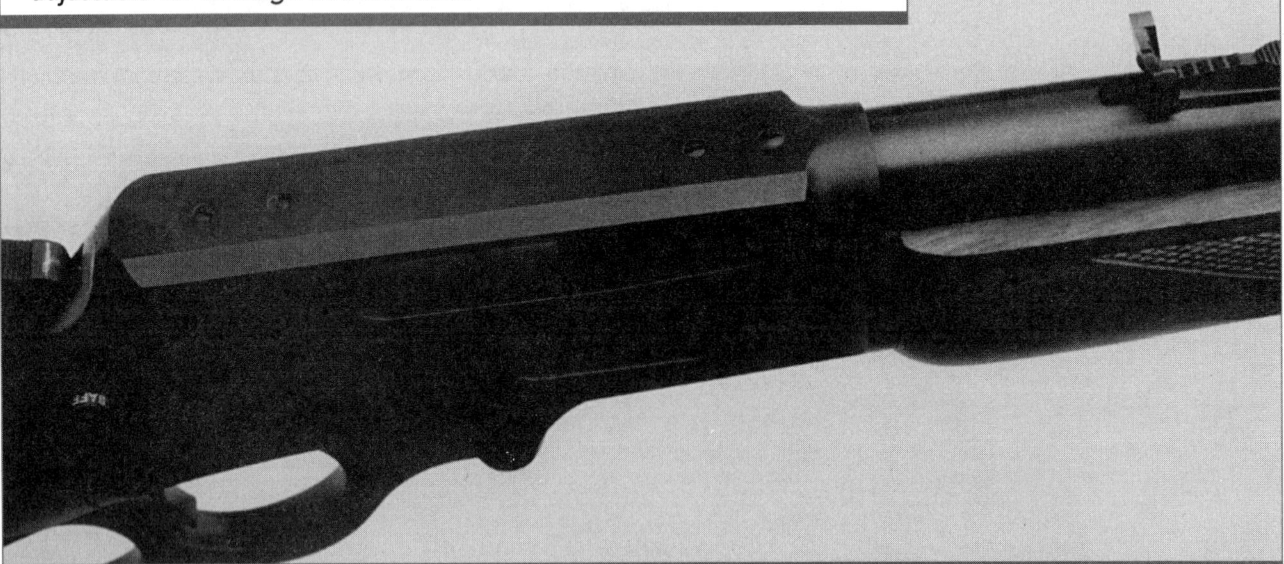
The sighting arrangements on the Model 336CS include easy adaptation to a telescopic sight (note the scope-mounting holes on the receiver drilled and tapped at the factory).

The author fired this 3.1-inch group from the 100-yard bench with the Model 336CS in .35 Remington.

own lever-action rifles. The safety button on the Marlin rifle works in conjunction with the hammer half-cock. The hammer, by the way, cocks very quietly, a desirable feature that allows hunters to carry the rifle in relative safety until the moment they're ready to take aim and shoot. The minuscule cocking noise made by the hammer is not likely to spook even the most noise-sensitive of wild animals. Another of Marlin's more desirable safety features is its finger lever plunger. Located just behind the trigger, this plunger deactivates the firing mechanism as the lever is opened up and downward, releasing the plunger. Only with the lever pushed all the way upward into battery is the plunger compressed, allowing the trigger to release the firing mechanism and fire.

The sighting system on the 336CS is typical of those found on many lever-action rifles: a rear sight of semi-buckhorn type adjustable for windage and elevation, and a front sight with a ramp and protective hood. The rifle is easily adapted to mounting a telescopic sight. The rear sight folds down, while the hammer is offset to one side. The receiver also has scope-mounting holes drilled and tapped at the factory.

Furniture on the Model 336CS is quite attractive, considering the gun's moderate price, especially the stock made from American black walnut, a durable and attractive wood. Current issues (since 1995) feature checkering on the pistol grip and forearm, with the traditional diamond pattern added in both places. White spacers separate the pistol-grip cap and buttplate from the wooden stock for a contrasting look that embellishes the traditional appearance of this gun. A clear protective coat of "Mar-Shield" lends wear-resistance to the wood. All metal parts feature an attractive bright, blue-black finish, with the bolt left white and highly polished.

My test rifle came in the traditional .30-30 cartridge, whose chief shortcoming relates to its rounded- or blunt-nosed bullet design—a necessity since most rifles chambered for the .30-30 employ a tubular magazine. To prevent detonation of the primer on the leading cartridge by the bullet of the round behind it, the bullet nose must be blunt. If the .30-30 were to use a pointed-nosed (spitzer) bullet, detonation would be a distinct possibility. Though bullet shape makes the .30-30 cartridge potentially lethal on game up to deer-size, it also results in a cartridge whose accuracy potential drops off rapidly at ranges beyond 100 yards. For most deer hunting in the Eastern United States, a 100-yard limitation is no problem, since deer hunting in many areas takes place in woods or other dense cover. Limiting one's shots to the 50- to 100-yard range helps ensure the impressive results of the .30-30 on deer. For those who dislike the .30-30, a .35 Remington (available since 1953) is also available in the Model 336. Accuracy with this cartridge is comparable to the .30-30, with muzzle velocities and power levels slightly less. The .35 Remington enjoys a fairly large following, though not as great as the highly popular .30-30.

The Marlin Model 336CS I tested (in .30-.30 Remington caliber) produced 100-yard groups as small as 3 inches across (3 MOA). That's not bad for a lever-action rifle, especially in light of the range limitations noted above. At 50 yards, which is a reasonable distance at which to take deer in close cover, 3 MOA translates into a 1 1/2-inch group. Assuming the hunter does his job, a rifle that shoots up to that standard will bring home the deer virtually every time with either a .30 or a .35 caliber bullet. To sum up, Marlin's Model 336CS combines reasonable price with excellent materials and workmanship, offering several desirable features not found on other, ompeting rifles.

The Model 336CS safety is a crossbolt hammer-blocking type located at the rear section of the receiver. It pushes from right to left to fire (exposing a red band to alert the shooter), then back the opposite way (covering the red band) to the safe setting.

MARLIN MODEL 336CS

	MODEL 336CS
Overall Length	38.5 inches
Barrel Length	20.0 inches
Weight	7.0 pounds
Caliber	.30-30 or .35 Remington
Magazine Capacity	6 rounds

Rossi Model 92

The Brazilian-made Rossi Model 92—or Puma—featured a Winchester Model 92-style mechanism and lower labor costs. The result: an exceptionally handy and affordable rifle in a wide choice of calibers and other options. This rifle (imported by Interarms) first appeared as the Puma and later, in 1965, as the Model 65. It quickly became popular in its native Brazil. Importation of Rossi Pumas (which began as the Model 92) to the U.S. started in 1978, and it has been popular in this country ever since.

Rossi has worked hard at creating a variety of Model 92 options and variants that appeal to every shooter's tastes. Current versions include caliber choices of .357 Magnum, .44 Magnum, .44-40 (introduced in 1995), and .45 Colt (also introduced in 1995). Adding to its versatility, the Model 92 in .357 Magnum can also fire the .38 Special, while the .44 Magnum version

The Rossi Model 92 (or Puma) appeals to the many fans of the John Browning-designed Winchester Model 92, of which this Brazilian-made Rossi is a close copy. The model pictured is the standard blued version with short (16-inch) barrel.

The Rossi Model 92 (center) is well suited to the role of pistol-caliber carbine, as are any of the more recently-designed models, including the Auto-Ordnance M1927A1 (top) or the Ruger Police Carbine (bottom).

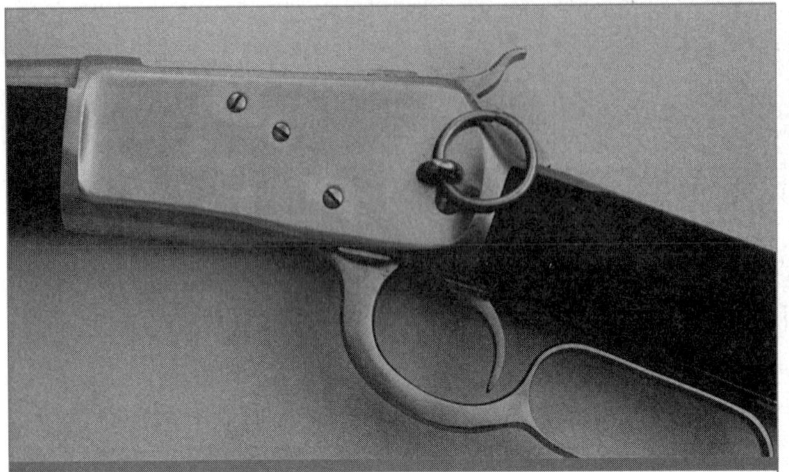

Some Rossi Model 92 "Puma" rifles, like this stainless-steel variant, include a saddle ring on the left side of the receiver. Popular with 19th-century rifles, saddle rings offer another way of carrying the rifle.

can accept the .44 Special cartridge as well. Since the .38 Special and .44 Special are shorter cartridges than the .357 Magnum and .44 Magnum, respectively, then it follows that more of them can fit in the tubular magazine. Power and accuracy, however, will both be impaired. Nevertheless, this dual-caliber capability offers considerable flexibility where the supply of ammunition is concerned. Barrel length options are 16 inches (carbine), 20 inches (rifle) and 24 inches (.45 Colt only). Another Model 92 option is the standard-sized lever, which is just large enough for an adult male shooter to operate with a gloved hand. A "Large Loop" variation, whose operating lever is much wider and larger, is still another variation. A saddle ring is also available with the longer (20- and 24-inch) barrel lengths.

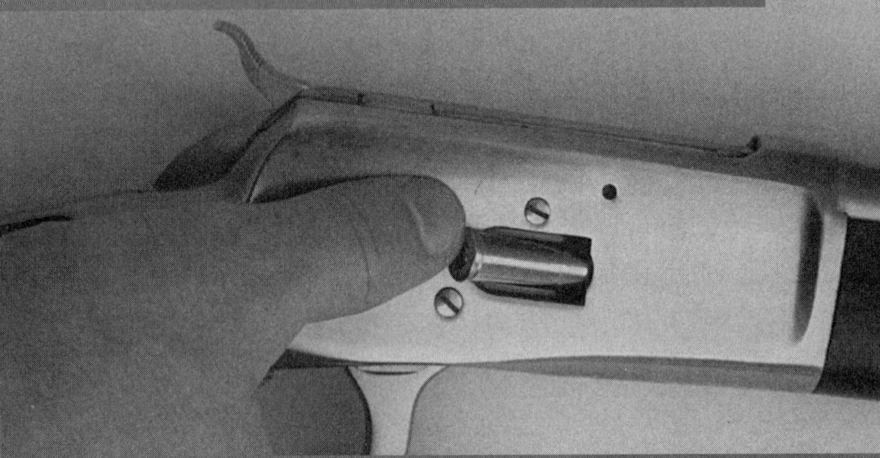

The Rossi Model 92 loads from a gate in the right side of the receiver. The cartridges enter a tubular magazine located beneath the barrel.

The Rossi Model 92 offers fast, close-range firepower beyond the capabilities of a handgun chambered for the same cartridge.

The Rossi's hammer must be cocked (as shown) for the gun to fire.

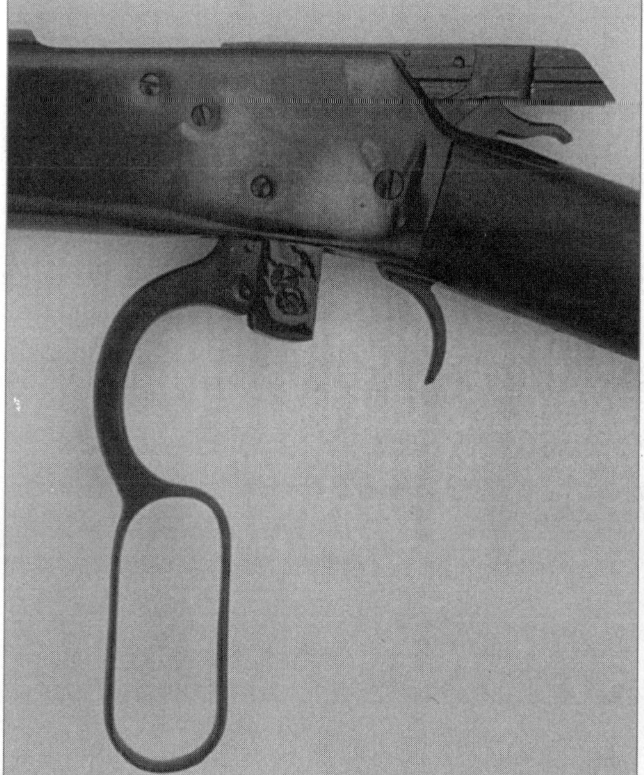

Midway through the loading cycle, the Model 92 loading lever is swung down and forward. The locking block is dropped, and the bolt is pushed back as far as possible, cocking the hammer. Note how the trigger stays put when the lever is moved.

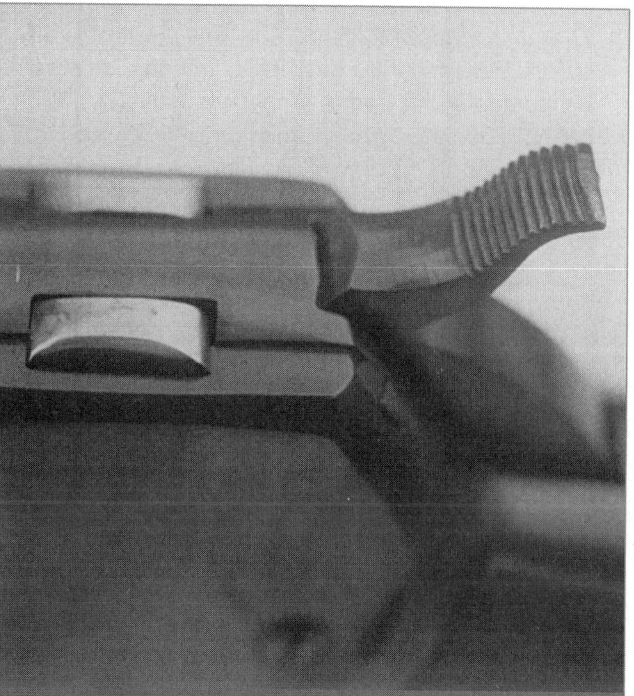

A Rossi Model 92 is shown ready to fire. Note the locking block, the light-colored metal on either side of the bolt, and the uncocked hammer.

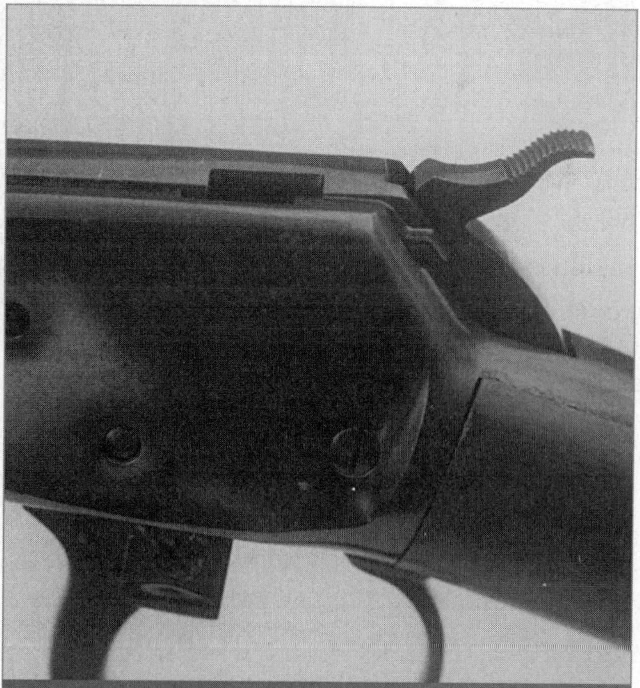

Once the loading cycle starts, the locking block falls into the receiver and the bolt begins to move to the rear, pushing against the hammer.

The blued Model 92 tested for this book proved surprisingly accurate despite its unsophisticated sights and short, carbine-length barrel. The .357 caliber 50-yard group measures 1.7 inches, which is good accuracy for a handgun cartridge, albeit a powerful one fired from this distance.

Standard finish on the Model 92 is blue, either high-polished or matte form. Rossi also offers a stainless steel option on the .357 Magnum Model 92. In the past, Rossi has even made Model 92s available in blue, gold or chrome engraving with deluxe wood furniture. These were all discontinued, however, around the late 1980s. The chief appeal of the Model 92 has always been that of a solid, reliable shooter in the best tradition of the classic lever-action rifles we've all read about and seen in movies about the Old West. It's easy to see why the Model 92 established itself so quickly in America. But since the early 1990s, due mostly to fierce competition with Forjas Taurus, Brazil's other premier firearms manufacturer, Rossi has been forced to expend great efforts to improve the quality and visual appeal of its products. The Puma/Model 92 has benefited from this improved quality control, with current examples offering a truly stunning appearance.

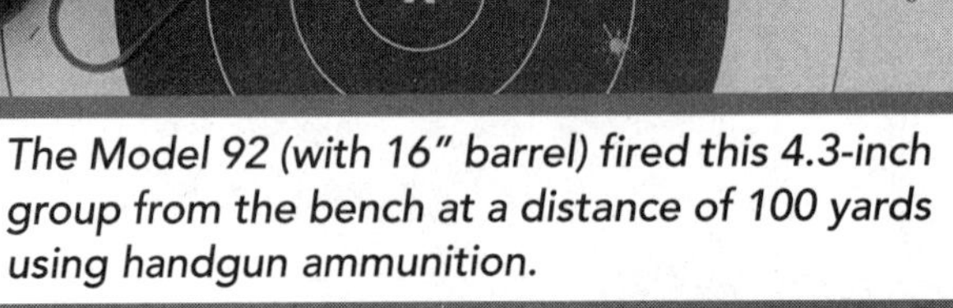

The Model 92 (with 16" barrel) fired this 4.3-inch group from the bench at a distance of 100 yards using handgun ammunition.

The Model 92 loads in the traditional manner for a lever-action model. To begin, its tubular magazine is accessed by a loading slot in the right side of the receiver. The exposed hammer indicates immediately, cocked or not, whether the rifle is ready to shoot. Because lowering and raising the operating lever automatically cocks the hammer, all that's needed to begin firing is to load the rifle and work the lever. While it's necessary to operate the lever between shots, it invariably works smoothly and easily enough to produce an impressive rate of fire.

As revealed in my tests, the Rossi Model 92/Puma shoots accurately. A .357 Magnum caliber model, tested at both 50 and 100 yards with both .357 Magnum and .38 Special ammunition, I fired 3-shot groups as small as 1.7 inches (.357 Magnum) and 2.3 inches (.38 Special)

The stainless steel Rossi Puma gave the author his best 100-yard benchrested group of 3.1 inches. Oddly enough, he did it with a .38 Special +P rather than .357 Magnum ammunition.

from the 50-yard mark. Although a short-barreled (16-inch) .357 Magnum caliber Puma hardly looked like a 100-yard shooter, I set up behind the bench and fired five shots. That little rifle rewarded me with a group measuring 4.3 inches across—and one of those shots opened the group up from the other four. While these results may seem mediocre compared with the sub-minute-of-angle (1 inch or less at 100 yards) groups achieved by some rifles, bear in mind that the Rossi rifle has simple open sights and fires a pistol-caliber cartridge with a looping trajectory at extended ranges. Keeping those things in mind, including its rapid-fire ability and ease of handling, plus its modest price, the Rossi Model 92 looks better and better.

The Model 92 has simple, old-fashioned sights, such as this semi-buckhorn rear sight, which is adjustable for elevation only. Still, the gun is capable of decent accuracy.

ROSSI MODEL 92 "PUMA"

	MODEL 92
Overall Length	33.5 or 37 inches
Barrel Length	16 or 20 inches (24 inches available in .45 Colt only)
Weight	5.5 or 5.75 pounds
Caliber/Capacity	.357 Magnum, .44 Magnum, .45 Colt/10-shot (13 in 24-inch .45)

Ruger Model 96

Ruger's Model 96 is a hammerless lever-action rifle inspired by Savage's classic Model 99 (see *Complete Guide to Classic Rifles*). Available in .22LR, .22 Magnum and .44 Magnum calibers, the Model 96 also shares Savage's cocking indicator located at the rear of the receiver. For a rifle whose firing mechanism is entirely concealed within the receiver, a cocking indicator is a good idea. Without one, shooters would be unable to readily determine the rifle's true state of readiness. In its .22 Magnum caliber version, the Model 96 has a detachable rotary magazine that holds up to 9 rounds.

The mechanism of Ruger's Model 96 boasts the same well-tested attributes of the company's Model 10/22, which is respected the world over. When adapted to the lever-action loading operation, the Model 96 mechanism operates smoothly through not quite 90 degrees. As with most lever-action rifles, the trigger remains in place while the lever moves; there's little danger, though, of pinching the trigger finger, because all

The Ruger Model 96 bears a striking resemblance to the now-discontinued Savage Model 99, one of the great classic guns.

Note that the Model 96 trigger stays put while the lever is pushed down. This lever-action mechanism closely resembles that of the Savage Model 99.

The Model 96 is a well-balanced rifle that is pleasant and easy to shoot.

more faithful to the Savage Model 99 design and overall style.

Thanks to Ruger's expertise and experience, the Model 96 shoots outstandingly well. A .22 Magnum caliber Model 96 tested for this book produced 5-shot offhand groups as small as 1.6 inches across from 50 yards, and 3-shot 100-yard benchrested groups measuring 1.5 inches—all without even placing a scope on the rifle (a task made easy by Ruger's inclusion of a

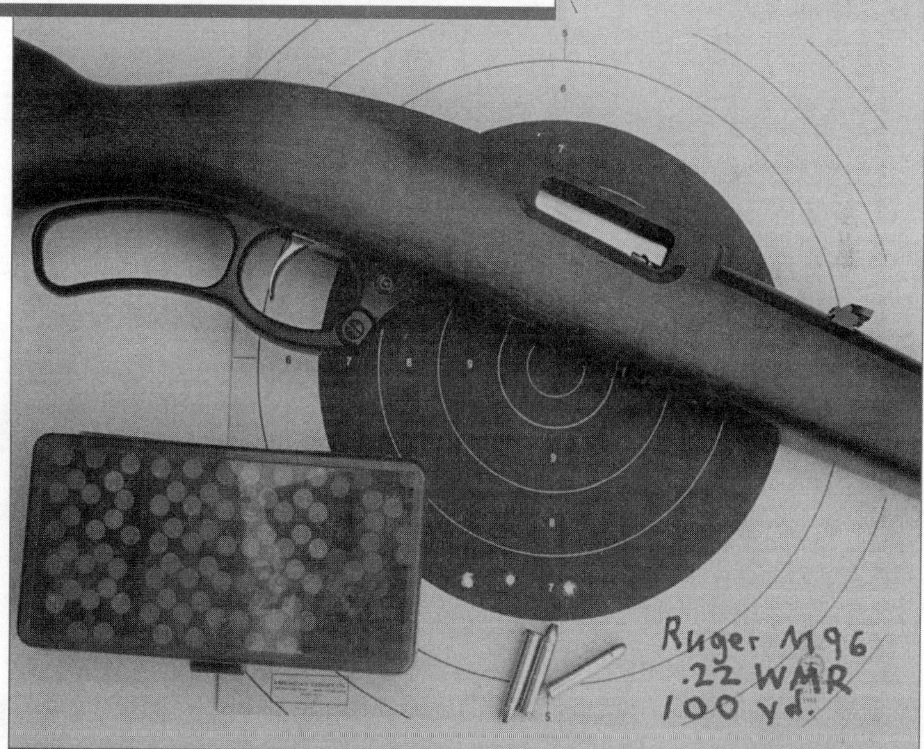

The Ruger Model 96 tested by the author performed sensationally on the shooting range, producing this 1.5-inch group from the 100-yard bench with the rifle's own iron sights (not a scope). Actually, the rifle shot very close to the point of aim at the bottom of the target.

four fingers fit into the lever loop when reloading. The lever operates briskly—but not noisily—and throws spent cartridges casings, and even complete cartridges, well clear.

Because the Model 96 lacks an exposed hammer, Ruger has added a manual crossbolt safety activated by a pushbutton located at the leading edge of the triggerguard. This makes sense when one notes that the rest of the triggerguard assembly moves each time the shooter reloads. Personally, I'd prefer a tang safety, which is more ambidextrous to operate than a crossbolt type and is folding rear sight, scope rings and receiver recesses ready for scope mounting). A little over 40 years ago, the .22 Magnum cartridge had a reputation for mediocre accuracy; but with modern ammunition offerings that reputation now lacks credence. In reality, the .22 Magnum offers superb accuracy in high-quality loadings such as CCI's Maxi-Mag and Winchester's sensational Varmint round with 34-grain hollowpoint bullet. This latter cartridge is an absolute terror to medium-sized varmints such as opossums, raccoons and such.

The test results of the Model 96, which were flawless, backed up all the expectations developed by the author following years of using all types of Ruger firearms. These are well-made guns supported by a host of well-conceived design features. The Ruger Model 96 is, moreover, a natural for the .22 Magnum (.22 WMR) cartridge, making this a reasonably powerful rifle with a sturdy, reliable operating mechanism well-suited to fast followup shots.

The Ruger Model 96 (bottom) and the Rossi Model 92 (top) prove that the lever-action rifle, far from being dead, remains a flourishing action type.

RUGER MODEL 96

	.22 LR/MAGNUM	.44 MAGNUM
Overall Length	37.25 inches	37.3 inches
Barrel Length	18.5 inches	18.5 inches
Weight	5.25 pounds	5.9 pounds
Magazine Capacity	10/9	4 rounds

PART IV:

MODERN PUMP-ACTION RIFLES

Pump-action (also called "slide-action") rifles date back to the late 1800s, when the pump-action technology—first developed for shotguns under John Browning's 1893 patent—were applied to rifle. It all began with rifles that fired rimfire rounds and later, as the metallurgy and breech-locking mechanisms evolved, graduated to more powerful centerfire models. The earliest commercially successful pump-action rifle was the Winchester Model 1890 designed by John Browning. Winchester made over 849,000 of these rifles from 1890 to 1932. Unfortunately, this gun was so popular in shooting galleries that, despite the enormous quantities made, it is difficult now to find one in great shape. Winchester followed the Model 1890 with the smaller Model 1906 (1906-1932), the Model 61 (1932-1963) and the Model 62 (1932-1958).

Still another pump-action design by John Browning—the legendary "Trombone"—went into production at Fabrique Nationale (FN) in Belgium. With just over 150,000 made from 1922 to 1973, this rifle remains popular around the world, but not in the U.S. The only importation here took place when Browning brought in 3,250 during 1970. Back in 1909, Remington had introduced its Model 12 rimfire pump-action rifle to compete with Winchester for the "gallery gun" market. Though not as successful as the Winchesters, sales of the Model 12 were good enough for Remington to introduce a number of slight variations—Models 12B, 12C and so on. It remained in production until 1936 before it was replaced by the improved Model 121, which lasted until 1954. Remington's current pump-action rimfire rifle—the Model 572 or Fieldmaster—took over in 1955 and remains in production.

Remington's success with these rimfire models encouraged the company to develop its centerfire pump-action Model 14 series rifles firing the same .25, .30, 32 and .35 Remington cartridges also used by the Remington Model 8 Autoloading rifle. The Model 14 remained in production from 1912 to 1936, when it was replaced by the improved Model 141A (1936-1950), which in turn was replaced by the Model 760, or "Gamemaster" (1952). In building the Model 760, Remington eliminated the early Remington autoloading calibers in favor of more popular and effective chamberings, such as the .222, 223, 243, .308 and .30-06, among others. This was made possible because the rifle had a strong built in action using multiple locking

Remington Model 572

Rossi Model 59

lugs on a rotating bolt. The Model 760 proved a popular gun, remaining in production for 30 years. An improved version—the Model 7600—came out in 1981 and remains the industry's premier centerfire pump-action rifle (although Browning's BPR promises to challenge that statement).

Among the advantages of the pump-action rifle is the superior ambidexterity of its operation compared to most rifles. They are also very fast to operate. Although early pump-action rifles were limited by the cartridges they could use, modern materials and breech-locking designs allow these guns to handle the same powerful cartridges found suitable for semiautomatic sporting rifles. Of course, what causes less recoil in semiautomatic operation does not apply to the pump-action rifle. Like other manually-operated rifles (i.e., bolt-action and lever-action), pump-action rifles fired with powerful calibers kick the shoulder hard. Interestingly, while pump-action rifles can be operated successfully from the prone position (unlike lever-action rifles), most armed forces choose not to adopt pump-action rifles for military service. This is all the more curious when one notes that pump-action shotguns have always been used widely by the U.S. armed forces.

Even in civilian life, the market for pump-action rifles, while steady, is fairly small, with only a few companies competing for the business. The .22 caliber Remington Model 572 "Fieldmaster" remains the most advanced rimfire model. Because of its tubular magazine, the Model 572 can fire .22 Short, Long or Long Rifle ammunition at will. It also has a sleek, hammerless design that many shooters find attractive. Rossi's Model 59 (designed by John Browning and made originally by Winchester) uses only the .22 Magnum. The Model 62 SA, however, fires a .22 Short, Long or Long Rifle ammunition and has a 23-inch barrel. In addition, the Model 62 SAC fires .22 Short, Long or Long Rifle ammunition from a 16 1/2-inch barrel. In the more powerful centerfire calibers, Remington's classic Model 7600 is made for the .243, .270, .280, .308, .30-06 and .35 Whelen calibers. In 1997, Browning's Pump Rifle (BPR) made its debut. A modification of Browning's self-loading, gas-operated mechanism, the BPR retains all of the BAR features, including its strong breech-locking mechanism, which enable the BPR to handle calibers as powerful as .300 Winchester Magnum. While pump-action rifles exist in only a limited range of choices, they still offer many advantages for the sport shooter.

Browning BPR

Browning's BPR (Browning Pump-Action Rifle), which began production in 1998, is assembled, finished and test-fired at Browning's factory in Vianna, Portugal, from parts made by Fabrique Nationals (FN) in Herstal, Belgium. Essentially a pump-actuated adaptation of Browning's highly regarded semiautomatic BAR hunting rifle, the BPR shares all the features of the BAR except that the forearm must be operated manually between shots to reload. On its way back (towards the shooter), the forearm extracts the spent cartridge casing from the firing chamber and then ejects it well clear of the rifle. After it has traveled all the way to the rear, the pump mechanism cocks the striker. Then, on its way back toward the firing position, the forearm causes the mechanism to push a fresh cartridge into the firing chamber and prepare the rifle for firing.

While the mechanism of the BPR is in the firing position or at rest, none of the operating rods are visible, so that it is not immediately

The BPR's pump-action motion, while it looks odd, is really no harder to operate than any competing pump-action mechanism that moves back and forth in a straight line. The pump-action mechanism is shown as it appears all the way to the rear.

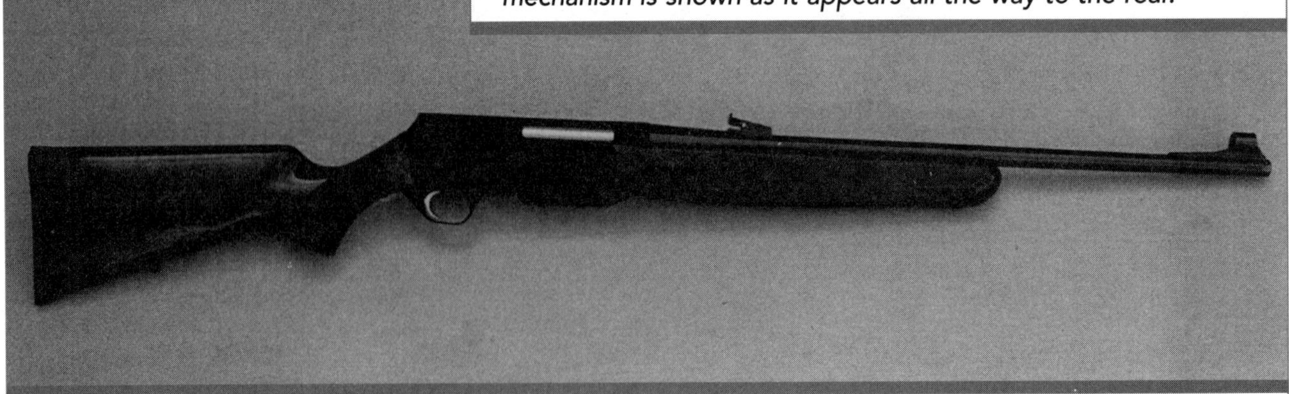

The pump (slide)-action Browning BPR strongly resembles the company's BAR semiautomatic rifle; indeed, the two rifles are mechanically identical except for the means by which the bolt moves to reload.

One way to distinguish Browning's BPR from the BAR: the BPR (shown) has no exposed extractor in the ejection, whereas the BAR does.

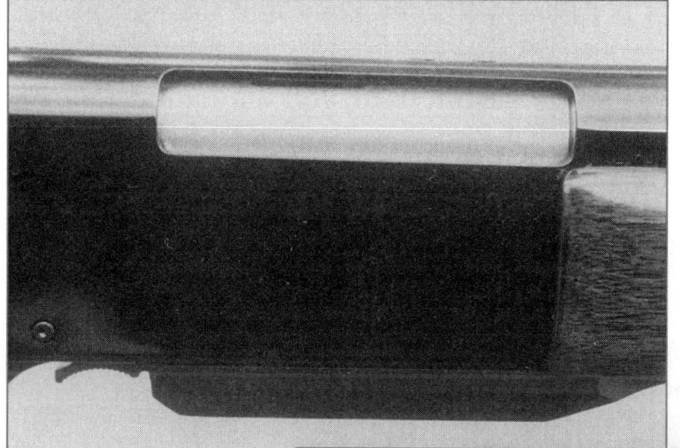

One problem faced by pump-action rifle and shotgun shooters is what to do—once the action loads and cocks the mechanism—in the event the shooter decides not to fire. Pulling back on the operating slide will not eject the chambered cartridge, because the mechanism is locked in its forward position to prevent any gas leakage that might occur should the rifle be fired with the breech partway open. To remedy this potential safety hazard, the BPR includes a slide-release control. Located on the right side of the triggerguard, it pushes forward and in, allowing the slide to open. The shooter can then eject a live round from the firing chamber.

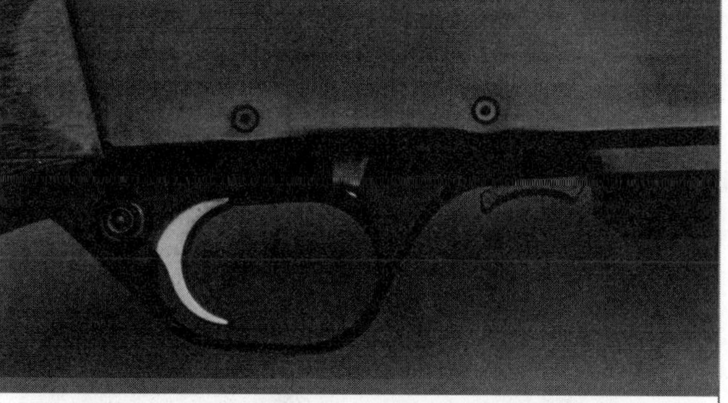

The BPR has a bolt-release latch on the left side of the receiver, in front of the trigger. This enables the shooter to unlock the action and eject a cartridge from the firing chamber after loading.

obvious that this is a pump-action rifle. In fact, the BPR resembles the parent BAR so strongly that a casual observer could easily mistake one for the other. The BPR is unusual also in that its forearm operating mechanism does not move straight back and forth, as do most pump-action rifles. Instead, the forearm hinges down slightly on its way back to the rear. Despite the slight up-and-down motion that accompanies this back-and-forth motion, the BPR remains easy to operate, its pump mechanism being so smooth and fast.

The BPR's other operating controls are logically arranged and easy to manipulate. The safety—a crossbolt push-button type—is located on the rear edge of the triggerguard. To operate, it pushes inward, from right to left, exposing a red band (fire setting) and back to safe (on request, Browning can fit a left-handed version of the safety button).

The BPR's magazine follows the same excellent design introduced by Browning in the A-Bolt and BAR rifles. This magazine release provides the shooter with an option: either load the magazine while still on the rifle or remove it altogether and replace it with a fresh one. To load with the

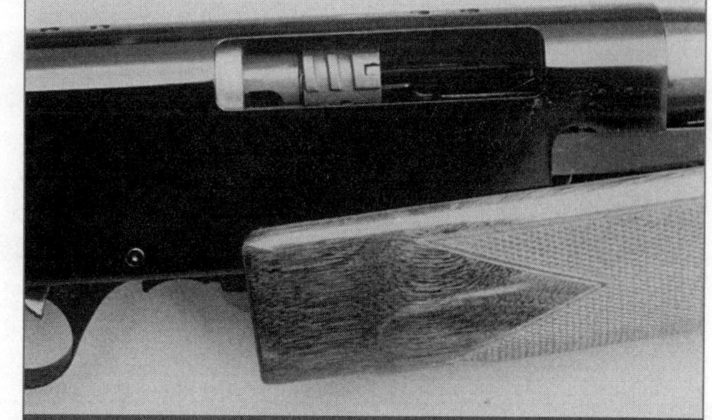

The BPR has the same massive rotating bolt, with seven locking lugs, as the self-loading BAR. Note also the action bars, about halfway through their reloading stroke, visible just ahead of the receiver as the forearm drops.

The Browning BPR is a pleasure to shoot, but recoil is more pronounced than in a BAR of the same caliber (the BPR's mechanism does not siphon off propellant gas when cycling the bolt).

The BPR magazine release lies just ahead of the triggerguard along with a crossbolt pushbutton manual safety on the trailing edge of the triggerguard.

magazine still attached to the rifle, the magazine release is pushed all the way to the rear, allowing the back end of the magazine to fall clear of the rifle while the front stays put. With the rear end hinged down, simply press fresh cartridges down into the magazine in the usual manner. If the shooter wants instead to remove the magazine completely from the rifle and replace it with a new one, proceed as above, grasping the magazine box near the front, squeezing it inward slightly, and pulling the box to the rear until it slides off the floorplate. Both methods have their time and place, and Browning should be commended for allowing the shooter to

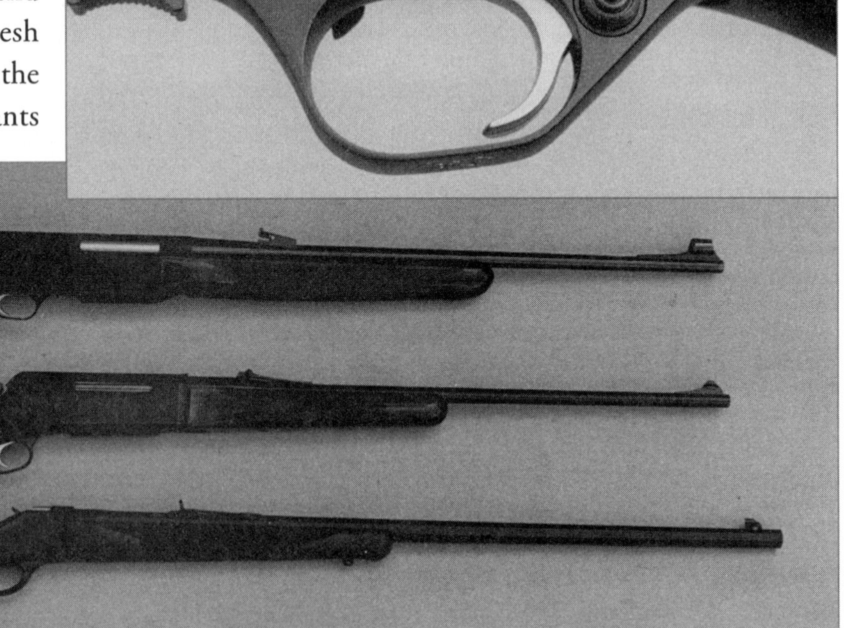

With the pump-action BPR (top), the lever-action BLR (middle) and the single-shot Model 1885 (bottom), the Browning company produces an excellent product line of heavy-duty, top-quality centerfire rifles.

decide. I really like the BPR's gold-plated trigger, too. Typical of Browning, it has a smooth face, which is unusual on a rifle, and it's slightly wider than you'd expect. These features combine to make the BPR trigger feel lighter, crisper and more comfortable to operate.

With its lightweight aluminum-alloy receiver, the BPR weighs slightly less than the steel-framed BAR. Moreover, the heavy recoil characteristics of the BAR's gas-operated mechanism are absent in the BPR. Recoil is therefore noticeably more pronounced in the BPR than in the BAR. This limits the BPR's largest caliber choice to .300 Winchester Magnum, whereas the BAR is available in an even more powerful round, the .338 Winchester Magnum.

In testing for accuracy, the BPR produced a best 3-shot benchrested group measuring 1.3 inches from 100 yards, with two bullet holes almost touching and the third "opening up" the group by landing only .75 inches away. These results are good for any rifle, especially one that uses iron sights. Recoil in

The BPR's sighting equipment includes this hooded front post.

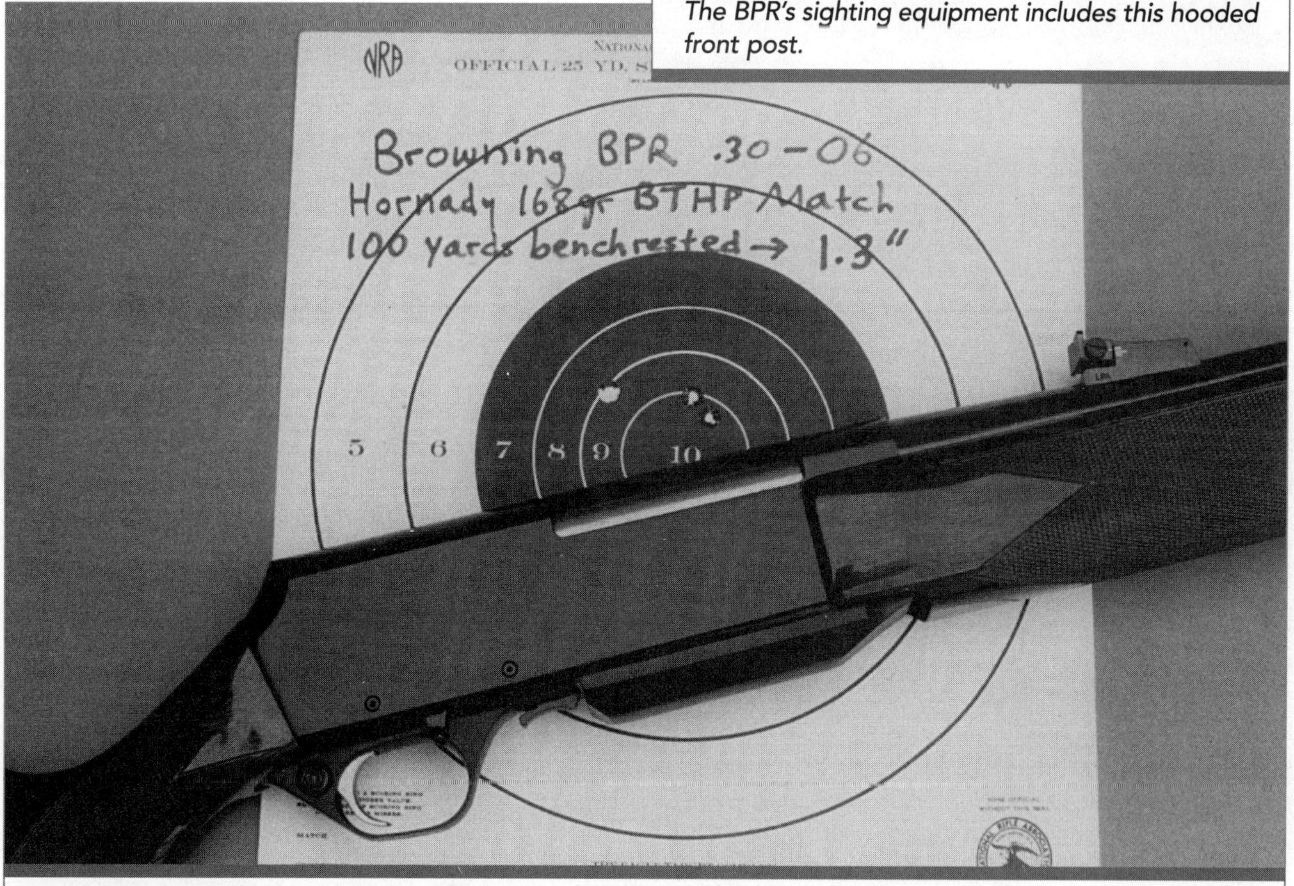

In testing for accuracy, the author found the Browning BPR exceedingly accurate, as this 1.3-inch, 100-yard group attests.

the .30-06 Winchester variant tested was more pronounced than in Browning's semiautomatic BAR, which is a relatively mild-mannered gun. The iron sights worked well, providing a clear and precise sight picture out to 100 yards. A scope might make a better choice in some hunting applications, so Browning has added four holes in the upper receiver for those who prefer telescopic sights. The pump mechanism is surprisingly smooth to operate, and though it may pull out and away from the receiver, this quick motion feels no different than the motion one encounters on a pump shotgun—or even on other pump-action rifles.. Certainly the BPR is an efficient rifle, and I am happy to note that another powerful centerfire rifle has become available in the efficient and useful pump mechanism.

The rear sights on the Browning BPR are the same fully-adjustable type found on the company's iron-sighted BARs.

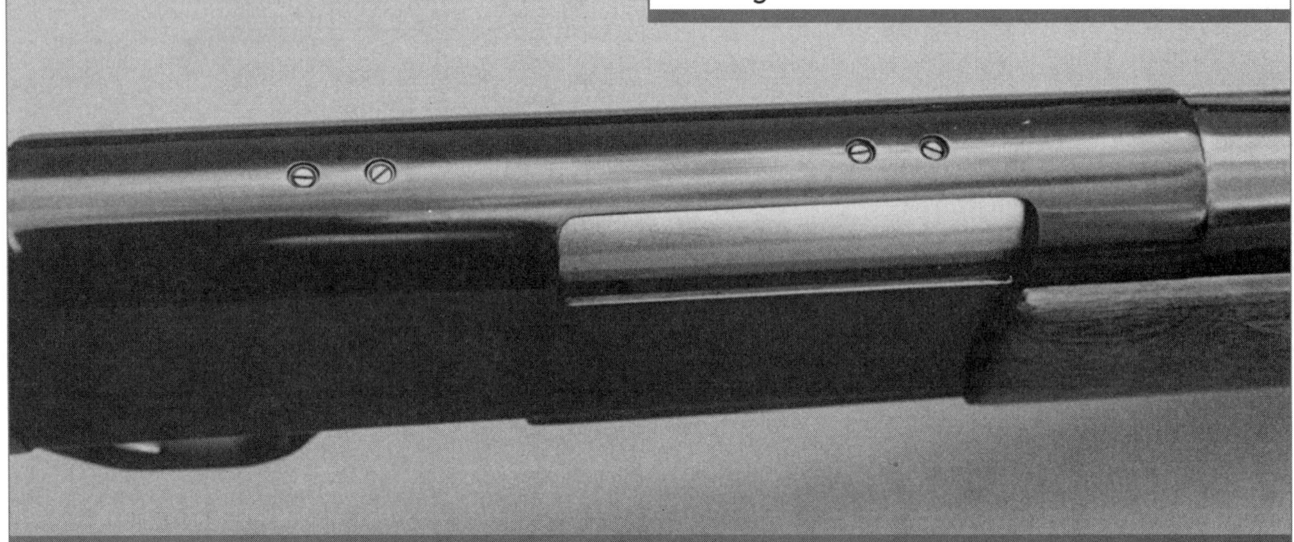

For those who prefer a scope for increased long-range accuracy, the BPR receiver comes already drilled and tapped for scope mounting.

BROWNING BPR

	BPR
Overall Length	43 (standard) or 45 (magnum) inches
Barrel Length	22 inches standard/24 inches in magnums
Weight	7.2 pounds
Years Produced	1977-present
Caliber & Capacity	.243, .308, .270, .30-06/4 rounds 7mm Remington Magnum, .300 Winchester Magnum/3 rounds

Remington Model 572 Fieldmaster

Remington's Model 572 Fieldmaster is one of those old reliables—it seems to last year after year while other, perhaps more dramatic designs, come and go. After spending some time recently working with a Model 572 BDL Deluxe Fieldmaster, I came to understand why this gun has survived while other models, even including Remington's classic contemporary Nylon 66 rifle, have gone out of production.

The Model 572 first appeared in 1955. Designed as a companion piece to Remington's Model 760 pump-action centerfire rifle and Model 870 shotgun, the 572 has a large, sleek-lined receiver, a tubular magazine beneath the barrel, and a reciprocating forend with which to load the firing chamber in a smooth pumping motion. As with most successful gun designs, Remington developed several variants along the way. The Model 572 A, for example, was basically a Fieldmaster type with a simple rear sight adjustable for elevation, a small front sight post, a plain uncheckered stock and a grooved forend. Then there is a smoothbore variant—the Model 572 SB—which was similar in all respects to the 572 A except it had no rifling inside the barrel. Next, the Model 572 Lightweight (introduced in 1958) featured an anodized aluminum alloy receiver and barrel, reducing its weight to only four pounds. The Lightweight model featured a choice of three colors—tan, black and blue—on its anodized metal parts. During the late 1950s and early 1960s this gun was considered too radical, forcing Remington to quit making it in 1962 after less than 35,000 had been built. Today the Model 572 Lightweight is considered quite a collector's item, especially in its "Teal-Wing Blue" color scheme.

The Model 572 BDL Deluxe Fieldmaster first appeared in 1966. Similar to the 572 A, this model added a fully-adjustable rear sight and a larger ramp front sight. The stock, made of better wood

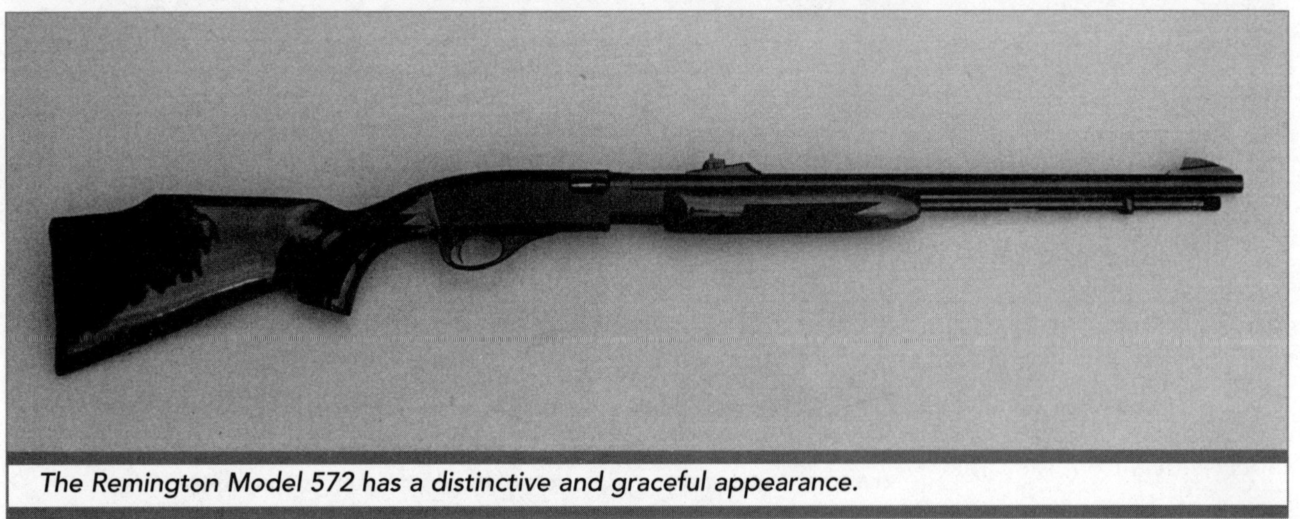

The Remington Model 572 has a distinctive and graceful appearance.

The Remington Model 572 balances and is sized right for an adult shooter. The rifle is shown with its forearm pulled all the way back.

than the 572 A's, also included checkering on the pistol grip (checkering replaced the 572 A's simple grooving on the forend, too). Since the BDL Deluxe cost only a few dollars more than the plain-looking 572 A Model, the latter's popularity declined to the point where, in 1988, Remington quite making it. The BDL Deluxe thus became the only Model 572 Fieldmaster variant Remington made, and so the situation remains today. The basic design has changed very little. Today's model differs from the same model of 20-odd years ago only in the improved, fully-adjustable rear sight similar to that found on Remington's iron-sighted centerfire rifles.

Why has the Model 572 survived even though Remington offers several other rimfire rifles for sale? Part of the explanation lies at the heart of the rifle: its ammunition feed and pump-action mechanism. Also, its tubular magazine allows conversion of the rifle to a single-shot and back to a repeating rifle simply by

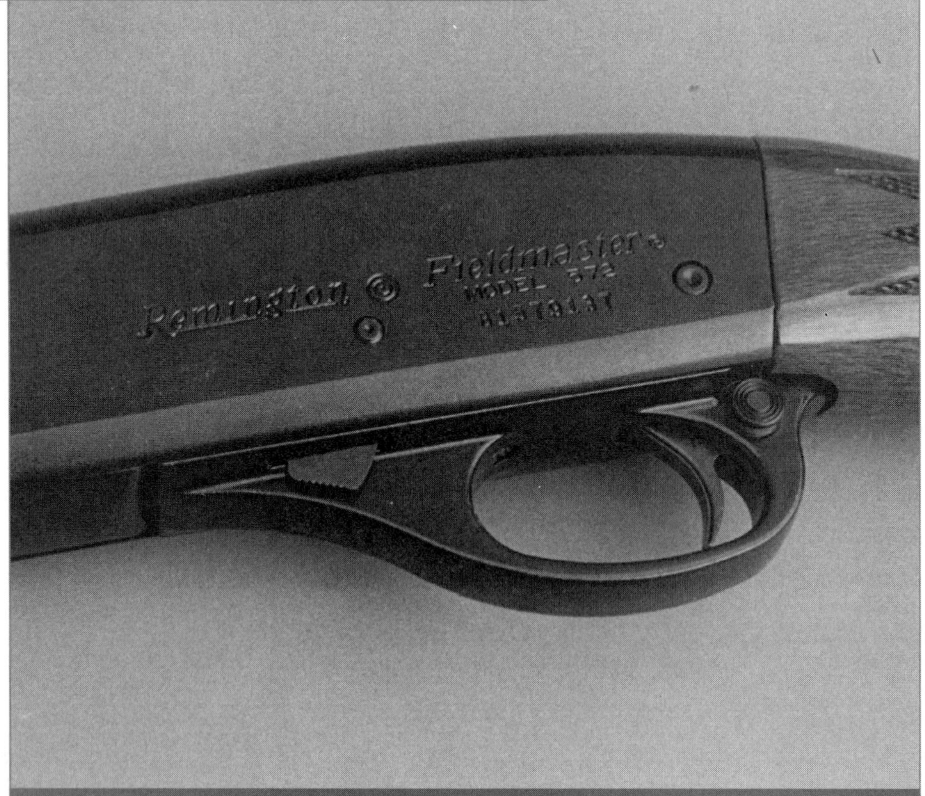

The controls on the Model 572 include a slide release at the leading edge of the triggerguard and a crossbolt manual safety at its trailing edge.

removing the inner magazine tube. This feature makes the rifle useful as a training weapon, where trigger control and sight alignment are more important than learning how to hose down a target with multiple rapid shots. The tubular magazine also gives the shooter the flexibility of choosing between .22 Short, Long and Long Rifle cartridges, a feature shared by no other rimfire repeater equipped with a box magazine. In fact, the Model 572 is so reliable, it can mix and match .22 Short, Long and Long Rifle cartridges in the same magazine without creating a problem.

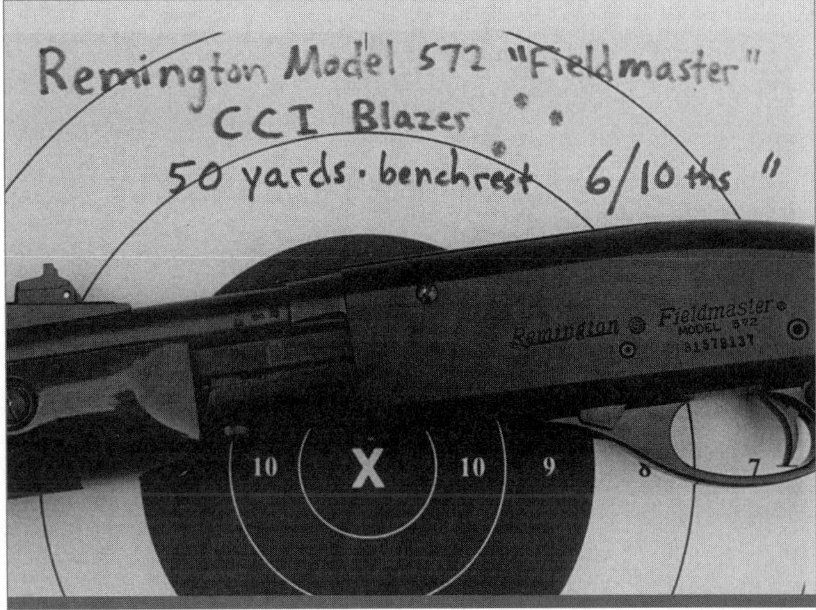

The Remington Model 572 proved highly accurate. The best 50-yard group produced this .06-inch effort fired with CCI Blazer. The three bullet holes appear just after the "Blazer" designation on the target paper.

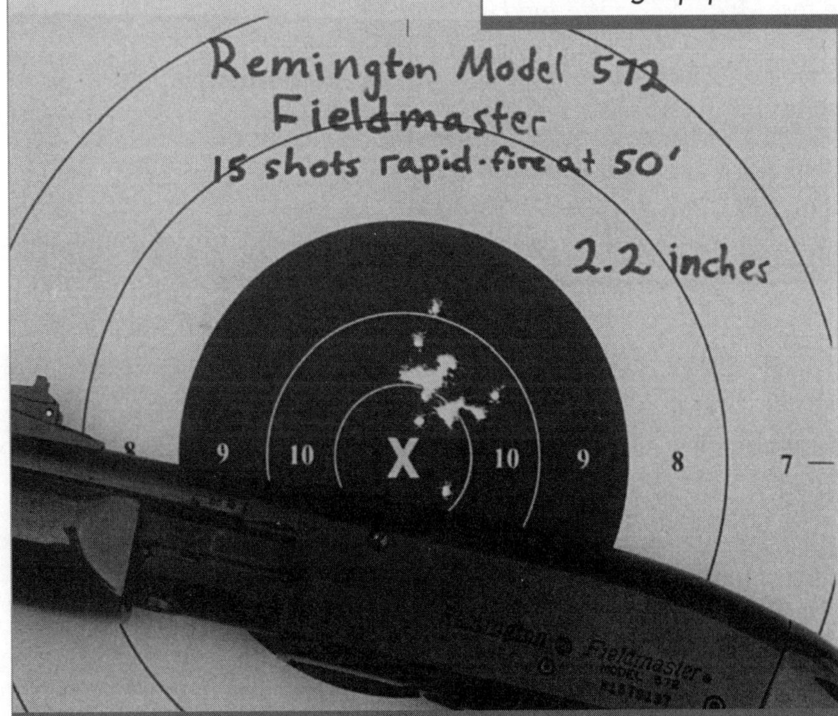

The author loaded up a Model 572 with a full magazine of ammunition and proceeded to fire as fast as he could shuck the forearm and press the trigger. The result: 15 shots into 2.2 inches at 50 feet. This is the kind of shooting that many pump-action, rimfire caliber rifles are capable of.

The Model 572 handles well in other ways, too. It's a good-sized rifle and can be handled comfortably by full-sized adults without feeling cramped, yet light and well-balanced enough for use by smaller shooters as well. The pump action is smooth and the gun's sleek beauty is something to be admired. The wood used on the rifle we tested was as beautiful as any I've ever seen on a mass-produced rifle.

Because the action locks when the slide is pumped back and then pushed forward, there's a slide release on the left bottom portion of the receiver. Pushing this up and in unlocks the action without having to fire the rifle in order to unlock the slide. The manual safety, which is located behind the trigger, is the pushbutton crossbolt type. Normally, that would be a handicap, but not in a pump-action rifle, whose pumping motion loads the rifle quickly and naturally.

The Model 572 excelled in both formal target shooting and plinking at targets of opportunity. Three-shot groups from the 50-yard bench were extraordinarily accurate for a .22LR rimfire rifle. The best 3-shot, 50-yard benchrested group (with CCI Blazer ammo) measured only .60 inches across, followed closely by .80-inch groups fired with Federal Classic and Aguila Super Extra. Still another 3-shot, 50-yard benchrested group fired with CCI Stinger ammunition spanned 1.8 inches, which is really not so terrible. In a final test of the Model 572's shooting qualities, I loaded up a tubular magazine with 15 rounds of Aguila SE and fired them all at the target 50 feet away as fast as I could pump the slide. The action was so smooth and its recoil so light that I was able to put all 15 shots into a pattern less than 2 1/2 inches across.

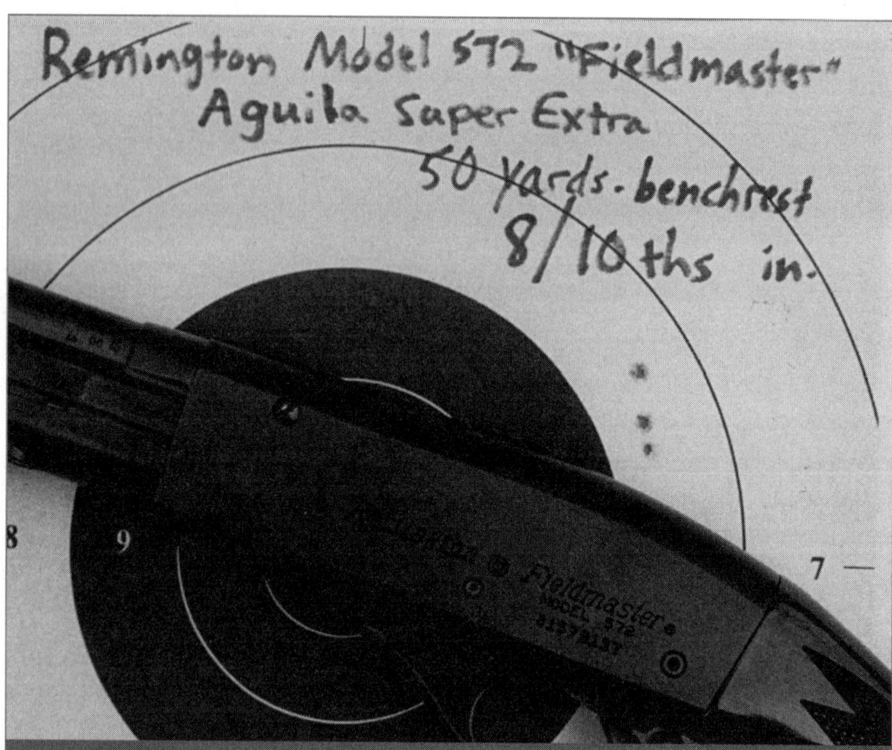

The test Model 572 performed well with Mexican-made "Aguila Super Extra" ammunition. In the author's experience, foreign rifles and ammunition often do as well as (and sometimes better than) their American counterparts.

The Remington Model 572 BDL Deluxe Fieldmaster is not the cheapest .22 rifle around by any means, but it ranks among the best and is well worth the price. For shooters who also own a Remington Model 760 or 7600 pump-action rifle (see below), or even a Remington Model 870 shotgun, this is a natural choice for a .22 Long Rifle. It's also very expensive to make, but I hope Remington will keep it in production for a long time to come. It's that good.

REMINGTON MODEL 572

	MODEL 572
Overall Length	40 inches
Barrel Length	21 inches
Weight	5.5 pounds
Years Produced	1957-present
Caliber & Capacity	15 rounds (.22 LR); 17 Longs; 20 Shorts

Remington Model 7600

Remington's Model 7600 dates from 1981, but its lineage goes back further than that, to the early years of the 20th century. That's when Remington's talented designer, John D. Pedersen, patented a tipping bolt used by Remington in its Model 14 pump-action rifle. Introduced in 1912, the Model 14 became the first practical pump-action rifle to fire modern centerfire cartridges. Equipped with a tubular magazine (under the barrel), the Model 14 held up to five rounds. The new rifle sold in the tens of thousands during a 23-year production run. The similar Model 141 "Gamemaster" came on line in 1936 and remained in production until 1950.

Unfortunately, the Models 14 and 141 were available only in Remington's own calibers, which were shared by the company's Model 8 self-loading rifle. Accordingly, one of Remington's top priorities in the early 1950s was to introduce a new pump-action rifle design capable of handling more powerful, commercially-available cartridges then in use. Thus did the Model 760, the immediate successor of the Model 7600 in terms of design and function, stake its claim to being one of the all-time great rifles of the world. Better known as the "Gamemaster," a title taken from the Model 141, the new rifle boasted a much stronger and efficient breech lock consisting of a rotating bolt and detachable box magazine. It was produced from 1952 to 1982 in a variety of popular commercial chamberings, from .222 all the way up to .35 Remington, and in a variety of finishes sufficient to satisfy every fancy and budget. The Model

Because the Remington Model 7600 (top) is a full-size pump-action rifle chambered for serious rifle cartridges, it must be made larger and heavier than the Rossi Model 59 (bottom), which is chambered for a relatively low-powered rimfire cartridge.

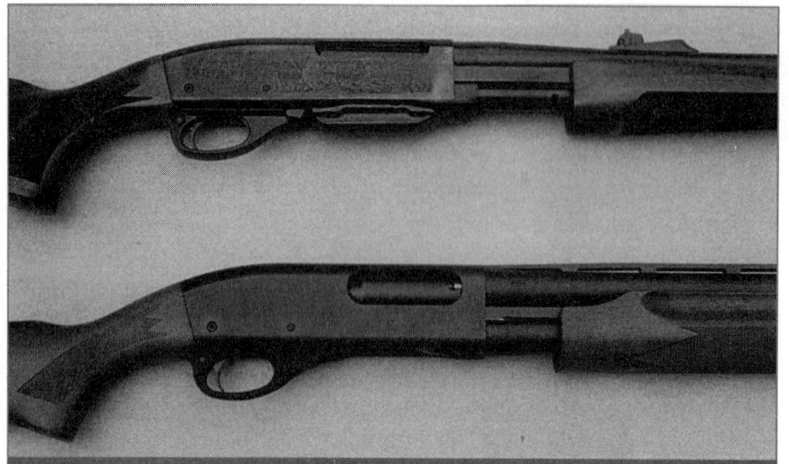
The one major difference between the Model 7600 centerfire rifle (top) and the Model 870 shotgun (bottom) concerns their methods of storing ammunition. The rifle has a detachable box magazine, whereas the shotgun employs a tubular magazine.

760 quickly became the choice of thousands of sportsmen. Unfortunately, it was also the rifle of choice used by James Earl Ray in the assassination of the Reverend Martin Luther King, Jr. In Memphis, Tennessee, in April 1968. Actually, the Model 7600 was not unlike its successor in terms of its design. A side-by-side comparison of the two rifles immediately made this observation apparent. The Model 7600, a versatile model used in a number of chamberings, was effective against a wide variety of game animals. Remington chambered it from the beginning in 6mm Remington, .243, .270, .308 and .30-06 calibers. The 6mm Remington version was dropped in 1984, but a few years later Remington added two Model 760s

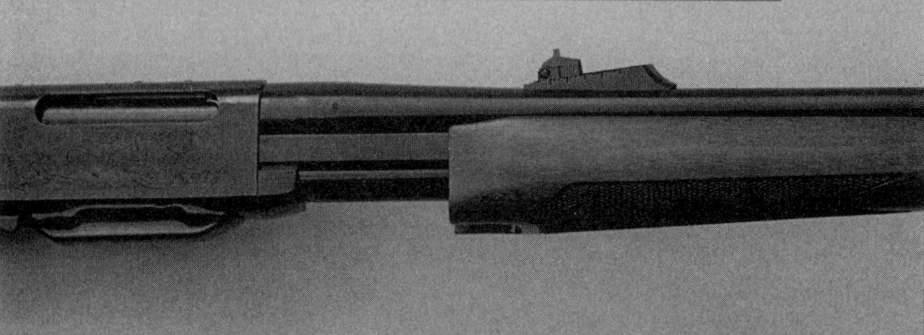
The magazine release on the Remington Model 7600 receiver is visible at the far left, next to the triggerguard. Note the exposed action bars between the receiver and forearm.

The Remington Model 7600 (top) rifle makes a logical companion piece for Remington's exceedingly popular Model 870 pump-action shotgun (bottom), with both firearms operating in almost exactly the same way.

chambered for the .280 Remington and .35 Whelen cartridges. The latter, while it had stiff recoil, raised the potential of this rifle against elk and other large North American game.

The Model 7600 is a straightforward, simple design, one that is surprisingly rugged despite its partially exposed operating rods that connect the forearm to the receiver. Among its controls is a crossbolt safety on the triggerguard. As with the rimfire Model 572 (see above), the Model 7600 includes a slide release on the left bottom portion of the receiver. This enables shooters to unlock the action after working the slide without having to fire the rifle. It also has excellent Remington iron sights, a ramped front post and an

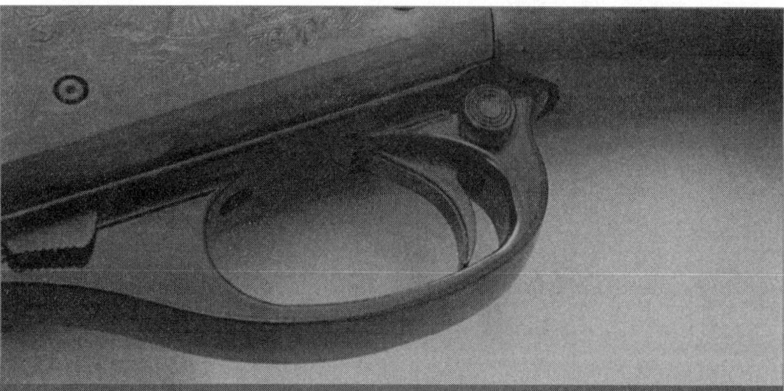

A pushbutton-type manual safety is located on the trailing edge of the Model 7600's triggerguard. The safety button shown pushes right to left to reach the fire position.

The Model 7600 includes a slide-release control located next to the leading edge of the triggerguard. Although its magazine resembles that of Remington's similar Model 7400 self-loading rifle, the two magazines are not interchangeable.

The Remington Model 7600 features factory engravings on its large, flat-sided receivers.

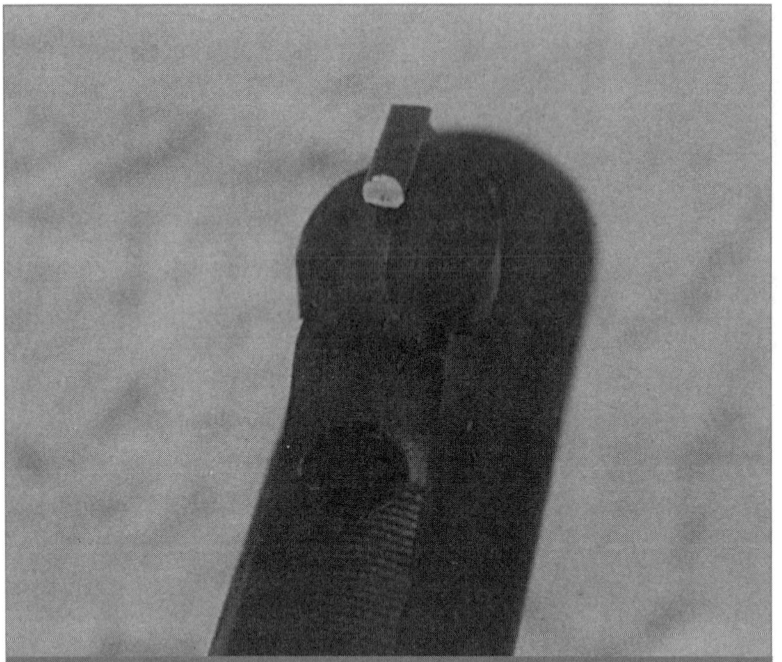

The front sight on the Model 7600 includes a prominent white dot as an aiming mark. It's so large, though, that it might actually obscure the target at longer ranges.

adjustable rear, with provisions for mounting a scope. Even without a scope, the Model 7600 comes close to being a 1 MOA rifle, delivering accuracy near the 1-inch mark at 100 yards.

I preferred the .270 Winchester caliber version tested for this book over every .270 caliber bolt-action rifle I've tried. The pump mechanism is smooth, fast and easy to operate, offering a rate of fire far in advance of what a bolt-action rifle can do. It's slightly faster, even, than a lever-action and only slightly slower than a semiautomatic rifle. Those who think only a bolt-action rifle can be

The Model 7600, firing a .270 Winchester cartridge, is capable of near minute-of-angle accuracy even without using a scope, witness this 1.1-inch group from a 100-yard benchrest. Point of aim was the "X" at the target's center.

The rear sight on the Model 7600 is the same sturdy, reliable pattern Remington uses on its other modern rifles equipped with integral sights.

The Model 7600 topped by Millett's excellent "Buck" scope makes an outstanding hunting package at a reasonable cost.

accurate, or that only a lever-action or semi-automatic rifle can produce a rapid rate of fire, should take a close look at Remington's Model 7600. For decades the Model 760/7600 was the pump-action centerfire rifle. Now Browning's BPR has appeared to challenge Remington's well-established heavyweight. It will be interesting to see if the market for pump-action rifles can sustain both models. Let's hope it will, because these interesting designs have a great deal to offer, including a wide range of cartridges.

REMINGTON MODEL 7600

	MODEL 7600
Overall Length	42 inches
Barrel Length	22 in. (18.5 in. for carbine variants in .30-06 only)
Weight	7.5 pounds
Years Produced	1981-present
Caliber/Capacity	.243, .270, .280, .308, .30-06, .35 Whelen/4 rounds

Rossi Model 59

The Brazilian-made Rossi Model 59 has long held the distinction of being the only pump-action rifle made to fire the .22 Magnum cartridge. The Amadeo Rossi company began manufacturing the Model 59 at its factory in Sao Leopoldo Brazil, in 1989, with Interarms of Virginia its importer in the U.S. The Model 59 is the most powerful of all Rossi Model 62-series guns—including the Models 62 S and 62 SAC (see following entry).

Rossi's Model 59, named after the year in which Winchester introduced its .22 Magnum cartridge, is a 10-shot .22 Magnum caliber version of the company's otherwise identical Model 62 in .22LR caliber. Both guns revived the proven design of the pump-action gallery rifle created in the late 1800s by John Browning and formerly made by Winchester, first as the Model 1890 (1890-1932) and then as the Model 62 (1932-1958). The Model 59 follows Browning's original design to a tee in both its internal mechanical details and its outward

The distinctive profile of the Rossi Model 59 evokes memories for many older shooters who once used Winchester prototypes in shooting galleries.

Though its basic design is now over a century old, the Model 59 (bottom) holds its own when competing against modern rifles like the Marlin 922M (top).

appearance, including the exposed hammer and tubular magazine below the barrel. There's also a reciprocating wooden forearm that provides shooters with a handle with which to operate the action. Pulling the handle smartly to the rear unhinges and opens the receiver, ejecting a live round or spent cartridge case. With the receiver fully open, extending the loading mechanism to the rear also cocks the spur hammer. To reload, the forearm handle is pushed all the way forward. Deep grooves in the wooden handle offer an excellent non-slip grip. For safety reasons, the gun will fire only in battery (fully forward and locked). The hammer has a half-cock notch that protects the shooter from accidental firing should his thumb slip while cocking the rifle. Unlike the Remington Models 572 and 7600 (see previous entry), the Rossi Model 62-series guns do not have separate

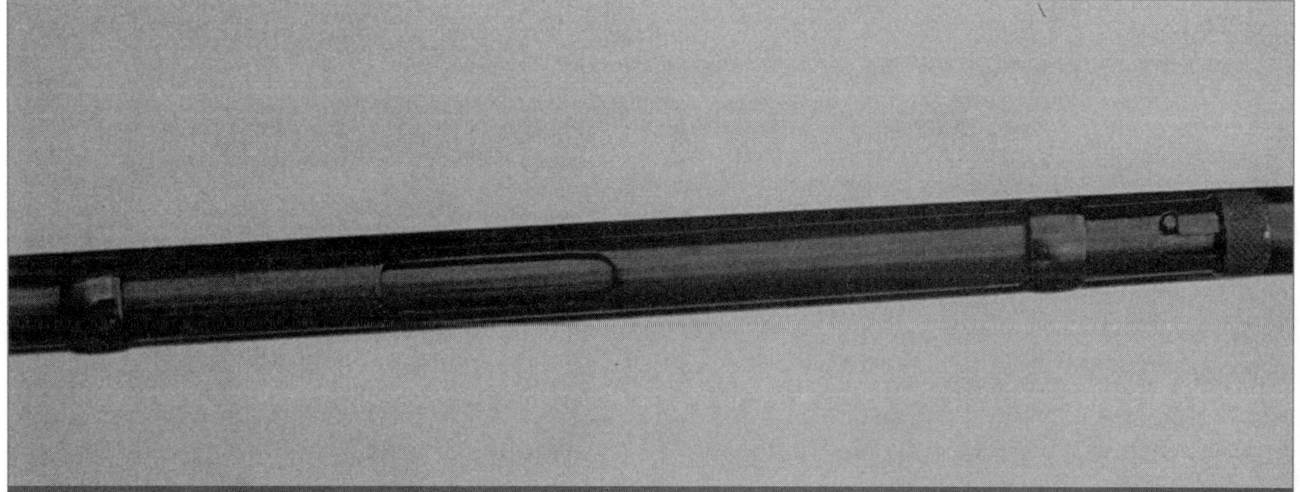

Reloading the Model 59 begins by turning the knurled front of the magazine tube until the detent button disappears.

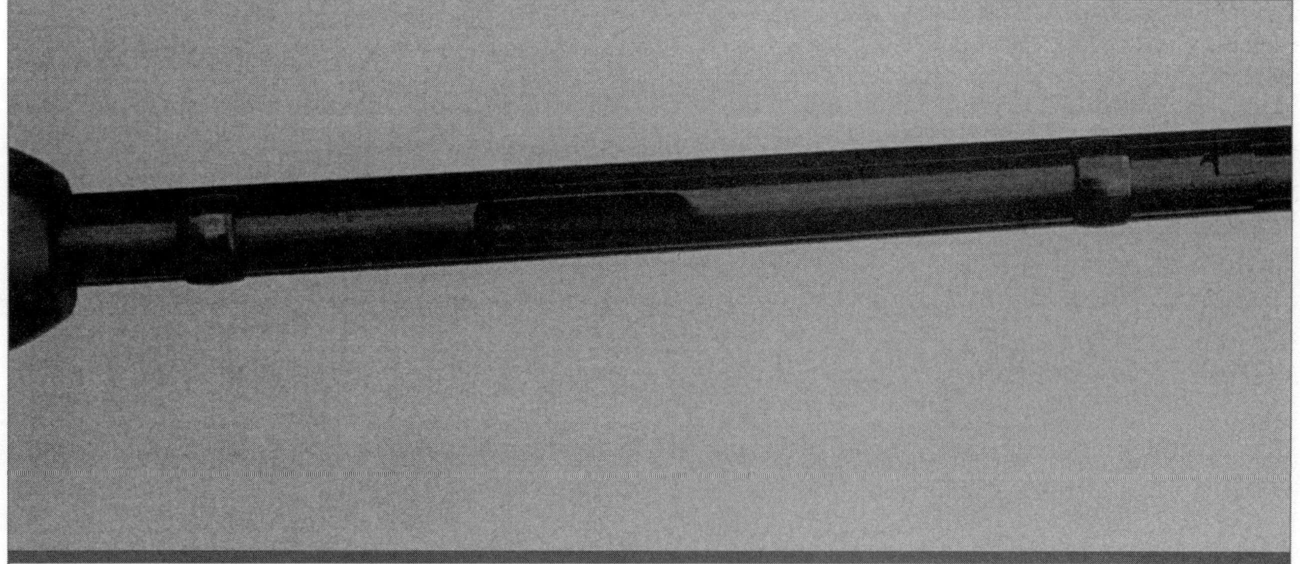

After turning the front of the magazine tube, the magazine follower is pulled forward until the loading gate opens up about midway down the magazine tube.

The Model 50's wooden forearm is deeply grooved for a tight hold. Despite its traditional semi-buckhorn rear sight (shown) the rifle is actually very accurate.

The Rossi Model 59 disassembles easily by loosening the large screw at the rear of the receiver. The hammer must be cocked, as shown, for the gun to fire.

slide-release controls. In the event a shooter with a loaded and cocked rifle in hand decides not to shoot and wants to disarm the gun, he simply unloads the tubular magazine, first removing the outer magazine tube and then tipping the cartridges out of the magazine. He must then gently lower the exposed hammer, controlling it with his thumb while pulling the trigger until it reaches its full-forward (not half-cock) position. The slide can then be operated as required to eject the chambered cartridge.

The front sight on the Model 59 is the fixed blade type and its adjustable rear sight is placed well forward on the barrel, several inches ahead of the receiver. The gun, which weighs only 5 1/2 pounds,

Disassembled, the Model 59 makes an extraordinarily handy package, measuring only a little over two feet long despite its 23-inch barrel.

is easy to disassemble. All that's required is loosening a screw.

In testing the Model 59 on the range, it performed superbly. With the exposed-hammer design clearly indicating the gun's state of readiness, no manual safety is necessary. Once the gun is leaded, you simply pump the handle and fire, then pump to eject and reload. This process continues until the magazine is empty. The pump action mechanism works smoothly and effortlessly. Since the Model 59 requires only a short stroke to load and unload the relatively small .22 Magnum cartridges and empty shell casings, anyone can learn to fire this rifle quickly with only a little practice. Loading the 10-shot magazine is easy and convenient, too. After removing the follower from the front, the cartridges (primer end first) are dropped down the tube until the rounds (up to 10) have been loaded. The follower is then re-inserted over the nose of the lead bullet and turned until it locks in place.

Despite its simple design and rudimentary sights, accuracy is impressive with the Model 529 we tested. Offhand groups fired from 50 yards went into 3-shot groups ranging in size from 0.9 inch to 1.5 inches, while at 100 yards the same

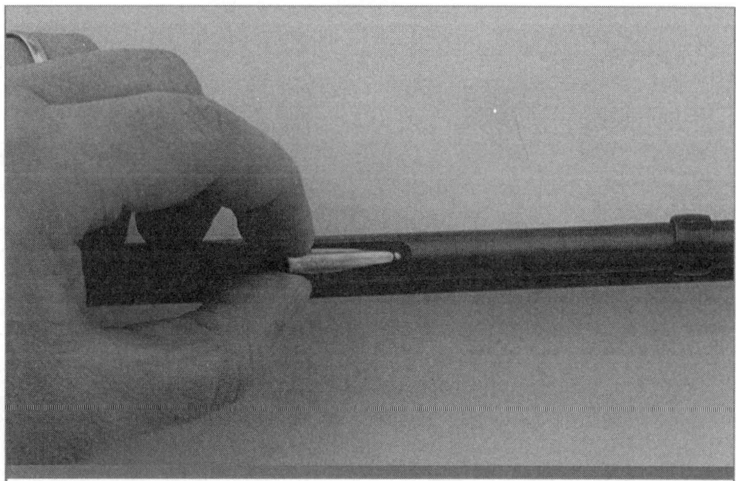

To load, insert up to ten .22 Magnum cartridges, bullet end forward, through the open loading gate in the magazine tube.

The sleek lines and compact dimensions of the Model 59 make it fun for people of all ages to fire.

This 50-yard benchrested group measures just under an inch, which is incredible given the author's average skill level. Point of aim was the bottom of the black area, or "6 o'clock hold."

sights are simple but more than adequate to serve their purpose.

The Rossi Model 59 combines excellent performance and workmanship at a reasonable price. The original Winchester Model 62 has been out of production since 1958; consequently, these guns command collector's prices that can soar in price double what Interarms (Rossi's Importer) asks for this same rifle. Bear in mind, too, that Winchester never made its Model 62 to fire the potent .22 Magnum round, an option Rossi has always offered in its Model 59.

This 3-shot, 100-yard benchrested group fired with the Model 59 measures a mere 1.4 inches across, which is a good result when using the .22 Magnum rimfire cartridge.

3-shot benchrested groups varied in size from 1.4 inches to 2.4 inches across. For an open-sighted rifle of ancient design, such accuracy is indeed impressive (in fact, all .22 Magnum rifles tested for this book proved exceptionally accurate). Because of the receiver's break-open design and its vertical ejection of spent cartridge cases, only limited choices exist in scope mounts. But for the type of shooting these rifles are most likely called upon to do, a scope is probably not necessary anyway. Like the rest of the gun, the

ROSSI MODEL 59

	MODEL 59
Overall Length	39.25 inches
Barrel Length	23 inches
Weight	5.5 pounds
Years Produced	1989-present
Manufacturer	Amadeo Rossi, S.A., Sao Leopoldo, Brazil
Importer	Interarms, Alexandria, VA
Caliber/Capacity	.22 Magnum (SMR)/10 rounds

Rossi Model 62 SA

Rossi's Model 62 SA is the .22 Long Rifle caliber version of the Model 59 (see above) and operates in exactly the same way. The "SA" stands for "Slide Action," another term for pump action, while "Model 62" recreates Winchester's term for that company's own final version of the classic John Browning design.

Like Remington's pump action Model 572, the Model 62 SA can use either Short, Long or Long Rifle cartridges or any combination thereof. Rossi offers the gun in a choice of blue or nickel finish, with a round or an octagonal barrel. With labor costs still quite low in Brazil, the Rossi factory is able to lavish plenty of workmanship on this gun, leading it with a high-polish blued finish of excellent quality. Like other Brazilian guns, the nickel finish is quite attractive and offers as well superior corrosion resistance compared to the standard bluing.

I tested a blued M62 with an octagonal barrel, a traditional look and feel that appealed greatly to me. As for accuracy, the Model 62 SA was impressive, with 5-shot groups benchrested at 50 yards covering an area as small as 1.1 inches with CCI Stinger. With both CCI Blazer and Mexican-made Aguila "Super Extra" brand ammunition, the hits measured 1.2 inches across, escalating slightly to

The Model 62 SA is well-balanced and easy to shoot. Its long barrel (23 inches) makes it more suitable for adult shooters than for younger ones.

The .22LR caliber Rossi Model 62 SA is available in a round-barreled variant (shown here) or in a variant with an octagonal barrel.

1.4 inches using Federal Classic. In a comparative test with the Model 62 SA, similar to the one I used with the Remington Model 572 (see previous entry) and with a full magazine (14 rounds), I fired at a target 50 feet away as fast as I could pump the mechanism and work the trigger. The result was a 4.2-inch group for all 14 shots fired. While the result was a full two inches wider than the Remington group fired under comparable conditions, I still consider it acceptable. The result represent the most grueling test of accuracy one is likely to put a .22LR caliber rifle through at short range (generally 50 yards or less) where .22 rimfire cartridges are most effective. The Rossi Model 62 may not be quite as well balanced nor its contours quite as smooth as those of the Remington, but it's still a fine gun. In addition, the full-sized Rossi Model 62 SA balances better than the short-barreled Model 62 SAC (see below), at least for adult shooters, but both guns are equally fast to load.

For this accuracy test, the author loaded up a Model 62 SA with a full magazine of ammunition, stood 50 feet from the target, and fired as fast as he could, placing 14 shots into a 4.2-inch pattern.

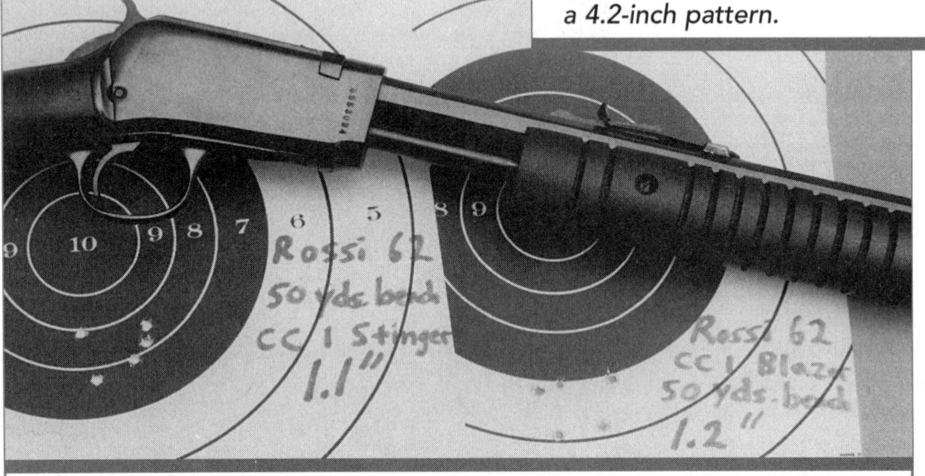

In testing, the Model 62 SA delivered 50-yard benchrested groups of slightly over an inch. Accuracy with both standard- and hyper-velocity loads was remarkably consistent although it did print slightly higher with hyper-velocity rounds like CCI's Stinger (left). Note the high-polish finish on the blued receiver and the octagonal barrel.

ROSSI MODEL 62 SA

	MODEL 62 SA
Overall Length	39.25 inches
Barrel Length	23.0 inches
Weight	5.75 pounds
Manufacturer	Amadeo Rossi, S.A., Sao Leopoldo, Brazil
Importer	Interarms, Alexandria, VA
Caliber/Capacity	.22 Short, Long or Long Rifle/20, 16 or 14 rounds

Rossi Model 62 SAC

Rossi's Model 62 SAC is a .22 Long Rifle caliber carbine version of the Model 62 SA (see above), differing only in its barrel length (16.5 inches) compared to 23 inches. Using this short, carbine-length barrel explains the additional "C" in its model designation. As with the other Rossi pump-action rifles, Interarms has imported this gun and handled North American sales since its beginnings in 1988.

In both these models, the magazine capacity can also be increased by using .22 Shorts or Longs instead of Long Rifle cartridges. *[Personally, I advise against this. Prolonged use of shorter cartridges may in time cause erosion of the firing chamber, making it difficult to use .22 Long Rile cartridges.]* In general, the .22 Long Rifle cartridge is the best choice for use with a Rossi Model 62 SA or SAC. The .22 Long Rifle, after all, delivers more power, velocity and accuracy than either the .22 Short or .22 Long cartridge. The .22 Long Rifle cartridges are also far more plentiful than those other cartridges. Neither the Model 62 SA nor the Model 62 SAC can fire the .22 Magnum cartridges used in the Model 59, nor can the Model 59 fire the .22 Short, Long or Long Rifle cartridges.

The Rossi Model 62 SA (top), with 23-inch barrel, is pictured with the Model 62 SAC (bottom), which is identical other than having a shorter barrel (16"). Note, however, that their magazine tubes are of almost equal length.

Despite its shortened barrel, the Model 62 SAC includes a full-length magazine tube extending almost to the muzzle, making it possible for this carbine variant to carry an impressive 12-round magazine load. That means the Model 62 SAC loses only two rounds of magazine capacity from the full sized Model 62 in the same caliber. It actually holds two more rounds than the larger Model 59, since the Model 59's .22 Magnum rounds are appreciably larger than the .22 Long Rifle rounds used by the Models 62 and 62 SAC.

Despite its short barrel, the Model 62 SAC can produce better than average accuracy. Typical 50-yard benchrested 3-shot groups went into 2 inches using Mexican-made Aguila "Super Extra" brand ammunition and 3_ inches with Federal Classic. One oddity about this gun is its ejection pattern. It sends empty cartridge casings straight up into the air—about 9 inches or so. No matter how hard you work the action, the ejected brass seems always to take the same path.

Thanks to its light weight and compact dimensions, Rossi's Model 62 SAC has fine potential as a first gun—or at least a first repeating gun—for novice shooters. And even for an experienced adult, this is a fun rifle to shoot. Moreover, its takedown feature promises extraordinarily good handling and storage potential, the two halves each measuring less than 20 inches. In short, the Rossi Model 62 SAC is a well-made gun with a proven design and a price that is reasonable considering its top-notch quality.

The Model 62 SAC used in our tests preferred high-intensity ammunition, such as CCI Stinger, which produced this 1.75-inch group and came close to point of aim from 50 yards away.

Here the Model 62 SAC is shown with its breech fully open. The ejection pattern during tests was straight up, almost a foot, with seemingly no change in direction or height regardless of how hard the action was opened.

The Rossi Model 62 SAC, disassembled, being less than 20 inches long, makes a remarkably handy package

ROSSI MODEL 62 SAC

	MODEL 62 SAC
Overall Length	32.75 inches
Barrel Length	16.5 inches
Weight	4.25 pounds
Manufacturer	Amadeo Rossi, S.A., Sao Leopoldo, Brazil
Importer	Interarms, Alexandria, VA
Caliber/Capacity	.22 Long Rifle/12 rounds

PART V:

MODERN SELF-LOADING RIFLES

The self-loading rifle—also called the automatic or semiautomatic rifle, depending on whether it gives multiple shots ("automatic"), or only one shot ("semiautomatic"), each time the shooter presses the trigger—powerfully influenced the 20th century. Appearing in prototype military form in the first decade of the 1900s, self-loading rifles virtually replaced earlier bolt-action designs in military service with the major powers by the 1950s. The first self-loading rifles suitable for sport shooters also appeared by 1910, and while many sport shooters prefer other types of rifles covered elsewhere in this book, the self-loading rifle has become an important firearm for hunters as well.

Compared to single-shot rifles and the various types of manually-operated repeating rifles—including lever-action rifles, bolt-action rifles and pump or slide-action rifles—self-loading rifles offer significant advantages (and some disadvantages as well) about which the shooter should also be aware. The self-loading rifle's chief advantage, a high rate of fire, convinced armed forces to abandon virtually all their bolt-action rifles (a few specialized applications, notably sniping, being the exceptions) once sufficiently reliable self-loading rifles became widely available. Given the same or a similar cartridge, self-loading rifles also have less recoil than single-shot or manually-operated rifles, since in a self-loading rifle part of the energy released upon firing goes back into the reloading process instead of exerting that energy against the shooter.

Compared to the operating mechanisms of other rifle types, the self-loading rifle arrived with some inherent disadvantages of its own, including less accuracy. For instance, while it is theoretically possible to build a self-loading rifle as accurate as a premium bolt-action model, doing so involves difficulty and expense. Part of the reason for the generally inferior accuracy of self-loading rifles is mechanical—too many parts moving around, too much recoil on rapid follow-up shots, and even some psychological reasons.

Century L1/A1 Sporter

Armscor M-1600

Self-loading rifles are also expensive to make. They require close tolerances to work well, they may fail to function properly when exposed to mud, sand, snow or powder fouling. While many self-loading rifles are surprisingly reliable even when abused, few hold up under these circumstances as older, manually-operated rifle types. On the subject of cleaning, the maintenance needs of self-loading rifles are invariably greater than those of older, simpler action types; in addition to cleaning the barrel and chamber, the reloading mechanism must also be maintained. While some of these systems—notably those used on the modern AK and FAL rifles—are robust and easily accessed, the operating mechanisms of many other self-loading rifles are difficult to service.

Self-loading rifles also tend to be fussy in terms of their ammunition requirements. Underpowered ammunition may fail to cycle with enough force to reload; it also causes feeding malfunctions and even parts breakage. Along with bolt-action rifles, self-loading rifles are generally a poor choice for left-handed shooters, simply because most eject their spent cartridge casings from the right side of the receiver, sometimes with considerable force. Some manufacturers—notably Colt with its AR-15/M16 series of rifles—have, it should be acknowledged, catered to the needs of left-handed shooters by offering spent cartridge deflectors and ambidextrous safety controls. Nevertheless, the self-loading rifle is, by and large, more adapted to right-handers than to their left-handed shooters. Despite these various complications and shortcomings, self-loading rifles offer such an advantage in firepower over competing types that they have become universally accepted by the armed forces of the world and enjoy a huge following in the sporting arms market as well.

Next, we shall consider the development of self-loading rifles for the military,

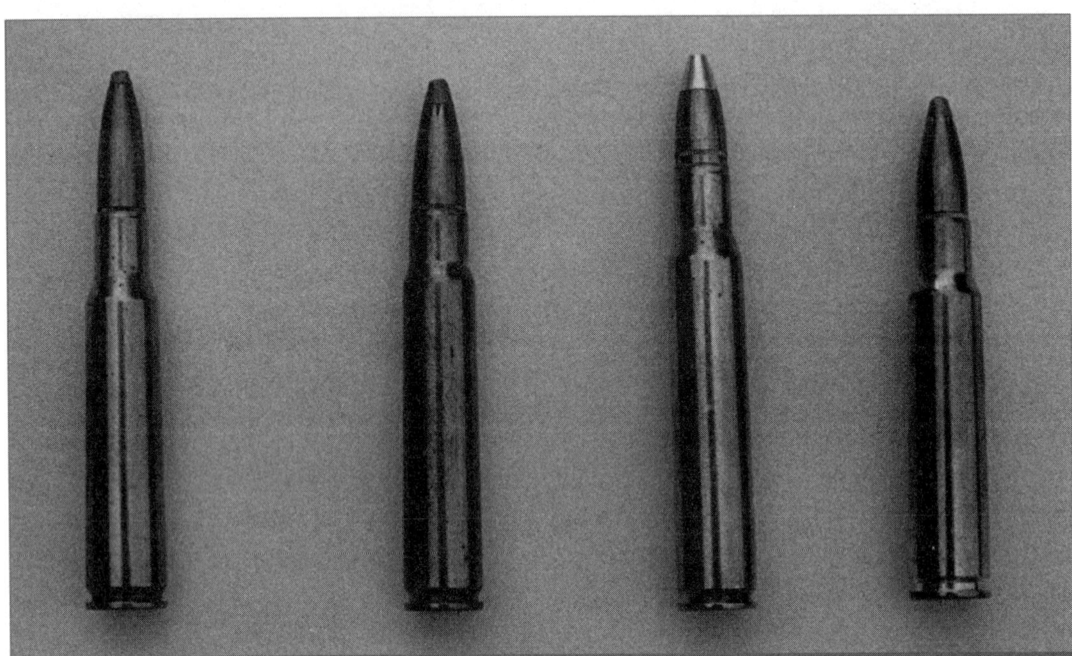

The Mauser-type cartridges used in military bolt-action rifles challenged the designers of self-loading rifles because of their considerable power and excessive length. They are (left to right) the 7mm Mauser (7x57mm), 8mm Mauser (7.92x57mm), .30-06 Springfield (7.62x63mm) and the .308 Winchester (7.62x51mm) cartridges. Only the .308 Winchester was originally designed to work in a self-loading mechanism.

followed by a brief history of these rifles for civilian use. During the first quarter of t he 20th century, many talented firearms designers—including Rossignol and Meunier of France, Pedersen, Browning and Garand of the United States, Mannlicher of Austria, Mauser of Germany, Cei-Rigotti of Italy, Mondragon of Mexico, Federov of Russia and Schouboe and Bang of Denmark—were all hot on the trail of a self-loading rifle that was mechanically and militarily viable. With a little more development and official encouragement, some of their clever and innovative ideas could have served successfully in World War I (1914-1918). The widespread use of self-loading rifles in that war would have undoubtedly helped unfortunate infantrymen of that period deal more successfully with the opposition they faced from enemies armed with machine guns.

Regrettably, the universal issue of bolt-action military rifles less than two decades earlier delayed their replacement by self-loading rifles. Moreover, the ammunition developed for the bolt-action service rifles usually developed too much power for early self-loading mechanisms. The rimmed and tapered cartridge cases used in Russia, France and Britain were poorly shaped for automatic loading. Only the Mexican-designed Mondragon and Mauser ***Flieger-Karabine*** *("Aviator Carbine)" issued by Germany, the French Chauchat, Meunier and RSC, Vladimir Federov's* ***Avtomat*** *in Russia, and the U.S. Browning Automatic Rifle (BAR), along with some commercial Winchester self-loading carbines, all saw service in World War I. Considering the millions of soldiers who served in that war, the number of self-loading rifles involved was limited. While other self-loading firearms—mostly rifle-caliber machine guns and pistol-caliber submachine guns—came of age in World War I, none could replace the bolt-action rifle for issue to the bulk of the infantry.*

Between world wars, considerable developmental work on reliable self-loading rifles continued. These efforts culminated in the U.S. in the truly excellent M1 Garand. Adopted in 1936, this rifle went on to arm most U.S. troops in World War II, with production exceeding five million rifles between 1940 and 1945. The semi-automatic M1 Garand was accurate, powerful, rugged and reliable. In combination with the equally rugged, fully-automatic Browning Automatic Rifle, the M1 Garand gave American soldiers an enormous advantage over their opponents who were armed mostly with obsolescent bolt-action rifles. Another wartime innovation was the M1 Carbine, which supplemented M1 Garand issue in the U.S. and was actually produced in greater numbers. The secret to the M1 Carbine's success was the relatively low-powered round it used, thereby allowing a lightweight mechanism in a short, handy rifle offering adequate power at close ranges.

While no other countries approached the accomplishments of the U.S. in arming its troops with self-loading rifles during World War II, other nations did manage to field self-loading rifles in smaller quantities. In the Soviet Union, slightly over 30,000 AVS-36 rifles of Simonov design went into Soviet service from 1937 to 1938, some lasting into World War II. During that conflict, the Red Army fielded over a million Tokarev-

Beretta AR-70

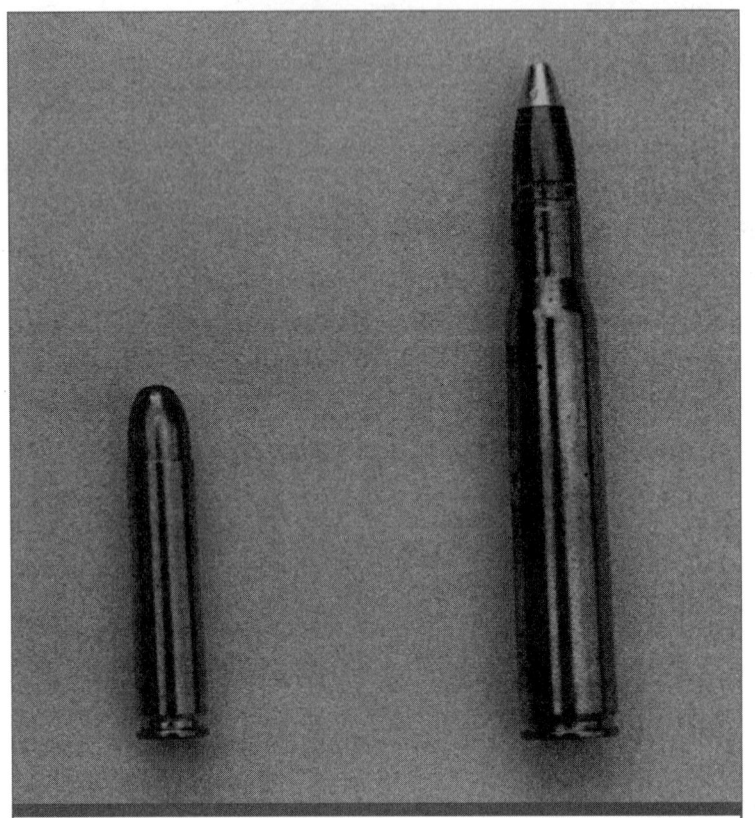

The .30 Carbine round (left) was among the first cartridges adapted specifically to the self-loading military rifle, the M1 Carbine. A .30-06 cartridge is also shown for size comparison.

designed SVT-38 and improved SVT-40 rifles. Shortly before World War II began, Fabrique Nationale (FN), located in Herstal, Belgium, developed a military self-loading rifle design. Though the German invasion of Western Europe in the spring of 1940 temporarily disrupted the development of this rifle, the FN staff, which was in exile in England during the war, perfected it. When the resulting SAFN rifle finally entered production in 1949, it became quite successful. When Sweden feared it might be invaded by Germany or the Soviet Union, it quickly developed its AG-42 Ljungman rifle, which went into limited service in 1943. After several false starts, the Germans eventually developed a good semi-automatic rifle of their own—the ***Gewehr*** *(Rifle) 43 or G-43—based in part on the Tokarev mechanism. Developed by the world-renowned armsmaker Carl Walther Waffenfabrik, the G-43 incorporated some of the most advanced design features of the day. This rifle would have been even better had conditions in Germany allowed its production from higher-quality materials, but the dislocation of the German industry brought on by the war prevented the G-43 from reaching its full potential. Ultimately, fewer than half a million were built, far less than the wartime German armed forces needed to re-equip themselves with a modern self-loading rifle. As a result, most German soldiers served to the end of the war armed with a hodgepodge of mostly obsolete bolt-action rifles.*

Near the end of World War II, Germany made the next big advance in military self-loading rifle design by fielding the Hänel

StG-44. Early development of this weapon, as with so many other developments in firearms design, occurred with changes in ammunition. As early as World War I, German military planners realized that their 7.92mm Mauser cartridge possessed more power and range than was required for a futuristic, general-purpose, self-loading rifle. Conversely, the 9mm Parabellum pistol cartridge, while usable in submachine guns, lacked sufficient power and range. By the late 1930s an experimental cartridge of intermediate power was well on its way to production. This eventually took the form of a shortened 7.92mm Mauser rifle cartridge. The result—a 7.92x33mm round—easily outperformed the 9mm Parabellum cartridge and yet was small enough to adapt to a reasonably compact self-loading rifle mechanism that provided both semi-automatic and fully-automatic fire. Experimental rifles using this ammunition appeared in 1942, and by 1943 the Hänel design, which was easy to mass-produce (owing to its extensive use of medium-quality stamped steel), was ordered into full-scale production. An estimated 300,000 units saw service by war's end. Arming Germany's

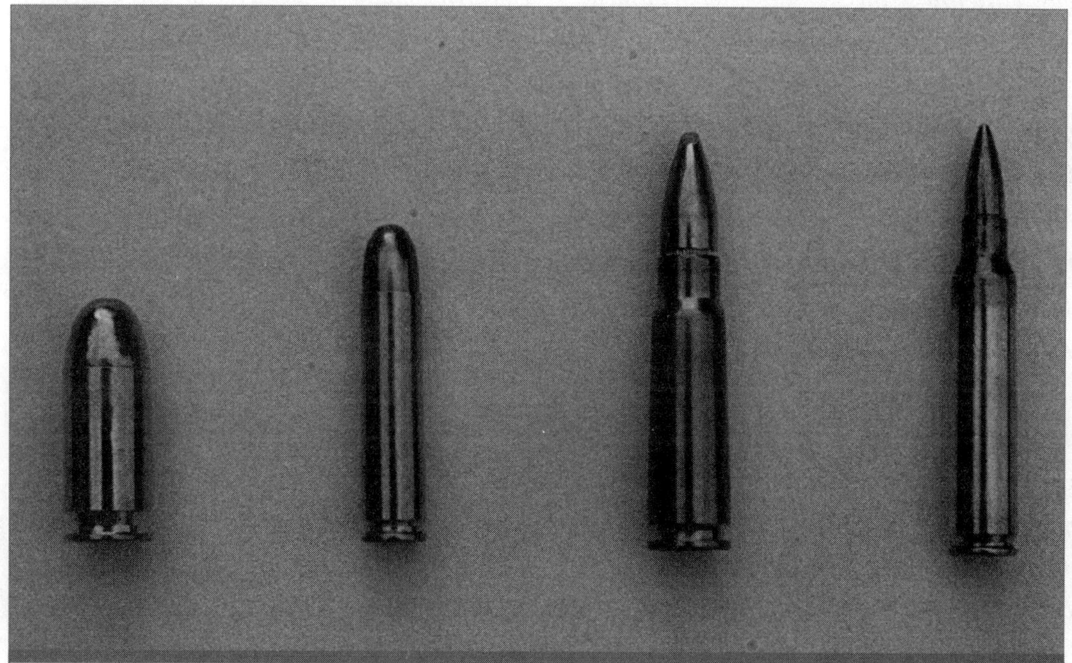

As self-loading firearms became more prevalent at military arsenals, designers created new or updated cartridges for them. From left to right are the .45 ACP, originally a pistol cartridge but now used in submachine guns and some carbines; the .30 Carbine round created in 1942 for the M1 Carbine; the Soviet 7.62x39mm Model 1943 cartridge used in the SKS, AK-47 and other military weapons; and the 5.56x45mm (.223 Remington) developed for the AR-15/M16 U.S. military rifle and since adapted to a wide range of sporting guns.

Auto-Ordnance Model 27A-1 & Ruger Police Carbine

most elite units (the MP44, later renamed StG44) made a powerful impression on Germany's enemies, who adapted most of its principles into a postwar, self-loading rifle design. Its designation, ***Sturmgewehr****, which was allegedly given it by Adolf Hitler himself, means "Assault Rifle." The name was eventually applied to a broad class of related weapons currently in military use around the globe. Intended for combat at ranges of 400 yards or less, the StG-44 has proven the most enduring rifle design to emerge from World War II in terms of its effect upon subsequent military weapons development. By the late 1950s, self-loading rifles had come into virtually worldwide issue among military forces, with only the poorest nations still clinging to their bolt-action designs for general issue.*

Self-loading rifle development in the postwar era took two distinct paths. Some countries followed the lead of the wartime Garand and Tokarev rifles by developing large, powerful self-loading "battle rifles," which used the same (or similar) full-power rounds as the last generation of military bolt-action rifles. These weapons had to be large and heavy enough to handle the stresses imposed by firing such powerful cartridges. Big battle rifles—the U.S. M14, the Belgian-designed FN FAL, the German-designed G3—are all typical of this design trend.

The second design path for postwar military self-loading rifles followed the trail-blazing ***Avtomat*** *and* ***Sturmgewehr*** *prototypes, creating self-loading rifles firing smaller cartridges of intermediate size and power. These cartridges were consistent with shorter, lighter and handier weapons capable of fully-automatic fire, albeit by sacrificing the range and long-distance* *power and accuracy possible with the larger battle rifles.*

The most significant postwar intermediate cartridge has been the Soviet 7.62x39mm, followed by the 5.56x45mm (.223) cartridge developed in the U.S. in the late 1950s for the AR-15 (M16) rifle and since used in many other military assault rifles. A third intermediate round, the 5.45x39mm, appeared in Soviet service with the modified Kalashnikov AK-74 assault rifle from 1974 onward. The 5.45x39mm cartridge has since been adopted by Russia's military service and has gradually supplanted the 7.62x39mm assault-rifle cartridge, especially in areas formerly under Soviet influence.

Weapons of the intermediate-power, selective-fire type, generally referred to as assault rifles, have become standard issue in virtually every army the world over. Many countries, however, retain smaller quantities of the older, larger battle rifles that use full-power cartridges for such specialized duties as sniping. Other elite troops continue to make good use of the increased power these big rifles offer compared to the smaller, handier assault rifles.

Self-loading rifles first appeared in commercial use for sale to private citizens. Not bound by military specifications in terms of existing ammunition supplies, designers of semiautomatic rifles aimed at sportsmen had much more freedom in design. John Browning, the world's most brilliant firearms designer, created several highly successful self-loading designs for commercial exploitation prior to World War I, notably the Remington Model 8 centerfire rifle, the Auto-22 rimfire rifle and the Auto-5 shotgun. During its decades-long manufacturing run, Remington sold about

M14 & MAS-49/56

Norinco MAK-90

60,000 Model 8 rifles and another 56,091 improved Model 81s—no mean feat in a period that saw a major depression and two world wars. Winchester also introduced promising self-loading rifle designs, specifically the Model 1905, 1907 and 1910. These rifles featured an unlocked-breech or blowback design. For this line of related guns, a talented designer named Thomas Johnson decided to use cartridges specially designed for, and unique to, these guns. Winchester's self-loading rifles sold well for the times, with slightly more than 100,000 built by the 1940s.

With the end of World War II, a large demand arose within the postwar commercial market for semiautomatic sporting rifles. In addition to surplus sales of these rifles to civilian shooters and collectors, rifle manufacturers developed a number of excel-

Norinco L1A1 Sporter & M14

lent new self-loading designs specifically for sporting use. These included Remington's Model 740 and the improved Model 7400. The Browning BAR (not to be confused with the infantry squad automatic weapon mentioned above) appeared in 1967 and remains in production. Sturm, Ruger and Company has also built several outstanding semiautomatic rifles, including the Model 44, the Mini-14 (and similar Mini Thirty) and, most recently, the Police Carbine.

Another direction taken by commercial semiautomatic rifles concerning ammunition is the rimfire cartridge, usually the .22 Long Rifle. The Auto-22 (designed by Browning) and Marlin's Model 60 have had impressive success in this field. Other self-loading rimfire classics have included Winchester's elegant Model 63, Remington's innovative Nylon 66 and Ruger's Model 10/22.

A final trend in self-loading rifles for commercial sale to private citizens is the development of "sporterized" versions of arms created originally for military service. Typically, the sporterization process involves reworking the receiver mechanism to make fully-automatic firing impossible. Since 1989, the elimination of such military-style features as high-capacity magazines, pistol grips, flash suppressors and bayonet lugs has been widespread. Sporterized versions of military designs have included, at one time or another, various AK models, the M14, AR-10/15/M16 variants, the FAL, the Heckler & Koch G3, the similar Spanish CETME, and several SIG self-loading rifles.

Barring any radical advancements in the field of ammunition, self-loading rifles will undoubtedly provide most of the world's military armaments for the foreseeable future. In terms of non-military shooting enthusiasts and collectors, the future of the self-loading rifle is cloudy at best. Many governments have severely restricted or outlawed private ownership of self-loading rifles, particularly the fully-automatic variety. The history of the self-loading rifle in the decades to come will undoubtedly depend as much upon political and legislative events as it will upon technical and mechanical advances.

Brno ZKM 611

The AR-7

The AR-7, originally a creation of the ArmaLite firm, dates from 1959, when it emerged from the fertile mind of Eugene Stoner (see the following entry for more details about ArmaLite and its history). In the early 1950s, the U.S. Air Force—and especially the Strategic Air Command (SAC)—led the search for a survival rifle designed to arm air crews forced down over enemy territory. Such a weapon would, they felt, outperform the Model 1911A1 pistols then in general issue, which many servicemen found too heavy and difficult to shoot accurately. The Air Force demanded that any survival rifle they considered for adoption must be compact and lightweight, while at the same time accurate and powerful. To meet these seemingly contradictory requirements, Eugene Stoner created the AR-5 Survival Rifle, which took the form of a bolt-action takedown rifle in .22 Hornet caliber whose component parts all fit into the hollow buttstock. The Air Force liked what it saw and took modest quantities of the AR-5 into service along with a combination .22 Hornet rifle/.410 gauge shotgun known as the M6 Scout (made by Springfield, Inc.)

Eugene Stoner then developed a semiautomatic version of the AR-5 for sale to private firearms enthusiasts. This rifle, which was chambered in the popular .22LR round, retained the unique takedown/storage feature of the Air Force survival model. Adoption of the .22LR, however, led to considerable loss of power. Whereas the .22 Hornet could drive a 45-grain bullet to a muzzle velocity of 2,700 feet per second or more, the .22LR could muster less than half that. Still, the

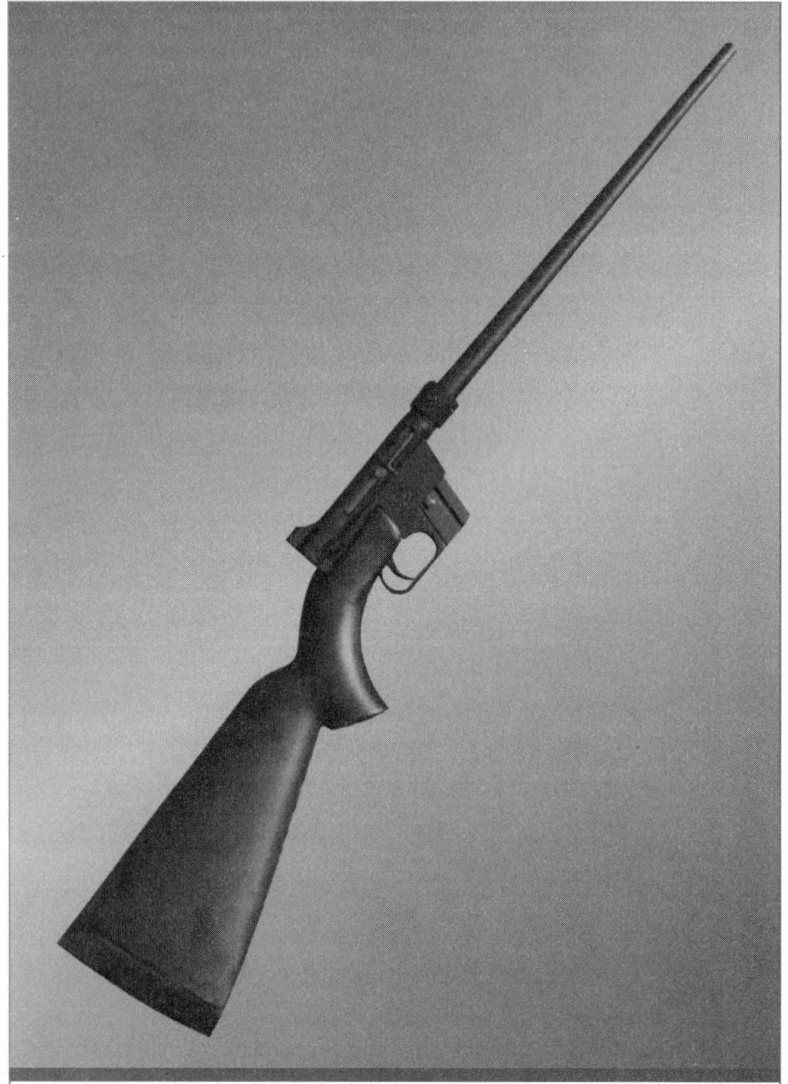

The AR-7 is a rugged rifle well suited to arduous outdoor use.

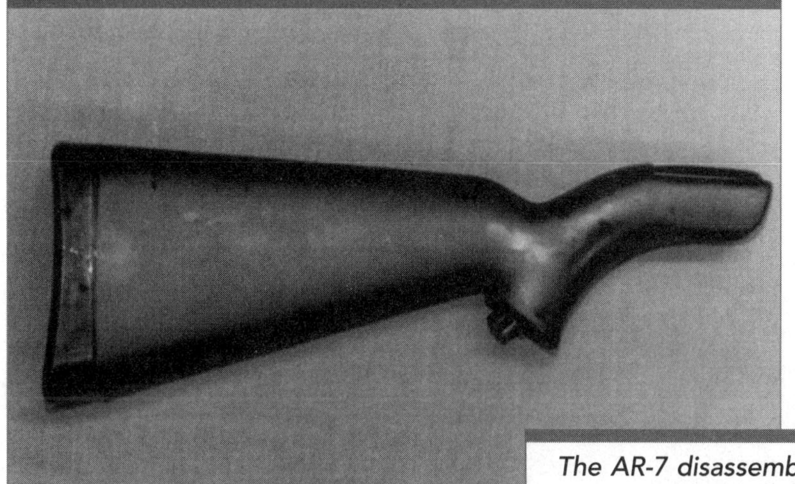

The AR-7's component parts all fit into the buttstock, which is less than 18 inches long, corrosion-resistant, and can even float.

Advertised as the AR-7, or "ArmaLite Explorer,: Stoner's modified rifle finally went into production in 1959. When Stoner left the company two years later, ArmaLite kept the AR-7 in production until 1973, when Charter Arms took over its manufacture for the next 17 years. Survival Arms (Cocoa, Florida) then bought the AR-7 design and produced the rifle from 1992 to 1997. Henry Repeating Arms Company (Brooklyn, NY) acquired the AR-7

.22LR round is no toy. It is accurate, comparatively quiet, widely available and inexpensive. Switching to this less powerful cartridge also helped designers in modifying the AR-5 design to semiautomatic operation without having to include the complicated breech-locking mechanism required by the .22 Hornet. In short, the new .22LR chambering was a wise choice.

The AR-7 disassembles into the following components (top to bottom): watertight rubber buttplate, barrel, hollow plastic buttstock, receiver and magazine. This Model AR-7 was made by Charter Arms, one of several manufacturers of this rifle during its 50-year history.

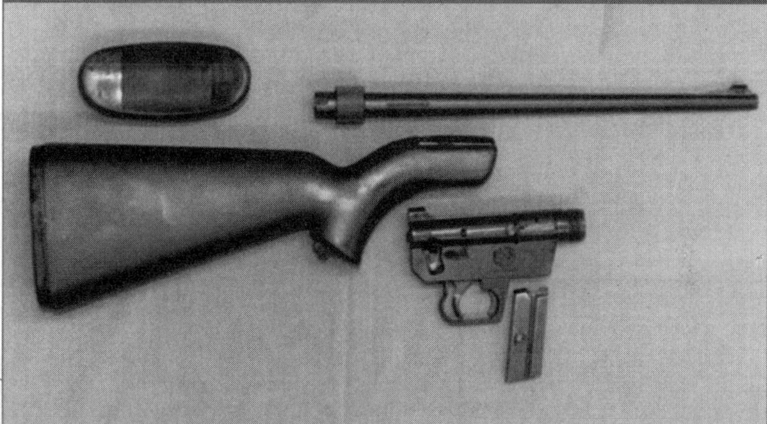

The only real competition for the AR-7 is Marlin's Model 70P, the so-called "Papoose." Its barrel can be unscrewed to shorten the rifle for storage (photo courtesy of Marlin Firearms Company).

in 1998 and, as of this writing, continues to produce it.

The most interesting feature of the AR-7 is, of course, the way it disassembles and stores. The best way to go about this is to unload the gun by removing the magazine, then pulling back the operating handle to eject any round that might be left in the firing chamber. Next, loosen the threaded ring at the front of the receiver, allowing the barrel and receiver to separate. The receiver (or action) is then lifted up and out of the stock. The rubber buttplate is now removed from the stock, which has been hollowed out to receive the barrel, magazine and action. After the three major assemblies have been put into the buttstock, the buttplate is replaced on the rear end of the stock and sealed firmly. The result is a short, lightweight, durable package that can even float on water. To save weight, the stock is made of lightweight ABS, or cycolac plastic, and being hollow, it becomes lighter still. Three color options are available for this hollow plastic stock. At various times in the AR-7's long history, these have been silver, black and camouflage (Henry Repeating Arms now offers only the silver finish). Interestingly, no major manufacturer has come up with a truly competitive product, the closest being Marlin's Model 70P "Papoose," with its takedown barrel that divides into two pieces.

Still another weight-saving measure is the AR-7 barrel, which is aluminum on the outside and has a rifled insert made of steel. This composite barrel design works perfectly with the relatively low-pressure .22LR cartridge; in fact, Smith & Wesson uses the same technology in its Model 317 AirLite revolver. Adapting this technology to larger, more powerful guns proved elusive for almost 40 years following Stoner's first successful attempt. Originally, Stoner tried to use a similar type of barrel construction with his early prototype assault rifles (1956-1957); but his composite barrel was unable to handle the more powerful cartridges, forcing Stoner to use a conventional all-steel barrel and accept the added weight. In late 1998, Remington announced it had solved the problems inherent in producing composite barrels for large-caliber rifles. As for the .22 Long Rifle caliber, the AR-7's composite barrel has never been a problem, offering a significant weight savings compared to the all-steel barrel.

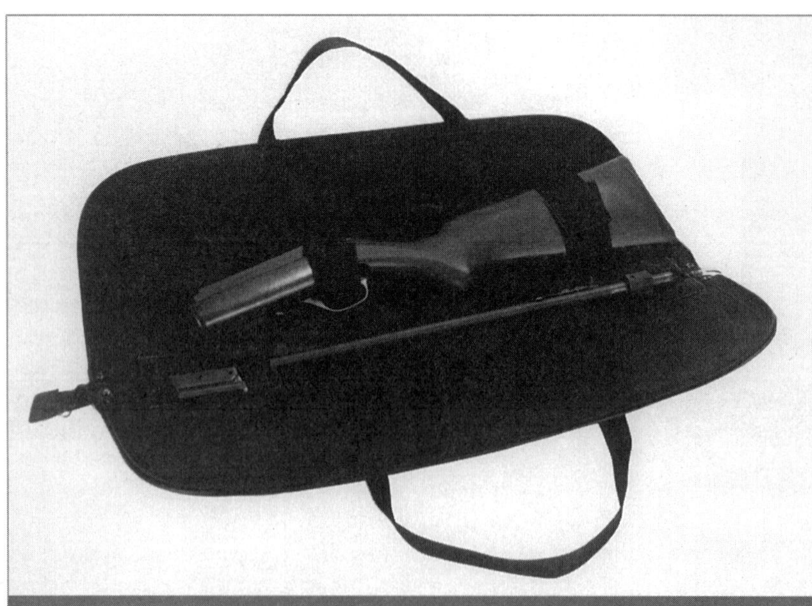
Once its barrel is unscrewed, the Marlin Model 70P "Papoose" stores in a padded carrying case (photo courtesy of Marling Firearms Company).

Between 1964 and 1970, ArmaLite also made a "Custom" version of the AR-7. It differed from the standard model by having a more conventional fixed wooden (walnut) buttstock. While less common than the standard AR-7, its scarcity has made it a collector's premium. During its AR-7 production run, Survival Arms also made a similar wooden-stocked version, called the "Wildcat." For those who seek a useful, portable survival rifle, my recommendation is to pass on the AR-7 Custom and Wildcat and invest in a hollow AR-7 with the plastic stock.

Make no mistake, the AR-7 is no toy. It has good sights consisting of a prominent square front post sight on a ramp and useful rear aperture ("peep") sight adjustable for elevation. As for accuracy, it shoots about as well as any .22LR semiautomatic sporting rifle tested for this book. Fully assembled, it balances well and is about the size of the ultra-handy U.S. M1 Carbine. When stowed away in its padded carrying case, the AR-7 is less than a cubit long (the distance from an adult elbow to the tip of the middle finger), which means it stores easily in a car, truck or boat. Despite the frequent changes in manufacturers, the AR-7 should not be considered a flawed or unreliable design. Conceived as a handy survival rifle, it serves admirably in that role, while shooting well enough to appeal to most consumers intent on acquiring a good, general-purpose .22LR caliber rifle.

The AR-7 (left) is almost the same length as the ultra-handy U.S. M1 Carbine (right) and is even lighter.

AR-7

	AR-7
Overall Length	34.5 inches (open); 16.5 (Stowed)
Barrel Length	16.0 inches
Weight	2.5 pounds
Years Produced	1959-present
Manufacturers	Various (see text)
Caliber & Capacity	.22 Long Rifle/8 rounds (25 rounds in a "Sporter" variant formerly offered by Survival Arms)

ArmaLite AR-10

The ArmaLite AR-10 story began in 1952, when Charles Sullivan and George Dorchester founded the ArmaLite firm in Hollywood, California. Two years later the Fairchild Engine & Airplane Corporation bought the company and formed an ArmaLite Division to promote a series of then-radical rifle designs. After hiring Eugene Stoner as its chief engineer, the new ArmaLite firm developed a whole series of self-loading rifles with mostly plastic furniture, including an AR-5 Survival Rifle (for the U.S. Air Force) and its commercial equivalent, the AR-7 Explorer (covered above). Stoner, who was a U.S. Marine Corps veteran, developed an interest in rotating-bolt, selective-fire military assault rifles using a direct impingement of propellant gas onto the bolt carrier via a narrow tube that ran alongside (or above) the barrel. The first AR-10 prototypes appeared in 1955, followed by a series of tests, until ArmaLite was ready to market the gun. Artillerie-Inrichtingen of Zaandam, Holland, took on production of the AR-10 under license with ArmaLite, which also created a network of various importers/distributors for the AR-10 (including a relatively new firm, called Interarmco, which evolved into the well-known Interarms). Unfortunately, the timing for the AR-10 was not good. The FN FAL from Belgium and the M14 from America both had superior designs.

The gas tube on the AR-10 is bent slightly in order to lengthen the path the gas must take and also to follow the contours of the barrel.

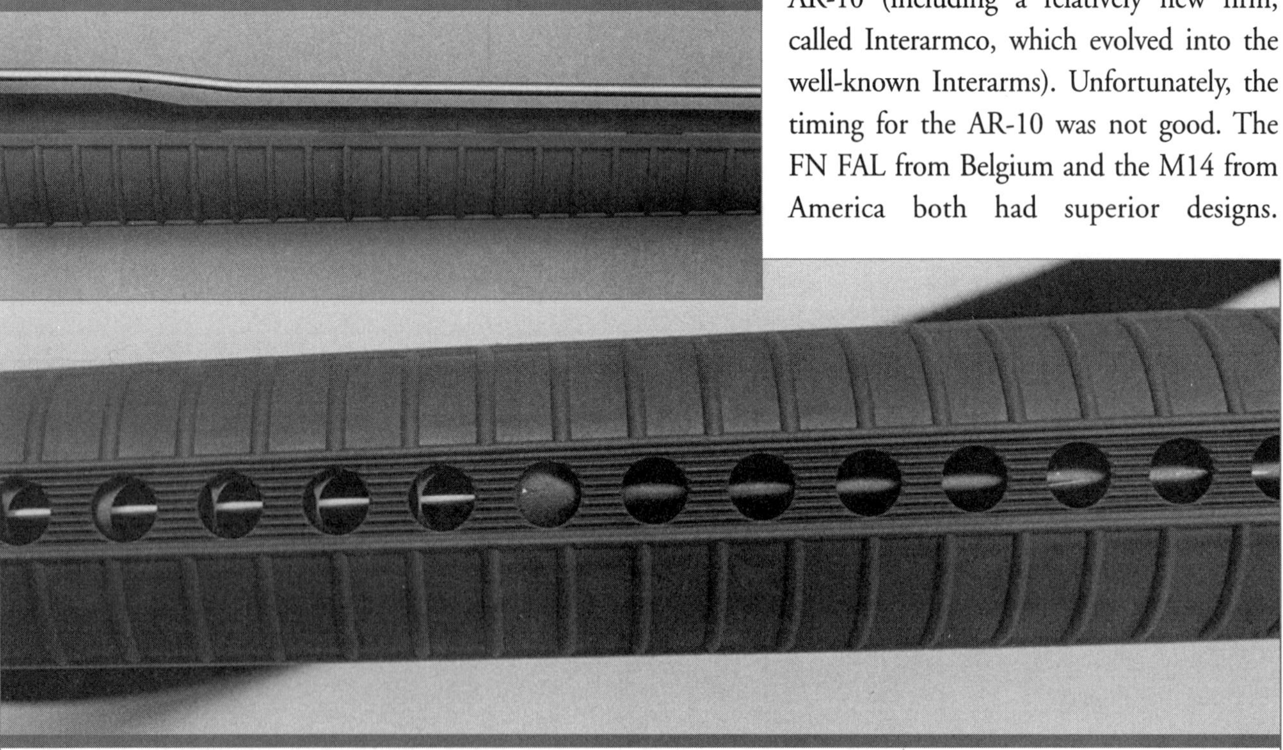

Like other self-loading rifles designed by Eugene Stoner, the ArmaLite AR-10A4 employs a gas tube to operate the rifle's reloading mechanism.

Maintenance is easy with the ArmaLite AR-10A4, especially when compared to the complicated disassembly procedures required with early self-loading rifles.

Because it is limited to semiautomatic fire (one shot for each pull of the trigger), the ArmaLite AR-10'' manual safety includes only two settings, "SAFE" and "FIRE."

Moreover, they were already in full-scale production and had a momentum of initial orders to work with. While the AR-10 attracted some interest in South Africa, Nicaragua and Holland, the FAL outsold it in all three areas. And in Sudan, Portugal, Burma and Guatemala, the AR-10 proved a commercial failure.

Ultimately, Fairchild (parent firm of ArmaLite) became discouraged with this lack of success and, in 1959, licensed the entire ArmaLite rifle development program over to Colt. Two years later, Fairchild abandoned ArmaLite altogether, enabling Colt to reap huge benefits from the development of a new version of the AR-10, called the AR-15, or M16 Series, which sold in the millions. Meanwhile, ArmaLite was reorganized in 1961 as ArmaLite, Inc., now located in Costa Mesa, California. The new company first pinned its hopes on the AR-16, a 7.62mm (.308 caliber) rifle designed by Eugene Stoner. Nothing much came of this design, with only three prototypes being made. Discouraged by ArmaLite's lack of progress, Stoner left the company in 1961 and joined Cadillac Gage company, where he eventually developed the innovative Stoner 63 Weapons System.

ArmaLite next pinned its hopes on the AR-18, a selective-fire assault rifle in 5.56mm (.223), a scaled-down version of the AR-16 (just as the AR-15 had been a scaled-down AR-10). The AR-18 showed considerable promise, performing in competition with the AR-15/M16 at only a fraction of its cost. The AR-18 featured a conventional tappet-type gas system and stamped steel receiver as opposed to the direct-impingement gas system and machined aluminum-alloy receiver found in the AR-15/M16. This made the AR-18 more suitable for production with simple machine tools in contrast to the AR-15's complicated

The muzzle brake on the ArmaLite AR-10A4 works extremely well, blasting large objects off the author's bench during range testing of the rifle.

manufacturing process. U.S. Army tests in 1964 and 1965 revealed that the AR-18 did indeed have merit, but the army was unfortunately heavily committed to the M16, hence it could not order large quantities of the AR-18. ArmaLite then licensed its production of the AR-18 to Howa in Japan, which produced small quantities in 1872-1973. But Japan's constitution prevented it from exporting war materials to countries at war, causing Howa to drop the AR-18. The foreign license then passed to Sterling in England (1976-1978), which did eventually modify the rifle into a folding-butt design. Further modifications included the SA-80 and the SR-88, both introduced by CIS (Chartered Industries of Singapore). These rifles proved modestly successful, arming Singapore's armed forces and being sold to various other countries, but ArmaLite failed to profit from these sales and the company folded.

As shown, the ArmaLite AR-10A4 breaks open, M16-style, to allow quick, easy access to the bolt and other internal operating parts.

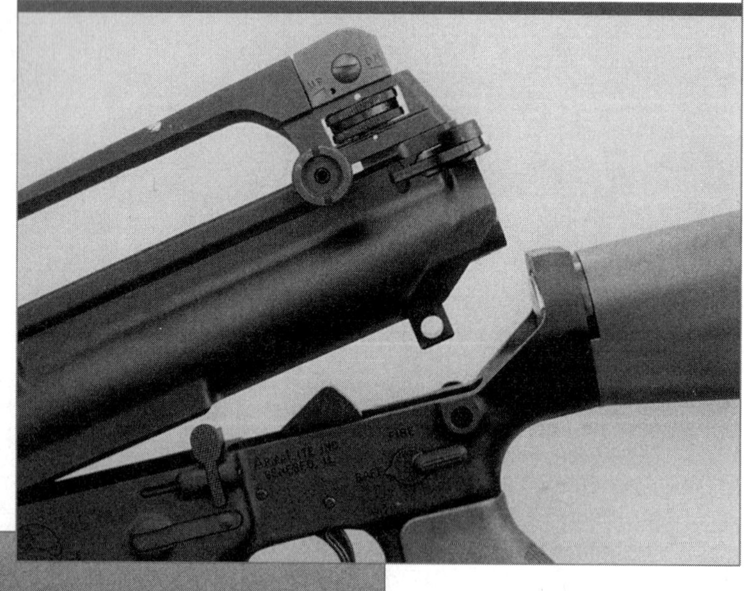

The bolt found on the AR-10A4 is much larger than the AR-15's/M16's because of the larger, more powerful .308 cartridge it fires.

Despite its failure in the marketplace, the AR-10's original design was, nevertheless, an interesting gun. Those who liked the handling and features of the AR-15 (M16), however, distrusted its light 5.56mm (.223) cartridge, but they found the idea of an AR-15 type rifle in 7.62x51mm (.308) caliber highly attractive. The idea of manufacturing such a rifle appealed to various people, notably Knight's Manufacturing (Vero Beach, Florida), which retained Eugene Stoner as a consultant and reintroduced a 7.62mm version of the AR-15. Thus did a reconstituted ArmaLite company reintroduce the rifle in 1995, calling it the "AR-10A4."

The bolt on the AR-10 has seven locking lugs, plus a plunger-style ejector and claw extractor.

The main difference between ArmaLite's newest version of the original AR-10 and the military-style M16 series is its flattop receiver with integral Weaver-type scope rail. Shooters armed with an AR-10B could now mount a much wider variety of scopes than was possible with the AR-15/M16, whose fixed carrying handle got in the way. On the other hand, the AR-10B could be ordered with an easily detachable carrying handle (located atop the receiver), which included an aperture-type rear sight. The AT-10A4 also has a case deflector located on the rear surface of the ejection port as a protection for left-handed shooters who might otherwise be struck by spent cartridge cases. With its rounded handguard and spent shell deflector, the AR-10B now resembles an overgrown M16A2, except that it lacks the bolt assist plunger found on most AR-15 series rifles.

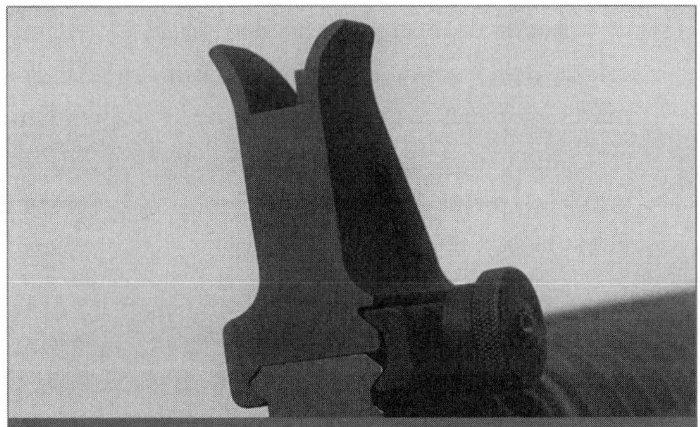

A front sight assembly can be attached to the ArmaLite AR-10A4 rifle. When a telescopic sight is attached, the front sight partially blocks the view and must be removed.

Testing the AR-10B for accuracy produced excellent results. My best 3-shot benchrested group fired from 100 yards spanned 0.90 inches. Indeed, every group that was fired using iron sights measured less than 1 1/4 inches. The test rifle also provided an amazing level of consistency with several different types of Federal, Hornady and Winchester commercial-grade ammunition. Some guns shoot particularly well with one brand of ammunition but deliver mediocre performances with

The ArmaLite AR-10A4 offers an iron-sight option in which a carrying handle with rear sight attached is bolted to the scope rail.

This close-up view of the right side of the receiver on the ArmaLite AR-10A4 reveals the scope rail, dust cover in its open (down) position, and brass deflector at the rear of the ejection port, which prevents left-handed shooters from being struck by ejected cartridge cases.

or a standard Springfield Armory M1A in 7.62mm caliber. It all boils down to this: the ArmaLite AR-10B makes a top choice for shooters who like the handling, looks and performance of the .223 caliber M16/AR-15 but who prefer the superior power of a 7.62mm NATO (.308 Winchester) cartridge.

With the rifle unloaded and the mechanism unhinged for disassembly, the AR-10's charging handle (top) and bolt (bottom) are easily removed from the receiver.

others. The AR-10B, however, excelled with every type of ammunition we tried. Moreover, its reliability proved flawless with all types of 7.62x51mm (.308) ammunition tested.

Today, the ArmaLite AR-10B costs less than $1500, which means that it sells for about the same as a .223 caliber Colt Sporter AR-15 variant

The ArmaLite AR-10A4 is extremely accurate, delivering 100-yard benchrested accuracy of one minute of angle (MOA) or even better (as shown here).

The ArmaLite AR-10A4 (shown with its top handguard removed) reveals the gas tube atop the barrel. Note also the reflective inner lining, which radiates heat back toward the barrel and away from the shooter's hand.

ARMALITE AR-10B

	AR-10B
Overall Length	41.0 inches
Barrel Length	20.0 inches
Weight	9.6 pounds
Years Produced	1995-present
Caliber/Capacity	7.62x51mm (.308)/5 or 10 rounds

Armscor M-1600 Auto Rifle

The M-1600 Auto Rifle, a product of the Arms Corporation of the Philippines (located in Manila) is now known as "Armscor." The company began by manufacturing revolvers in both rimfire and centerfire chamberings, from which a flourishing business has evolved. Since the late 1970s, Armscor has built a .22 Long Rifle caliber semiautomatic rifle, called the Model 20, which has the simple blowback operation common to .22LR caliber rifles. The Model 20 appears in several different versions, plus a military-replica rifle resembling such famous weapons as the M16, PPSh-41, AK-47, and so on. The Model 1600 we tested was the M16 with features common to Armscor's rimfire rifles, including wooden stocks, detachable box magazines, and a simple blowback mechanism. The stocks, made of Philippine mahogany hardwood, are sized for adult shooters, but being light in weight they also work reasonably well for shooters of smaller stature. The stock on the M-1600 Auto Rifle fired for this book was painted matte black (to resemble the black plastic stock on the M16), but it's still wooden like the other Armscor rifles.

The Armscor M-1600 is shown with the top of its barrel exposed, unlike the M16, which employs an all-enveloping handguard.

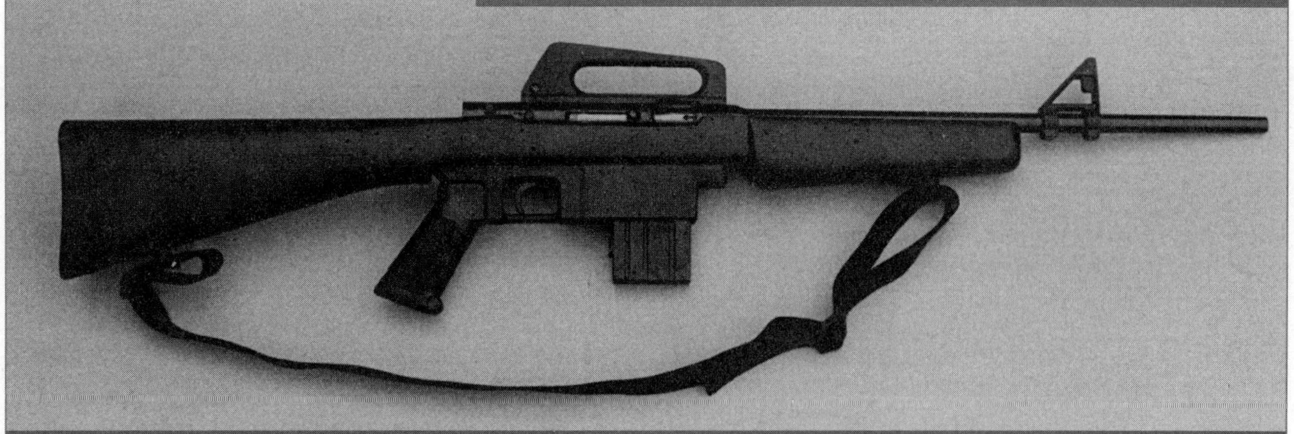

The Armscor M-1600 may be fitted with a smooth barrel (shown) or a muzzle brake may be mounted at the end of the barrel. While it is styled after the famous U.S. military M16, the M-1600 is not an exact copy. It has, however, been optimized for the .22 Long Rifle cartridge.

The Armscor M-1600 safety is located on the right rear portion of the receiver, forward to fire ("F") and rearward to safe ("S"). Note the carrying handle, which closely resembles the M16's, and the cartridge-case deflector immediately behind the ejection port.

At one time or another, I've fired an Armscor Model 20 rifle, an AK-47 lookalike and most recently the M-1600 Auto Rifle. Test results with the Armscor rifles included 3-shot groups, benchrested, measuring less than 1 1/3 inches from 50 yards. Reliability was excellent, especially for a rimfire rifle. Even though an occasional jam is to be expected with a .22LR caliber autoloading rifle, the M-1600 we tested never jammed, even after repeated firing. Still, the long profile and rimmed case of the .22LR round are not conducive to reliable feeding. That makes meticulous cleaning a must, followed by a very light application of gun oil (too much oil will attract dirt and powder fouling) after every shooting session with a rimfire rifle.

Like most rifles that fire the .22 Long Rifle cartridge, the Armscor models are somewhat fussy about which particular brand and configuration of ammunition they use for optimum reliability and accuracy, so it is wise to experiment. Fortunately, doing this is not too difficult with a .22 Long Rifle, either in terms of recoil or cost. This particular Model 1600 was fired with virtually every brand we tested with equally commendable results.

The Armscor M-1600's accuracy is reflected in this 1.3-inch group using Aguila Super Extra ammunition. The author conducted these tests with guns chambered for the .22 Long Rifle.

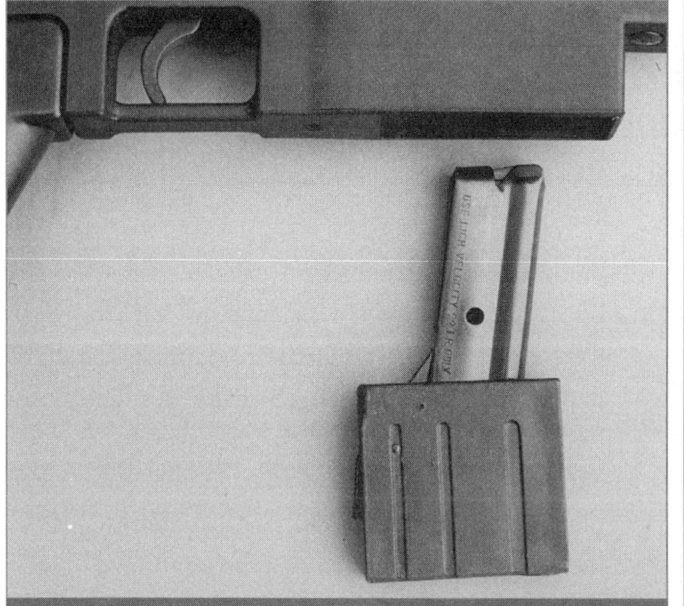

The Armscor M-1600 magazine is surrounded by an enlarged shroud so that it more closely resembles the M16's much longer magazine (designed to hold the longer .223 cartridge).

The Armscor M-1600 magazine release is located at the trailing edge of the magazine shroud and is convenient for both right-handed and left-handed shooters.

The Armscor M-1600's wide magazine shroud and narrow magazine make possible a fast magazine load, similar to the beveled magazine wells found on some competition automatic pistols.

ARMSCOR M-1600 AUTO RIFLE

	M-1600
Overall Length	38.5 inches
Barrel Length	18.25 inches
Weight	6.2 pounds
Years Produced	1987-present
Caliber/Capacity	.22 Long Rifle/10 rounds

Auto-Ordnance Model 27A-1 Thompson

The Auto-Ordnance Model 27A-1 Thompson is a recreation of the infamous Thompson submachine gun, or "Tommy Gun," the favorite of many gangsters in bygone years. It was also a favorite of the U.S. Marines and British Commandos. The original Thompson submachine gun was designed by John T. Thompson and developed during World War I as a so-call "Trench Broom." It was a little late getting into production to join that war, however, and has been designated a "Class 3" weapon in the U.S. since passage of restrictive legislation in 1934. The Federal Firearms Act requires that any fully-automatic and/or short-barreled weapon be registered with the government and a $200 transfer fee paid. The sales transaction itself must be handled by a Federal Firearms License holder who has a Class 3 license, all of which can create considerable paperwork. In an effort to make the Thompson design more accessible to the average firearms enthusiast, the Auto-Ordnance company introduced in 1985 its Model 27A-1 variation. It was identical to the notorious "Tommy Gun," except that it didn't fire fully automatically and its barrel was 6 inches longer.

Other features of the Model 27A-1 included a quality hardwood buttstock, pistol grip and vertical forend. The finned barrel came complete with a Cutts Compensator at the muzzle. The cocking handle lay atop the receiver and was slotted to give

The Auto-Ordnance Model 27A-1 (top) is well positioned to capture some of the booming pistol-caliber carbine business. Another example of this genre is the Ruger Police Carbine in 9mm Parabellum or .40 S&W caliber (bottom). The Model 27A-1, however, fires the .45 ACP cartridge favored by many handgun experts.

the shooter a clear view of the front sight. A manual safety located on the left side of the receiver, just above the pistol grip, pivoted forward to fire and back to its safe setting. The rear sight was adjustable for ranges up to 600 yards in 100-yard increments. The magazine release was a large C-shaped piece of blued steel located on the left side of the receiver, ahead of the triggerguard. When the shooter pushed up on the checkered rear portion of the magazine release, the magazine dropped slightly and could then be pulled free.

Among the most recognizable features on most of these "Tommy Gun" models was the Cutts Compensator located at the end of the muzzle. Equipped with four gas ports that vent upwards, this device holds the muzzle down during fully-automatic fire, reducing the tendency to "climb," which is the ruination of accuracy for many automatic weapons. The Auto-Ordnance company has continued this Thompson tradition by including a Cutts Compensator on the Model 27A-1. Though it is not as functional as it was on the original fully-automatic Thompson, the compensator makes the Model 27A-1 look like an original except for its longer barrel.

Auto-Ordnance currently offers several variations on the Model 27A-1 theme. In addition to

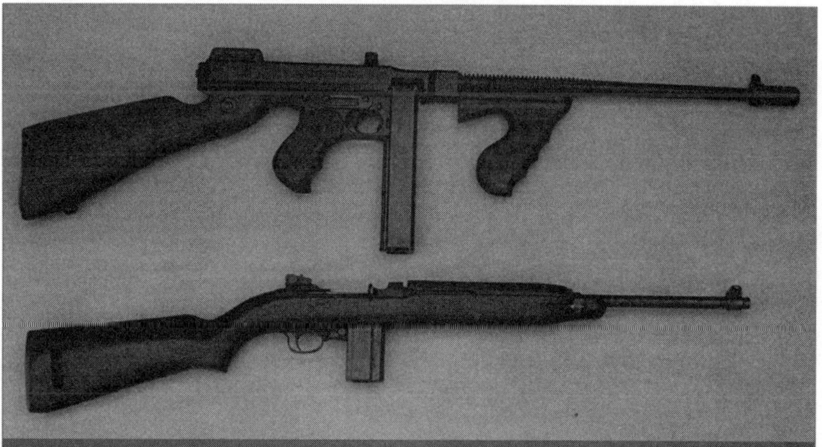

The Auto-Ordnance Model 27A-1 (top) is about the same size as the popular M1 Carbine (bottom), but it is bulkier and much heavier.

Because it fires the .45 ACP cartridge, the Auto-Ordnance Model 27A-1 is a useful companion to the many Model 1911-type pistols offered by various manufacturers, including Auto-Ordnance's own Model 1911A1 (top).

The Auto-Ordnance Model 27A-1 can outshoot most pistols in this caliber. This 3-shot, 50-yard offhand group measuring 3.1 inches would be difficult, if not impossible, to surpass with a .45 caliber handgun.

the standard model, with its dual pistol grips and finned barrel spanning half its length, there's a military model with a plain, unfinned barrel and plain rear sight. There's also a Lightweight model with a finned barrel and aluminum alloy frame, and a Thompson M1 (styled after the M-1 version used in World War II) with a side-cocking handle, horizontal forend and smooth, unfinned barrel.

The carbine, while on the heavy side, handles nicely. Its weight, though, helps control recoil. The sights, which are better suited for rapid target engagement at close distances than for long-range accuracy, are quite appropriate. Despite the less-than-ideal sighting arrangements, results with a Lightweight Model 27A-1 tested well for accuracy. Results typically included a 3.1-inch offhand group fired from a distance of 50 yards. And at 100 yards the two best benchrested 3-shot groups measured 3.6 inches and 4.4 inches, respectively.

As for reliability, the Model 27A-1 performed best with standard military-style ball ammunition using 230-grain FMJ bullets. The factory advises against +P ammunition (because it is potentially too powerful), and discourages reloads using cast lead bullets (because shavings can build up in the compensator) and hollowpoints, which do not always travel into the firing chamber over the long feed ramp with consistency. Limited testing with ammunition containing hollowpoint bullets, however, revealed no particular problems. Moreover, the greatly extended barrel length of the Model 27A-1

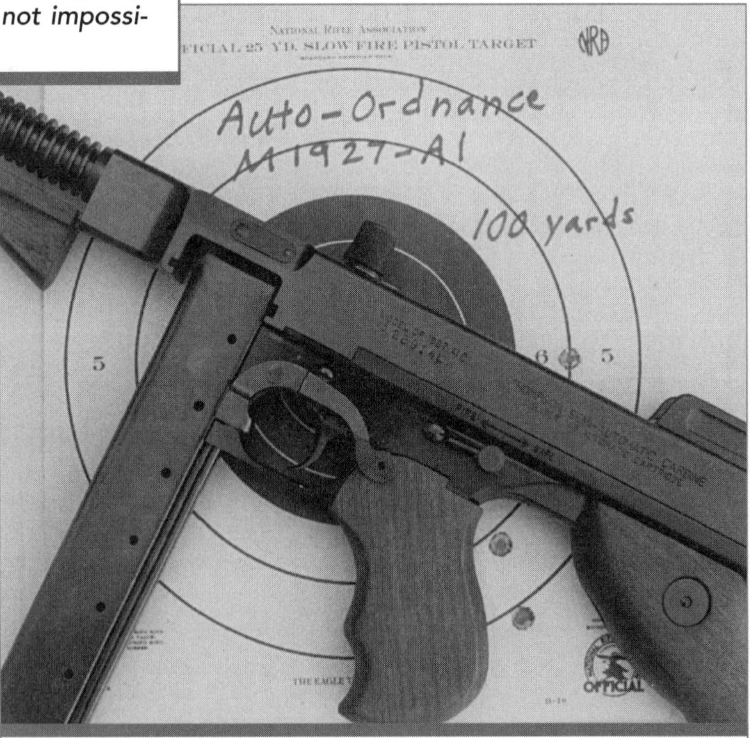

The Auto-Ordnance Model 27A-1 tested by the author produced 3-shot, 100-yard benchrested groups as small as 3.6 inches, a much better result than with a pistol in the same caliber.

compared to a pistol guaranteed that virtually any modern hollowpoint round that was fed through the carbine would expand upon hitting flesh—a real plus when firing a relatively low-powered pistol cartridge. The .45 ACP may have a fearsome reputation, true, but it exists only in comparison with other handgun ammunition. By rifle standards, the .45 ACP is nothing to boast about. Even the .30 carbine round, which is termed puny by many, possesses about twice the energy level of the .45 ACP. Those who use a Model 27A-1 that feeds hollowpoint ammunition reliably should by all means use that instead of FMJ "hardball" for self-defense purposes. Like all handgun rounds, the .45 ACP needs all the help it can get in order to stop an assailant reliably.

For close-range shooting the Auto-Ordnance Model 27A-1 employs a battle sight setting.

Once the range increases beyond 25 yards or so, better results come with the rear sight raised and adjusted to point of aim.

Purists rightly insist that the Model 27A-1 is no longer a "Tommy Gun." It is instead a pistol-caliber carbine that is easy to handle, fun to shoot and, except for its longer barrel, almost identical in appearance to the original "Tommy Gun."

AUTO-ORDNANCE MODEL 27A-1 THOMPSON

	MODEL 27A-1
Overall Length	42.0 inches
Barrel Length	16.0 inches
Weight	11.5 pounds (standard model) • 10 pounds (Lightweight)
Years Produced	1985-present
Caliber/Capacity	.45 ACP/10, 20 or 30 rounds

Beretta AR-70 Series

In 1965, the Pietro Beretta firm of Gardone Valtrompia, Italy, the world's oldest and perhaps most famous firearms manufacturer, recognized that lightweight, selective-fire assault rifles firing the 5.56x45mm (.223 Remington) cartridge represented the wave of the future in military armament. ArmaLite and Colt had already blazed the trail with the AR-15/M16, and Heckler & Koch of Germany was working on its own .223 caliber HK-33 (an adaptation of the company's enormously successful G3 service rifle). Meanwhile, FN of Belgium was creating the CAL, a downsized FAL with a modified locking system that was better suited to the .223 cartridge. So Beretta joined forces with SIG of Switzerland in the creation of a .223-caliber service rifle to compete in time for the military orders that were sure to come.

It was not until 1970, however, that Beretta announced its rifle—the AR-70—was ready for consideration (SIG had meanwhile gone its own separate way, eventually developing a .223 rifle series of its own). Beretta's AR70 departed considerably from the company's traditional practice of arduous hand-fitting and polished blued finishes; instead, it opted for the stamped metal technology developed by Nazi Germany late in World War II. SIG excelled in this same technology and was then working hard on its P220 pistol at about the same time Beretta was putting the finishing touches on it own rifle. The AR70 featured all-plastic handguards, pistol grips and buttstocks, as opposed to the wooden construction Beretta used previously on its long arms. There was also a selector switch to allow fully-automatic fire at a cyclic rate of

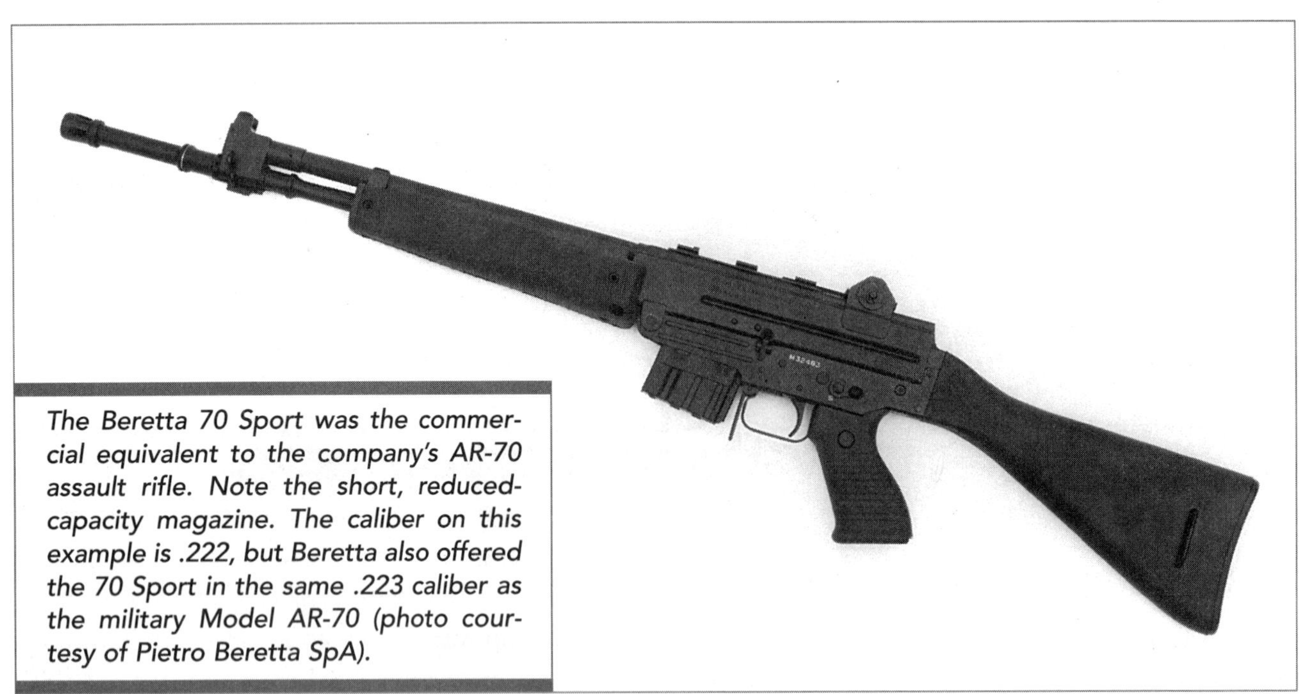

The Beretta 70 Sport was the commercial equivalent to the company's AR-70 assault rifle. Note the short, reduced-capacity magazine. The caliber on this example is .222, but Beretta also offered the 70 Sport in the same .223 caliber as the military Model AR-70 (photo courtesy of Pietro Beretta SpA).

Beretta's late-style AR70 rifle featured an improved handguard with a rounded cross-section. This series of rifles strongly resemble SIG's 500-series (Models 530, 540 and 550). Beretta and SIG worked on the designs together in the mid-to late 1960s (photo courtesy of Pietro Beretta SpA).

about 600 round per minute. This was considered by most experts to be an improvement over the M16/M16A1's hard-to-control cyclic rate of fire of some 900 rounds per minute. Another clever AR70 feature was a combination muzzle-brake/grenade launcher, somewhat like the French MAS-49/56 rifle. The protective handguard placed around the barrel of the AR70 was designed to shield the shooter's hand from heat. Later on, Beretta changed to a handguard with a round cross-section, in the manner of the later M16A2. Although the AR70 was already quite handy and lightweight, Beretta introduced a folding-stock version, called the SC-70, and later on an even smaller, abbreviated version (the SC70), which first appeared in 1974. The SC70's 12.6-inch barrel makes this rifle especially handy.

Despite its attractive appearance and advanced design features, the AR70 did not enjoy the success Beretta had envisaged. For one thing, the Italian army uncovered a major design flaw: the guide rails for the bolt were liable to warp in heavy service, causing the bolt to jam. As a result, orders for the AR70 from the Italian military were limited to one order for 1200 rifles, perhaps a few follow-up orders, and some small purchases by two Italian elite anti-terrorist units. Italy's air force favored the standard AR70, while the special forces went for the more compact folding-stock derivatives. Unfortunately, the smallest variant, the SC70, lost its grenade-launching capability along with some striking power and accuracy. The Malaysian armed forces bought 5,000 AR70s, and the Jordanian armed forces also ordered a few thousand. The bolt-jamming problems reported by the Italian army finished the AR70 as a serious competitor for international business in the booming market for military assault rifles, forcing Beretta to halt its production in 1983. A totally redesigned and improved rifle—the AR70/90—came on line in 1985. But that is not relevant to our story, because this gun was apparently earmarked almost entirely for the Italian army.

Soon after production of the AR70 stopped, Beretta decided to create a semiautomatic variant, called the "AR70 Sport" (or "70 Sport"). Beretta U.S.A. imported a modest quantity of these, in both full-sized rifle and short-barreled carbine

Beretta made the AR-70 in carbine form as the SC70 (also called the SCS70 or SC70 Short). Note the much shortened barrel and folding stock. This late model has the rounded handguard, replacing the earlier pattern with its triangular cross-section. This gun is similar in concept and layout to SIG's Model 552 "Commando" (photo courtesy to Pietro Beretta SpA).

variants, during the mid-1980s. The company also imported selective-fire AR70s and SC70s for sale to law-enforcement agencies in the U.S. These Beretta guns still show up from time to time, especially the 70 Sports, but the high prices are gradually reducing these rifles to collectors-only status.

As for its controls, the magazine release (a long lever) on the 70 Sport is located between the magazine well and the triggerguard. Extending down to about an inch below the triggerguard, the release must be pushed forward to drop the magazine, which makes this a very convenient control to operate. The manual safety lever (on 70 Sport variants restricted to semiautomatic fire) goes up and back, pointing to the number "1" for semiautomatic fire (one shot for each pull of the trigger) and to the letter "S" for the safe setting. In the selective-fire versions, the safety switch/fire selector points all the way up for automatic fire, down for safe, and midway between those two for single shots. The manual safety control is easily accessible for right-handed shooters who, while holding the pistol grip, simply extend the thumb. The cocking handle appears on the right side of the receiver, behind the handguard. It's large enough for positive actuation, even with a gloved hand.

The rifle sights are excellent, too. The front sight is a large post surrounded by two protective "ears," and the rear sight is an aperture ("peep") sight located well back on the receiver, close to the shooter's eye. The arrangement is well suited to quick acquisition and allows reasonable (but not target-grade) accuracy.

Interestingly, Beretta offered the 70 Sport in a .222 Remington version as well as the standard .223 Remington (5.56x45mm) military-caliber model. The .223 round was originally developed from the .222 by stretching the latter's cartridge case 2mm, thereby allowing greater power and scope for load development. Both cartridges use 55-grain bullets as their standard, though some .22s are loaded with 50-grain bullets instead. The .223 is sometimes loaded with slightly heavier bullets of 62 grains, which supposedly improves accuracy in some rifles, particularly at extended ranges. Compared to the .223, the .222 develops slightly less power in some loadings (notably Federal's), while Remington's own .222 loadings bear close comparisons with their .223 offerings. Obviously, the .222 cartridge has not experienced anywhere near the load development of the .223, which is not all that bad; indeed, there's been so much radical tinkering with the .223—including major changes in bullet configuration, rate of rifling twist in the barrel, and so forth—that some .223 rifle/ammunition combinations do not perform at all well together.

The 70 Sport in .222 or .223 caliber is a good performer for this rifle. I once fired a 3-shot, 100-yard benchrested group from a 70 Sport (chambered for the .222 cartridge) that measured 3.2 inches. Recoil was quite low, and I suspect the military version is quite controllable on full-auto compared with the M16A1, which I have fired on a fully automatic setting. In my opinion, the AR70 Sport also has better sights than the early M16 or M16A1, and without that annoying carrying handle. Alternate sighting arrangements thus become less problematic. The difficulties caused by warping bolts, which eventually caused this gun's demise, are not likely to show up among private enthusiasts or in police service. Anyone lucky enough to own one of these guns can rest assured that he has an excellent carbine on his hands.

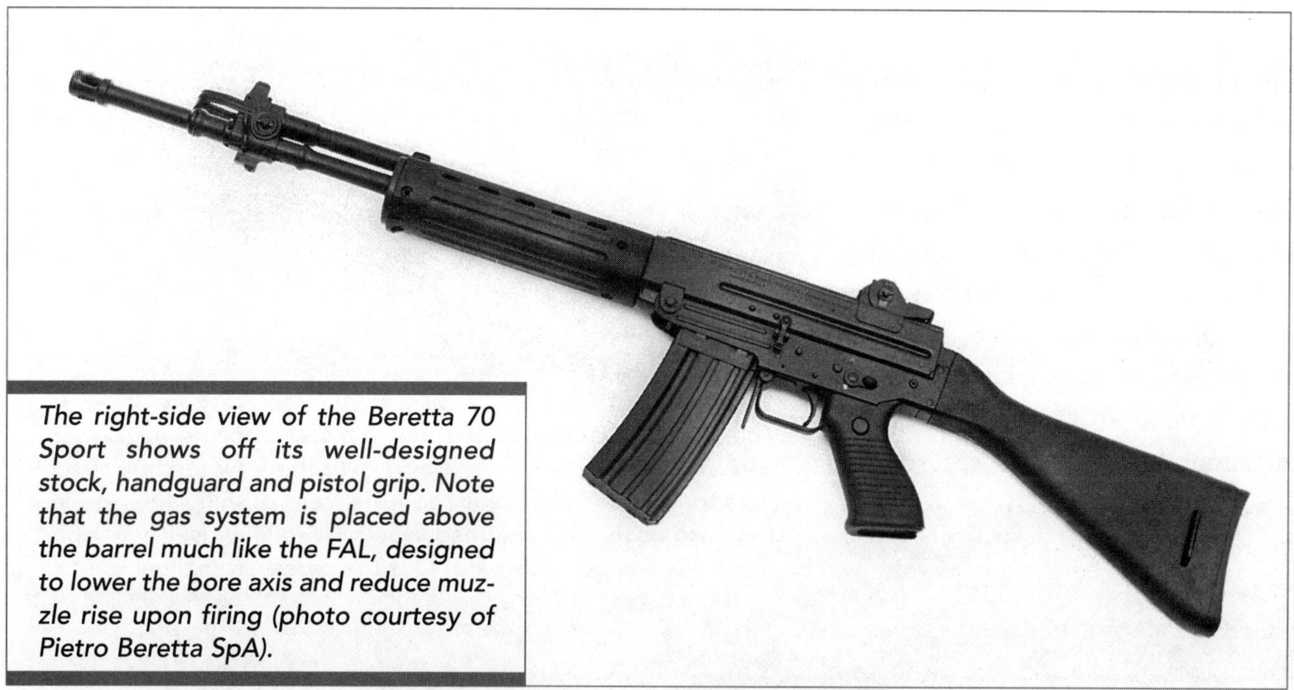

The right-side view of the Beretta 70 Sport shows off its well-designed stock, handguard and pistol grip. Note that the gas system is placed above the barrel much like the FAL, designed to lower the bore axis and reduce muzzle rise upon firing (photo courtesy of Pietro Beretta SpA).

BERETTA AR-70 SERIES

	AR-70
Overall Length	37.6 inches
Barrel Length	17.8 inches
Weight	8.3 pounds
Years Produced	1970-present; U.S. importation halted 1989
Caliber/Capacity	.222 or .223/5, 8 or 30 rounds

Brno ZKM 611

The Model ZKM 611 rifle is a product of Zbrojovka Brno (Brno, Czech Republic), but it is not made in the same factory as the famous CZ series of automatic pistols. It's produced in Bohemia, a region of the Czech Republic that has been famous for gun-making and the manufacture of other iron goods for centuries.

The ZMK 611 is a .22 Magnum caliber self-loading rifle with a 6-shot magazine that comes standard (the factory offers 2-shot and extended 10-shot magazines as well). It also has a 2-piece stock made of walnut separated by a massive forged steel receiver. The pistol grip and forend are hand-checkered the old-fashioned way. Sling swivels are already attached. The stock has an odd shape—a kind of "hog's back" comb—that is fairly common in Europe.

The manual safety is a crossbolt-type push button located above and in front of the trigger. When pushed from right to left, a red warning band visible on the left side indicates the rifle is ready to fire. When pushed from left to right, the firing mechanism is deactivated, preventing the bolt from moving. The magazine release, located

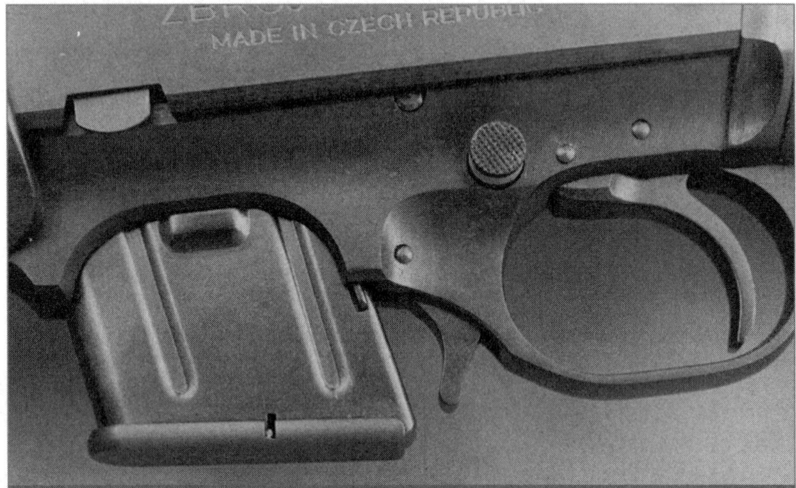

The ZKM 611 comes standard with a 6-shot magazine (2-shot and 10-shot magazines are also available). Note the raised magazine stop to prevent shooters from pushing the box in too hard or too far. The magazine release lever is just behind the magazine box. Also visible is the crossbolt manual safety.

The ZKM 611 may look odd, but shooters soon learn to enjoy its design features and excellent workmanship.

in front of the triggerguard, is pushed forward to drop the magazine. ZKM 611 also has a magazine disconnect as an added safety measure (the best safety device, though, is always good courtesy and common sense). In addition to these mechanical safety features, the hammer, which is visible when the rifle is cocked, comes into play. This same feature is found in the M1 Garand and AK-47 rifle families. The takedown mechanism of the ZKM 611 is similar to the John

The SKM 611 comes equipped with a sling swivel on the forearm. Note also the attractive checkering on the forearm.

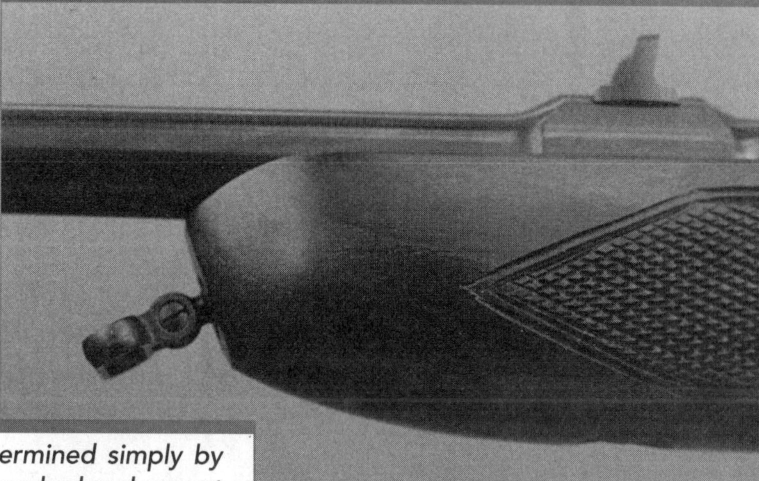

The ZKM 611's firing status can be determined simply by looking at it. In this view, the hammer is cocked and cannot be seen in the slot at the rear of the receiver, slightly behind the polished, white-metal bolt. This gun is ready to fire.

Browning-designed Winchester gallery rifles: simply loosen the thumbscrew on the left side of the receiver and this handy, compact gun divides into even handier and more compact halves, the longer half measuring just under 25 inches. This feature is popular among campers and backpackers of all kinds.

Because of its unusual stock, handling the ZKM 611 takes some getting used to, but it shoots superbly. Its extraordi-

Here the ZKM 611 hammer, which is not cocked, rises far enough to be seen through the slot at the rear of the receiver. With the hammer in view, the firing mechanism is at rest and the gun is not ready to fire.

narily fine workmanship makes this little rifle a pleasure to handle and a delight to shoot. The sights, consisting of a covered front post and a fully adjustable rear sight, is easy to use out to 50 yards, and probably well beyond. The receiver is grooved for a scope mount. Recoil, which is mild, has a distinct two-stage feel typical of self-loading rifles, with the action hanging back after the last shot is fired. Several benchrested groups at 50 yards ranged as small as 0.60 inches across and were never larger than 1.3 inches. Unlike the .22 Long Rifle, which drops off quickly beyond 50 yards, this rapid, flat-shooting .22 Magnum round is extremely accurate to 100 yards or perhaps even more with the right rifle. Any shooter who desires a compact, lightweight but powerful rimfire rifle ought to give the Brno ZKM 611 a close look. It's definitely my first choice in a .22 WMR caliber rifle.

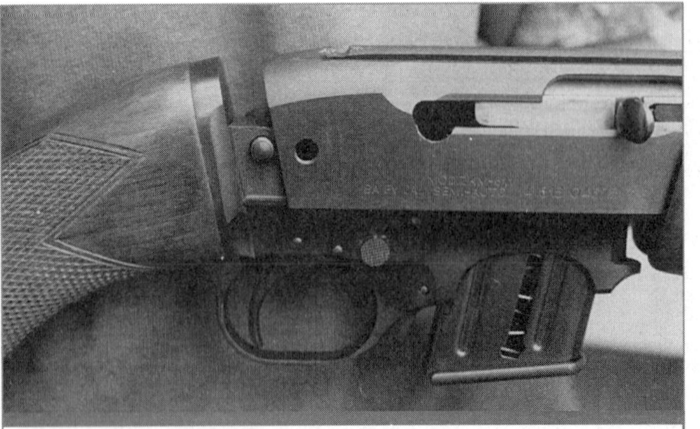

With the receiver screw loosened and partially withdrawn, the shooter separates the ZKM 611 into two pieces.

When the large knurled screw at the rear of the receiver has been loosened, the ZKM 611 rifle can be separated into two pieces for easy storage and cleaning. The shooter must first remove the magazine and check the firing chamber by withdrawing the bolt, verifying that the gun is completely unloaded.

Once the ZKM 611 has been separated into two parts, it becomes a remarkably compact package suitable for carry and use by those who require a firearm that is at once small and handy yet also accurate with powerful cartridges.

The ZKM 611's front sight is a hooded post, which is easy to spot even when zeroing in on a moving target.

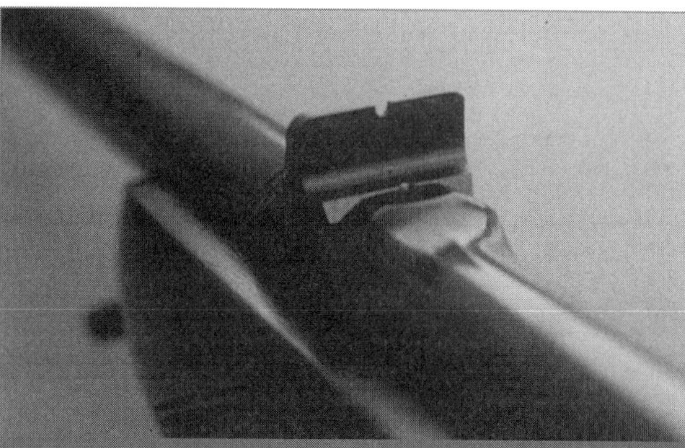

The rear sight notch on the ZKM 611 is quite narrow. A square cut at the bottom, rather than a rounded U, would also enhance the sight picture. Still, the rifle is capable of excellent accuracy at distances where one is likely to use a .22 Magnum rifle.

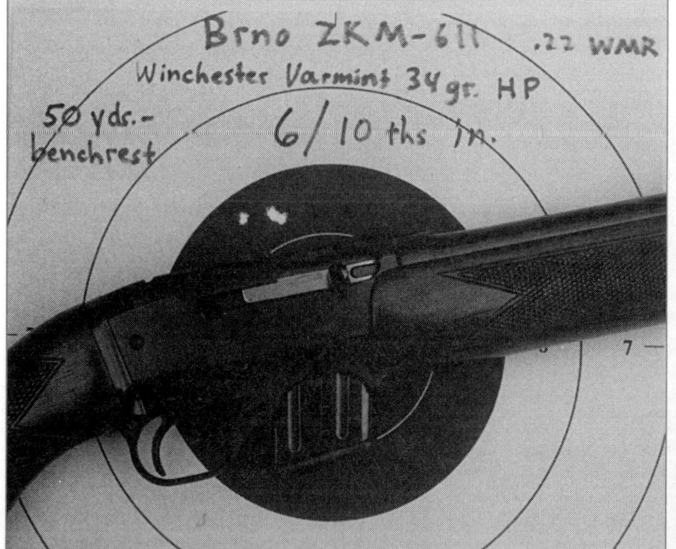

The ZKM 611 tested by the author at 50 yards produced amazing results using his favorite Winchester-brand ammunition.

Even with ammunition the ZKM does not usually respond well to, it still fired more than an acceptable 1.3-inch group.

BRNO ZKM 611

	ZKM 611
Overall Length	37.0 inches
Barrel Length	20.0 inches
Weight	6.1 pounds
Years Produced	1994-present
Importer	Euro Imports, El Cajon, CA
Caliber/Capacity	.22 WMR (.22 Magnum)/2, 6 or 10 rounds

Browning BAR Mark II Safari

The Browning BAR, which is totally unlike the military BAR of half a century earlier, became available in 1993 in the form of Browning's improved Mark II Safari version. Although John Browning himself had died decades before anybody came up with the idea for this rifle, his son (Val) and grandson (Bruce) continued the family's design magic with the new BAR. Its features include a short-stoke piston/gas system similar to that of the U.S. M1 Carbine. The bolt is a rotating piece with seven locking lugs, strong enough for most rifle cartridges. Compared to the original BAR, the gas system in the current version is smoother to operate, thus contributing to the longevity of its mechanism and improving the rifle's already commendable accuracy. It also boasts a clever detachable magazine which the shooter can, at will, either hinge down at the front to reload or remove completely and replace with a fresh one. The BAR Mark II Safari may operate the same magazine system as the original version, but they are not interchangeable. The stock on the BAR is a two-piece affair, with the buttstock and forend separated from each

The Browning BAR Mark II Safari (right), while by no means small, is more compact than first-generation military self-loading rifles like the SVT-40 Tokarev (left).

other by a massive, flat-sided receiver. The rifle is available with or without iron sights, or with a simple rear sight (adjustable for windage and elevation), and a bead front sight protected by a semicircular hood. The manual safety is a crossbolt button, which pushes in from right to left, exposing a red band (to fire) and from left to right (for safe). Typically, this safety arrangement favors right-handed shooters, but Browning can, upon request, reverse the safety button for left-handed shooters.

The BAR, along with other FN/Browning products, has a special coded serial number identifying the type of gun and the year in which it was made. The number begins with the BAR Mark II product code 107, followed by the code for the year of manufacture (NT=1996).

Two changes representing great improvements in the BAR Mark II Safari are (1) the addition of a bolt release on the right side of the receiver and (2) making the Ballistic Optimizing Shooting System (B.O.S.S.) an option for buyers. The B.O.S.S. is a device attached to the muzzle that enhances accuracy by dampening barrel vibrations. It also vents gases through a series of holes for a muzzle-braking effect. In addition to the BAR, Browning offers the B.O.S.S. on its A-Bolt bolt-action rifle. Winchester's Model 70 is also available now that Browning and USRAC, Winchester's parent firm, have become subsidiaries of the same French company. The original B.O.S.S., with its muzzle-braking holes, made the gun painfully noisy to shoot, until Browning introduced an optional B.O.S.S. without the additional holes, thus losing the braking feature but without reducing accuracy. Regret-tably, Browning can provide neither B.O.S.S. system as an option on any of the iron-sighted rifles. It's one or the other.

Test results firing a .308-caliber BAR Mark II Safari rifle (with iron sights and no B.O.S.S.) included a 1.8-inch benchrested group fired from a distance of 100 yards using Norinco commercial ammunition. Another benchrested 3-shot group measured 2.1

The BAR Mark II Safari offers fine checkering on the pistol grip to help shooters get a good hold on the rifle.

inches from 100 yards with aged surplus NATO-type ammunition (made in Portugal). Neither type of ammunition is anywhere near the top of the heap in terms of quality, so these groups would shrink still more with better ammunition. Reliability was near-perfect throughout the course of fire; and recoil, thanks to the gas-operated mechanism, was less than one would expect with a manually operated repeating rifle of similar caliber and weight.

Performance with the BAR is excellent in every way, and it can compete with any high-quality bolt-action rifle. Its self-loading mechanism provides remarkably soft recoil, while accuracy, especially with the

The BAR Mark II Safari tested for this book yielded groups as small as this 1.8-inch effort from the 100-yard bench with open sights. A telescopic sight would have made this result even better.

The BAR Mark II Safari includes a bolt-release latch whose lever is located at the bottom front corner of the receiver. This useful addition gives the BAR (in the Mark II version that has been produced since 1993) better handling than the original BAR introduced in 1967.

B.O.S.S. mechanism in place (and a scope fitted), is on a par with the finest bolt-action rifles. Quality of manufacture is enough to please even the most discerning shooter, and yet the BR's price is competitive. With its wide range of calibers—from .243 Winchester and .22-250 up to .338 Winchester Magnum—the BAR Mark II Safari remains one of the most versatile sporting rifles ever made, with enough firepower to take down all but the largest, most dangerous game.

The BAR Mark II Safari comes with a thick recoil pad made of soft rubber. This pad, plus the relatively smooth gas operation of the rifle's self-loading mechanism, lessens recoil.

Browning's famous "Buck Mark" logo (introduced in 1977) appears on the bottom of the triggerguard of the BAR Mark II Safari and other FN-type rifles sold by Browning.

BROWNING BR MARK II SAFARI

	MARK II
Overall Length	43.0 inches (45 in Magnum calibers, 41 in Lightweight)
Barrel Length	22.0 inches (24 in Magnum calibers, 20 in Lightweight)
Weight	7.4 pounds (Standard), 8.4 (Magnum), 7.1 (Lightweight)
Years Produced	1967 (1993 in Mark II configuration, 1997 in Lightweight configuration)-present
Caliber & Capacity	*Lightweight models:* .243, .308, .270, .30-06/4 rounds *Standard models:* .22-250, .243, .25-06, .308, .270, .30-06/4 rounds *Magnum model:* 7mm Magnum, .300 Win. Mag., .338 Win. Mag./3 rounds

Century L1A1 Sporter

Century International Arms (St. Albans, Vermont) introduced its L1A1 Sporter in order to make the excellent L1A1 service rifle, which has been surplus in British service since the early 1990s, available to U.S. shooters. The L1A1 was nothing more than a British version of the Belgian-designed FAL (made to British inch measurements rather than metric). Great Britain adopted the FAL in 1953 and, five years later, commenced licensed production of the L1A1 version. By the time production ended in 1975, two British manufacturers—the state-owned RSAF Enfield and the privately-owned BSA Guns Ltd.—had made more than a million L1A1s.

Steps taken to convert a military L1A1 into an L1A1 Sporter included removing the former's flash suppressor. This also eliminated the bayonet lug, which lay on the flash suppressor in this model (FALs made by FN had a bayonet with a tubular handle that slipped over the flash suppressor instead). Other changes involved removing the buttstock and

The Century L1A1 Sporter has had a new sporterized thumbhole stock fitted, a muzzle brake and bayonet lug removed, and a new receiver fitted (for semiautomatic fire only).

In keeping the British-style safety/fire selector, only the safety ("S") and semiautomatic settings ("R"="Repetition") still function on the Century L1A1 Sporter. The fully-automatic or "A" setting has been deactivated, while a new receiver is limited to semiautomatic fire.

The Century L1A1 Sporter uses the British-style bolt carrier with grooves cut into it so that dirt and fouling can work their way out of the action. Note that the carrying handle has been pushed down out of the way for firing.

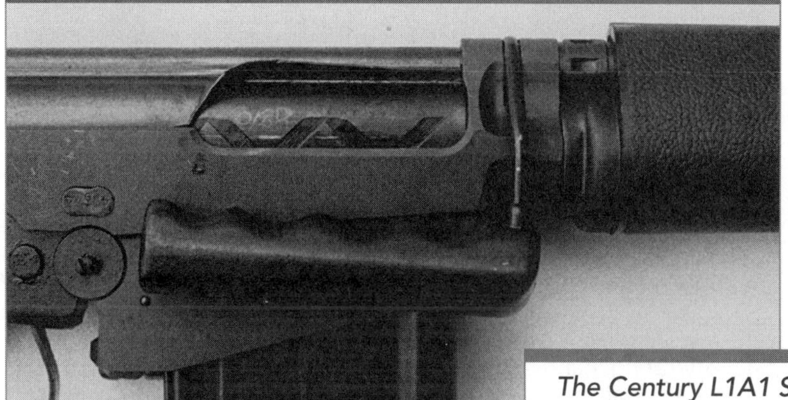

pistol grip of the military L1A1 and substituting a one-piece, thumbhole-type stock instead. Early L1A1 Sporters featured a Bell & Carlson thumbhole stock, but later Century made it own. The shape of these stocks remained the same, with sling swivel studs making a definite improvement. Century's stock was available in matte black or a camouflage pattern.

The removal of the original L1A1's selective-fire receiver and the substitution of a Brazilian-made receiver limited the L1A1 Sporter to semiautomatic fire only. Since it has a metric receiver, the Sporter fits only metric-pattern FAL magazines rather than the inch-pattern magazines Century supplied to its British, Canadian, Australian and Indian accounts. Fortunately, metric FAL magazines are far more common than inch-pattern magazines anyway. Everything else—sights, gas system,

The Century L1A1 Sporter retains the typical FAL rear sight, which is shown in the raised position for shooting. When a scope is fitted, the rear sight can be lowered out of the way simply by pushing it forward.

The Century L1A1 Sporter has retained the distinctive carrying handle typical of the FAL rifle design. The improved stock on this later version includes sling swivels.

trigger mechanism and so on—remain the same as the military FAL/L1A1.

The L1A1 Sporter retains the typical strong points of the FAL: good accuracy, reliability and handling. Some shooters complain that the angle of the pistol grip on the thumbhole sporter stock is too steep, while other like it the way it is. Certainly the Shorter L1A1 Sporter is handier and better balanced than the original L1A1 or FAL. The adjustable gas system is an advantage on a military weapon, which might fire hundreds of rounds without cleaning. When encountering feeding or ejection problems with an L1A1 Sporter or any other FAL-type rifle, shooters need to be sure the gas port is open wide enough to operate the system reliably.

The Century L1A1 Sporter has also retained the British-style folding operating handle, which is less likely to catch or snag on clothing, equipment or foliage. Here the handle is shown pulled back, allowing the shooter to retract the bolt for loading.

In testing the Century L1A1 Sporter for accuracy, the author placed three shots into a 1.3-inch group from the 100-yard bench. However, this gun occasionally jammed, while another test rifle, though less accurate (a 2 MOA shooter firing groups of 2 inches or more at 100 yards), proved utterly reliable.

In early 1998, President Clinton banned further import of the L1A1 Sporter and other semiautomatic rifles, which were misleadingly dubbed "assault weapons." As a result, the supply of L1A1 Sporters has grown scarce. Nevertheless, the L1A1 Sporter is a good, inexpensive version of what many consider to be the best military rifle ever made.

CENTURY L1A1 SPORTER

	L1A1 SPORTER
Overall Length	41 1/8 inches
Barrel Length	20 3/4 inches
Weight	9 pounds, 13 ounces
Years Produced	1993-present
Caliber/Capacity	.308 (7.62x51mm NATO)/20 rounds

Century International Arms G-3 Millennium Sporter

As one might expect from the name, the G-3 Millennium Sporter, which appeared in early 1999, is mostly a straightforward copy of the world-famous Heckler & Koch G3/HK91 design. Among the changes made by its importer, Century International, is an aluminum-alloy receiver instead of H&K's standard receiver made of stamped steel. Using aluminum for the receiver allows the manufacturer to make the rifle without the expensive equipment needed by Heckler & Koch for its stamped steel process. Switching from steel to aluminum, however, means a noticeably thicker receiver; thus, some handguards and other accessories that ordinarily interchange easily between H&K's G3 variants may not make a perfect fit with the G-3 Millennium Sporter.

The G-3's safety mechanism is also modeled after early H&K 91 rifles. That is, it offers two positions: down to fire and up to safe (S). Again typical of Heckler & Koch rifles, the safety, though well-positioned and large, is stiff to operate. This makes the manual safety difficult to operate without taking the trigger hand off the pistol grip, in full or in part.

The sighting system on the G-3 Millennium Sporter is typical of the Heckler & Koch G3 rifle series. It features a rotary three-position rear sight and a front sight with a sturdy post and protective hood. To mount a telescopic sight, an integral Weaver rail has already been milled into it, thanks to the machined-aluminum receiver that only this model offers. As for furniture, the G-3 Millennium Sporter has a pistol-grip stock and a

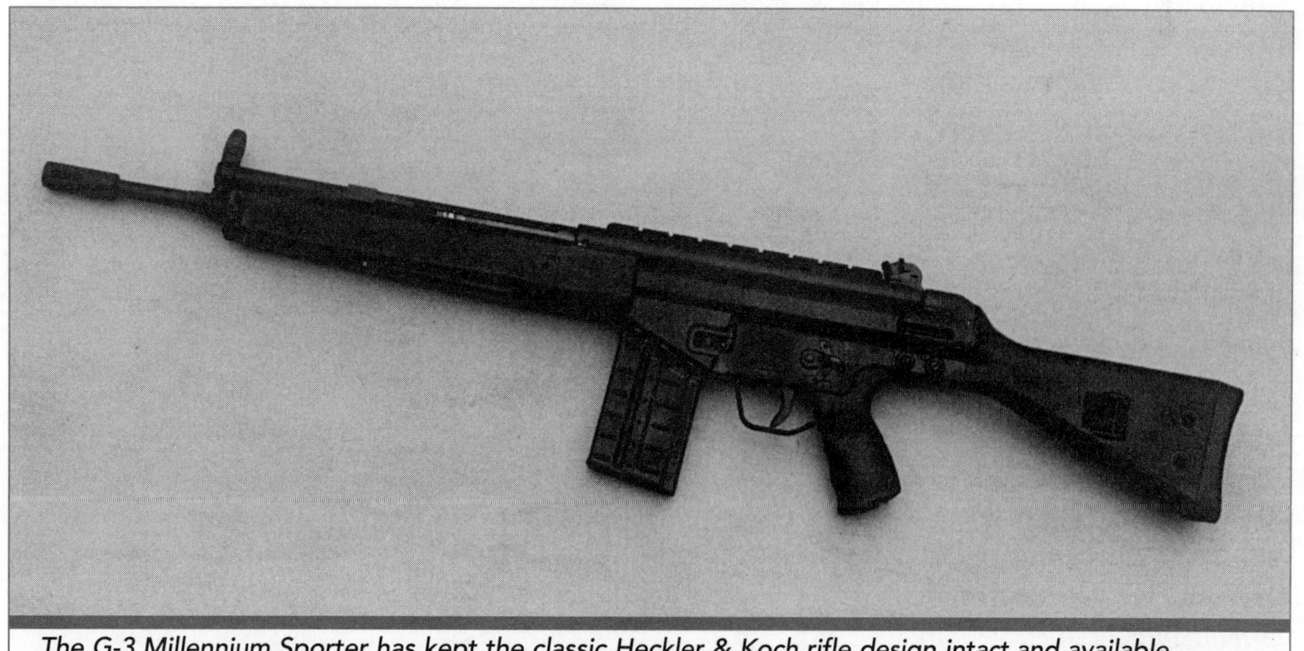

The G-3 Millennium Sporter has kept the classic Heckler & Koch rifle design intact and available.

The G-3 safety features two positions: down to fire (pointing to a red E) and up (pointing to a white S). This design retains H&K's excellent rotary-adjustable rear peep sight.

Its magazines, which are also the standard G3 type, come in plastic, aluminum and steel, with capacities of up to 20 rounds. The Millennium Sporter employs the less desirable push-button magazine release—the same as the commercial HK91 model, rather than the more ambidextrous lever-type release found in the original G3. The magazine release pushes in from right to left; remember, though, that these magazines must be "rocked" into place. That means the front portion must be first inserted all the way, with the narrow, round handguard that was in use until the early 1980s. Although I prefer the wide "tropical" handguard that came later, many shooters—small-handed ones in particular—prefer the early "slimline" type.

Like other Heckler & Koch service-type rifles, the G-3 Millennium Sporter fires the popular .308 Winchester (7.62 x51mm NATO) cartridge—a good choice because of its power level and availability. The .308 makes a fine intermediate rifle cartridge, with enough power to be useful both for hunting and for military/police/defense work, yet still without excessive recoil.

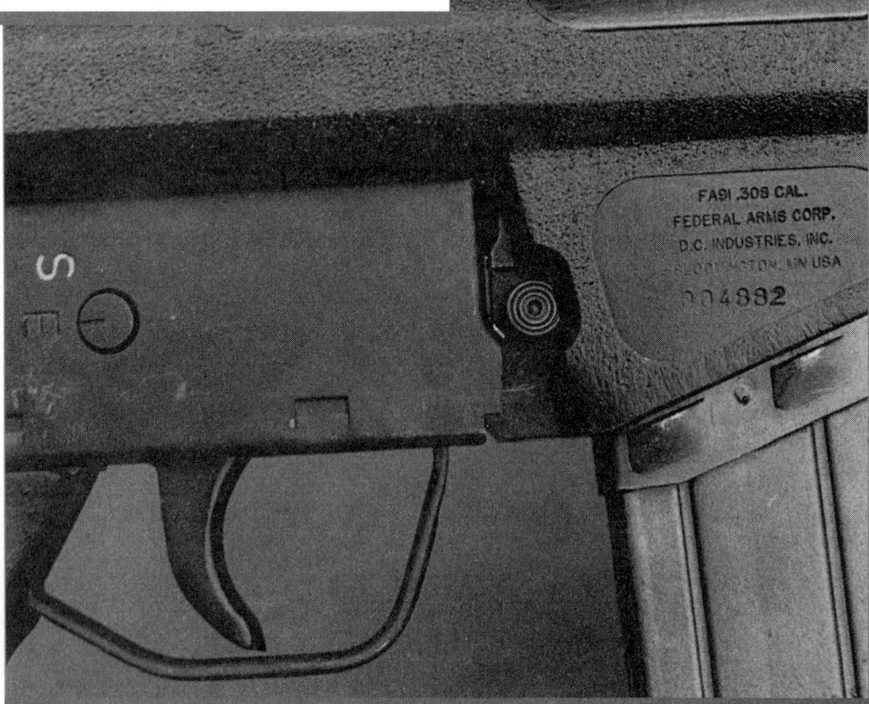

The G-3 employs a pushbutton rather than the more desirable lever-type magazine release specified by the West German military for its original G3 service rifle.

rear part swung up until it clicks. The AK-47, M14 and FAL magazines all operate the same way. The G-3 Millennium Sporter's bolt does not hold open when the last shot is fired, a fault shared by all G3-type rifles. Some shooters also complain about how hard it is to operate the left-sided charging handle. Shooters may want to test this feature before buying the G-3 rifle. Try cocking the rifle using both overhand and underhand grips. In the former instance, your triceps muscle comes into play, while in the latter your biceps muscle will supply most of the energy required to move the charging handle, then load and cock the rifle.

In testing this rifle, I found the G-3 Millennium Sporter pleasingly accurate, providing 3-shot benchrested 100-yard groups measuring as little as 0.8 inch across. Ironically, the test rifle did its best with the Winchester Ballistic Silvertip, not the Hornady Match ammunition which had

The G-3 operating handle folds out from the left side of the barrel, as shown.

The G-3's sighting arrangement includes a factory-machined, Weaver-compatible scope rail.

performed so well in previous tests. The best 100-yard benchrested group fired with the Hornady, however, was still a perfectly respectable 1.8 inches wide. The moral of this story is: test your rifle/ammunition combination until you discover what works best.

Trigger pull, like that of most factory-stock G3 rifles, is not as crisp as some shooters would prefer. It's not bad, either, unless you're shooting extremely fast or trying to hit a target more than 300 yards away. The G3's mediocre trigger is a regrettable but typical feature on other rifles originally designed as selective-fire weapons. Between the FAL, G3 and M`14, the last-named typically has the best trigger and the G3 the worst. In general, though, the G-3 Millennium Sporter offers the best Heckler & Koch features and performance at a reasonable price.

Century International Arms' G-3 Millennium Sporter in .308 Winchester caliber provided the author with consistent groups of less than two inches across from the 100-yard bench.

CENTURY G-3 MILLENIUM SPORTER

	SHORT ACTION
Overall Length	40.5 inches
Barrel Length	23.5 inches (includes 2.5-inch muzzle device, permanently attached)
Weight	7.0 pounds
Caliber	.308 Winchester
Magazine Capacity	20 rounds
Production	1999-

Colt Match Target Series

Since Colt took over the 5.56mm (.223) AR-15 program from ArmaLite, the company has been selling the military variant M16-series rifles with great success. Colt has also offered commercial AR-15 variants (limited to semiautomatic fire) since the early 1970s. These rifles have sold well to private citizens, many of them former servicemen looking for replicas of the famous M16 they remember from several decades earlier. Likewise, many police departments have requested a rifle whose performance, reliability and handling closely approximated those of a U.S. service rifle without the legal and tactical complications of fully-automatic fire.

The adoption of the M16A2 by the U.S. Marine Corps and later by the U.S. Army had a positive effect on Colt's subsequent production of the AR-15 for the commercial market. Mechanical changes introduced from the early 1980s on included improved handguards with a rounded cross-section, a thicker barrel contour in front of the handguard—or thickened throughout

A hinged dust cover over the ejection port on the AR-15 pops open once the charging handle has been pulled back. It stays closed at other times to prevent dust and dirt from entering the mechanism.

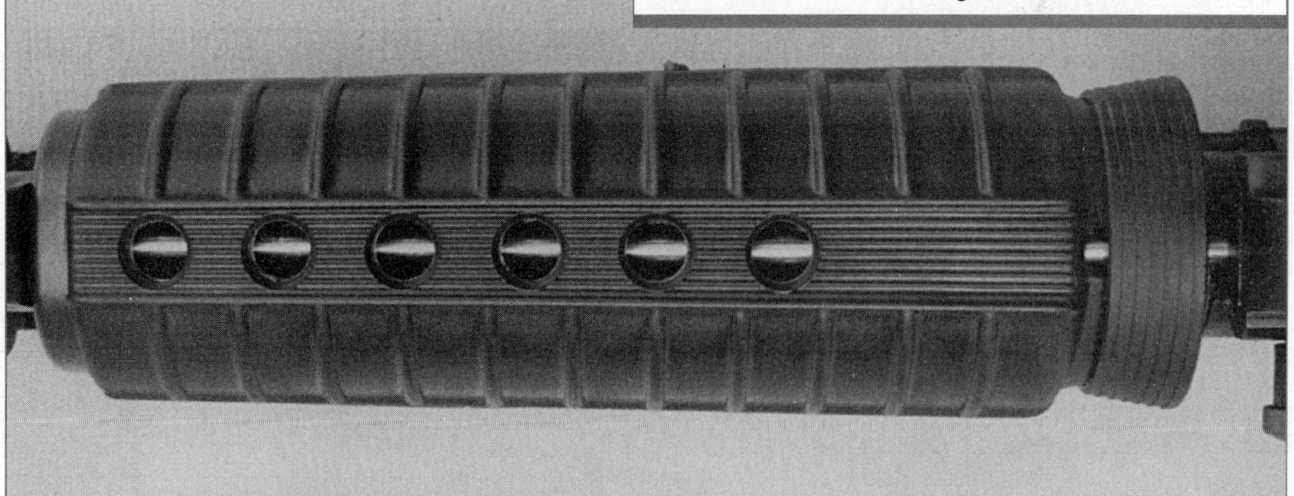

This view from the top of an AR-15 displays the stainless steel gas tube from which expanding gas from the burning powder strikes the bolt carrier directly.

This Colt Match Target HBAR II balances easily and shoots quickly and with reasonable accuracy.

the whole length as in the HBAR series—improved front and rear sights, and a new rifling twist to the barrel.

Rifles of the commercial AR-15 type offered by Colt in recent years include the Colt Match Target Lightweight and the Colt Match Target Competition HBAR II (which is available in several variations). This series, which was known as the Colt Sporter Lightweight series, began production in 1991. Its rifles differ from earlier semiautomatic-only AR-15 variants in that no bayonet lug was included and its magazines were limited to a five-round capacity.

Two modern Colt AR-15 commercial rifles were tested for this book. First came a Sporter Lightweight (which later was named Match Target Lightweight model) chambered for the 7.62x39mm cartridge, which was popular in countries formerly under Soviet domination.

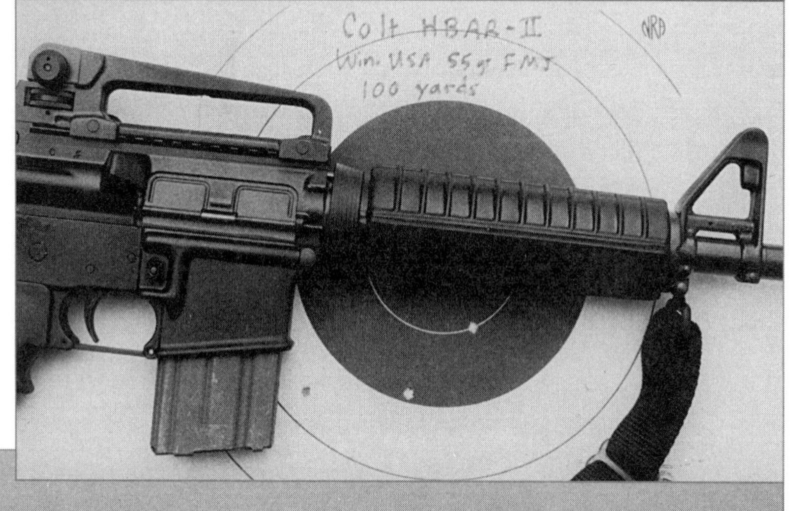

In testing the AR-15 for accuracy at 100 yards, results were acceptable for a .223-caliber rifle. Point of aim was the bottom on the black part of the target (the famous "six-o'clock hold" taught in the armed forces).

An 8-round magazine on Colt's Sporter Lightweight almost disappears into the magazine housing.

I also tested a Match Target Competition HBAR in .223 caliber with a 16-inch barrel (a 9mm Parabellum variant of the Match Target Lightweight). The Match Target Competition and HBAR rifles are available with 20- and 24-inch barrels.

Both rifles produced little recoil and accuracy was good in either the .223 or 7.62x39mm chamberings. The best 3-shot offhand target fired with the Match Target Lightweight in .223 caliber clustered inside 1.3 inches from 50 yards. From the 100-yard bench, the same .223 caliber Match Target Lightweight rifle fired a 3.6-inch group. The Sporter Lightweight in 7.62x39mm chambering did even better, producing a 100-yard benchrested group measuring only 2.8 inches across. That is better accuracy with the .223 cartridge than with almost any other rifle tested in that caliber, including the Chinese

The AR-15 (left) is appreciably more compact than rifles of the German G3 type (right).

The adjustable rear sight found on current AR-15 rifles are better than those used on earlier M16s, M16A1s and early commercial AR-15s. The charging handle for the bolt and the head of the bolt forward-assist plunger are visible in this photo.

SKS, Chinese and Hungarian AK-47s, and even the Ruger Mini-Thirty. Only a Yugoslav AK-47-type rifle—the Zastava M-90—scored higher.

Except for their limitation of one shot for each press of the trigger, the Colt Match Target Lightweight and Competition series work much like their military counterparts. Colt's commercial rifles are by no means inexpensive, though, costing about twice as much as Ruger's Mini-14. But their similarity to the military M16—and their greater sturdiness compared to the Mini-14—make them useful and versatile rifles in their class.

This AR-15 rifle has a rotary manual safety. Civilian models of this type have non-ambidextrous, two-position manual safeties and semiautomatic-only receivers.

The carrying handle on the AR-15 is one of its more distinctive features.

COLT MATCH TARGET LIGHTWEIGHT & COMPETITION SERIES

	MATCH TARGET LW	MATCH TARGET COMP HBAR II
Overall Length	34.5 inches	34.5 inches
Barrel Length	16.0 inches	16.1 inches
Weight	6.7 pounds	7.1 pounds
Years Produced	1991-present	1995-present
Caliber/Capacity	.223 or 9mm/5 rounds	.223 or 9mm/5 rounds

Dragunov "Tiger" Carbine

The Dragunov "Tiger" carbine was a short-lived commercial variant of the Soviet-designed SVD sniper rifle. A 10-shot weapon of modified Kalashnikov action, the original *Snaiperskaya Vintovka Dragunova* ("Sniper Rifle Dragunov," most often referred to as "SVD" or "Dragunov") appeared in 1965, replacing the Mosin-Nagant Model 1891/30 bolt-action rifles for sniper issue. Using the AK-47 assault rifle as a starting point, the design team, led by Yevgeniy Feodorovich Dragunov, altered the rifle to improve its role as a sniper. The major change from Kalashnikov's AK-47 was to substitute a short-stroke piston for the AK's solid operating rod. With this system the piston, bolt and bolt carrier all travel together throughout the entire operating stroke. Dragunov's initial attempts to scale up the AK-47 mechanism to a size large enough to operate the longer and more powerful 7.62x54mm cartridge resulted in a rod that was too heavy, spoiling the shooter's aim as it reciprocated with each shot. In the short-stroke arrangement that was eventually adopted, the piston derived its initial energy from the powder gas. As it was forced to the rear, the rod struck the bolt carrier, to which it imparted all of its energy. The Kalashnikov-style bolt carrier then traveled to the rear, rotating the bolt inside to unlock the mechanism, eject the empty cartridge case, and so on.

The Dragunov Tiger (left) is far more compact than the SVT-40 "Tokarev" (right), one of the USSR's first self-loading rifles.

As might expect, the safety and trigger mechanisms of the Dragunov rifle also adhere to the Kalashnikov principles, operating in much the same way except that, unlike military-issue AK-47 and AKM rifles, the Dragunov is limited to one shot for each pull of the trigger. Fully-automatic fire, though useful in the AK-47 and AKM at close ranges, were counterproductive in a sniper rifle intended for precision strikes at ranges of 500 meters and beyond.

The Dragunov rifle first saw service with North Vietnamese troops in Vietnam, probably beginning with the siege of Khe Sanh in early 1968. Later on, it was widely used by Soviet troops against Afghanistan forces and has been copied in Bulgaria, Communist China, Egypt, Hungary and Poland.

SVD versions designed for civilian use include the "Medved" (translation: "Honey eater" or "Bear"), which has a sporting-style pistol grip stock and scope, along with the "Tigr" ("Tiger"). The latter has a military Dragunov-style stock and scope, but its barrel length (20.8 inches) is much shorter than the original (24 inches). The thumbhole stock on the Dragunov Tiger is made of laminated wood, with the forend sporting a black composition material.

As interesting as this rifle is on its own, its telescopic sight deserves close scrutiny, too. Called

The PSO-1 sight is crude by Western standards but has a number of useful features, notably a good rangefinder, a lighted reticle and passive infrared-detection capability. Note the skeletonized stock which has been cut away in strategic sports for weight-saving purposes.

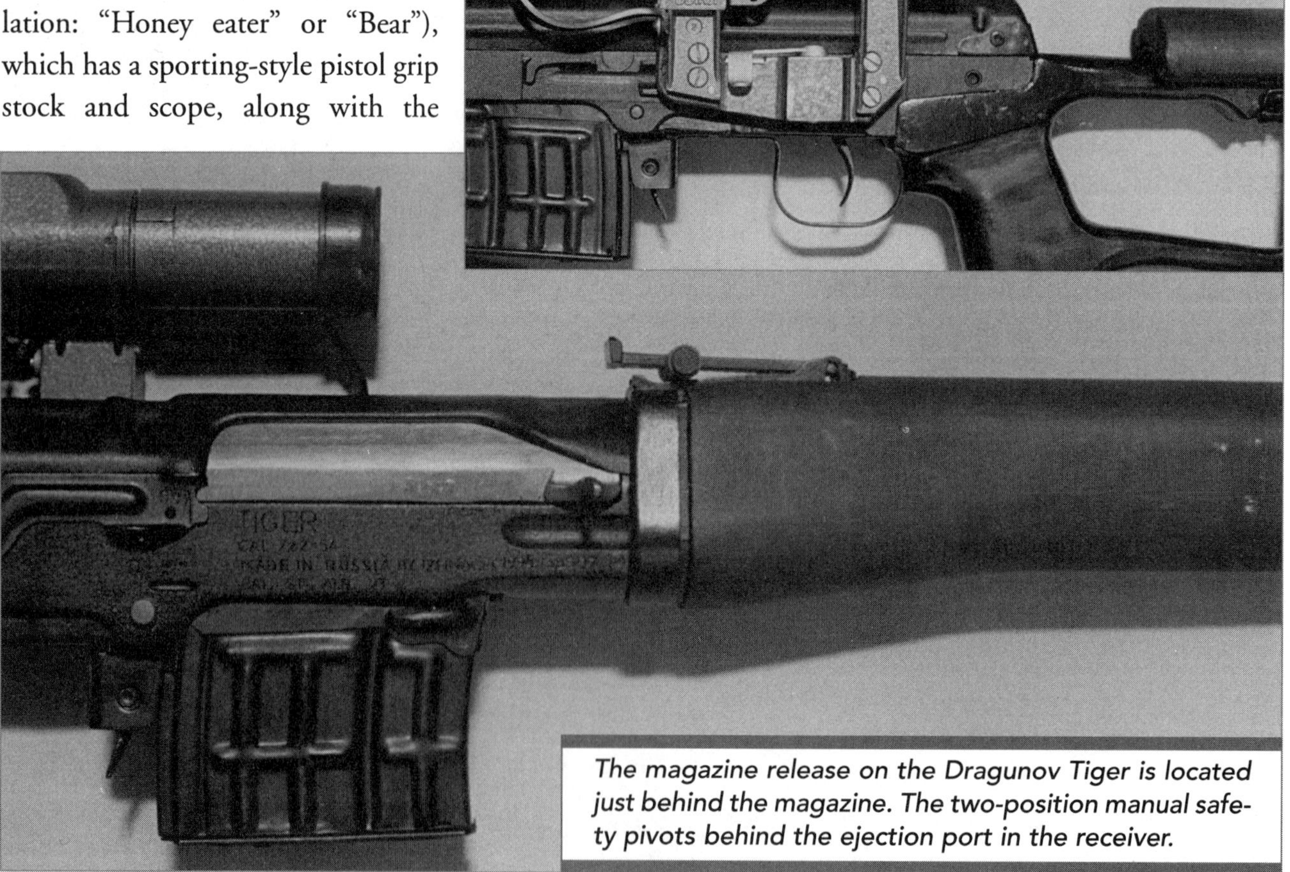

The magazine release on the Dragunov Tiger is located just behind the magazine. The two-position manual safety pivots behind the ejection port in the receiver.

the PSO-1, this 4-power optical scope boasts a good internal rangefinding system and a lighted reticle for nighttime use. It also has passive infrared capabilities in which sensors emitted by enemy forces appear as blobs on the PSO-1 reticle, thus enabling nighttime shooters to target the emissions. While this was a remarkable effort for the 1960s, the PSO-1 has become rather archaic by modern standards. Its fixed 4-power (4x) magnification setting is severely limited by comparison with superior American and Western European rifle scopes, most of which can magnify at least twice as much as the PSO-1. Nevertheless, the Dragunov's telescopic sight offers aiming precision well beyond the capabilities of the rifle's standard but crude iron sights.

The inherent accuracy of the Dragunov family of rifles is a subject of fierce debate in the West. Critics cite the rifle's thin barrel and questionable optics. However, the Soviets would certainly have discontinued the type long ago had its performance not attained the same standard as the Mosin-Nagants these rifles replaced. The Mosin-Nagant is easily a 2 MOA (capable of 2-inch groups at 100 yards) rifle, and they can approach 1 MOA with certain rifles and ammunition. The Dragunov "Tiger" tested for this book grouped into less than 2 MOA without difficulty, even though we were limited to the use of old military-surplus ammunition of questionable quality.

The Dragunov "Tiger" offers an interesting and exotic rifle with good capabilities for about the price of a Springfield M1A. Regrettably, it has been unavailable in the U.S. since 1996 following the government's edict preventing the Russians from exporting firearms to the United States.

The Dragunov Tiger's AK-type manual safety is limited to two positions: down, as shown here, allows the gun to fire, while up is the safe setting.

DRAGUNOV "TIGER" CARBINE

	TIGER
Overall Length	42.9 inches
Barrel Length	20.8 inches
Weight	8.5 pounds
Years Produced	1993-1996
Caliber/Capacity	7.63x54mm/5 rounds

FÉG (K.B.I.) SA-85M

The SA-85M hails from Hungary, which has been making copies of the Kalashnikov AK-47 and AKM assault rifles since early in the Cold War. Its stock is made of blonde European hardwood and is quite attractive, much like the grips on Hungarian pistols of the "High Power" type. The SA-85M's metal parts are coated with a black phosphate finish. Compared to other AK-47/AKM variants, the SA-85M feels lighter and handier than most. In keeping with its compact style, the rifle comes standard with a shortened magazine that holds only six rounds, though higher-capacity AK magazines can be used as well.

Distinctive features of the FÉG SA-85M include a short 6-round magazine, an AKM-style stamped sheet metal receiver cover with stiffening ribs, and attractive blond hardwood for the thumbhole buttstock and handguard.

The FÉG SA-85M, like other Kalashnikov-type rifles chambered for the ex-Soviet 7.62x39mm round, is no great shakes beyond 50 yards. This 5-shot benchrested group at 100 yards measures 4.2 inches across.

Mechanically, the SA-85M is identical to other rifles of the Kalashnikov type. Because of its lightweight, stamped metal receiver, however, it proved less accurate than the beefier Yugoslav type. My best 100-yard group placed five shots into 4.2 inches. Still, as a light and handy variant of the AK, it's an interesting rifle whose 7.62x39mm round has been documented at close ranges.

FÉG (K.B.I.) SA-85M

	SA-85M
Overall Length	34.7 inches
Barrel Length	16.3 inches
Weight	7.6 pounds
Years Produced	1995-present
Caliber/Capacity	7.62x39mm/6 rounds

Marlin "Camp Carbines": Model 9 and Model 45

The Marlin Camp Carbines revived the concept—popular in the Old West over a century ago—of a long gun and handgun both chambered for the same ammunition. After falling out of vogue in the early 1900s, the concept of a short, light rifle firing relatively low-powered ammunition enjoyed a spectacular resurgence in the form of the M1 Carbine. This gun, however, fired a rifle round created specifically for it, one that was modified from the existing Winchester .32 self-loading rifle cartridge rather than a commercially available pistol cartridge. It remained for the Marlin company to fully restore the pistol-caliber carbine concept with its "Camp Carbine" Model 9 (introduced in 1985) and 45 (introduced the following year).

The Camp Carbines are handy and sleek, with many quality features available at reasonable prices. The stocks are made of Maine birch and stained to resemble walnut. The pistol grip and forend areas are press-checkered for a secure, non-slip grip. Sling swivel studs are standard, too, a feature Ruger omitted from its competing Model PC-9. Whether a 9mm Parabellum caliber Model 9 or a .45 ACP caliber Model 45, the Camp Carbines are virtually identical in appearance, operation and dimensions. The Model 9's magazine, however, accepts up to 12 rounds (but is limited to 10 for civilian use) whereas the Model 45 holds up to 7 rounds. Although Marlin supplies the Model 45 with its own magazines marked "Marlin," it will accept any magazine made for a

The Marlin Camp Carbine Model 45 (top) in .45 ACP was heavily influenced by the U.S. M1 Carbine (below) in size and general layout.

standard Government Model/Model 1911-type pistol, a definite selling point for the Marlin carbine. Unlike the Ruger PC-9, whose pistol magazine is partially exposed, the Model 45's sleek, streamlined magazine well fully encases and protects the pistol magazine and prevents mud, dirt or sand from entering the counter holes. The Model 45's magazine release—a pushbutton type located on the left side of the magazine well—is designed much sturdier than the type used on Marlin's similar Model 922M (see below).

The Model 45 also utilizes Marlin's excellent Garand-type safety. The sights are strong and functional, its front sight a simple ramp highlighted by an orange-colored post and an adjustable, open rear sight mounted toward the front of the receiver. Marlin has already drilled and tapped the receiver so shooters can mount scopes. Factory sights are more than adequate for shooting at those distances (or even further in the hands of an expert shot); but shooting at targets much farther than 50 to 100 yards with a .45 ACP caliber firearm is not advisable.

Results of testing for accuracy with a Model 45 carbine were not disappointing. Benchrested 3-shot groups measured as small as 2.2 inches from 100 yards, making this the most accurate weapon in .45 ACP caliber the author has ever experienced.

The Marlin Model 45's operating controls (visible from the left side) include a Garand-style manual safety (pushed forward to its fire setting), a bolt-release control, and a pushbutton magazine release at the front of the magazine housing.

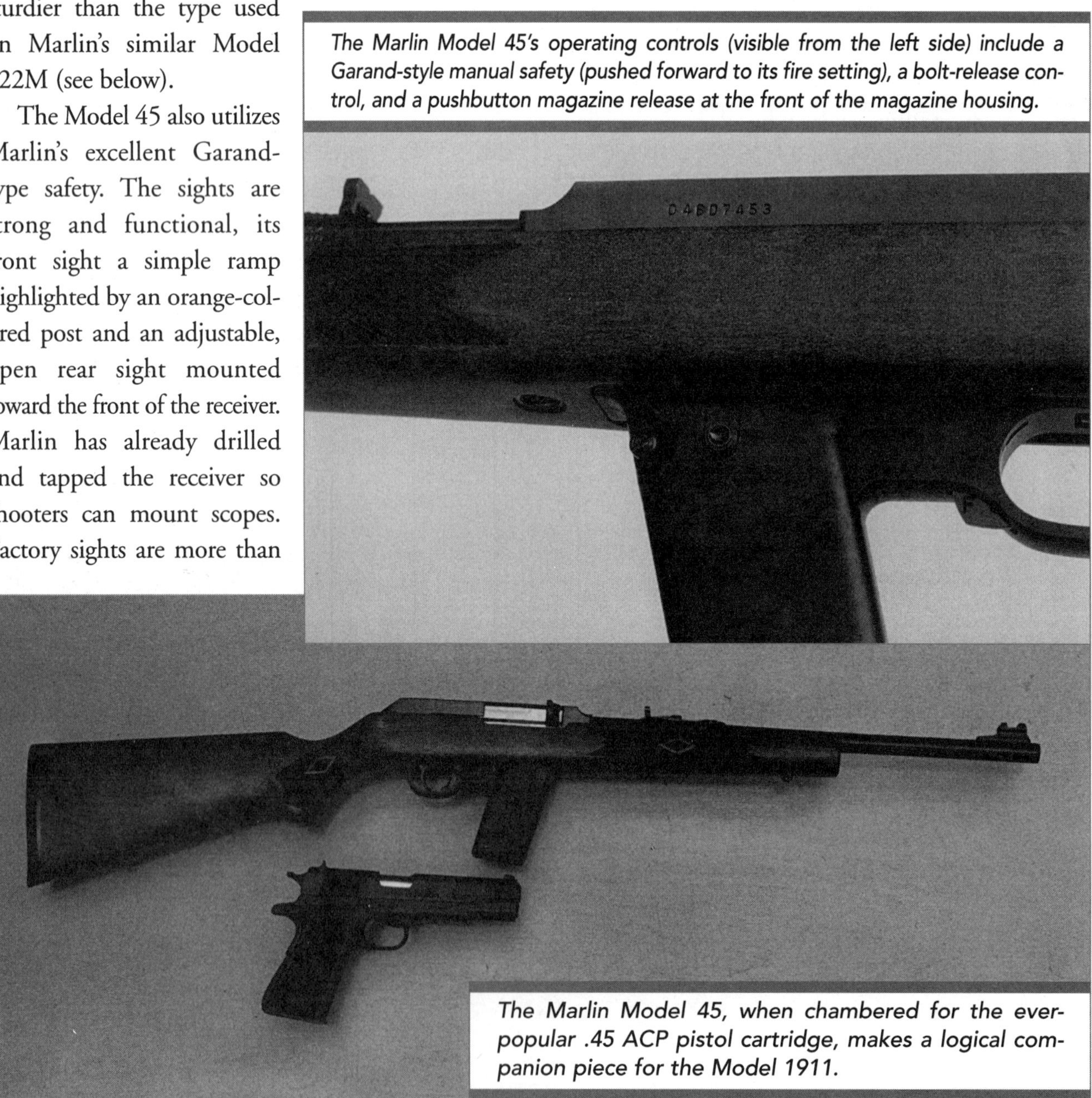

The Marlin Model 45, when chambered for the ever-popular .45 ACP pistol cartridge, makes a logical companion piece for the Model 1911.

Reliability was perfect with all rounds tested, which included several brands of FMJ (ball) as well as jacketed hollowpoints in 165-grain, 185-grain and 230-grain bullet weights (in deference to the manufacturer's suggestions, +P ammunition was not used). Although the Marlin Models 9 and 45 were made primarily for civilian use, they saw some police work as well. In some instances, a pistol caliber offers advantages over arms of similar size but higher-powered, such as the M1 Carbine, Colt AR-15 and Ruger Mini-14, where over-penetration and risk to innocent bystanders could be serious consequences. This commonality of ammunition—i.e., between a Marlin carbine and a service pistol—must gladden police officials in charge of supplies. The chief advantage of the Marlin Camp Carbine over the Auto-Ordnance models for police work was the former's less threatening image as a sporting rifle. In any event, both Models 9 and 45 have proven quite successful and highly popular with those who insist on a light, handy rifle that utilizes widely available calibers. As a self-defense firearm, either model is an excellent choice.

The Marlin Model 45 chambered for the .45 ACP cartridge displayed excellent accuracy. This 2.2-inch group was the most accurate of the many guns fired in tests with that caliber.

MARLIN CAMP CARBINES

	MODEL 9	MODEL 45
Overall Length	35.5 inches	35.5 inches
Barrel Length	16.5 inches	16.5 inches
Weight	6.75 pounds	6.75 pounds
Years Produced	1985-present	1986-present
Caliber/Capacity	9mm Parabellum/12	.45 ACP/7

Marlin Model 922M

Marlin's Model 922M, introduced in 1993, strongly resembles the company's centerfire caliber (9mm and .45 ACP) "Camp Carbine" series (see above). Indeed, it was derived from them. For example, the 922M has borrowed the Camp Carbine's Garand-style safety (located in the front portion of the triggerguard). Unlike the Garand's safety, which can be applied only with the hammer cocked, the 922M safety is operative with its firing mechanism cocked or uncocked. In addition, a magazine safety device prevents firing a round in the firing chamber when the magazine is not in the gun. To advise the shooter when it's safe to reload, the bolt stays back on the last shot. Even with no empty magazine in the action, the bolt can be locked open using a locking latch on the left side of the receiver.

During its first year of production, the Model 922M sported a plain walnut stock, but since 1994 the pistol-grip and forearm areas have been checkered. Sling swivel studs are fitted to the front and rear of the stock, which includes a rubber

The bolt hold-open latch on the Model 922 is a useful device for cleaning the firing chamber and bore of the barrel. The bolt stays back after the last shot has been fired. Note also the impressed wood checkering.

Marlin's Model 922 displays its clean lines. Note the slight Monte Carlo comb on the upper end of the stock (for those who want to scope this rifle and make the most of the .22 Magnum round it fires).

recoil pad on the butt (not really a necessity with the low-recoiling .22 Magnum cartridge fired with this rifle of moderate weight). The receiver is made of aluminum alloy and comes standard with iron sights (but already drilled and tapped for mounting a scope). The front sight has a prominent bead and is protected by a removable hood. The rear sight is the semi-buckhorn adjustable type. While light and handy (only 6 1/2 pounds), Marlin's Model 922M feels solid and sturdy. The only flimsy thing about it is the magazine release. This narrow strip of sheet steel, located to the right of the magazine, must be pressed inward to release the magazine.

The magazine release on the Model 922 is located to the right of the magazine. It constitutes a weak point in an otherwise nearly flawless design.

The Garand-style manual safety on the Model 922 is shown after being pushed forward into its "fire" setting. The bolt hold-open release latch on the receiver is also visible.

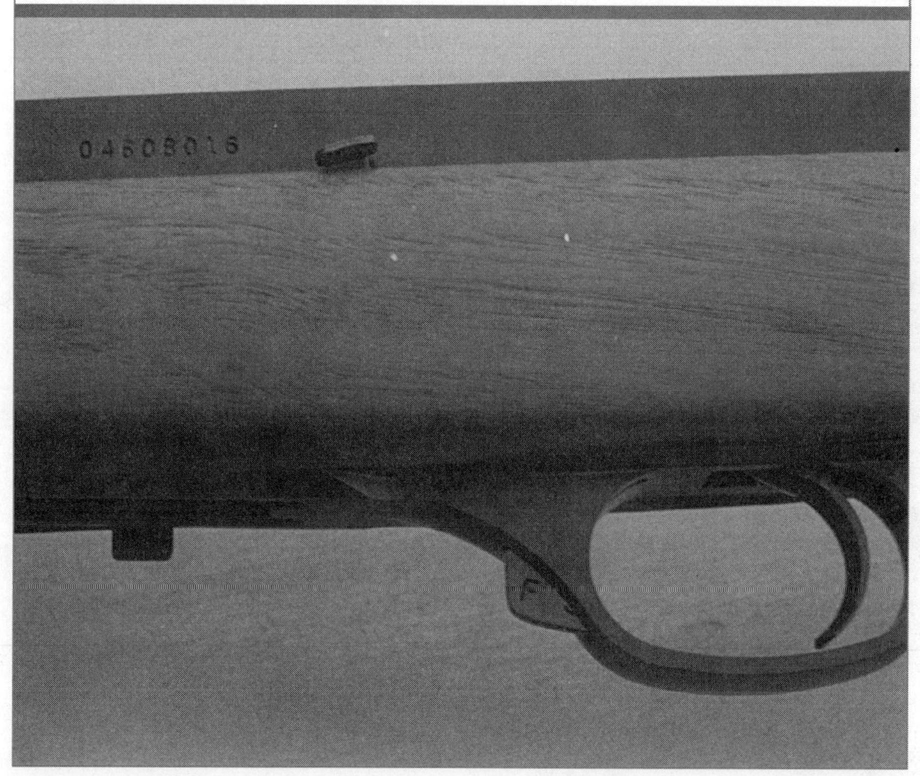

Accuracy results, typical of Marlin rifles, were excellent using the Model 922. The tightest group fired from 50 yards placed three shots into 0.80 inches. The best 3-shot 100-yard group spanned a mere 1.6 inches. Reliability was perfect, which is quite an accomplishment for a long rimfire cartridge fed through a semiautomatic weapon.

All things considered, Marlin's Model 922 is a most

impressive specimen from a company excelling in small semiautomatic rifles. While the less expensive Remington Model 597 in .22 Magnum offers stiff competition, the 922M, with its all-round performance and classical styling, can hold its own. Personally, I prefer the Marlin's Garand-style safety and wooden stock to Remington's crossbolt safety and plastic stock. On the other hand, the magazine release on the Model 922M remains a weak spot in an otherwise flawless design. As noted, the magazine release is too delicate, and its latching mechanism does not grip the magazine as tightly as one might like. In fact, with the Model 922 tested for this book, I was able to pull the magazine out without pressing the release at all.

From a 100-yard benchrested position, the same rifle fired this 1.6-inch group.

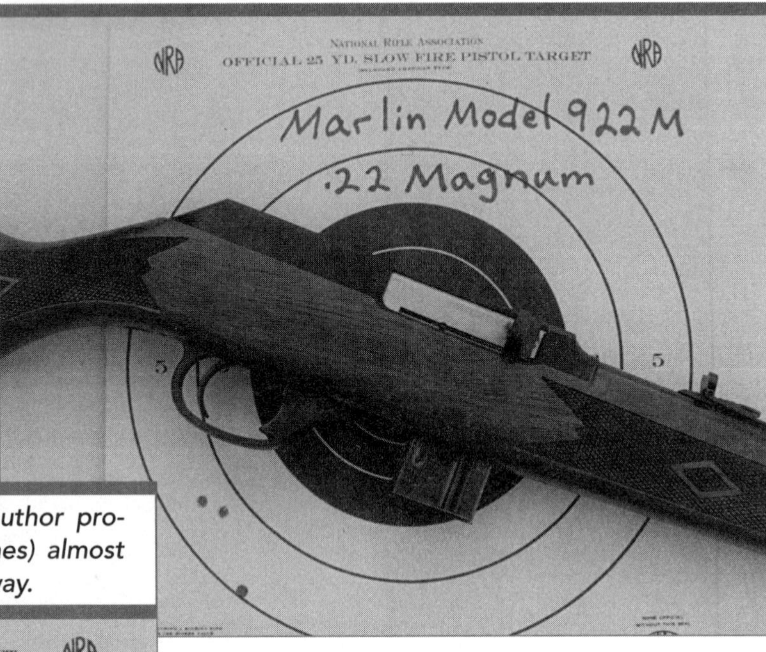

The Marlin Model 922 tested by the author produced this spectacular group (0.80 inches) almost exactly on point of aim from 50 yards away.

So far, Marlin's rifle has held its own in the .22 Magnum autoloader field; it was, in fact, the only such gun available for several years. But once a .22 Magnum version of the Remington Model 597 becomes available in quantity, the Model 922M will become less competitive. Even now, Brno Arms' excellent ZKM 611 offers better performance, workmanship and features.

MARLIN MODEL 922M

	922M
Overall Length	39.75 inches
Barrel Length	20.5 inches
Weight	6.5 pounds
Years Produced	1993-present
Caliber/Capacity	.22 WMR/7 rounds

MAS Modele 49/56 .308 NATO

The 7.5mm MAS 49/56 rifle was only the second self-loading rifle (following the Swedish Ljungman) to feature direct gas operation of the bolt, thereby eliminating the pistons and operating rods of other semiautomatic rifle designs. This simple mechanism became world-famous in the AR-15/M16 series of rifles after Eugene Stoner had adapted its design for his own purposes. The French designers, however, had perfected the design more than a decade before Stoner used it.

The MAS 49/56 can now be considered a "modern rifle" because of a recent conversion

The converted MAS-49/56 (center) offers .308 caliber performance at a much lower cost than rifles like the Springfield, Inc. M1A (top) or the ArmaLite AR-10A4 (bottom).

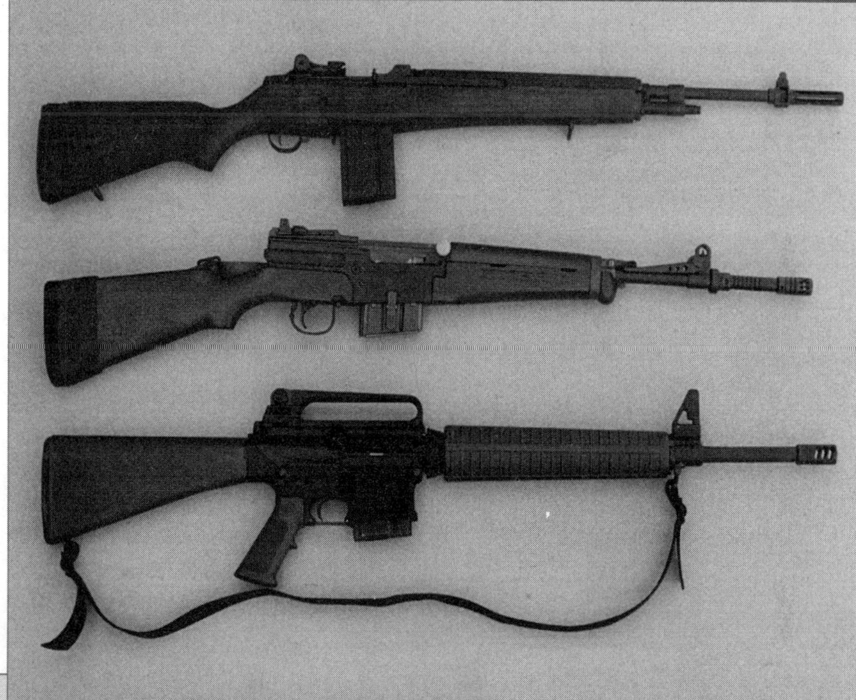

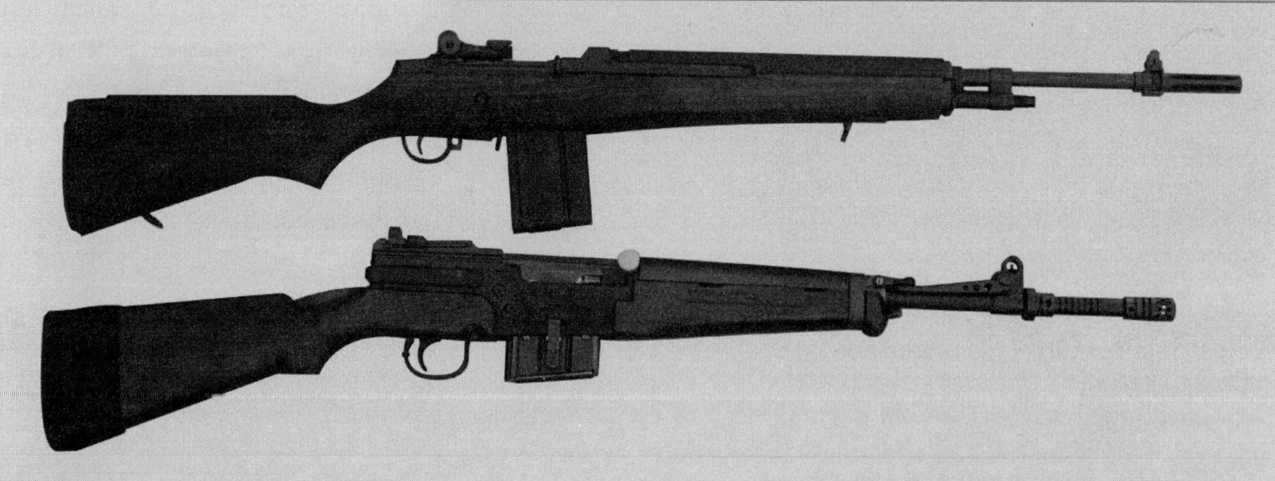

The MAS-49/56 (bottom), a contemporary of the M14 (top), was in many respects a more advanced design.

now offered by Federal Arms Corporation (Fridley, MN), which allows shooters to fire the more common .308 Winchester (7.62x51mm NATO) round instead. The idea for this conversion did not originate with Federal Arms Corporation; indeed, the French themselves had explored the interchangeability possibility with their NATO allies beginning in the 1950s, successfully converting both MAS-36 bolt-action and MAS-49/56 self-loading rifles to .308 caliber. When France withdrew from NATO in 1970, the .308 Winchester conversion project languished. Today, all the desirable mechanical and operational features of the MAS-49/56 .308 caliber conversion have been retained. Among those desirable features that have proven so conducive to accuracy and reliability are the rifle's good sights, its crisp trigger pull, and its overall quality of construction. Indeed, the rifle I rested outperformed the original French 7.5mm Model 1929 chambering. With the .308-caliber conversion, my best 3-shot benchrested group, fired from 100 yards using Federal Hi-Shok ammunition, created a pattern measure a scant 1.2 inches across. That is considerably better than the group fired earlier with an unaltered 7.5mm version. The conversion makes a great deal of sense, actually. The French 7.5mm round and the .308 are both derived from Mauser-system ammunition and are not only similar in power levels, they are almost exactly the same size. The original French 54mm cartridge casing is only 3mm longer than that of the .308 cartridge. Moreover, high-quality .308 ammunition is much easier to find around the globe than the 7.5mm French. It's a well-made gun, as most French military arms are, and it handles well by virtue of its compact dimensions. In short, the MAS Modele 49/56 .308 caliber conversion offers good, solid performance for much less money than any other .308 caliber military rifle. That makes it an excellent choice for shooters on a budget, offering performance out of all proportion to its cost.

The MAS-49/56 converted to .308 caliber shot even better than an unconverted 7.5mm variant tested earlier.

MAS MODELE 49/56 .308

	MODELE 49/56 .308
OVERALL LENGTH	41.3 inches
BARREL LENGTH	20.5 inches
WEIGHT	8.5 pounds
YEARS PRODUCED/CONVERTED	1997-
CALIBER/CAPACITY	7.62x51mm NATO (.308)/10 rounds

Mitchell Arms AK-22 and M16A1/22

Mitchell Arms, a one-time manufacturer and importer based in California, was an importer of lookalike rifle in rimfire calibers emanating from the Armi-Jager Company of Milan, Italy. Its AP-74—an M16 lookalike—first appeared in 1974. Made in both standard M16A1 rifle and CAR-15 carbine variants, this rifle looks surprisingly like the real ArmaLite/Colt .223 caliber military rifle—much closer, in fact, than the Armscor M-1600. The AK-22, styled to resemble the Soviet AK-47/AKM, first appeared in 1980 and has seen some official service as a training rifle for the Egyptian armed forces. In addition to these replicas, Armi-Jager has also made .22 Long Rifle caliber copies of the French FA-MAS service rifle, the Soviet PPSh-41 submachine gun, and Israel's service rifle, the Galil.

Internally, considerable differences exist between the Armi-Jager replicas and the full-

The Mitchell Arms AK-22 (top) and M16A1/22 (bottom), along with the TU-KKW from Norinco of China, offer military rifle features in an inexpensive rimfire format.

The best 50-yard group produced by the M16A1/22 measured 2.3 inches. Note also how authentic in appearance this M16 copy is.

powered military rifles after which they are styled. The former, limited to .22LR, .22 Magnum, or .32 ACP chamberings, use a simple blowback mechanism. The magazines resemble a rimfire target pistol magazine, but they fit into an enlarged shroud styled to resemble the M16/AK-47's larger magazine box. In that regard, the enlarged fake magazine on the M16A1/22 is a better facsimile than the AK-22's, which is undersized for the real AK-47/AKM magazine. Original Armi-Jager AP-74s featured a rotary safety inspired by the M16 unit; but the later M16A1/22 (imported by Mitchell Arms) was converted to a crossbolt safety. The Armi-Jager AP-80 (AK-22) safety works much like the full-powered AK-47/AKM's, but it includes a notch that enables shooters to lock the bolt open for cleaning or inspection—an improvement over the AKM, which lacks this useful feature.

The excellent sights on these rifles closely resemble those found on the military originals on which they're based. Both Armi-Jager rifles tested performed well, with 50-yard groups measuring 2.3 inches (for the AP-74/Mitchell Arms M16A1/22) and 1.9 inches

The Mitchell Arms AK-22's best 50-yard group measured 1.9 inches with five shots fired.

(for the AP-80/AK-22). Best accuracy was achieved with the highest-velocity ammunition, in this case CCI Stinger. Regrettably, reliability was spotty even with the best-functioning brands; indeed, with some brands of .22 Long Rifle ammunition the rifles jammed frequently, with spectacular results, including squashed and deformed bullets and bent cartridge casings. In short, these guns looked great but performed on the fussy side, even more than usual compared to other rimfire rifles tested for this book.

The Mitchell Arms AK-22's notched safety lever allows the manual safety to double as a bolt hold-open device.

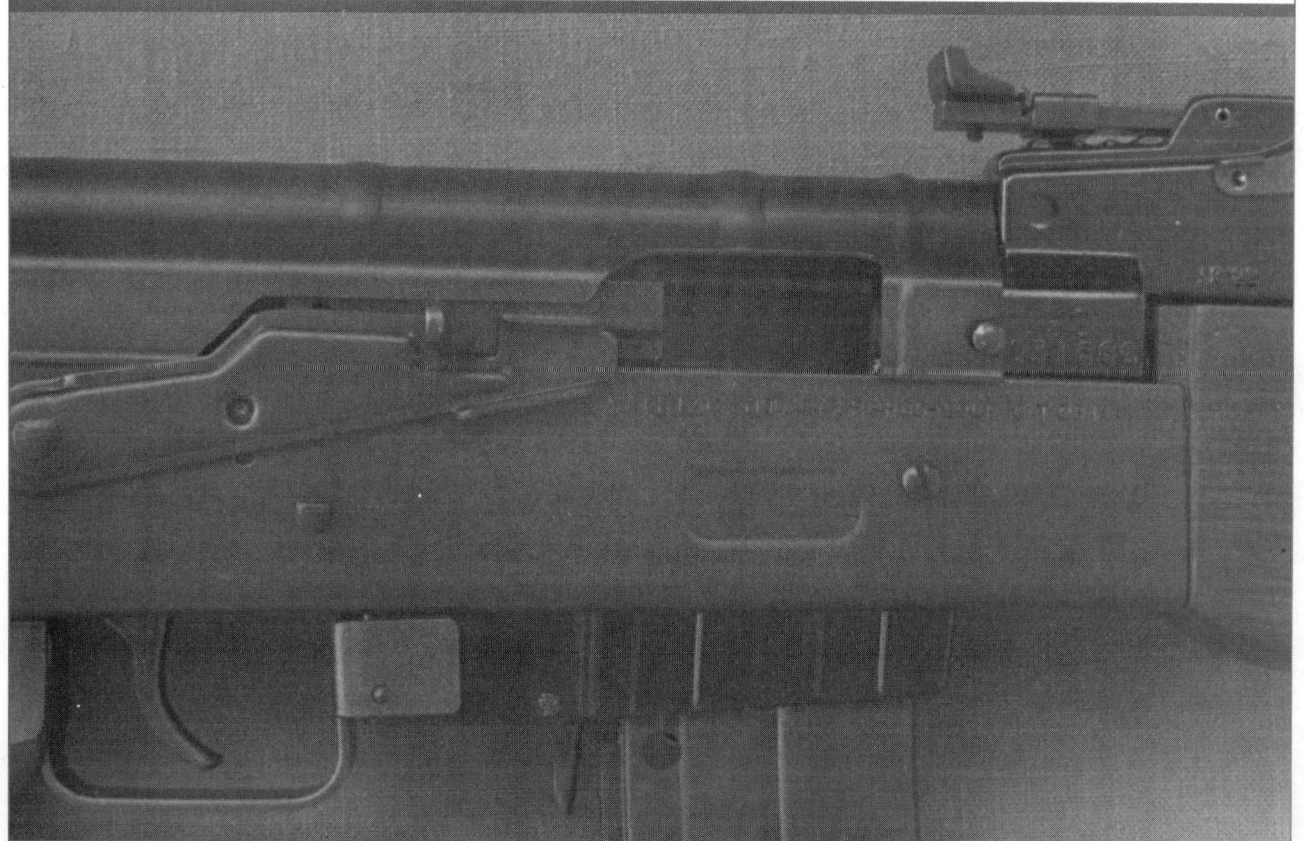

MARLIN CAMP CARBINES

	M16A1/22	AK-22
Overall Length	38.5 inches	36.0 inches
Barrel Length	20.5 inches	18.0 inches
Weight	7.0 pounds	6.5 pounds
Manufacturer	Armi-Jager, Milan, Italy	Armi-Jager, Milan, Italy
Former Importer	Mitchell Arms	Mitchell Arms
Years Introduced	1974	1980
Years Imported	1987-1993	1985-1994
Caliber/Capacity	.22LR/15 rounds	.22 LR/20 rounds • .22WMR/10 rounds

Norinco (China North Industries Corporation) 22-ATD

Norinco's 22-ATD was a Browning product (an Auto-22 copy formerly imported by Interarms) made in China. It was initially announced in 1987, with importation beginning in 1989. In its 1989 catalog, Interarms made the following statements: "You'll recognize it as a modern interpretation of one of the world's most famous designs . . . the 22-ATD . . . high quality workmanship and performance—without a high price!"

Interarms clearly sought customers who liked the excellent mechanical features of the Browning Auto 22 but were willing to give up some quality for a break on the price. Apparently, Interarms found quite a few buyers, because even though the 22-ATD had a less elegant surface appearance than the genuine Auto-22, it was mechanically and functionally identical—and the price reduction was significant. For example, in 1993 the least expensive (Grade 1) Browning Auto-22 sold

The Norinco 22-ATD (bottom) follows the Browning Auto-22's appearance (top) very closely. The Norinco's receiver, however, has a less rounded outline, and its rear sight does not fold down so that a scope can be mounted.

for $344.95 (suggested retail), while the Norinco 22-ATD sold for only $158.33.

In fairness to Browning, it should be pointed out that the Norinco clone's accuracy—at least with the example I tested—was not nearly the equal of either Belgian- or Japanese-built Browning Auto-22s I have fired, nor did its workmanship approach that of the Browning rifle. The 22-ATD also lacked some of the small refinements that have continued to make the genuine Brownings hard to beat. For instance, the rear sight on the Auto-22 folds down to facilitate mounting a scope. In contrast, the 22-ATD's rear sight was fixed, forcing those who wanted a scope to remove the rear sight or mount the scope high enough to clear the sight. At any rate, when the U.S. Government banned all further imports of firearms from China in 1995, the 22-ATD was effectively rendered a dead issue.

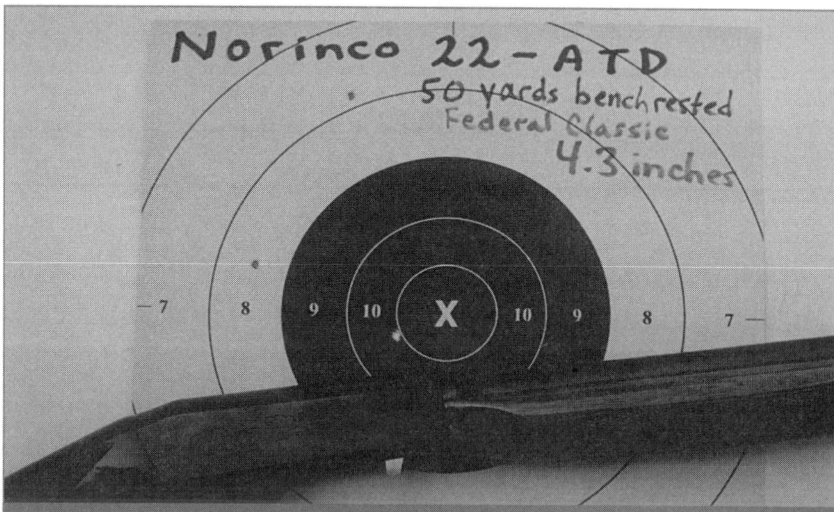

The Norinco 22-ATD tested poorly with some brands of ammunition. This 4.3-inch, 50-yard benchrested group using Federal Classic was the author's worst group with any rifle chambered for .22 Long Rifle caliber. Another group shot with Aguila SE, also a highly regarded ammunition brand, went into an almost equally bad 3.9-inch group from 50 yards.

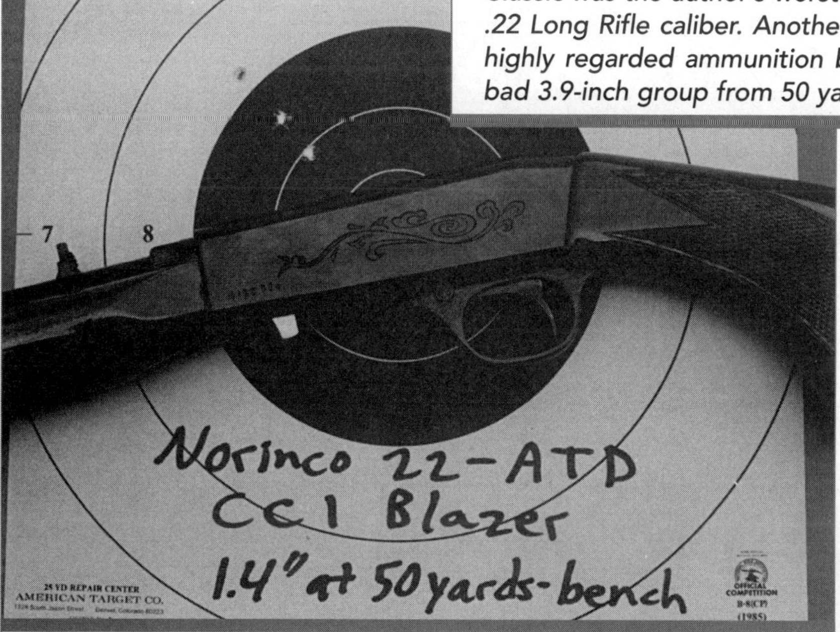

This 1.4-inch, 50-yard benchrested group using CCI Blazer was the author's best effort in test-firing the Norinco 22-ATD.

NORINCO 22-ATD

	22-ATD
Overall Length	36.6 inches
Barrel Length	19.4 inches
Weight	4.6 pounds
Years Produced	1989-95
Caliber/Capacity	.22LR/11 rounds

Norinco M14

A close copy of the U.S.-owned M14 rifle, this Norinco facsimile fires the same 7.62x51mm (.308 caliber) cartridge as the M14 but has no bayonet lug and lacks the capability of fully-automatic fire. Some have no flash suppressor at all, while others have a fake one at the end of the barrel, but without slots to break up the ball of hot gases emerging from the barrel behind the bullet, hence nonfunctional. Briefly imported into the U.S. by Century International Arms (1991-1995), Norinco M14s are still legal to buy, sell and own, but none may be imported.

The Norinco M14 (bottom) and the L1A1 Sporter (top), both once imported by Century Arms, tried unsuccessfully to offer slightly modified versions of two of the world's most famous 7.62x51mm (.308 caliber) battle rifles at a relatively low cost.

Features of the Armscor rimfire rifles include 5- or 20-shot detachable magazines (any magazine made to fit the M14 will work in the Norinco copy). The stocks, made of hardwood (stained to resemble walnut) are also similar to the M14's. Early M14 copies made by Norinco used a rubber recoil pad on the butt, while later models adopted the M14's hinged buttplate from the M14 for a more authentic appearance. As for accuracy, the Norinco M14 rifle produced decent results, but certainly not up to the best M1A or M14 standards. Reliability, though, was perfect with the two examples tested for this book.

Though not as well made as a Springfield M1A, the Norinco M14, particularly in its later variations, offers a reasonably faithful M14 copy at a far lower price. As a matter of principle, I don't like to buy products made in Communist China. I'm willing to pay more for something not made there. For those who don't feel that way, the Norinco M14 offers good performance for the money.

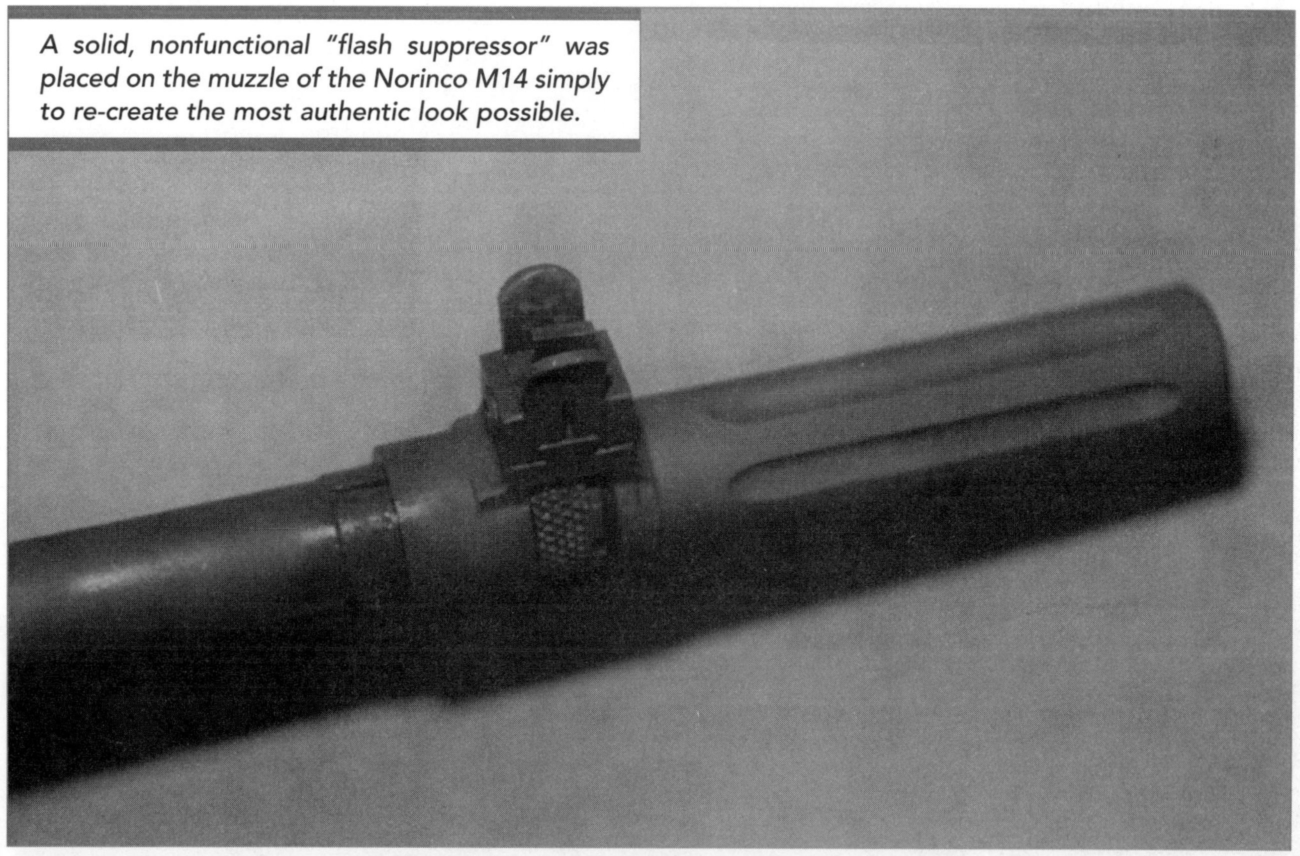

A solid, nonfunctional "flash suppressor" was placed on the muzzle of the Norinco M14 simply to re-create the most authentic look possible.

NORINCO (CENTURY) M14

	M14
Overall Length	40.8 inches
Barrel Length	22.0 inches
Years Produced	1991-1995
Weight	8.25 pounds
Caliber/Capacity	.308/5 or 20 rounds

Norinco MAK-90

Norinco's MAK-90 is simply a Chinese clone of the commercial AK. As such, it consists of the basic Kalashnikov-designed action (limited to semiautomatic fire only) with a sporterized thumbhole stock. A 5-round magazine is standard, but those with greater capacities and drums built for the AKs work effectively in this rifle. While the stock design—specifically the angle of the thumbhole cut—definitely favors a right-handed shooter over a left-hander, the MAK-90 handles well. Thanks to the rifle's considerable weight relative to its size, recoil is mild.

As for accuracy, I was able to fire 3-shot target groups at 100 yards measuring as little as 2.9 inches across with a Chinese-made MAK-90 using Winchester ammunition

The Norinco MAK-90 was an attempt to civilianize the basic AKM design, known throughout the world as one of the most formidable assault rifles ever created.

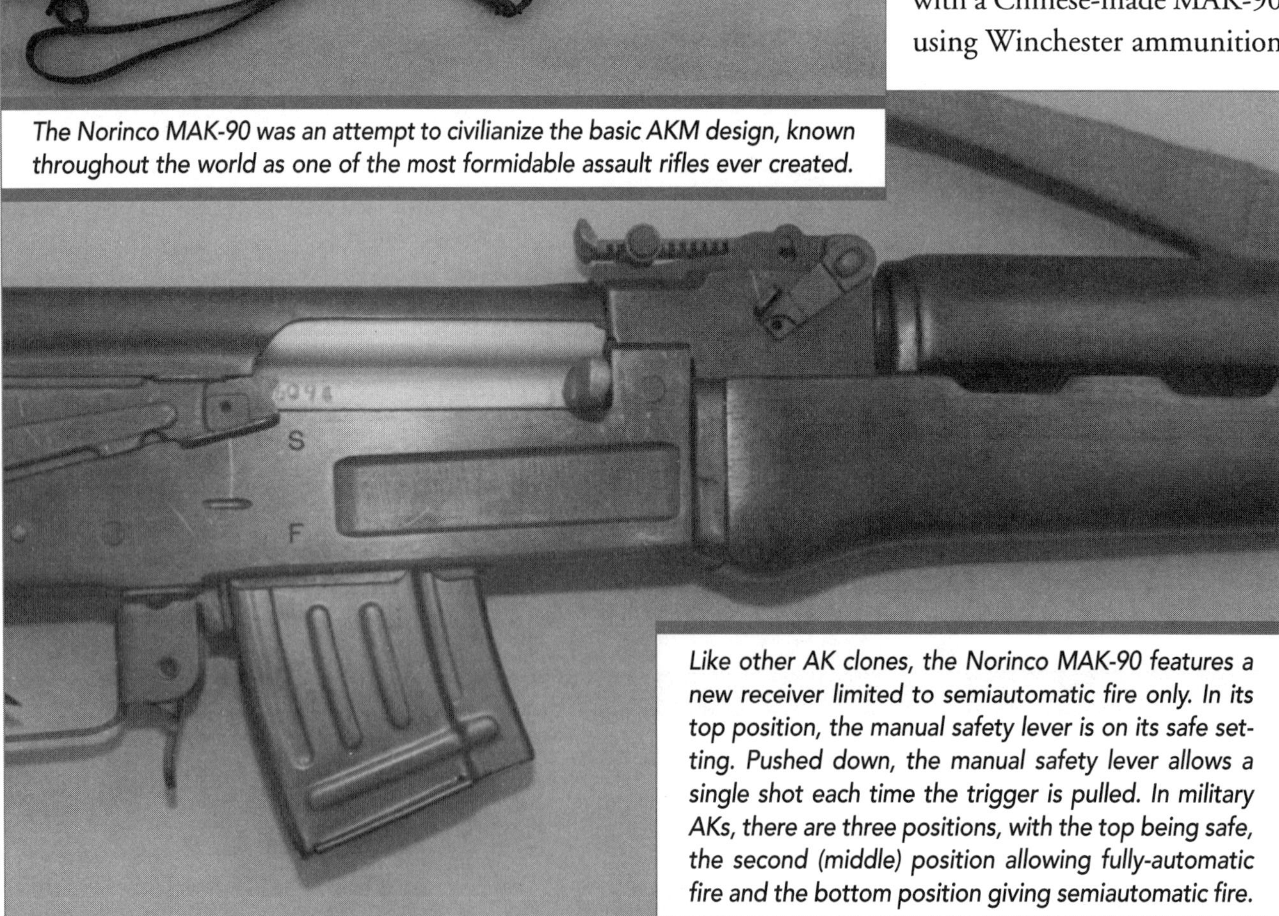

Like other AK clones, the Norinco MAK-90 features a new receiver limited to semiautomatic fire only. In its top position, the manual safety lever is on its safe setting. Pushed down, the manual safety lever allows a single shot each time the trigger is pulled. In military AKs, there are three positions, with the top being safe, the second (middle) position allowing fully-automatic fire and the bottom position giving semiautomatic fire.

(groups fired under the same conditions with Chinese-made Norinco ammunition have run several inches wider). This experience suggests to me that the reputed poor accuracy performance of AK-type rifles may not be entirely the fault of the rifle after all. Certainly modern Federal and Winchester ammunition brings out the accuracy potential of a rifle better than military-surplus 7.62x39mm ammunition emanating from China. The MAK-90 has also been advertised in .223 caliber (I have never come across one made to fire that cartridge, however).

The Norinco MAK-90 uses the shortened five-shot magazine shown here, but any extended-capacity magazine for any AK-type rifle in 7.62x39mm will also work fine in this rifle.

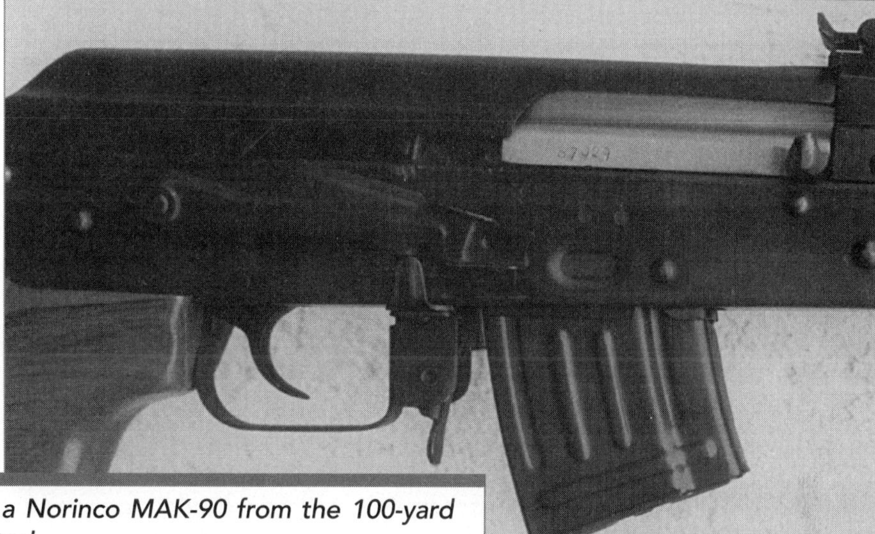

This 2.9-inch group fired from a Norinco MAK-90 from the 100-yard benchrest is better than expected.

Until it fell under the U.S. import ban of 1995, the MAK-90 was once the least expensive AK variant available in the U.S. and remains so, albeit in reduced numbers, on the used gun market.

NORINCO MAK-90

	MAK-90
Overall Length	35.5 inches
Barrel Length	16.25 inches
Weight	8.2 pounds
Years Produced	1990-1995
Caliber/Capacity	7.62x39mm/5 rounds

Ohio Ordnance BAR Model 1918A3

The BAR Model 1918A3 is an adaptation (semiautomatic only) of the world-famous Browning Automatic Rifle. Designed in 1917 by John M. Browning, this weapon reflected the need for a rugged, yet relatively lightweight automatic weapon capable of giving troops what the French called "walking fire." Though France had originated this concept, the automatic rifle they had chosen to implement it—the Model 1915 Chauchat—was chronically unreliable and suffered continuous parts breakdown. Early experiences in the U.S. with the Chauchat in both the 8mm Lebel and U.S. .30-06 service calibers were no better than the French results. Adopted by the U.S. Army in May, 1917, the Browning Machine Rifle went quickly into production, in time to see action in combat during the later stages of World War I. During this conflict, the Browning Automatic Rifle designation, usually shortened to "BAR," largely replaced "Browning Machine Rifle" as the weapon's official name.

Despite its considerable weight (16 pounds, unloaded) the BAR ranked high among the handiest fully-automatic weapon, one that worked extremely well in adverse conditions. As such, it added greatly to the firepower of troops armed with slow-firing, bolt-action rifles. Following the war, several changes were made, both to reduce weight and, paradoxically, to add accessories in an effort to improve the rifle's utility in the role of a light machine gun. Thus did the original BAR—a true rifle, albeit a heavy one—go though several

The BAR Model 1918A3 may look big and clumsy, but it actually handled well in our tests, especially with the bipod and carrying handle removed (as shown).

The Model 1918A3, which is limited to semiautomatic fire, has only a two-position manual safety. When the safety lever is pushed forward, the rifle can be fired. Pushing it back (as shown) renders the rifle safe.

variants, including the BAR itself, the Colt Monitor (a failed commercial development), the M1918A1 and the M1918A2.

The M1918A1, created in 1937, featured a bipod and a buttplate (both foldable additions) that made the BAR a light machine gun more than a true automatic rifle. The M1918A2, created in 1941, kept the folding buttplate but moved the bipod from the gas cylinder beneath the barrel to the flash suppressor on the muzzle. The buttstock on the A2, which was usually made of plastic instead of wood, also included a mounting point for a monopod. This accessory allowed precise shooting on a particular compass heading, a useful add-on for sustained fire. Monopods were popular in light machine guns of the period, but they were rarely used on the BAR. The forend was cut down to expose more of the barrel for cooling purposes. A machine-gun style rear sight replaced the M1918 Enfield's, and the semiautomatic setting on the selector switch was eliminated. Later, in the early 1950s, a carrying handle was also added to the design. These changes added four pounds to the weight of the M1918A2.

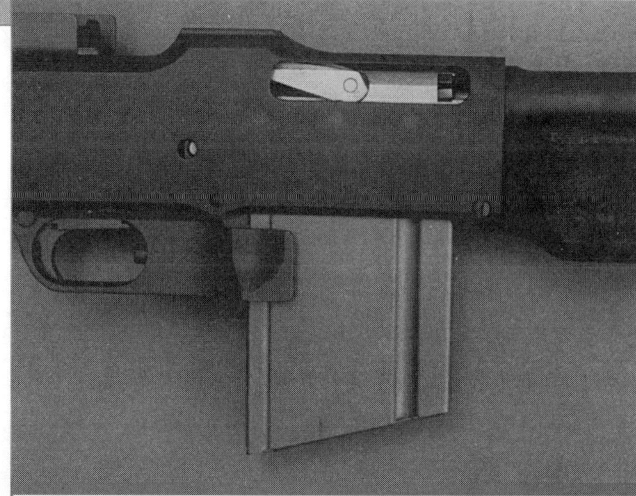

The Model 1918A3's breech-locking toggle mechanism is visible in the ejection port. Note also the prominent magazine guides slightly ahead of the triggerguard.

While all three types were used in World War II, the M1918A2 was the most common. In the field, though, many troops stripped this rifle down by removing the bipods and other gadgets. They wanted to keep the original M1918 configuration so the weapon could be used once again in direct fire support, rather than in a machine-gun role. With its 20-shot box magazine and its lack of a quick-change barrel, the BAR did indeed prove unable to provide the level of sustained fire needed in a light machine gun.

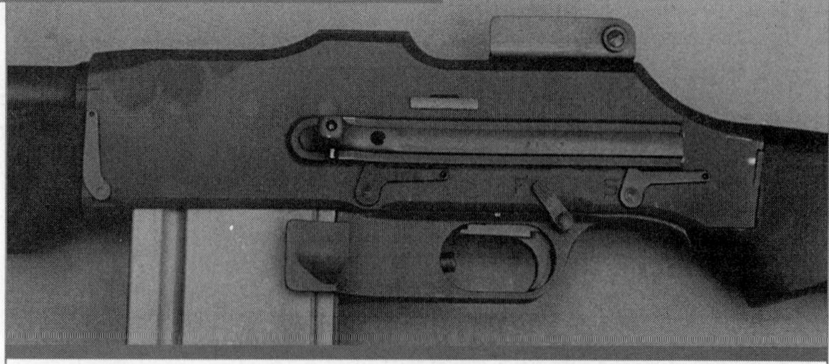

The Model 1918A3's cocking handle appears on the left side of the receiver, much like the MP40, FAL, G3 and other self-loading rifles. It allows right-handed shooters to keep their shooting hand in position to fire while reloading.

These original BARs all had the capability of fully-automatic fire. Each one, in fact, included a selector switch for shooters seeking an adjustable rate of full-auto fire (as in the M1918A2) or an alternate semiautomatic setting. Despite its considerable weight (for a rifle) and its limited sustained-fire capability as a light machine gun, the rugged and reliable BAR provided good service for U.S. armed forces as a front-line weapon right into the 1950s, and later with U.S. reserve forces up to the 1970s and even longer elsewhere.

Overseas, the BAR was licensed to FN in Belgium and Sweden's Carl Gustav state-owned rifle factory. Because of its widespread use in warfare since 1918, and its extensive manufacture and distribution, BARs can still be found virtually anywhere in the world. They are so well designed and built so solidly that they should endure for many years before wearing out.

Bob Landies, who was the spark in the BAR's re-creation, first attempted to make a replica BAR. It was a straight-pull, repeating version similar in concept to a bolt-action rifle. His latest effort, however, is the BAR Model 1918A3, a true repeating rifle that differs from the military BAR only in its inability to make repeated shots with a single pull on the trigger. It's gas-operated, has a locked breech, and fires from the closed-bolt position. This last characteristic means that fire must be limited so the barrel can cool off between long strings of fire. Otherwise, a "cook off" could occur should a round explode in the firing chamber and fire unintentionally because of excess heat in the barrel and firing chamber.

The BAR Mod 1918A3 (made by Ohio Ordnance) utilizes almost all surplus U.S. or Swedish parts, which makes it almost fully authentic to the original. It differs from the military model in one important respect: because Federal regulation has severely restricted private ownership of fully-automatic firearms, the BAR Model 1918A3 must have an investment-cast receiver containing a modified trigger group (hammer, sear and trigger) that limits the gun to semiautomatic

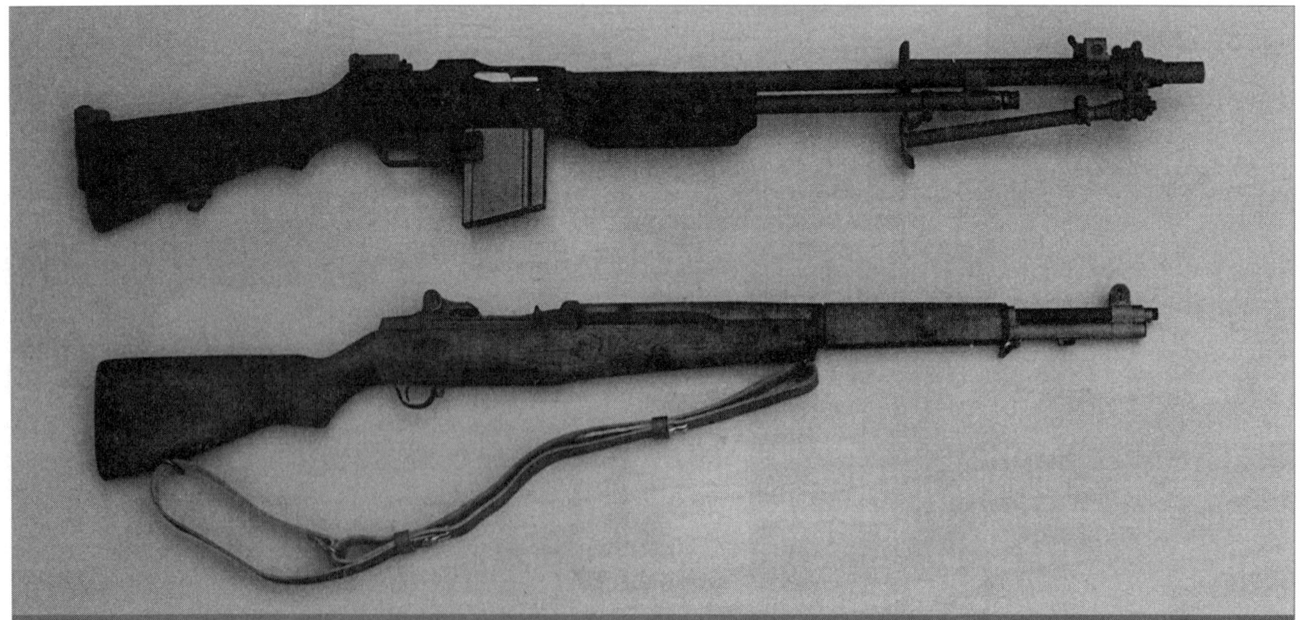

The Model 1918A3 (top) is only slightly longer than the M1 Garand (bottom), but weighs about twice as much. Both rifles fire the .30-06 round.

fire only. Some internal dimensioning has also mandated that all original BAR selective-fire trigger parts will not fit, hence the new model designation. This new trigger group has also changed the disassembly procedure of the BAR Model 1918A compared to that of the original

The Model 1918A3's best 100-yrd benchrested group (actually fired from the bipod) was a sensational 0.90-inch pattern. Point of aim was at the bottom of the target's black portion.

BAR variants. With the new rifle no longer possessing full-auto capability, a two-position manual safety has replaced the original three-position safety/fire selector. All other parts are authentic and original.

Two versions are planned: the first—the M1918A3—re-creates the World War II-era Model 1918A2, including parkerized finish, bipod, small handguard and synthetic stock. The second version—the A-1918 (which some have nicknamed the "Doughboy") is still under development. This design harks back to John Browning's original 1917 design, but without a bipod and with a high-polish blued finish. It also has a M1917 rifle-style rear sight adjustable for elevation only, a different gas regulator, a larger handguard, and a wooden buttstock. To build this World War I-style A-1918 "Doughboy" variant, Bob Landies, without any surplus wood available, was forced to commission newly-manufactured wooden stock furniture. More polishing of the investment-cast new receiver is also required before the metal will accept the labor-intensive, bright blued finish appropriate to World War I. This extra work delayed the "Doughboy's" introduction until the fall of 1998, with the price rising higher than the parkerized version. Landies has anticipated total production of the parkerized, bipod-equipped version to

Despite its size, the Model 1918A3 functioned well in offhand shooting. This 1.8-inch group fired at 50 yards was typical of what one can do with this rifle without a benchrest.

approach 3,000 complete rifles, limiting manufacture of the costlier World War I "Doughboy" variant to about 270 in number.

The BAR Model 1918A3 is equipped with a bipod, two original 20-round magazines, a canvas sling and a detachable carrying handle. For our tests I elected to fire the gun in its usual combat configuration, which meant extra parts had to be removed, reducing the gun's weight as close to the World War I BAR as possible. Off came the two-pound bipod and the ten-ounce carrying handle, and what I was left with was something similar to that which our Marine gunners carried into combat at Belleau Wood and, much later, Iwo Jima.

The BAR Model 1918A3, with all its heft, handles well and displays excellent shooting characteristics. A button located in the forward portion of the trigger-guard serves as a magazine release. The charging handle is located on the left side of the rifle. This enables right-handed shooters to keep their dominant right hand in position while loading the gun (Dieudonné Saive, a close follower of John Browning, designed a similar charging handle for the world-famous FAL). The BAR's considerable weight reduces recoil to relatively low levels despite the powerful .30-06 cartridge it fires.

Accuracy was excellent and reliability was flawless. At 100 yards our test produced less than two minutes of angle with Hornady match ammunition.

To be sure the BAR Model 1918A3 will not become a commonplace item. Ohio Ordnance charges close to $3000 for one, and the "Doughboy" runs considerably higher. Nevertheless, for well-heeled shooters and collectors, the BAR Model 1918A3 offers an historically interesting gun that is well off the beaten path. Certainly it will increase distribution of the BAR design, what with original fully-automatic BARs growing scarce and tightly controlled by government regulation.

Even the Model 1918A3's worst 100-yard benchrested/bipod group (1.8-inch) was more than acceptable.

OHIO ORDNANCE BAR MODEL 1918A3

	MODEL 1918A3
Overall Length	47.9 inches
Barrel Length	24.0 inches
Weight	20.0 pounds
Years Produced	1997-present
Caliber/Capacity	.30-06/20 rounds

Remington Model 552 Speedmaster

In 1957, two years after the pump-action Model 572 first appeared, Remington introduced the semiautomatic Model 552 or "Speedmaster." The two guns were quite similar, the chief difference being the way they operated. The Model 572 had a manually-operated slide mechanism, while the Model 552 featured a semiautomatic blowback operation. In addition, the Model 552 used the same tubular magazine feed, which gave it the flexibility of firing any type of .22 Short, Long or Long Rifle ammunition. In that respect, the Model 552 followed the example of an earlier Remington rifle: the semiautomatic Model 550.

Among its other features, the Model 552 included a shell deflector on the ejection port,

The Model 552 Speedmaster (bottom), is a classic design with great staying power, outlasting even Remington's venerable Nylon 66 (top).

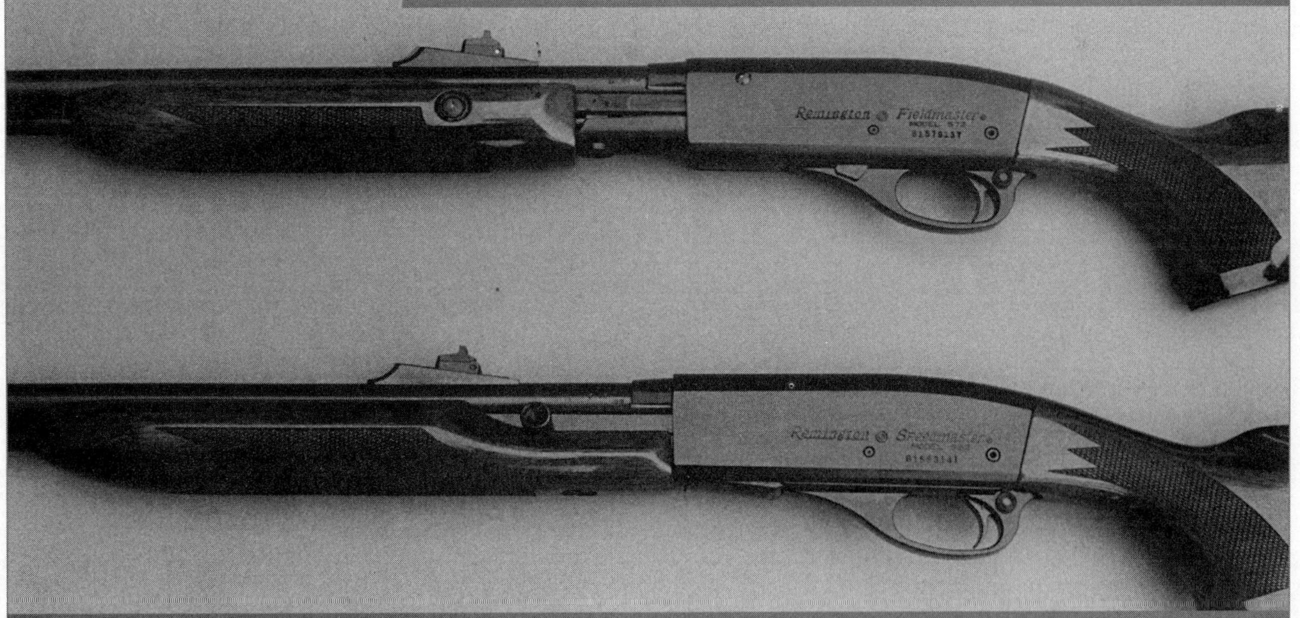

Slight differences exist between the self-loading Model 552 Speedmaster (bottom) and the pump-action Model 572 Fieldmaster (top). The Model 552 has an operating handle for cycling the bolt and no exposed parts in the loading mechanism. On the other hand, pump-action Model 572 has exposed action bars in front of the receiver and an added slide release lever next to the triggerguard.

which protected left-handed shooters from being pelted by hot brass from spent cartridge casings (another feature inherited from the company's earlier Model 550). In a further concession to left-handers, the Model 552's cocking handle was placed on the left side of the receiver rather than the right side. This switch also worked well for right-handed shooters, since it allowed right-handers to keep their dominant hand on the pistol grip while operating the handle with their left hand. Several well-known military weapons have this left-sided operating handle system, notably the U.S. Browning Automatic Rifle, the German MP38/MP40, Walther's MPK/MPL submachine guns and G3 Rifle, and the Belgian-designed FN FAL rifle.

Like the Model 572—a companion piece to the pump-action Models 870 (shotgun) and 7600 (rifle)—the Model 552 is analogous to Remington's own Model 7400 semiautomatic centerfire rifle. Having guns of similar action types like these examples allows shooters to train with the rimfire models prior to firing the more powerful centerfire types.

Like the 572, the Model 552 Speedmaster has also progressed through several different variants. The basic Model 552 A had simple sights and a plain stock of medium-quality, uncheckered wood. Remington offered this model in 1966 as part of its 150th anniversary edition (giving it somewhat of a collector's premium today over the standard A model). In 1961 Remington shortened the barrel on the Model 552 from 23 inches to 21 inches, calling it the Model 552 C ("Carbine"), which the company kept in production until 1977. The fancier Model 552—the BDL Deluxe—was introduced in 1966 and is the only Model 552 type still being made. It has a fancier wood stock cut in a Monte Carlo pattern with checkering on the pistol grip and forend.

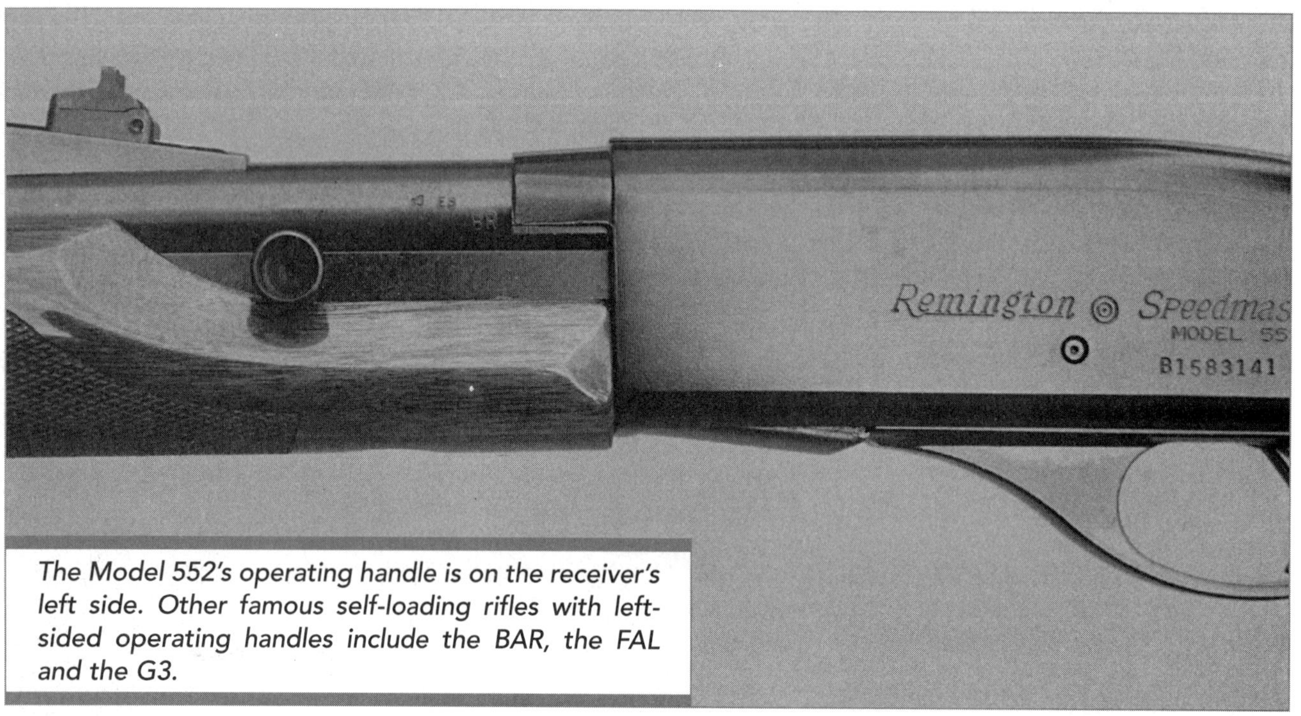

The Model 552's operating handle is on the receiver's left side. Other famous self-loading rifles with left-sided operating handles include the BAR, the FAL and the G3.

The Model 552 shoots with impressive accuracy and flawless reliability. Even when mixing .22 rimfire ammunition types in the same magazine load, reliability in feeding, firing and ejection is not adversely affected. Personally, I'd like to see Remington offer a version of its Model 552 in the more powerful .22 Magnum caliber. Also, a tang safety on this semiautomatic model (once used on the now-discontinued Nylon 66) would be more useful than the pushbutton type currently in use. On the other hand, Remington's similar Model 572 (a pump-action rifle) doesn't require a tang safety.

As for accuracy, my best 3-shot benchrested group fired from 50 yards using Aguila SE ammunition printed a tight group only 0.40 inches across. Because of the gun's substantial weight and well-shaped stock, recoil was negligible.

The Model 552 Speedmaster's longevity is a direct result of its excellent handling, versatile tubular magazine, and attractive appearance. It may be more expensive than Remington's own Model 522 and 597, but the Model 552 has a classier look and feel that appeals to gun fanciers who prefer rifles with more traditional materials and styling.

The Remington Model 552 tested by the author delivered this sensational 0.40 inches group from 50 yards. Another 3-shot group spanned 1.1 inches, but two of the bullets made one slightly enlarged hole.

REMINGTON MODEL 552

	MODEL 552
Overall Length	40 inches
Barrel Length	21 inches
Weight	5.5 pounds
Years Produced	1957-present
Caliber/Capacity	15 rounds (.22LR); 17 Longs; 20 Shorts

Remington Nylon 77/Model 10-C

By 1970, Remington's original high-tech rimfire rifle, the Nylon 66 (introduced in 1959), was showing its age. The company decided, therefore, to update the design by altering the ammunition feed mechanism. The result was the Nylon 77, which had a 5-round detachable box magazine or "clip" instead of the 14-round tubular magazine found on the Nylon 66. Remington decided to adopt the 5-round magazine, rather than a larger one, mostly to avoid upsetting the gun's sleek contours, a major selling point for the Nylon 66. A longer magazine box, it was felt, would be too unsightly, whereas the 5-round type fit nicely underneath the receiver. Altering the ammunition feed may seem a relatively minor change, but actually it required a major redesign of more than a dozen components. As a result, parts interchangeability with the Nylon 66 was seriously degraded. Reloads became much faster, but only if shooters kept spare magazines on hand. The 5-shot magazine capacity was simply too small for such a fast-firing little rifle. Largely because it gave up so much magazine capacity to the Nylon 66, the Nylon 77 proved unpopular and few were sold. Its production run lasted only two years, expiring in 1971.

That same year, Remington announced the Nylon 10-C, a Nylon 77 with a longer 10-round magazine replacing the original 5-round unit. This model designation was somewhat confusing, since Remington had already made a Model 10, a single-shot variation of the Nylon 66 autoloader (1962-1964). The recycled name did make sense, though, with reference to its increased magazine capacity compared to the aborted 5-shot Nylon 77. The Model 10-C, with its new 10-round magazine, proved more competitive and, along with the Nylon 66 and its tubular magazine, remained a

The Nylon 77 was equipped with a 5-shot plastic box magazine, while the Model 10-C used a 10-shot magazine. Otherwise, the two guns are identical and their magazines interchange. Both types of magazine are shown (a 10-shot unit is in the receiver).

commercial success for most of a decade. Remington stopped production of the Model 10-C in 1978. The rifle was then out of production for almost a decade, while the Nylon 66 remained in the company line until 1987 following an illustrious production history of 28 years. That same year the final variant of the Nylon 77/Model 10-C line, the "Nylon 77 Apache," made a brief appearance. The K-Mart store chain had contracted with Remington to reintroduce a run of Model 10-C type rifles. The result was the "Nylon 77 Apache," a 10-round box magazine Model 10-C rifle with a bright green stock reminiscent of the long-discontinued Seneca Green finish used on the Nylon 66 back in 1959-1961. Remington made a few thousand of these Nylon 77 Apache rifles for K-Mart, but production ended in late 1989, the same year in which it began.

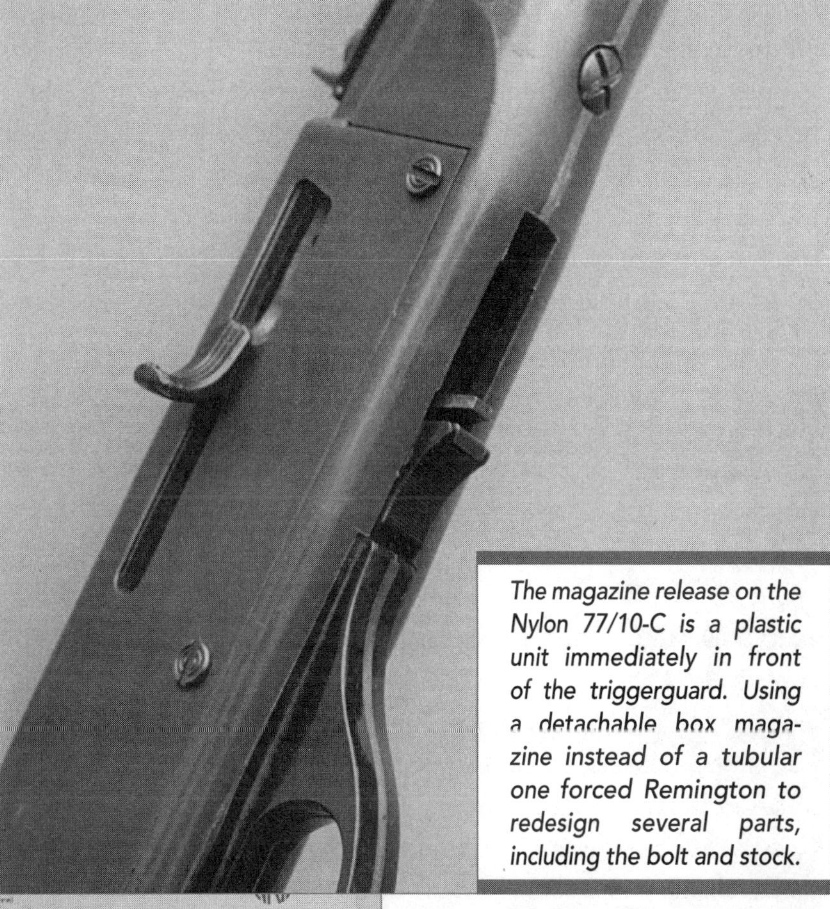

The magazine release on the Nylon 77/10-C is a plastic unit immediately in front of the triggerguard. Using a detachable box magazine instead of a tubular one forced Remington to redesign several parts, including the bolt and stock.

Using standard-velocity CCI Blazer ammunition, the Apache 77 turned in a perfectly adequate 1.3-inch group from 50 yards.

In tests using a Nylon 77 Apache, accuracy proved excellent with CCI "Stinger" hyper-velocity .22 Long Rifle ammunition. My best 3-shot benchrested group, fired from 50 yards, created a pattern half an inch across and only an inch above point of aim. Using standard-velocity .22 ammunition, however, results were less impressive. My best 50-yard benchrested group (using CCI Blazer) measured 1.3 inches.

Despite its limited commercial success, at least by comparison, the Nylon 77/Model 10-C shared virtually all of the Nylon 66's strong points. These included ruggedness (especially for a .22 caliber rifle), low maintenance (thanks to the self-lubricating nature of the DuPont Nylon 66/Zytel material used in the gun's construction), and excellent ergonomics, accuracy and reliability. For shooters with spare magazines on hand, a Nylon 77, Model 10-C or Nylon 77 Apache is arguably an even better choice for rapid .22 caliber shooting than the original Nylon 66 rifle. It is also an important link in Remington's autoloading rimfire history, bridging the gap as it does between the Nylon 66, the Viper, and current Model 597 rifles.

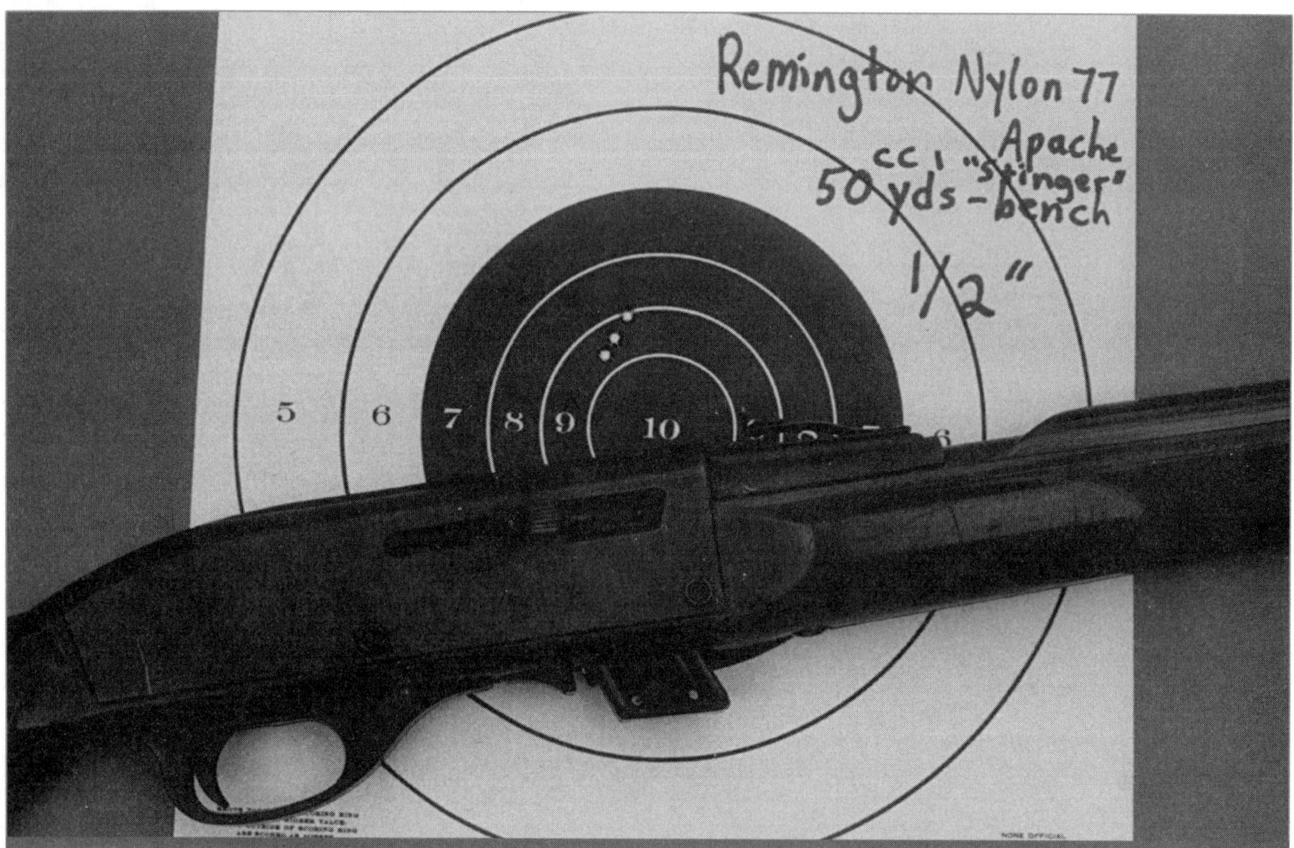

When firing the hyper-velocity CCI Stinger, the Apache 77 performed superbly, placing 3 shots in half an inch, close to point of aim at the center of the target.

REMINGTON NYLON 77/MODEL 10-C

	MODEL 10-C
Overall Length	38.75 inches
Barrel Length	19.6 inches
Weight	4.2 pounds
Years Produced	1970-1978; 1987 (see text)
Caliber/Capacity	.11LR/5 or 10 rounds (see text)

Remington Model 522 Viper

In 1993, in an attempt to reenter the .22 caliber self-loading market it had lost when the fabulous Nylon 66 rifle was discontinued in 1987, Remington decided to introduce its Model 522 Viper. This new rifle remained in production for five years before being replaced by Remington's more refined Model 597 (see following entry). Like the late lamented Nylon 66 rifle, the Viper was built almost entirely of polymer. The sights were similar in concept to those used on the Model 7400 centerfire self-loading rifle. They consisted of a bead front sight and an adjustable rear sight located just ahead of the firing chamber. The receiver also included grooves for easy scope mounting.

Safety features, which abounded on the Model 522, included a cocking indicator made of bright red plastic protruding from the rear end of the receiver with the striker cocked. This contrasted powerfully with the black receiver and stock. The manual safety device—the usual crossbolt affair—was located in front of the triggerguard. The rifle could not fire with the magazine removed, either. The bolt stayed open once the last shot was fired, and the shooter could also lock the bolt open manually. This convenient feature was typical of Remington's well-conceived designs.

The Viper's matte black plastic stock had a beavertail forend that ensured a comfortable grip; and the pistol-grip area itself had deep checkering for a positive hold as well. The "one-size-fits-all" stock was as well designed as any gun I've encountered. Indeed, everyone who shouldered the rifle I tested, including males and females of various sizes and ages, remarked on how comfortable the Viper felt. It also proved highly accurate, with perfect feeding and ejecting reliability using all ammunition brands tested, even after many shots had been fired without cleaning—a real accomplishment for a rimfire rifle. Even rifles firing ammunition in clean-burning centerfire calibers lose accuracy or become unreliable once dirt has gotten inside from extensive firing.

The Model 522 Viper represented a good first effort by Remington to recapture the market share

Remington's Model 522 Viper was the company's first attempt to replace the legendary Nylon 66 rifle with a gun similar in spirit, if not in its construction details.

surrendered when it dropped the superb Nylon 66 from the product line. As things turned out, however, the Viper became a transitional model only, never really establishing itself in the market. Some of its features—a sheet steel magazine release, for example—looked cheap. While it was highly efficient, the Viper lacked the elegance of the Nylon 66, nor was its appearance as attractive or refined as Remington's Model 597. In short, Remington's Model 597 (see below) caused the Viper to become obsolescent. Nevertheless, it was a great gun.

The Remington Model 522 Viper was superbly accurate. This effort (0.70 inches) was actually fired from 50 yards, not 100 yards as labeled. Note the plastic 10-round magazine (a more compact 5-round unit was optional).

The Remington Model 522 Viper (top) offered performance on a par with other .22 caliber self-loading rifles, such as the Norinco 22-ATD Browning copy (bottom). It failed to attract much of a following, however, and was quietly dropped after five years.

REMINGTON MODEL 522 VIPER

	VIPER
Overall Length	40.0 inches
Barrel Length	20.0 inches
Weight	4.6 pounds
Years Produced	1993-1998
Caliber/Capacity	.22 Long Rifle/10 rounds

Remington Model 597 Series: Standard (.22 Long Rifle)

In 1994, shortly after production commenced on the Model 522 Viper (see above), Remington began designing what it conceived as the ultimate rimfire rifle, which it planned to build in both .22 Long Rifle and .22 Magnum versions. Anticipating large orders of 100,000 units or more per year, Remington decided that its current production facility in Ilion, New York, which was already working at peak capacity, would be unable to take on this new model. Instead, the company built a new plant in Hickory, Kentucky, specifically for Model 597 production. By late 1995, design work on the new rifle had accelerated. Remington's plan was a good one: to build the .22LR variant first, then design a similar .22 Magnum model around a heavier bolt made of tungsten. Using tungsten, which was much heavier than steel, would cause a delay in opening the breech for the hard-kicking .22 Magnum round.

The tungsten bolt used on the Model 597 marked the first time in the history of firearms production that a major operating component has been made out of this space-age metal. The idea, while sound in principle, took some effort and several years to achieve what Remington's research

Remington's Model 597 (top) has at last succeeded in replacing the late, great Nylon 66 (bottom) with a rifle that is at once graceful, high-tech and functional.

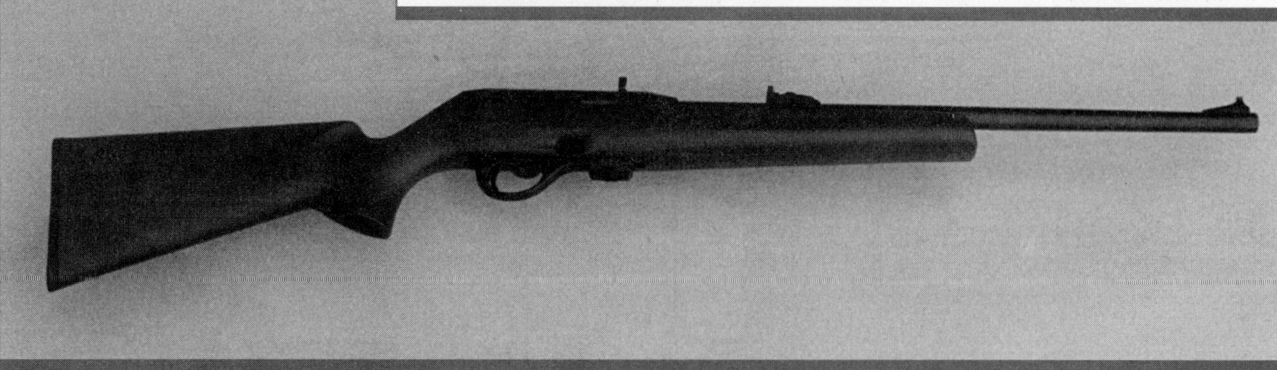

The Remington Model 597 is not the most attractive rifle, but form follows function—and its function is superb.

(See table on pg. 252)

The magazine release on the Model 597 is located on the right side of the stock just above the triggerguard. Note that the 10-shot magazine barely protrudes from the bottom of the stock, thanks to its double-column design.

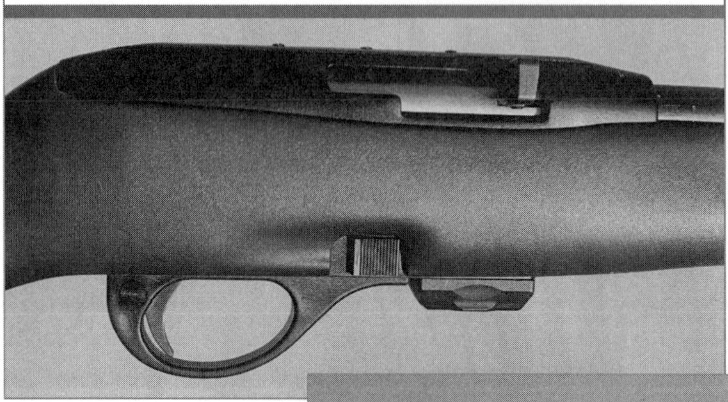

and development staff considered acceptable reliability. The company announced the .22 Long Rifle Model 597 variant in mid-1997 and announced, with considerable optimism, that the .22 Magnum variant would follow close behind. Unfortunately, the new model took almost a year longer than the .22 Long Rifle version to reach full production.

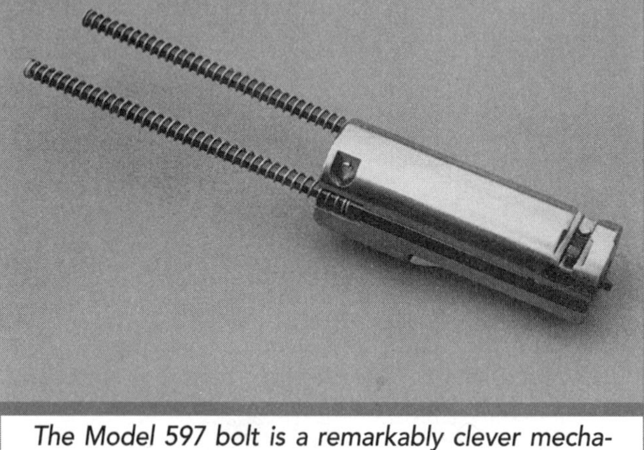

The Model 597 bolt is a remarkably clever mechanism and the only part, other than the barrel, that requires precision machining. Note the two recoil springs and guide rods at the rear of the bolt. This unit on the standard .22 Long Rifle caliber Model 597 weighs only 7 ounces, or not quite half a pound.

Today these polymer-stocked versions of the Model 597 are identical in outward appearance. The .22 Magnum version, however, by virtue of its heavier tungsten bolt, weights noticeably more. There's now a third Model 597 variant, called the 597 LSS (see below), which features a satin-finished stainless steel barrel, a gray-colored receiver made of aluminum alloy, a nickel-plated bolt, and a laminated wood stock. This model costs about $100 more than the standard .22LR model and about $50 less than the .22 Magnum version. In any of these three versions, the Model 597 offers excellent value. One of Remington's chief design objectives in creating this rifle, after all, was to minimize production costs and pass the savings on to the consumer.

Aside from the manual safety—a common crossbolt pushbutton type similar to that found on many rifles—the handling characteristics of the Model 597 are generally acceptable. For example, the bolt stays open when the last shot is fired, a good feature lacking in many .22 rifles. The polymer magazine is remarkably compact for a 10-shot unit, a welcome contrast from the long, downward-projecting box of the Savage Model 64. The secret of this compactness is the magazine's double-column feature. By

The Model 597's rear sight is rugged, offering a clear sight picture with its bold square notch. It is fully adjustable for windage and elevation.

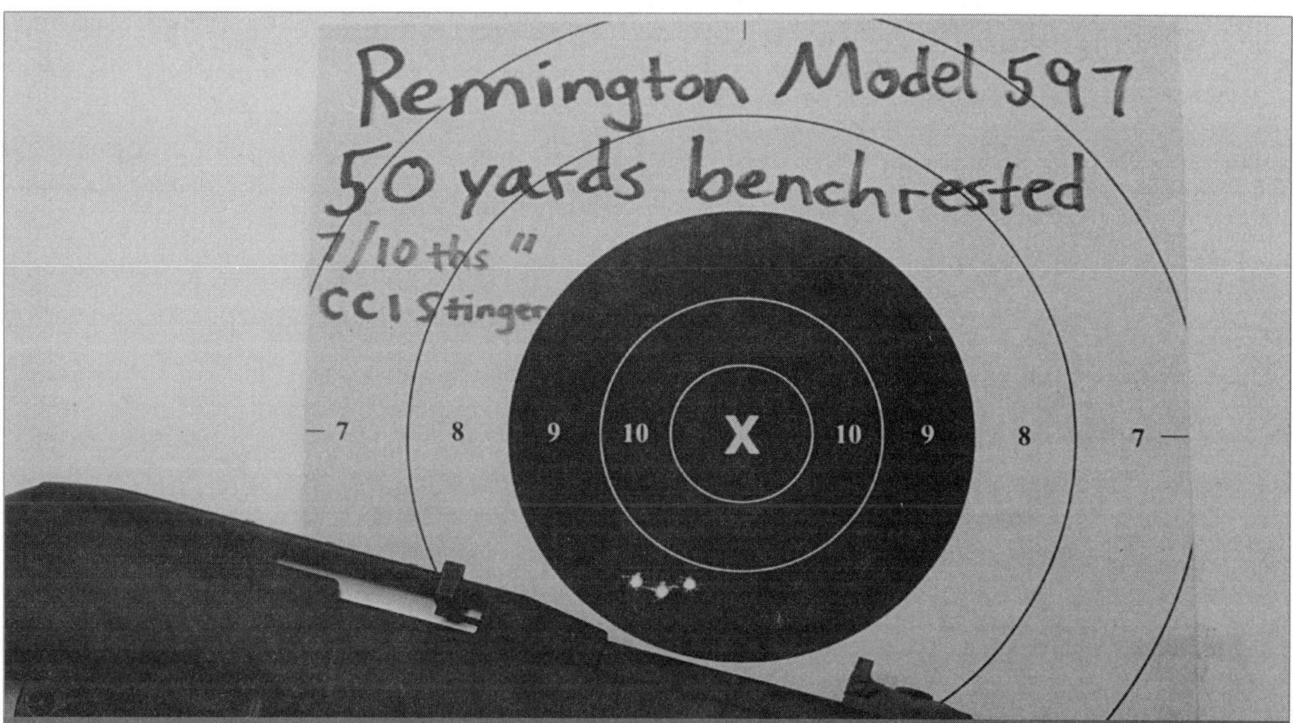

As with several other Remington rifles test-fired for this book, the Model 597 performed its best with maximum-intensity ammunition (in this case CCI's Stinger).

This 1.9-inch group fired from the Model 597 with Aguila "Super Extra" ammunition may not look like much but it is very close to point of aim at the bottom of the target's black portion.

stacking the ammunition both side-by-side and with one round on top of another, Remington was able to make the magazine shorter and thicker than would be possible if the cartridges sat in a single-column arrangement. The Model 597, I might add, should also have a magazine disconnect. This safety feature would help prevent shooters from firing a round inadvertently left in the chamber. Most rifles with detachable box magazine also lack this feature, so we can hardly find fault with Remington for not having it.

Benchrested groups fired from a distance of 50 yards using a standard Model 597 (with gray-black polymer stock and blued metal finish) measured from 0.70 inches up to 2.9 inches. As with most rifle built to fire the .22 Long Rifle round, the Model 597 has definite preferences in ammunition where accuracy is concerned. No brand used in our tests, however, produced really bad results; indeed, with some types accuracy was nothing less than stunning. In general, ammunition with the highest velocity provided the best results. Moreover, reliability remained flawless with all brands tested, an endearing feature in a .22 rimfire rifle.

While not as radical as the Nylon 66 was in its day, the Model 597 boasts a sleek, functional design with better efficiency than the Nylon 66 could provide. In .22LR caliber, the Model 597 is noticeably more refined and more attractive than the Viper. Its high-tech construction and racier styling are sure to appeal to modern shooters. In its .22 Magnum guise (see below), the Model 597 is even more impressive. Compared to the Marlin Model 922 rifle, its closest competitor, the Remington features more modern styling, more weather-resistant construction and an extra round in the magazine, all for less than what the Marlin rifle costs.

The Model 597 (top) should have offered more competition to Ruger's popular Model 10/22 (bottom). But Remington conceded the field for the better part of a decade after dropping the Nylon 66 from its line.

(See table on pg. 252)

Remington Model 597 LSS

The Model 597 LSS features a laminated wooden stock, with its barrel and action parts made of stainless steel (hence the "LSS" designation). Like the original standard Model 597, this is a .22 LR rifle. Typically, Remington put much thought into the design and ergonomics of this product. The sights, for example, are done in a contrasting black color so they'll show up against the lighter stainless steel barrel and thus help make the shooter's job easier.

The Model 597 LSS tested for this book, unlike most Remington rifles, preferred standard-velocity ammunition over high-velocity fodder. Using CCI "Stinger" hyper-velocity cartridges, my best 3-shot benchrested group fired from 50 yards away spanned almost two inches. By contrast, the rifle excelled when firing Aguila "Super Extra" (SE)-brand ammunition of Mexican manufacture, resulting in a 3-shot, 50-yard benchrested group measuring 0.40 inches across. U.S. manufacturers, by the way, are not the only ones who can produce quality arms and ammunition. In the course of testing many types of foreign rifles and brands of ammunition, I found that they performed in a manner fully competitive with anything U.S. arms-makers could offer—and frequently at a lower price.

While the Model 597 LSS is an attractive rifle, I question whether it offers enough advantages over the standard model to justify its considerably higher price. On the other hand, this rifle certainly makes a more attractive appearance than the standard grade with its somber gray-black plastic stock and matte blue metal parts. Its resistance to corrosion is also a definite step up from the standard Model 597. (See table on pg. 252)

Tests for accuracy with the Model 597 LSS produced this 0.40 inches group, just above the point of aim (six-o'clock hold).

For those who appreciate the Model 597's many excellent mechanical features but find the standard version (top) too plain, Remington offers the Model 597 LSS (bottom) with stainless steel metal parts and laminated wooden stock.

Remington Model 597 Magnum

In 1998, after two years of developmental work, the .22 Winchester Magnum Rimfire version of the Model 597 began to appear in quantity. The delay was caused mainly by Remington's desire to perfect a heavier bolt. This would allow the rifle to function with a more powerful cartridge but in the same size envelope as the .22 Long Rifle version. Remington met this challenge by making the bolt on the Model 597 from tungsten, which is, as stated earlier, heavier than steel. Although its bolt is exactly the same size as the standard model's, the Model 597 version weighs

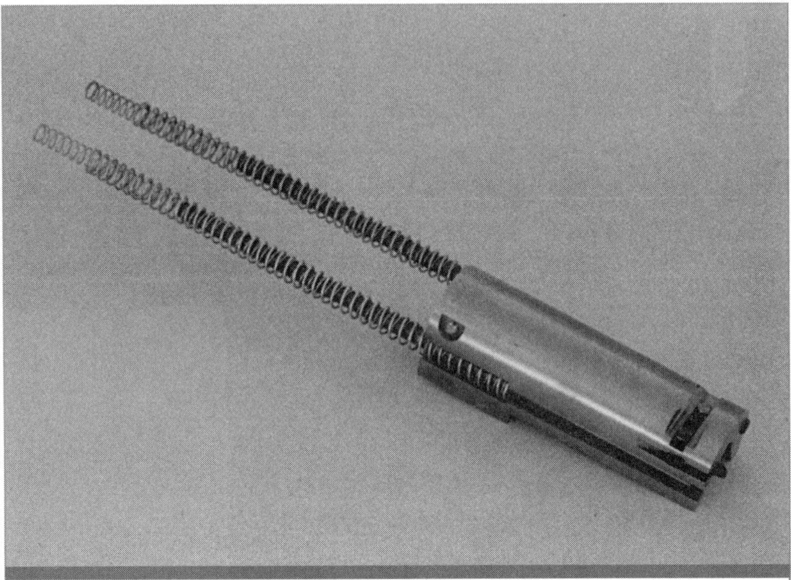

The bolt on a Model 597 Magnum looks like the standard version but weighs 15 ounces instead of only 7. It also has doubled recoil springs on each guide rod instead of single springs.

The Remington Model 597 Magnum receiver has a distinctive marking so that it will not be mistaken for the standard .22 Long Rifle model (both share the same length and shape).

a full 15 ounces in .22 Magnum, as opposed to only 7 ounces for the steel bolt on the .22LR variant. The Model 597 Magnum rifle also features two doubled recoil springs (not two singles), which return the bolt to the battery after each shot. This marvelous example of the art of firearms manufacturing allows the Model 597 Magnum to offer the .22 WMR (.22 Magnum) cartridge in a rifle exactly the same size as the company's standard .22LR Model 597, but only half a pound heavier. This was truly an impressive engineering feat.

All in all, the Model 597 Magnum is an excellent performer, witness my best 3-shot benchrested group fired from 50 yards. For ammunition, I selected Winchester's superb "Varmint" ammunition, which uses a 34-grain High Velocity Hollowpoint (HVHP) bullet. The pattern was a mere 0.70 inches across, only half an inch from point of aim. That is good shooting indeed for a rimfire rifle with open sights. While I ordinarily don't test rimfire rifles beyond 50 yards, this gun's flat shooting to point of aim intrigued me, so I fired a 100-yard

The Model 597 Magnum gave superb results at the 50-yard bench. Point of aim was at the bottom of the black portion of the target.

The Model 597 Magnum, when disassembled, displays the gun's simple construction and easy maintenance.

group that went into 1.6 inches. This was especially impressive because I used the rifle's standard sights. With a scope fitted, I could doubtless have done better. Indeed, a whole host of more expensive, more powerful centerfire-caliber rifles tested for this book failed to shoot as well.

To sum up: the Model 597 is an excellent rifle, and in .22 Magnum caliber it's even better. Moreover, the Model 597 Magnum is the least expensive .22 Magnum self-loading rifle currently available—and by a considerable margin at that.

Both the Model 597 Magnum (top) and the Brno ZKM 611 (bottom) offer superb accuracy in the versatile .22 Magnum cartridge.

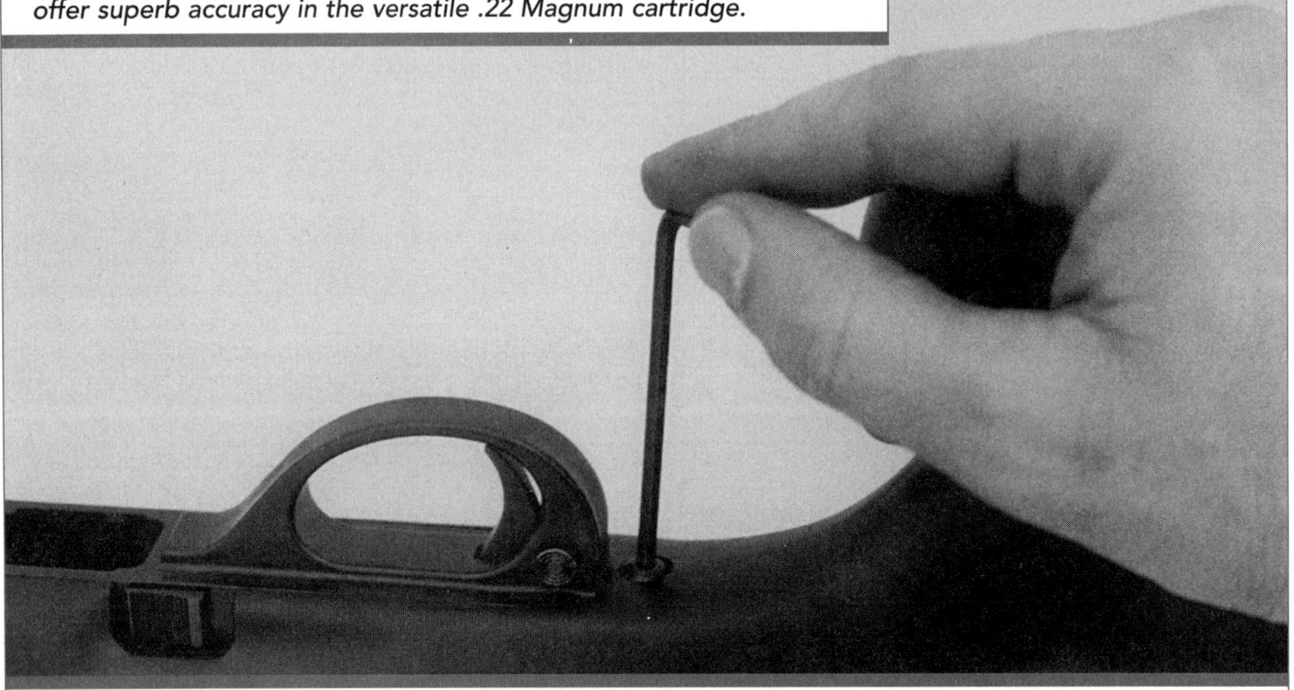

All Remington Model 597 types are disassembled with a 5/32-inch Allen wrench when removing the trigger group (but be sure to unload the gun first).

REMINGTON MODEL 597 SERIES

	MODEL 597
Overall Length	40.0 inches
Barrel Length	20.0 inches
Weight	5.5 pounds (.22 LR)/6.0 pounds (.22 WMR)
Years Produced	1997-present (.22LR); 1998-present (.22 WMR)
Caliber/Capacity	.22 Long Rifle/10 rounds; .22 Magnum (.22 WMR)/8 rounds

Remington Model 7400

Remington's Model 7400, an improved version of the 1955-vintage Model 740 Woodsmaster, first appeared in 1981. Remington also introduced at that time a Model 4, but it was essentially the same as the Model 7400 (the Model 4 had a fancier finish). Remington discontinued the Model 4 in 1987, transferring its deluxe features to the gas-operated Model 7400 line. The breech on the Model 7400 locks by means of multiple lugs on a rotating bolt, locking and unlocking into matching recesses cut into the barrel extension. The large receiver separates the wooden furniture into two parts: a stock (with pistol grip and, in some cases, a Monte Carlo comb) and a forend. The latter extends all the way back to the receiver. By contrast, the slide-action Models 760/7600 have shortened forends that move only partway back to the receiver, thus exposing several inches of operating rods. The

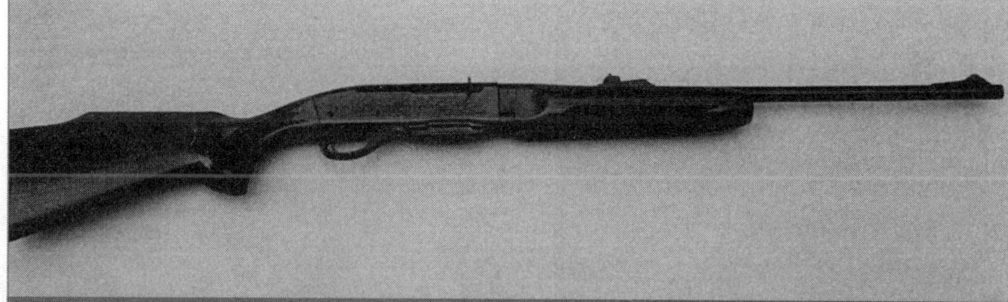

The semiautomatic (self-loading) Remington Model 7400 is similar to the pump-action Model 7600. Only the bolt operating method is different.

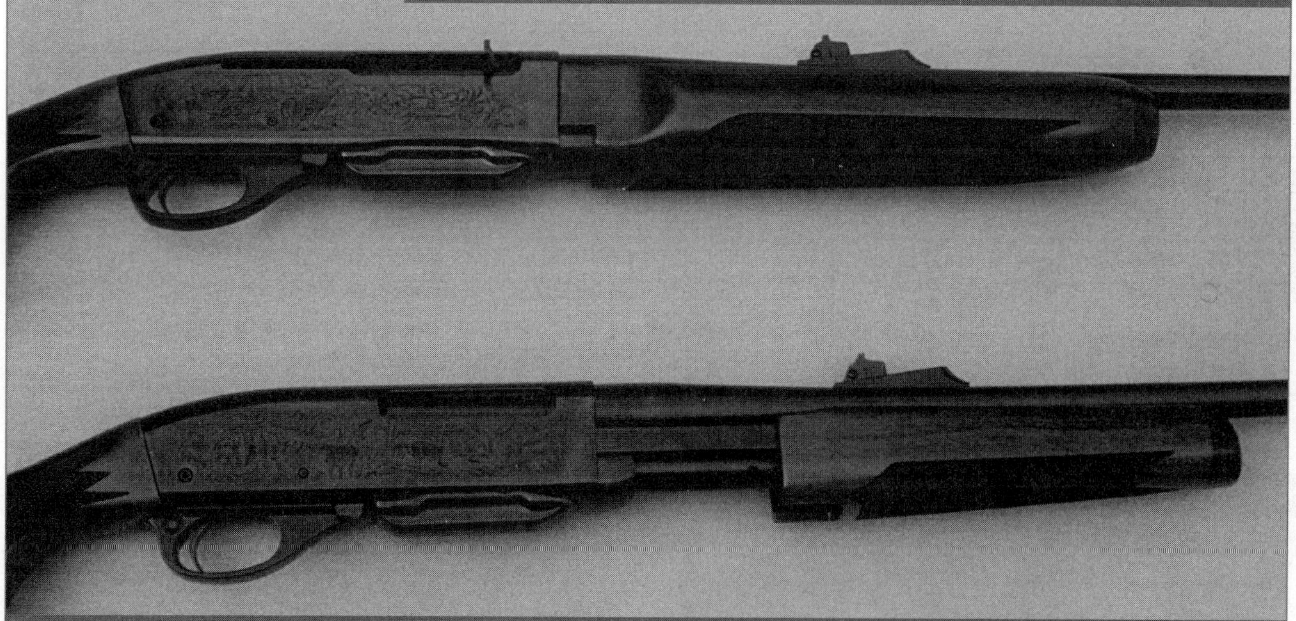

The forearm wood on the Model 7400 (top) extends all the way back to the receiver. The pump-action Model 7600, by contrast (bottom), has a shortened forearm with exposed action bars.

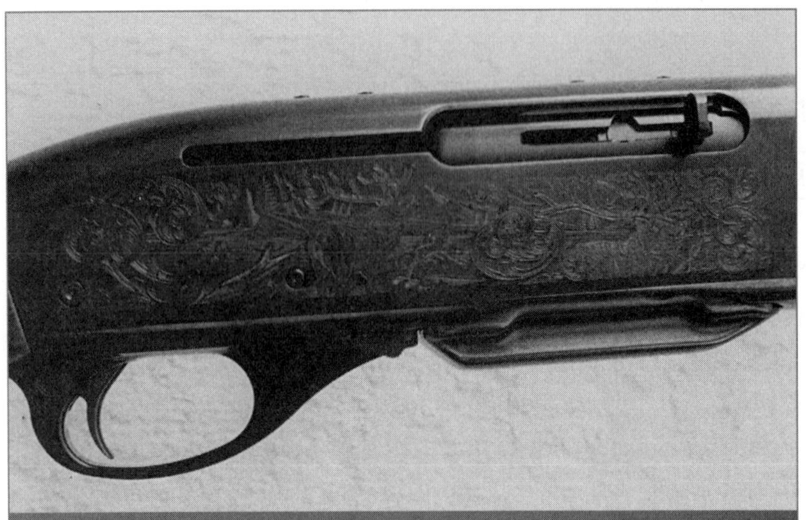

The magazine release on the Model 7400 is located at the leading edge of the triggerguard.

Model 7400 is a pleasant rifle to fire, with recoil occurring in two distinct stages (typical of self-loading rifles) rather than the single sharp blow one expects from a single-shot or manually-operated rifle. The mechanism itself seems to soak up a generous amount of recoil impulse as well; and when firing the .243 caliber, the Model 7400 hardly has any recoil impulse at all. Even in .270 caliber the recoil seems softer than that one expects from a bolt-action rifle in the same caliber.

magazine for the Model 7400, as opposed to the Model 7600, contains an integral hold-open device that keeps the bolt back should an empty magazine be placed in the rifle or upon the last shot being fired. Its front sights consist of a gold bead on a ramp, and there's a step rear sight a little more than halfway down the barrel. The receiver is drilled and tapped for mounting a scope (several manufacturers, notably Millett, make suitable scope mounts). The safety is a variation of the popular crossbolt mechanism, located as usual on the triggerguard.

Test results with the Model 7400 rifle reveal excellent accuracy. The best bench-rested 3-shot group measured 1.2 inches from 100 yards (with iron sights). The

This 1.2-inch group from the 100-yard bench indicates that the Model 7400 has excellent accuracy. Note the pushbutton manual safety at the rear edge of the triggerguard and the engraved receiver (standard on current models).

REMINGTON MODEL 7400

	MODEL 597
Overall Length	42.0 inches
Barrel Length	22.0 inches (18.5 inches .30-06 Carbine only)
Weight	7.5 pounds
Years Produced	1981-present
Caliber/Capacity	.243, .270, .280, .308, .30-06/4 rounds

Ruger Mini-14/Mini Thirty

In 1972, following the success of its Model 44 and Model 10/22 self-loading rifles, Sturm, Ruger & Company announced the 5.56x45mm (.223 caliber) Mini-14. After modest sales to various police and military organizations, full production for the commercial market began in 1976. Since then, "The World's Most Expensive Plinker" has become quite popular with sports shooters, hunters, police and paramilitary forces the world over.

Features of the Mini-14 rifle include a rotating bolt and manual safety/trigger mechanism modeled after the M1 Garand. The gas system and other mechanical features have been influenced by both the U.S. M14 service rifle and the older M1 carbine. Like many Ruger firearms, the receiver on the Mini-14 is an investment casting lightly machined to its final shape. The result is a component that is strong and yet relatively inexpensive to produce. This manufacturing method allows Ruger to offer the Mini-14 for significantly less than the Colt AR-15 and other competitive .223 caliber self-loading rifles.

The Mini-14 rifle accepts 5-, 10-, 20-, 30- or 40-shot detachable magazines (the 5-shot is standard issue for the commercial market, with Ruger supplying 20-rounders for police and military customers). Several companies have made aftermarket, extended-capacity magazines for the Mini-14 (and Mini Thirty) in the past, even though sales to private citizens of magazine exceeding 10 round capacity have been illegal since

Although they share many features, Ruger's Mini-14 (bottom), far from being a scaled-down copy of the M14 (top), boasts a new design in its own right.

The magazine release on the Mini-14 is the short lever protruding straight down from the stock immediately ahead of the manual safety.

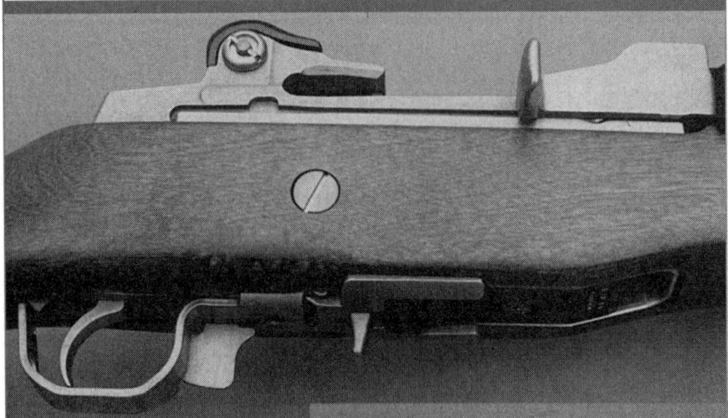

January 1995. The stock is usually a fixed, wooden half-stock type much like the M14's. The standard stock design works equally well for average-sized adult shooters and persons of small stature. A fiberglass handguard protects the shooter's hand from both the operating slide and the barrel, which heats up quickly when firing. Holes in the handguard also help cool the barrel.

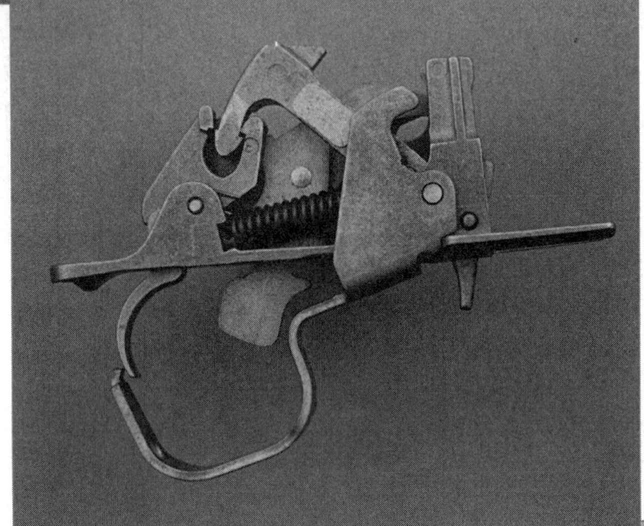

The Mini-14's trigger group, inspired by that of the M1 Garand, is a model of simplicity and efficiency.

Ruger builds several Mini-14 variations. The original version, still in production, has a fixed wooden stock that leaves the front portion of the barrel exposed, along with an M14/Garand-style adjustable rear sight. Ruger supplemented this model with a "Ranch Rifle" variant back in 1982. The Ranch Rifle has integral scope mounts and a rear sight that folds down and forward, out of the way, enabling a scope to be placed as low to the receiver as possible. Early Ranch Rifles featured a shotgun-style straight buttplate, but Ruger changed this to a curbed version much like the standard Mini-14.

A much heavier .243 Winchester and .308 caliber (7.62x51mm NATO) variant of the Mini-14—called the XGI—was developed by Ruger between 1984 and 1985. The company advertised this model briefly, but it never achieved full production status. It proved reliable enough, and it was significantly smaller and handier than the M14 in the same caliber, but Ruger was so dissatisfied with the XGI's accuracy that it stopped work on the rifle after making only 20 prototypes.

Fortunately for Ruger, the XGI led directly to the Mini Thirty. In 1987, with production for .30 caliber

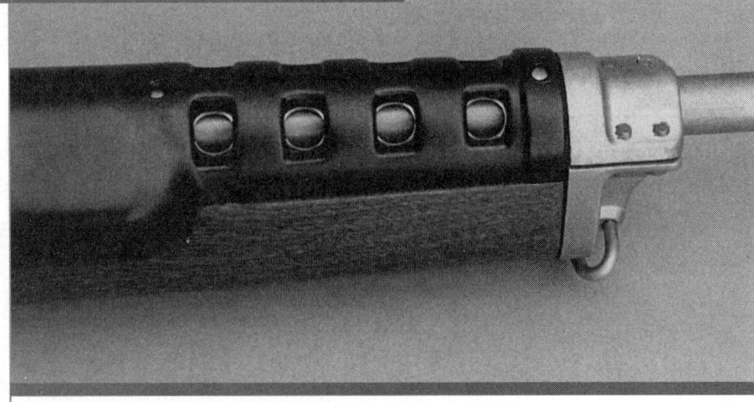

The handguard is pierced with holes to promote and hasten barrel cooling.

barrels established and with interest in the Soviet M43 round growing in the United States, Ruger decided to add a "Mini Thirty" variant to its Mini-14 line. Based on the Mini-14 Ranch Rifle variant, the Mini Thirty fires the 7.62x39mm cartridge, making it an attractive alternative to Russia's SKS and AK rifles, which are heavier and less accurate than the competition. All models are available in either blued or stainless steel finishes. The stainless Mini-14 Ranch Rifle dates from 1986 and the stainless Mini Thirty made its first appearance in 1990. Folding stocks on both blued and stainless standard Mini-14 versions offered during the period 1985 to 1989, thereby reducing the rifle's overall length still further, to a mere 27.5 inches.

Almost since the day Ruger announced it, the Mini-14 has attracted the attention of the world's armed forces. The first militarized version—the Mini-14/20GB—appeared early in the production run. This variant has a flash hider with an integral bayonet lug for use with the standard M8 bayonet

With the hammer cocked, the space behind the Mini-14's bolt appears open.

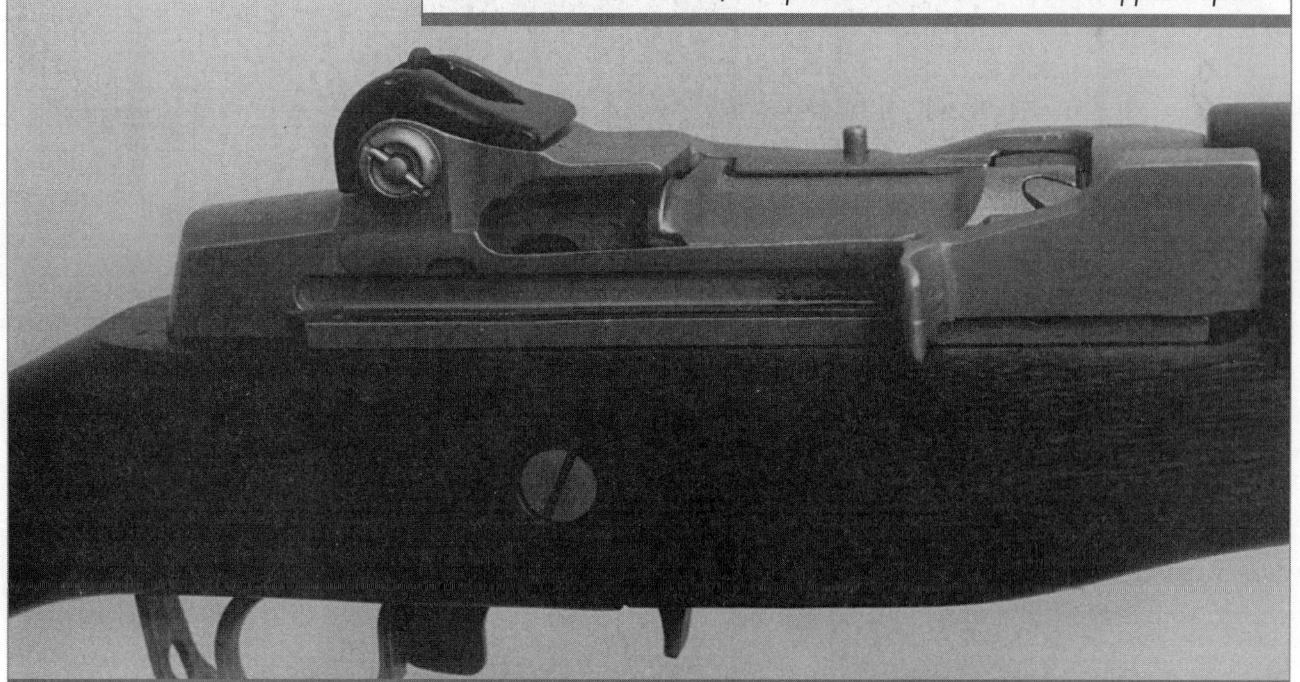

With the hammer uncocked and the rifle unable to fire, the hammer is visible (behind the bolt).

issued with the M16 rifle. Ruger followed this product in 1976 with the AC-556, basically the Mini-14/20GB with its trigger mechanism altered (by means of a selector switch) to allow single shots, 3-round bursts or fully-automatic fire. Ruger has offered these variants in fixed-stock and folding-stock versions, blued or stainless steel finishes, and in two barrel lengths, including the standard 18.5 inches.

In testing both the Mini-14 and Mini Thirty rifles, excellent performances emerged for this class of weapon. A Mini-14 typically produced benchrested 3-shot groups measuring slightly over 2 1/2 inches from 100 yards. A Mini Thirty performed almost as well, with a benchrested 3-shot group measuring 3.3 inches from 100 yards. As with other rifles chambered in the Soviet-designed 7.62x39mm round, superior groups were realized with ammunition made by U.S. manufacturers rather than with ammunition from China, whose military-surplus ammunition used corrosive primers that quickly rusted out the Mini Thirty's gas system. The only remedy in that event was to clean the system thoroughly within hours of shooting.

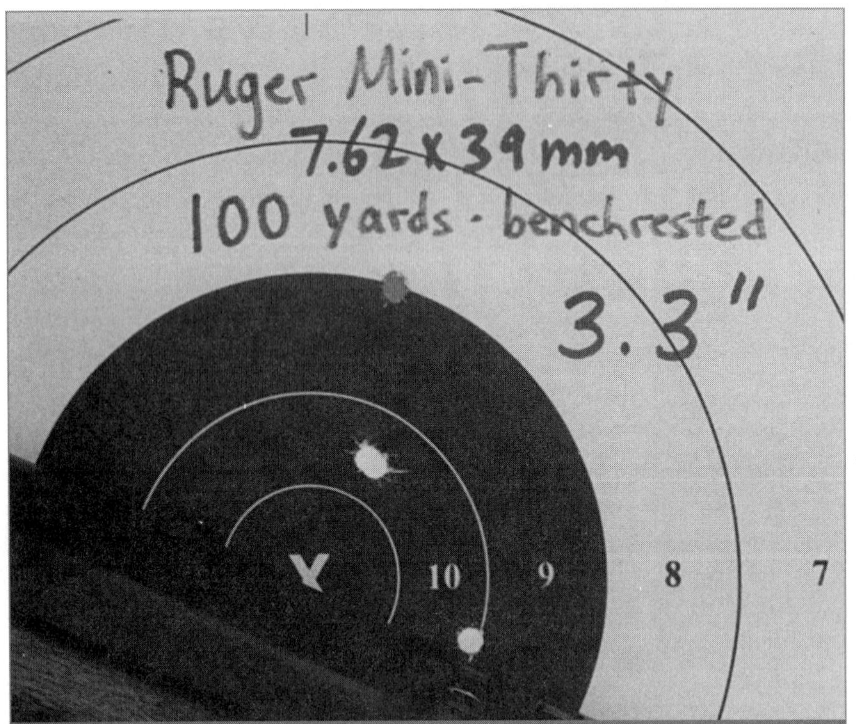

A Ruger Mini Thirty tested for this book fired 3-shot 100-yard benchrested groups as small as 3.3 inches across, which represents superior performance in most SKS and AK-47 rifles.

The Ruger Mini-14 tested for this book fired 3-shot 100-yard benchrested groups as small as 2.6 inches with American-made ammunition, which is good shooting for a semiautomatic .223 caliber rifle.

Reliability with both the Mini-14 and Mini Thirty was typically

DISASSEMBLY

To disassemble the Mini-14/Mini Thirty, first remove the magazine, draw back the bolt, and finish unloading (clearing) the rifle. Then pull down the rear edge of the triggerguard, unhinging it as shown.

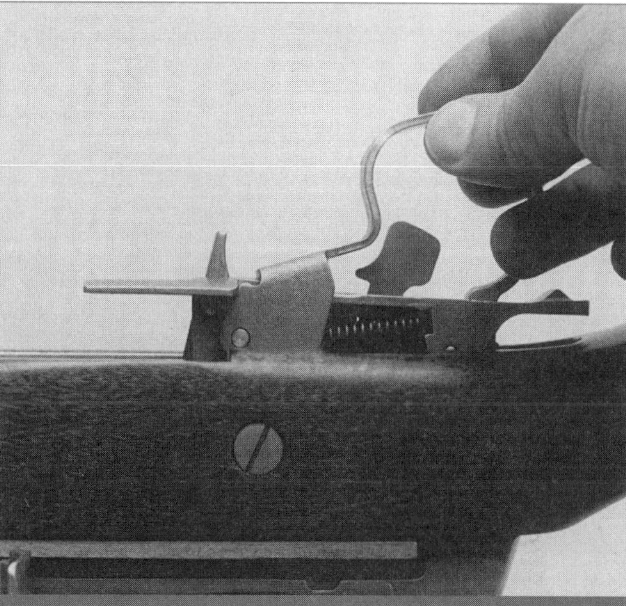

The disassembly sequence continues by withdrawing the trigger group from the stock.

With the trigger group removed, the barrel/receiver group can be unlocked from the stock.

DISASSEMBLY

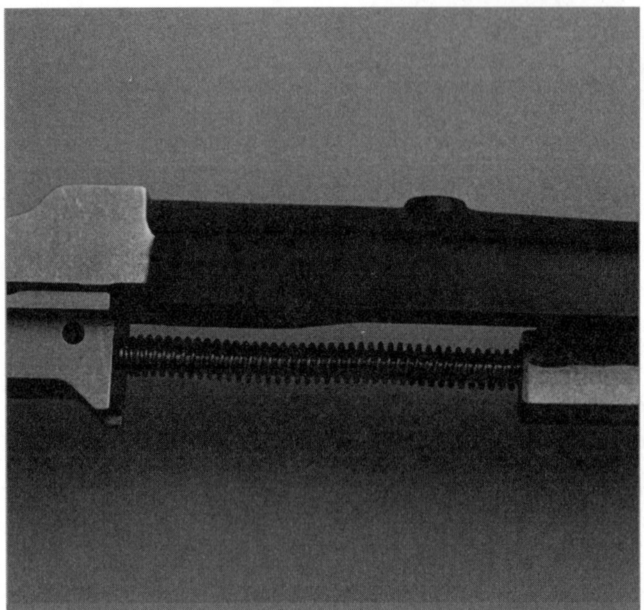

A return spring (underneath the handguard) connects the receiver to the operating slide.

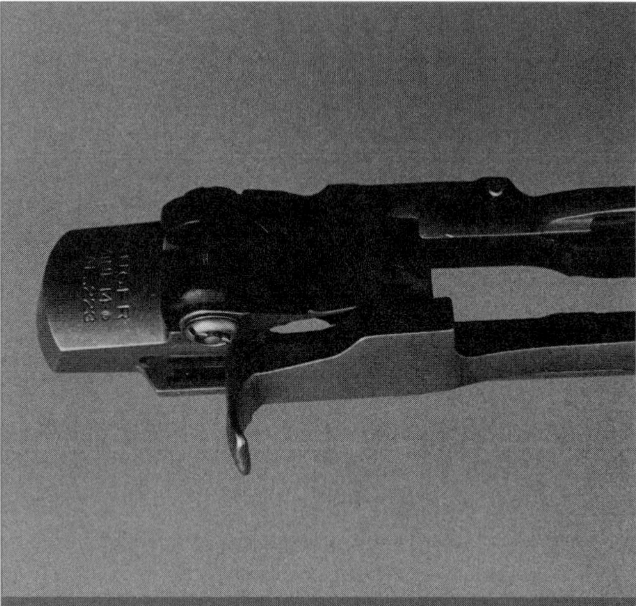

Once the bolt is out of the receiver, the operating handle can be removed.

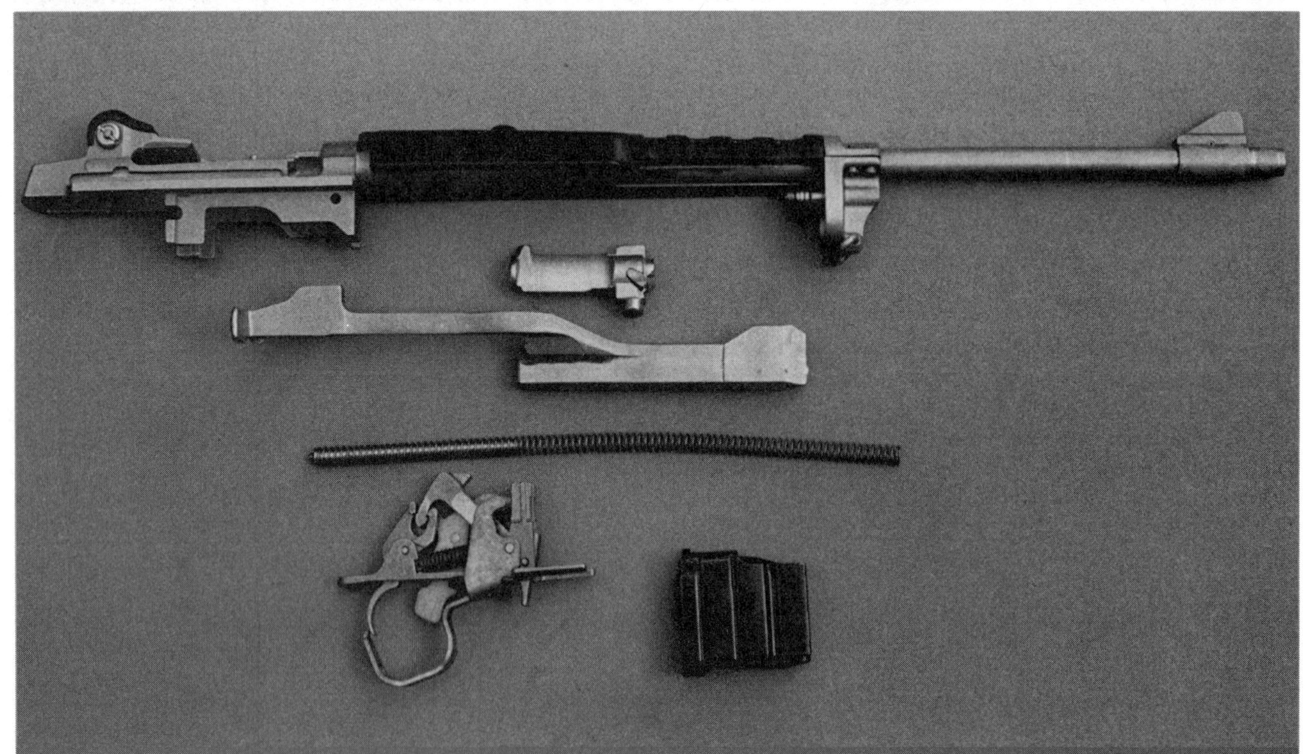

The Mini-14, disassembled, displays all of its major parts except the stock, as follows (top to bottom): barrel/receiver group, bolt, operating slide, return spring, trigger group and magazine.

flawless. Even after hundreds of rounds were fired, these rifles continued to feed, fire and eject without incident. However, it's important to clean these guns immediately after shooting them, especially the barrel bore and, even more so, the gas system. Failure to do so can result in carbon deposits that are very difficult to remove. Fortunately, Ruger-made rifles are easy to disassemble, especially when compared to the larger and heavier .308 caliber M14 and the .30-06 M1. On the other hand, neither the Mini-14 nor the Mini Thirty can withstand the same type of abuse one might expect a Steyr AUG, an FN FNC, an HK-33, or even an M16 to endure. But for the typical sport shooter or police officer, either one of these Ruger-made rifles offers excellent performance at a low cost. Moreover, they look less military than other rifles chambered in the same calibers, which makes them better choices for use by police officers or private citizens in gun-shy jurisdictions. A Mini-14 or Mini Thirty offers a significant step up in performance from an M1 Carbine, too, making it a better weapon for offensive operations, particularly beyond 75 and up to 100 yards. Those in need of a rifle that uses either .223 or 7.62x39mm should definitely consider Ruger's Mini-14 or Mini Thirty above all other rifles commercially available in these two calibers—and especially so where cost is a factor.

This left-side view of a Mini-14 displays the little rifle's exposed barrel, one of its most distinctive features.

RUGER MINI-14/MINI THIRTY

	MINI-14	MINI THIRTY
Overall Length	37.25 inches	37.25 inches
Barrel Length	18.5 inches	18.5 inches
Weight	6.4 pounds	7.2 pounds
Years Produced	1974-present	1987-present
Caliber/Capacity	.223/5 rounds*	7.62x39mm/5 rounds

**Ruger sells high-capacity magazines to police forces and government agencies only.*

Ruger Model 10/22

Without doubt Ruger's Model 10/22 ranks high among the influential guns of its type ever made. Since its debut in 1964, it has become an extremely popular gun; indeed, it's one of the best-selling .22 caliber repeating rifles made to date. Part of its appeal is its similarity in size, appearance and handling to the U.S. M1 Carbine of World War II fame. One of the most interesting features about the Model 10/22 is its magazine, a rotary unit that holds up to 10 rounds (9 rounds in the .22 WMR version). This

The magazine release, located just behind the magazine, pushes in as shown to drop the magazine.

The M1 Carbine (top) had a strong influence in the design of the Ruger Model 10/22, especially in its handling and appearance.

Like a number of rifles chambered for the .22 LR cartridge, the Ruger Model 10/22 tested for this book did its best work with maximum-intensity ammunition such as CCI's Stinger round.

maintenance requirements, caused U.S. Special Forces serving in Vietnam to prefer a Model 10/22 variant over a Nylon 66.

Another appealing characteristic of the Model 10-/22 is the large number of variants now available. These include the standard wood-stocked carbine version (with choice of blued or stainless steel finish), a heavy-barreled target version (without iron sights), an "International" model with Mannlicher-type stock, a Deluxe Sporter with fancy walnut stock, and a 10/22RP All-Weather stainless steel rifle with a synthetic stock. The Ruger Model 10/22 remarkably compact and efficient package enables the entire magazine to fit inside the stock—a huge improvement over the box magazine used by the Savage Model 64. The Model 10/22 is also fairly easy to disassemble. This fact, coupled with its relatively low

The Ruger Model 10/22 is a sleek, graceful and enormously popular rifle.

Ruger makes the popular 10/22 in a variety of configurations, including the "RBI International" 10/22, featuring a Mannlicher-style stock combined with stainless steel finish (photo courtesy of Sturm, Ruger and Company).

has attracted a large number of dedicated collectors intent on tracking down the basic rifle's numerous variants and sub-variants.

Those Model 10/22 rifles that are equipped with iron sights also have a rear sight that folds forward and down, a nice convenience for those who decide to install a scope. The 10/22 also allows shooters the flexibility of mounting a scope either with tip-off mounts or with screw-on scope bases placed in holes already drilled into the top of the receiver. In fact, the only *unlikable* feature on the 10/22 is its rather heavy trigger pull. Notwithstanding, the 10/22 tested proved more than adequate. Best results were obtained with CCI's hyper-velocity "Stinger" round, which can drive a lightweight bullet at an above-normal velocity. In testing the Ruger 10/22, a 3-shot group fired from the benchrest at 50 yards measured 11/2 inches across. The same rifle firing Federal Classic's .22LR round resulted in a 11/2-inch 3-shot group from the 50-yard bench.

With a little extra work, Ruger's 10/22 can produce stunning accuracy. In addition, this stylish and handy rifle responds well to various degrees of modification, along with a wide array of optional features at modest prices.

The Ruger Model 10/22 (bottom) arrived many years before Remington's Model 597 (top).

RUGER MODEL 10/22	
	MODEL 10/22
Overall Length	37.25 inches
Barrel Length	18.5 inches
Weight	5.0 pounds
Years Produced	1964-present
Caliber/Capacity	.22 Long Rifle/10 rounds or .22 WMR/9 rounds

Ruger Police Carbine (PC-9 and PC-4)

Ruger's new models—the PC-9 (Police Carbine) and its companion rifle, the PC-4 in 9mm Parabelum and .40 S&W, respectively—appeared in 1997 and 1998. Originally, Sturm, Ruger and Company had planned to market these handy pistol-caliber carbines solely to police forces and government agencies. But soon after beginning series production, the company decided to offer the guns for sale to private citizens as well. Ruger's Police Carbines are lightweight but strong despite their diminutive size. They bear close resemblance to the famed U.S. M1 Carbine of World War II fame, which is not a bad ancestry for a company in search of a light, handy weapon when a handgun won't do.

Like the Marlin Camp Carbines covered in the preceding entry, the PC-9 and PC-4 have revived the concept, popular in the Old West more than a century ago, of long guns and handguns chambered for the same ammunition. After falling out of fashion in the early 1900s, the concept of a short, light rifle capable of firing relatively low-powered ammunition enjoyed a resurgence, thanks to the M1 Carbine. That rifle, however, fired a proprietary cartridge adapted from a Winchester commercial self-loading rifle, one that offered considerably higher levels of power than all but the most powerful handgun cartridges. It remained for Marlin to restore fully the pistol-caliber carbine concept with its "Camp Carbines"—specifically, the Models 9 (1985) and 45 (1986).

I tested the 9mm Parabellum Model PC-9 and found it extraordinarily easy to handle and pleasant to shoot. Controls include a crossbolt safety, located just behind the trigger, which pushes in

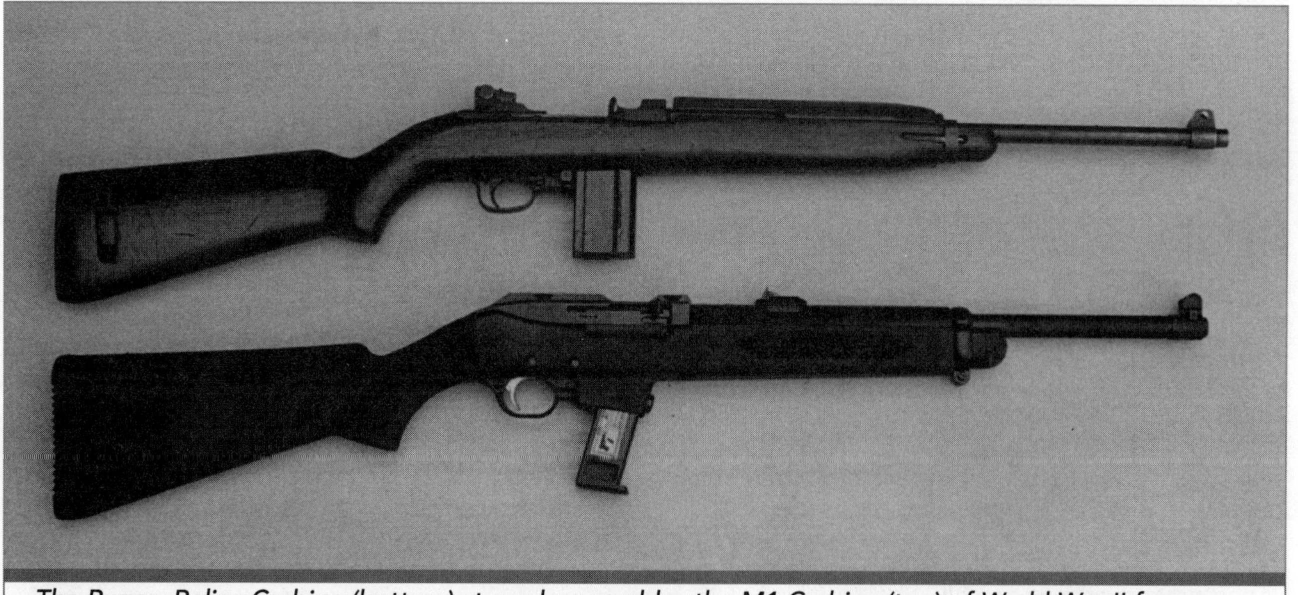

The Ruger Police Carbine (bottom) strongly resembles the M1 Carbine (top) of World War II fame.

from the right to its "fire setting" (exposing a red band) and from the left to its "safe setting" (the red band is not visible). An internal firing-pin lock, which prevents firing until the trigger is pulled all the way to the rear, is not actually a separate control, but an excellent safety device commonly found on contemporary automatic pistols and revolvers (but not on long arms). The magazine release, located in front of the trigger-guard, pushes in to remove the magazine. The carbine contains Ruger's pistol magazines with capacities of 10 rounds up to 11 rounds (.40 caliber) and 15 rounds (9mm). Like the Ruger pistols, the PC-9 also lacks a magazine safety, which means a single round left in the firing chamber (after the magazine has been removed) will still fire. The bolt stays to the rear after the last shot has been fired. After removing the spent magazine and replacing it with a loaded one, a bolt release button unlocks the bolt and lets it run forward to chamber a round. The operating handle, usually located on the right side of the receiver, works only to load a round initially from the magazine. When the bolt is locked back, the last bullet has been fired and the magazine is empty, the bolt release button must then be pushed in to close the bolt. Drawing back the operating handle and releasing it, which is how most self-loading rifles operate, won't work in this model.

The Police Carbine's manual safety is a crossbolt button located at the rear of the triggerguard. When pushed fully to the left, as shown, the rifle is ready to be fired.

Ruger's Police Carbine is a logical backup to a 9mm or .40 S&W caliber handgun, useful for police forces and private citizens as well.

This left-side view of a 9mm Ruger Police Carbine (PC-9) reveals its pistol-type magazine.

Lest one conclude that a handgun cartridge in a long arm is grossly underpowered, remember that muzzle velocities rise dramatically in a 16-inch-long barrel compared to pistol0length barrels measuring five inches or less. For instance, 9mm subsonic rounds with muzzle velocities of less than 1000 feet per second in a 9mm pistol rise to 1200 feet per second and more, greatly enhancing +P+ levels of performance. Because of the increased bullet velocities conferred by its longer barrel, the Police Carbine hits harder than a pistol in the same caliber. Also, the Police Carbine's reduced power levels, compared to other carbine and assault-rifle cartridges, actually make it a better choice for home defense, urban police use and other close-quarter fighting. Rising penetration levels, which can increase the risk to innocent bystanders, shrink dramatically compared to

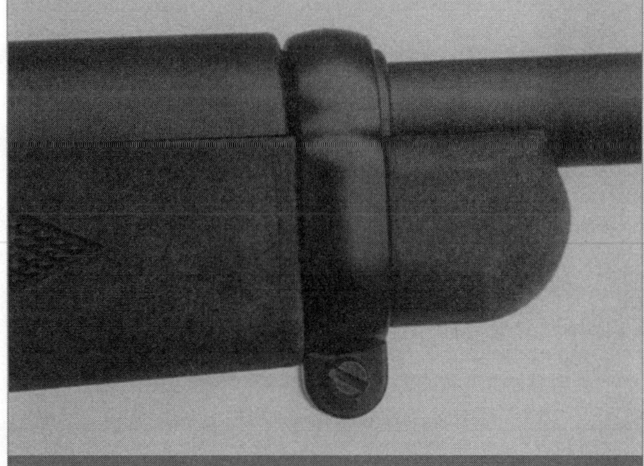

Like the M1 Carbine which inspired it, the Police Carbine's disassembly begins by removing the steel band that holds the barrel/receiver group to the stock.

The Police Carbine's sights are sturdy, both front and rear. The front sight has military-style protective "ears" on either side, while the rear sight, an open-notch blade type, is fully adjustable for windage and elevation. The Police Carbine also features grooves in the receiver for fitting scope rings (not included in the purchase price). For the distances at which one is most likely to use this gun, scope mounts are perhaps a luxury, but Ruger was thoughtful enough to include them. If somebody wanted to scope a Police Carbine for precise shot placement at 75 to 150 yards, this rifle will not likely disappoint them. It also has a sturdy black polymer stock with a recoil pad molded on the butt. Impressed checkering in the pistol-grip and forearm areas improves handling.

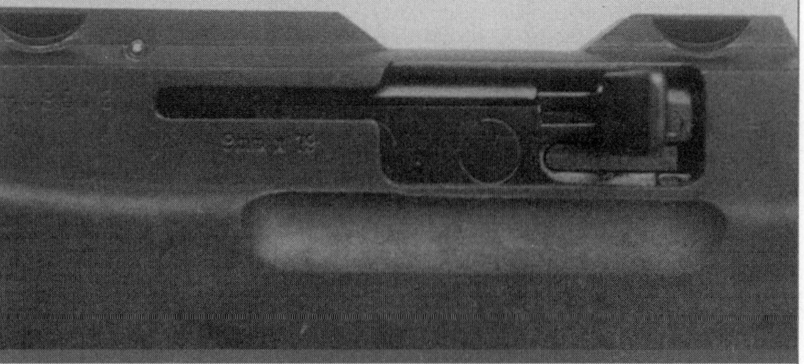

Careful attention to detail on the Police Carbine extends to easy mounting of a telescopic sight. Note the indentations machined into the receiver top for scope rings.

other short rifles that use .30 Carbine, .223, 7.62x39mm and other high energy rounds.

Accuracy with a Police Carbine is much superior to that of a service pistol, largely because recoil is practically nonexistent. Also, bracing the carbine's stock against the shoulder allows much better stability than what even a two-handed pistol can hold. At typical close-encounter handgun engagements (up to 25 feet), there's little to choose between Ruger's Police Carbine and a good pistol—although even at such close ranges a novice shooter may find the former produces better accuracy. Once the range opens up, though, the Police Carbine's longer reach and greater precision come to the fore. As an example, at 50 *feet* offhand the PC-9 fired a 1.7-nch 3-shot group, while at 50 *yards*, the same gun fired a 1.8-inch 3-shot benchrested group. The PC-9's best 3-shot benchrested group fired from 75 yards away measured 2.2 inches across, while at 100 yards it spanned just 2.7 inches. No service pistol, even the vaunted SIG P210, is likely to produce those results unless used by the most expert shots, whereas Ruger's Police Carbine in the

The Police Carbine has excellent accuracy. This 3-shot group, fired offhand from 25 feet, measures only 1.2 inches across.

The Police Carbine's rear sight is adjustable for both windage and elevation, resembling that found on some Ruger handguns.

At 50 feet, another 3-shot group was fired offhand from 50 feet and measured 1.7 inches across.

hands of an average shooter turned in such groups routinely. Consider also that a typical service pistol, with its fixed sights, rarely shoots to the point of aim beyond 50 feet or so. As a result, the shooter must know where a handgun shoots in relation to its sights. With the Ruger carbine, on the other hand, the bullets fly almost exactly to the point indicated by the sights.

While the Police Carbine's magazine arrangement may look somewhat improvised, I nonetheless found it worked well with practice. The gun's magazine setup is especially impressive when you consider how Ruger made the Police Carbine work effectively with existing pistol magazines, rather than following the usual path of creating new magazines especially for the gun. Another criticism concerns the Police Carbine's trigger, which suffered considerable military-style creep or slack before releasing the sear and firing the weapon. The trigger pull itsel is fairly heavy—almost 10 pounds—which in itself is not a problem. In fact, it's a useful level of resistance for high-stress situations; but I felt this pronounced trigger slack might frustrate beginning or out-of-practice shooters, especially on long-distance shots. As I continued to work with the Police Carbine, though, I concluded that Ruger, in its wisdom, had fitted the trigger best-suited to the little rifle's most likely mission: keeping criminals at bay. In that kind of situation, you most assuredly don't want a trigger that is so crisp, clean and light that it goes off by surprise! Furthermore, my test-firing results indicate that the Police Carbine's trigger works fine for longer-range (50 to 100 yards) shooting.

With all its virtues, the Police Carbine could, with a few slight improvements, become an even better design. Adding sling swivels to the stock, for

At 100 yards the author fired this 2.7-inch group with the 9mm version of the Police Carbine. No 9mm service pistol can produce results like this.

example, would allow police officers to carry the gun while keeping their hands free. The operating handle could be easily redesigned so the bolt traveled forward on an empty chamber in the usual way: by drawing the operating handle back, then releasing it to run forward. This would eliminate the separate bolt release button altogether. It might also be worthwhile for Ruger to develop an additional wood-stocked version of the Police Carbine to compete more directly with Marlin's competing Camp Carbines. With its matte black metal parts and Zytel stock, the Police Carbine still looks somewhat like an assault weapon, whereas the Marlin carbines look like sporting arms. Ruger might also develop a .45 ACP caliber version of the Police Carbine, once again in direct competition with Marlin. Creating a "PC-45" should present no great engineering problems. Ruger already produces a superb .45 ACP pistol—the P90.

To summarize: Ruger's Police Carbine is a short rifle that handles well and boasts impressive credentials. Like the famous M1 Carbine, which helped inspire it, this little rifle offers accuracy and power levels above and beyond what any service handgun can. Rugged, accurate and reliable, the Police Carbine has great potential for a variety of uses. And though it costs a little more than Marlin's Camp Carbine, the Ruger Police Carbine does have a sturdier operating mechanism and stock. It could well become still another great success story for Sturm, Ruger and Company.

RUGER POLICE CARBINES

	POLICE CARBINES
Overall Length	34.5 inches
Barrel Length	16.25 inches
Weight	6.7 pounds
Years Produced	1997-present
Caliber & Capacity	PC-9:9mm Parabellum/15 (10*) rounds PC-4: .40 S&W/11 (10*) rounds

**Mandated by federal law for civilian use.*

Savage Model 64

When it was first introduced in 1990 by Savage, the Model 64 was designated "Model 64B." Current variants include the standard 64G, which features a walnut-finished hardwood stock with impressed checkering, a Model 64GXP "Package Gun" (the standard model with a 4-power scope added), and a Model 64F with black synthetic stock.

The operating controls on the Model 64 are more than acceptable. There's a knurled latch near the magazine well which, when pushed forward, releases the magazine. The manual safety consists of a lever on the right rear portion of the receiver. When pushed to the rear, the letter "S" ("safe") is exposed. To remove the safety prior to firing, the lever is pushed forward, covering the letter "S" and exposing a red dot. The bolt does not stay open once the last shot has been fired. The bolt is locked open simply by drawing it all the way to the rear,

The Savage Model 64 is a graceful, well-balanced weapon, but its long protruding magazine can create some complications.

The magazine release on the Model 64 is located ahead of the magazine itself.

The Savage Model 64 is gracefully styled, in large part because the receiver slopes down smoothly to blend into the contours of the stock.

scope. The slight Monte Carlo comb on the stock makes it suitable for an optical (telescopic) sight as well.

Accuracy is excellent, as it was for all Savage rifles tested for this book. The gun handles well, too, but the box magazine protrudes too far beneath the stock than one looks for in a rifle.

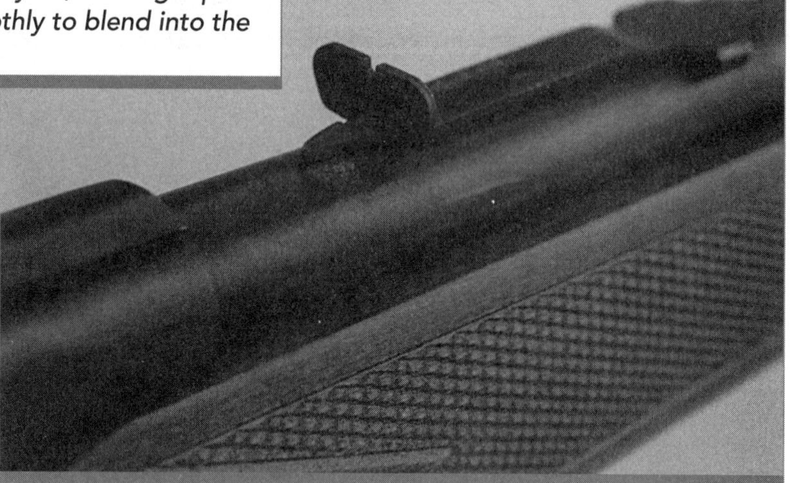

The rear sight on the Model 64 is a simple semi-buckhorn type adjustable for elevation only. A Model 63FV variant has no iron sights but includes a heavy, target-type barrel and Weaver scope bases on its receiver.

then pushing it up and into a matching recess in the rear of the receiver. The barrel is now exposed on both breech and muzzle ends for cleaning.

The sights are simple and straightforward. Typical of many .22 rifles, the front sight is a post with a sighting bead, while the rear sight (adjustable for height) is located immediately in front of the receiver. The receiver itself has grooves for mounting a rimfire

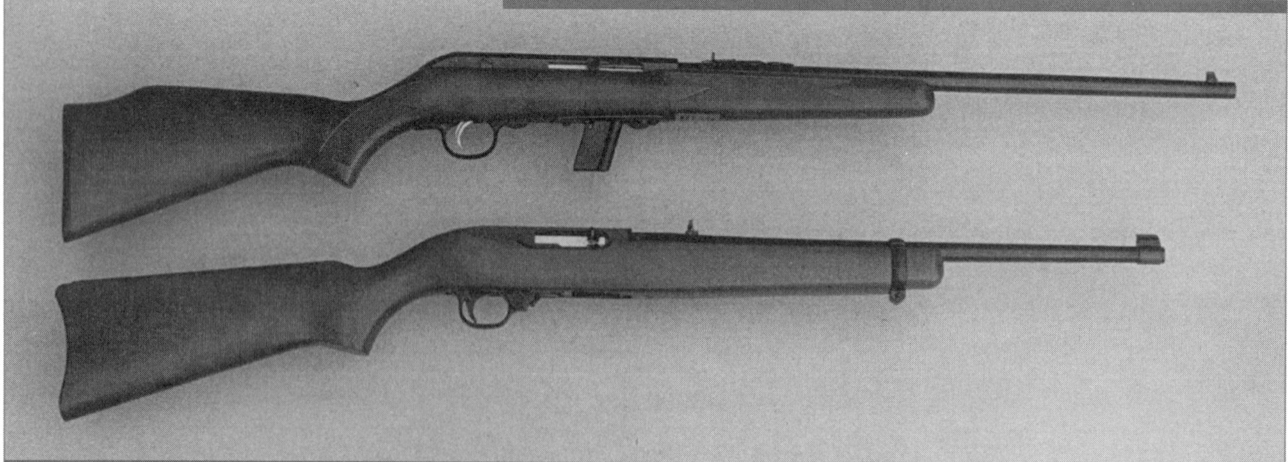

Savage's Model 64 (top) is probably not quite as capable as Ruger's Model 10/22; but it's considerably less expensive and a good buy.

For a shooter who is accustomed to automatic pistols, such as the Makarov and Walther P38, the magazine release operates completely backwards. The release catch is located in front of the magazine and must be pushed forward to remove an empty magazine and/or to insert a loaded one. In general, this plain and simple rifle offers commendable performance at about half the price of the Ruger 10/22. It costs less than the Remington Viper or Model 597, too, and yet it features more traditional styling than either of those two competitors. Fix that troublesome magazine arrangement and the Savage Mode 64 would be among the top .22 rifles on my list. Even with the current magazine setup, I give this rifle high marks indeed.

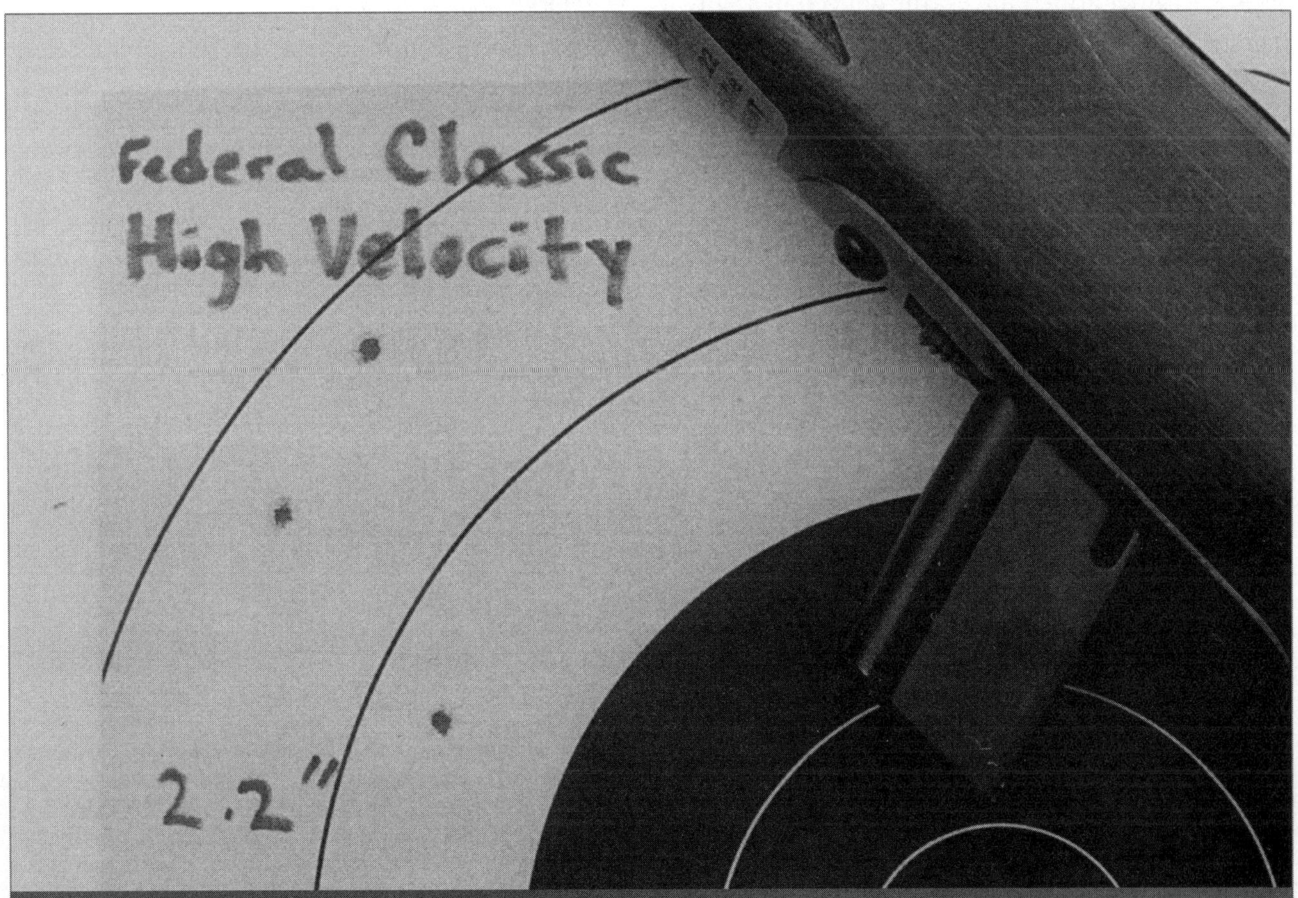

The Model 64 tested for handling well but its accuracy was disappointing, witness this 2.2-inch 3-shot group from the 50-yard bench.

SAVAGE MODEL 65G

	MODEL 65G
Overall Length	40.0 Inches
Barrel Length	20.0 inches
Weight	5.5 pounds
Years Produced	1990-present
Caliber/Capacity	.11LR/10 rounds

Springfield M1A

Springfield's M1A is a commercial version of the M14 rifle used by the U.S. and other armed forces. Introduced in 1971, it won approval in 1973 from both the Director of Civilian Marksmanship (DCM) and the National Rifle Association (NRA) as a satisfactory substitute for the M14 in service rifle competition. The M1A differs from the M14 primarily in its lack of any provision for fully-automatic firing. All other features of the M1A are similar to those of the M14. The M1A is extremely well-made and has found favor among private citizens and police forces alike, including those who need a powerful, highly accurate semiautomatic rifle for counter-sniper purposes.

The M1A is available from Springfield in a variety of configurations, as follows:

- *The Standard Model (with a choice of walnut or fiberglass stocks).*
- *The National Match, which has a slightly heavier barrel, a glass-bedded walnut stock, improved gas cylinder and flash suppressor, finely-adjustable sights, and an improved trigger assembly.*
- *The Super Match, which has an even heavier barrel and thicker stock for greater rigidity, accuracy and control in precision long-range shooting.*
- *The M21 Law Enforcement Rifle, which is the same as the Super Match rifle but with an adjustable cheekpiece and rubber recoil pad added to the butt-stock, plus provisions for mounting a scope.*
- *The M1A-A1 Bush Rifle, featuring an 18-inch barrel and a choice of walnut or fiberglass stocks.*

In all, Springfield has made well over 100,000 M1A-type rifles. The standard version with a

With the short 5-round magazine fitted, the Springfield M1A bears some resemblance to its distant ancestor, the M1 Garand rifle of World War II fame.

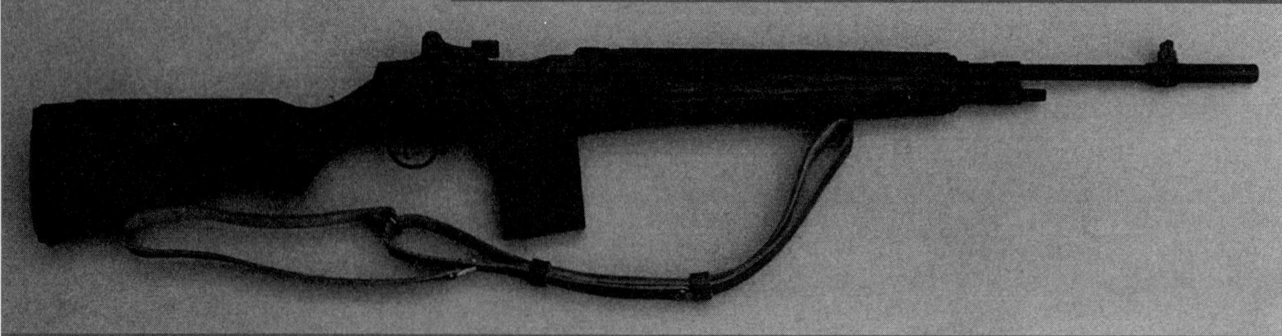

With the usual 20-round magazine fitted, the standard Springfield M1A looks a great deal like a semiautomatic-only version of the U.S. armed forces' M14 rifle—which, of course, is exactly what it is.

walnut stock and a National Match barrel were used in the accuracy tests for this book. Consistent 1.5 minute of angle (MOA) accuracy, which translates into 1 1/2-inch 3-shot groups at 100 yards, proved easily attainable with this combination. Groups as small as 1 MOA are possible with the National Match, Super Match and M-21 variants.

Like the M1 Garand and M14 on which it is based, the M1A should not be routinely disassembled because doing so can introduce excessive play between the parts, especially the stock and the barreled action. In time, this can degrade accuracy. The M1A is not as easy to maintain as an FAL or M16 type, although in most cases involving civilian shooters this should present no serious problems.

The Springfield M1A can be relied upon to shoot 3-shot, 100-yard benchrested groups of 1.5 inches or smaller.

Despite its considerable size, the Springfield M1A balances well and is a pleasure to shoot.

With its excellent manufacturing quality and impeccable pedigree, the Springfield M1A comes highly recommended. Because of legislation affecting imports it may soon become the only service-type rifle available to private citizens in the U.S. Certainly it is the most prolific.

SPRINGFIELD M1A

	M1A
Overall Length	44.25 inches
Barrel Length	22 inches (25.1 with suppressor)
Weight	8.8 pounds
Years Produced	1973-present
Caliber/Capacity	7.62x51mm NATO (.308)/20 rounds

Springfield M1A Super Match

Springfield created the Super Match from the standard Model M1A, but only after several small changes were made to produce a heavier, more accurate rifle. Compared to the Standard model, the Super Match comes with a heavier barrel, and an improved gas cylinder and flash suppressor. Its walnut stock has been built up in the forend and pistol-grip areas for improved rigidity and control. Fiberglass bedding now holds the receiver more firmly against the stock. A micrometer click rear sight ensures precise adjustments and an improved trigger assembly all contribute to the greater accuracy potential and improved control of the Super Match compared to the standard M1A. The difference is especially noticeable in long-range shooting out to 300-500 yards. To facilitate firing from a prone position (a good choice for long-range shooting), the M1A Super Match rifle comes standard with a 10-round magazine, but the M14's 20-round box magazine is also useable along with the "politically correct" 5-rounder.

The Springfield M1A Super Match represents the company's attempt to achieve maximum accuracy from the basic M1A design.

The M1A Super Match has a heavier stock and a fuller pistol grip area than the standard M1A.

When limited to the integral sights, the M1A Super Match shot superbly. This best 3-shot 100-yard benchrested group patterned a mere 0.70 inches wide, one of the best the author shot with any rifle tested in this book. Note the two shots into the slightly enlarged upper hole.

The M1A Super Match turned out to be the most accurate self-loading rifle tested for this book; indeed, it's one of the most accurate rifles of any type I've ever fired. My best 3-shot, 100-yard benchrested group measured 0.70 inches across using Winchester Ballistic Silvertip ammunition. Another 3-shot, 100-yard benchrested group fired with the M1A Super Match measured 0.90 inches with Hornady's fine "Match" 168-grain boattail hollowpoint (BTHP) cartridge. These are sensational results, true, but I still prefer the way Springfield's standard M1A rifle handles compared to the heavier Super Match variant, which felt bulky and clumsy. While the fiberglass bedding contributes significantly to the stellar accuracy of the Super Match, it also degrades the rifle's serviceability, simply

Even the M1A Super Match's worst 100-yard benchrested target group placed three shots into a 1.25-inch pattern, which is good shooting by almost any standard.

Accuracy with the M1A Super Match (top) is competitive with the ArmaLite AR-10A4 (bottom) in the same .308 caliber but in a more traditional package.

because fieldstripping it for a thorough cleaning is made that much more difficult. A weapon that's difficult to maintain probably won't get the same care as one that's easily serviced. This is one area where the AR-10, the FAL and the G3 all outperform the M14 series of rifles, including the commercial M1A and its many variants. But even compared to the standard M1A, the Super Match presents a much greater challenge in terms of maintenance. The solution may be to follow the Army's approach with its M21 sniper-rifle variant of the National Match: employ professional full-time armorers who will maintain the weapons on a regular basis. This may work with a SWAT team or whatever, but it's obviously not a solution for the private owner. The Super Match variant also costs appreciably more than the Standard M1A—more than $800 over the lowest-priced model, and more than the upscale M1A National Match.

The M1A Super Match's rear aperture ("peep") sight is larger than that of the standard M1A and capable of more precise adjustments.

For these reasons, I do not foresee the M1A Super Match approaching Springfield's enormously popular standard M1A in sales. On the other hand, since the Super Match outshoots the standard M1A by a slight but noticeable margin, the Super Match variant may well be the answer for those interested only in improving accuracy. The main advantage it has over the most accurate bolt-action rifles is its ability to fire repeat shots at a faster rate.

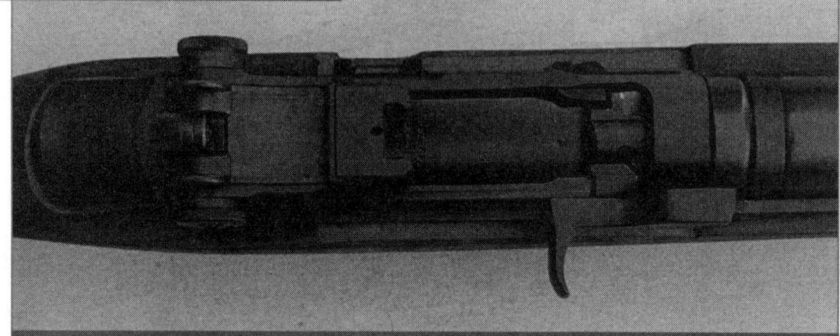

The M1A Super Match features a fiberglass-bedded stock in the receiver area.

SPRINGFIELD M1A SUPER MATCH

	M1A SUPER MATCH
Overall Length	44.3 inches
Barrel Length	22 inches (25.1 inches with suppressor)
Weight	11.0 pounds
Years Produced	1987-present
Caliber/Capacity	7.62x51mm NATO (.308)/10 rounds (see text)

Springfield M1A-A1 Scout Rifle

When it was introduced in 1997, the MIA-A1 Scout rifle represented Springfield's innovative attempt to create a rifle whose specifications were set forth in the early 1980s by Jeff Cooper, the well-known firearms expert. Cooper's specifications included a weight of 7 pounds (with scope), a 37-inch length (overall) and a .308 caliber. The result would be a truly versatile rifle in a package that was considerably handier than the usual rifle chambered for the first NATO standard cartridge. Cooper's plan also called for a long-eye relief scope mounted well forward, allowing shooters easy access to the action for reloading with stripper clips. The scope would have low magnification—no more than 2.5 power or so—enabling the shooter to keep both eyes open for a wide field of view and rapid target acquisition. While several firms, including Clifton Arms and Steyr GmbH, have created their own scout rifle from scratch with Cooper's help, Springfield is the only manufacturer of self-loading Scout Rifles (Cooper called for bolt action only).

The M1A-A1 Scout Rifle (bottom), which is barely larger than the .223 caliber Ruger Mini-14 (top), offers the much more powerful .308 caliber cartridge.

Like other M14 and M1A variants, the M1A-A1 Scout Rifle comes with a stripper-clip guide just forward of the rear sight. Part of the rationale behind mounting the sight well forward is to retain access to the stripper-clip guide.

Enough rifles have incorporated Cooper's concept to give shooters a chance to test the validity of his basic idea—and it passes muster with ease. Springfield liked the concept so well, in fact, that it built one of its own. The company deviated, however, enough so that it could use existing parts and supplies made for Springfield's semiautomatic M1A rifle. As a result, the company has been able to offer one of the least expensive rifles of this type ever made. The M1A is such a large rifle, however, that the Springfield Armory M1A-A1 Scout Rifle, though considerably smaller than the M14/M1A, ended up both longer and heavier than what Cooper had in mind. To reduce its overall length from that of the M14-sized M1A, Springfield adapted the short barrel from its Bush Rifle variation of the M1A. Its barrel is only 18 inches long and has no flash suppressor, which actually makes it an inch shorter than Steyr's own Scout Rifle (which has Cooper's seal of approval). Adding a flash suppressor, which comes standard on Springfield's rifle, adds three inches to the gun's overall length (but the suppressor can be easily removed). The M1A-A1 Scout Rifle has a standard M1A receiver, so overall weight remains at 8.5 pounds,

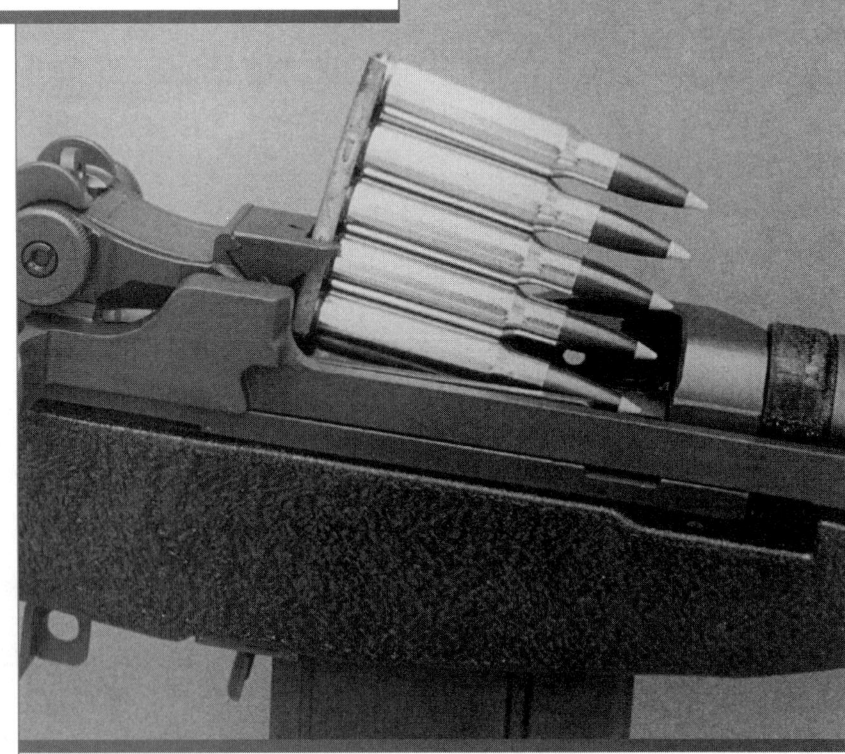

Stripper clips in the M1A-A1 Scout Rifle enable shooters to load five rounds at a time until the magazine is full.

The Aimpoint sighting system's intensity is easily adjusted through a series of clicks.

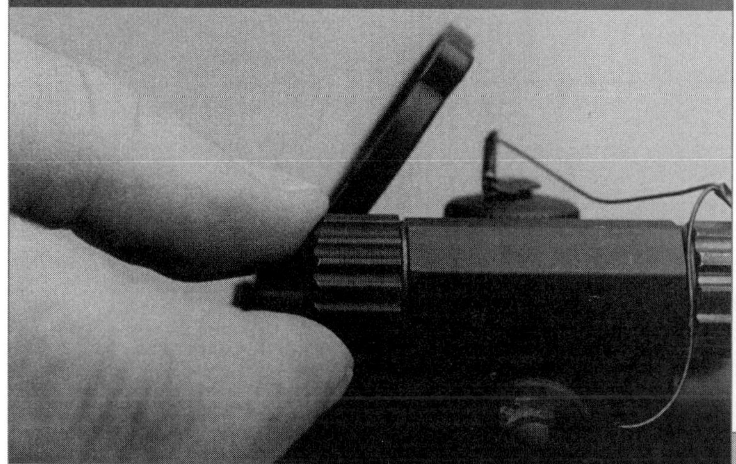

which is lighter than the M1A but still 1 1/2 pounds over Cooper's original maximum.

The stock on the M1A-A1 Scout Rifle used in testing was the black fiberglass type that comes standard with this model. Its matching black fiberglass handguard is pierced for a scope rail (a regular M1A or M14 handguard will fit but is not compatible with the scope mount). All other controls—including the stripper clip guide on the receiver, the manual safety and the magazine release—are the same as those found on a standard M1A rifle. Springfield's Scout Rifle relies on an Aimpoint scope for its primary sighting apparatus, which turns out to be a good choice. While the Aimpoint scope lacks aiming marks or reticules of its own, the shooter can look through it to the front sight, which then aligns on the target. The Aimpoint also allows shooters to keep both eyes open, thus securing a wide field of view. This ability to see all around the target is important, both in hunting dangerous game and in military applications. Shooters in general want to avoid becoming so fixated on the immediate target that they lose track of other possible threats in their vicinity. With all of these abilities, the Aimpoint scope also ensures considerable precision in target work. It's also quite compact and sturdy, with eyepiece covers that remain in place and yet will flip up and out of the way when needed.

When viewed through the Aimpoint sighting system mounted on an M1A-A1 Scout Rifle, the target looks like this.

In testing for accuracy, the Springfield M1A-A1 Scout Rifle revealed impressive accuracy. Best results included a 0.90-inch offhand group fired from a distance of 50 yards, while a benchrested 3-shot group measured 1.7 inches from 100 yards.

The M1A-A1 Scout Rifle comes with a low-power telescopic sight or with Aimpoint's innovative sighting system as shown.

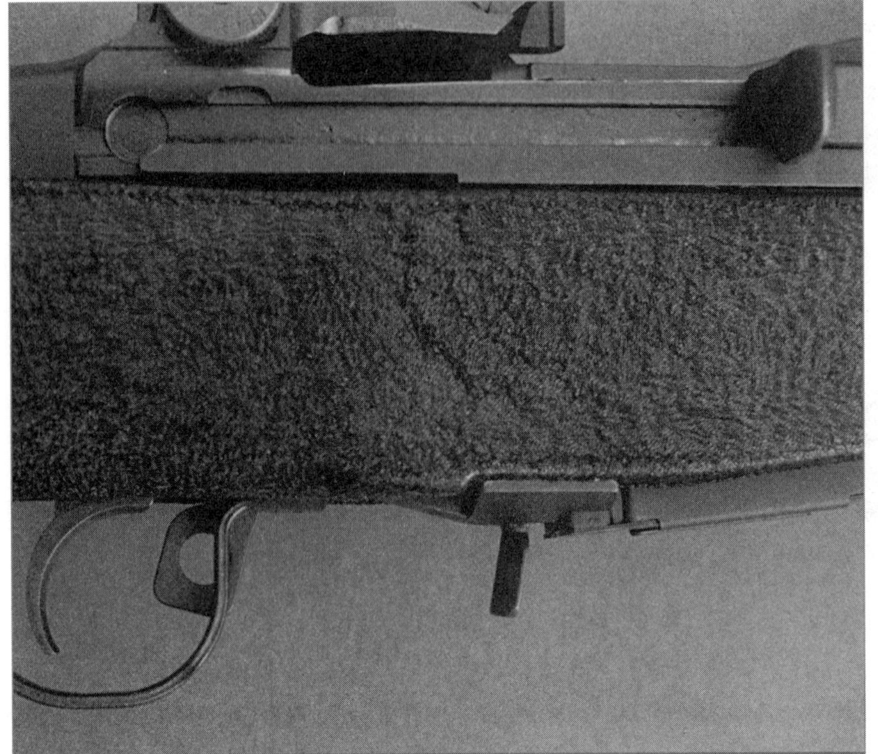

Like other rifles descended from the M1 Garand, the M1A-A1 Scout Rifle's manual safety is located in the front of the triggerguard. The rifle is shown with its hammer cocked and the manual safety pushed back to its safe setting. Note the five-round magazine flush with the bottom of the stock.

Handling the rifle was impressive when sighting in quickly on targets at 50 yards or less during offhand shooting. Reliability was flawless, too, with all ammunition brands tested, including military surplus, hunting and match ammunition.

Jeff Cooper once called this rifle a "Pseudo Scout," and while he correctly states that it is not a true Scout Rifle by his specifications, he does have some respect for it. Actually, its deviations from Cooper's Scout Rifle concept make it a more versatile rifle, thanks mostly to its self-loading action and slightly greater weight than Cooper's "genuine" Scout Rifle. It may be easier to carry afield for

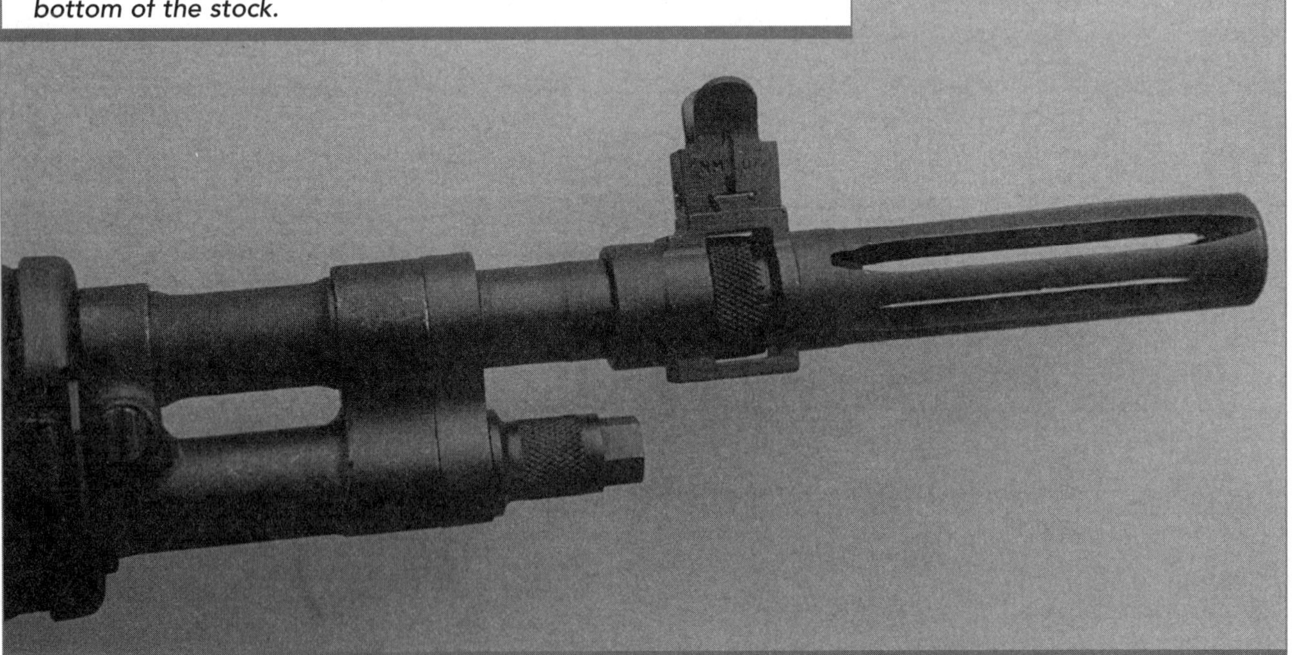

The M1A-A1 Scout Rifle's abbreviated muzzle barely extends past the gas cylinder, but fitting a flash suppressor extends the length another three inches.

long periods of time, and it may be a little faster on target; but Springfield's M1A-A1 Scout definitely has the edge with its semiautomatic mechanism as opposed to Cooper's bolt action. While an experienced shooter can accomplish amazing feats with a good bolt-action rifle, most can get far better rapid-fire shooting results with a semiautomatic. Moreover, the M1A-A1 Scout Rifle costs hundreds less than a standard M1A, and about $1,000 less than Steyr's Scout Rifle.

When all is said and done, the Springfield M1A-A1 Scout Rifle is a remarkable firearm, one that combines the excellent operating features of the classic M1 Garand/M14 with a more compact, updated stock and high-tech sights. Those who desire a high-performance self-loading rifle in .308 caliber should be quite content with this one.

The M1A-A1 Scout Rifle is impressively accurate, with the 50-yard target on the left measuring 0.90 inches, and at 100 yards (right) the group measured 1.7 inches.

SPRINGFIELD M1A-A1 SCOUT RIFLE

	SCOUT RIFLE
Overall Length	37.75 In (no flash suppressor)/40.75 (suppressor)
Barrel Length	18.0 inches (21.0 with suppressor)
Weight	8.5 pounds
Years Produced	1997-present
Caliber/Capacity	.308/5 or 20 rounds

Springfield SAR-8

Springfield's SAR-8 is a sporterized version of the Heckler & Koch G3 military rifle. It differs from that popular service rifle, however, by replacing the H&K pistol grip with a Bell & Carlson synthetic thumbhole stock. This eliminates the bayonet lug and flash suppressor; it also removes the provision for fully-automatic fire. The rifle was introduced in 1990, dropped in 1993, and reintroduced in 1995. Finally, the SAR-8 was among those rifles restricted from further import into the U.S. by the executive order of 1998.

Springfield's SAR-8 is an EBO (i.e., Greek-made) G3 clone of high quality. In extensive firing to derive data for this book, the Springfield SAR-8 proved not only one of the most accurate semiautomatic rifles, but among the most accurate of all types tested. Three-shot groups fired from the 100-yard bench went into groups as small as 0.90 inches.

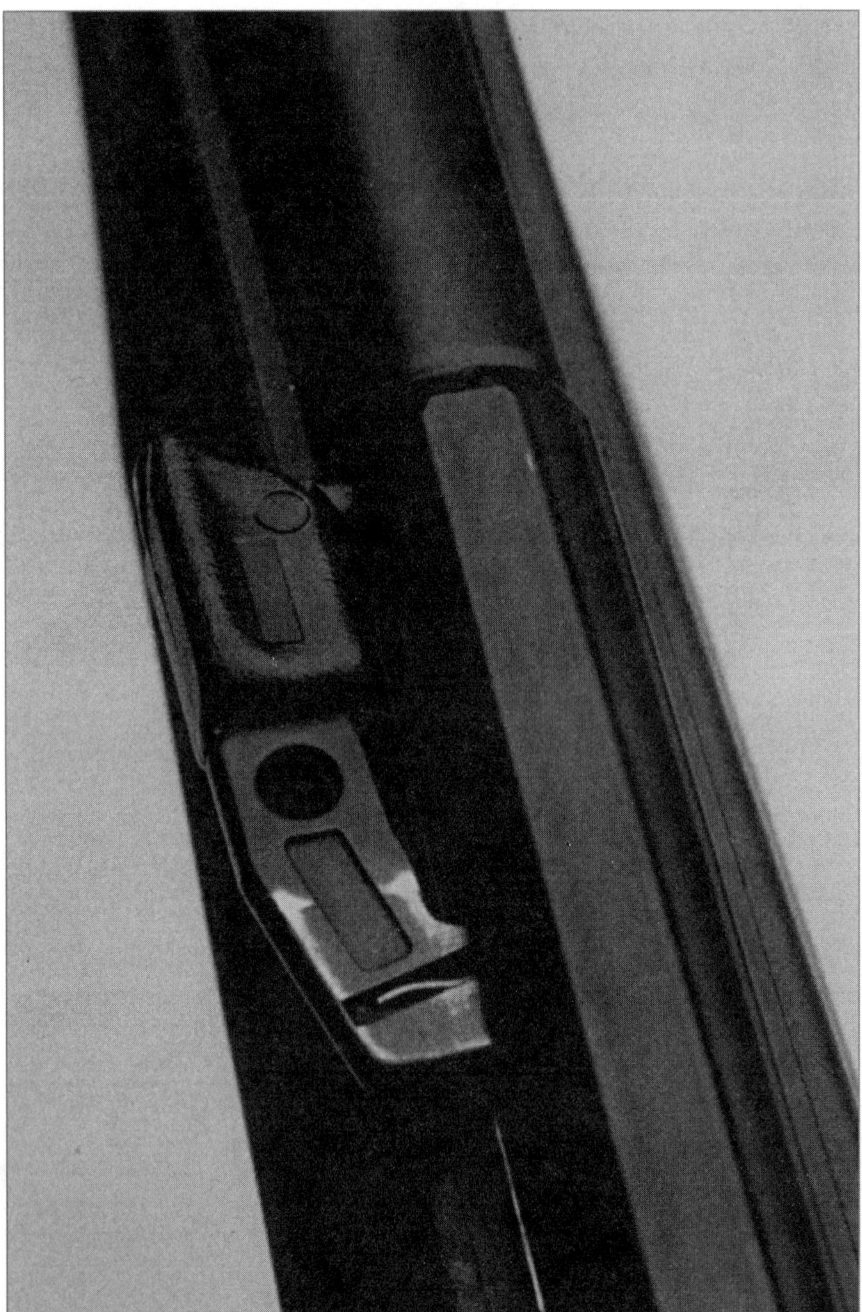

The SAR-8 uses a folding charging handle, shown here in its folded position.

Because of the unusual H&K roller-locked mechanism, the SAR-8 does offer some unusual handling characteristics. These include unusually vigorous

The SAR-8, like other G3 variants, disassembles quickly and easily into the following components: barrel/receiver group; bolt carrier with bolt; buttstock assembly with return spring; trigger group and magazine.

The SAR-8 (bottom) was, like the Century L1A1 Sporter (top), an attempt to re-create one of the world's most famous military rifles in modified form for civilian enthusiasts.

ejection of spent cartridge casings, which consistently soar 15-20 feet to the right and slightly forward of the shooter. In addition, the rifle has a fluted firing chamber—a necessary aid in all G3-type rifles for extracting fired cartridge cases—which can cause scoring of the cartridge cases. This in no way degrades their reloadability, however.

Because it is limited to semiautomatic fire only, the SAR-8's manual safety features only two positions: straight back, pointing to the red letter "F," indicates the fire position, while halfway up, pointing to the white letter "S," deactivates the firing mechanism, placing the rifle on the safe setting.

The SAR-8 design places the charging handle on the rifle's left side rather than the right side. This enables right-handed shooters to keep their dominant right hand in the shooting position.

SPRINGFIELD SAR-8

	SAR-8
Overall Length	40.3 inches
Barrel Length	18 inches
Weight	8.7 pounds
Years Produced	see text
Caliber/Capacity	.308/20 rounds

Steyr AUG

Steyr introduced its Model *Armee Universal Gewehr*—better known as the AUG—in the late 1970s. The company's intention was to introduce a service weapon using the most modern materials and whose modular construction would allow the rifle to serve various tactical roles simply by adding or switching accessories. The Austrian armed forces accepted the AUG immediately as a replacement for their Model StG 58 FALs. The AUG's official Austrian designation is the *Sturmgewehr* (Assault Rifle) 77 or StG 77 (for its year of introduction). Since Austria adopted the AUG, it has also become the official service rifle as well in Australia, Ireland, Morocco, the Netherlands, New Zealand, Oman, Saudi Arabia and others.

Like most military selective-fire rifles—i.e., those capable of either semiautomatic or fully-

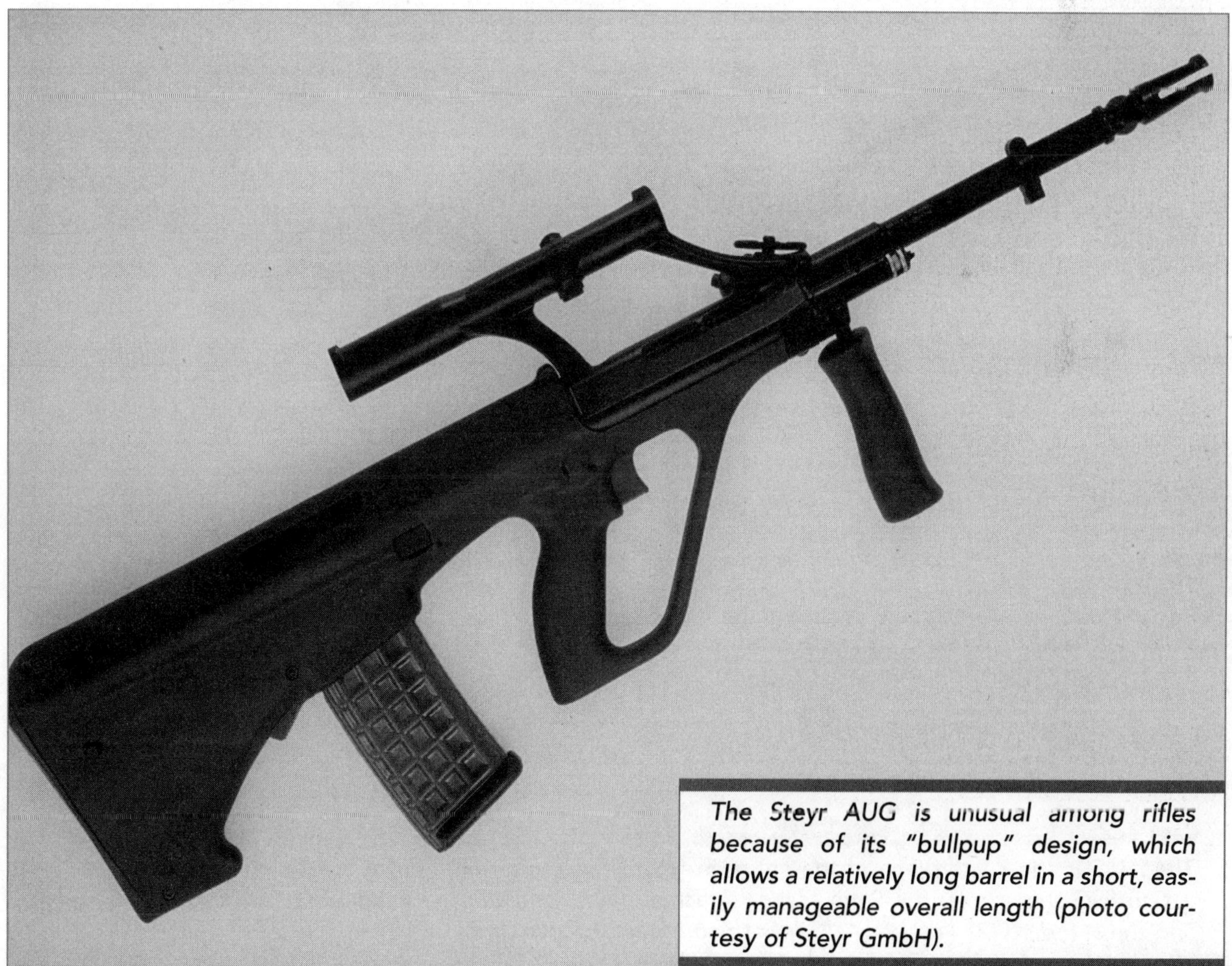

The Steyr AUG is unusual among rifles because of its "bullpup" design, which allows a relatively long barrel in a short, easily manageable overall length (photo courtesy of Steyr GmbH).

The AUG is the centerpiece of the entire Steyr military/police line. From top to bottom are the bolt-action SSG sniper rifle; the 9mm Tactical Machine Pistol or TMP; the 9mm AUG Para submachine gun; and the standard .223 caliber AUG (photo courtesy of Steyr GmbH).

automatic fire—the AUG is gas-operated. Expanding powder gas following each shot strikes the piston and drive it back to rotate the bolt. The metal lugs are then unlocked at the rear of the firing chamber. Interestingly, the piston does double duty, functioning as one of two guide rods for the bolt as it moves back.

Steyr's AUG certainly has a futuristic look. It has a bullpup design, with the receiver (and the magazine beneath it) set well back on the butt-stock, behind the pistol grip. That gives shooters the advantage of a short overall length—only 31.1 inches for the standard rifle—and a fairly long barrel (20 inches). By contrast, other modern carbine designs in the more traditional form place the receiver well forward, sacrificing barrel length to gain a short overall length. As an example, the overall and barrel lengths for Heckler & Koch's Model 53 (.223 caliber) submachine gun are 29.7 and 8.3 inches, respectively. The Colt Model 723 (U.S. M4) .223 caliber carbine has an overall length of 33 inches (barrel length: 14.5 inches). Several earlier designs featured this bullpup layout, including the French FA-MAS service rifle, which was introduced in 1975 and became a commercial success. The AUG was next in line, followed by several other bullpup rifle and shotgun designs, notably the British L85A1 service rifle and a variant of the Mossberg 500 pump shotgun. Still, the AUG is arguably the best of them all—and certainly the most versatile.

An important disadvantage of the bullpup design is its inability to be switched from shoulder to shoulder because the ejection port opening must be set on one side or the other to suit right- or left-handed shooters. It's possible to switch the ejection port to open on the opposite side, but doing so means the rifle has to be disassembled. Otherwise, a shooter cannot shift the rifle to fire from either side of his body instantaneously. This also means that soldiers armed with bullpup rifles are at a greater disadvantage when patrolling down one side of a city street as opposed to the other. Nevertheless, the AUG is a reliable and well-liked weapon.

Other AUG features include its all-plastic furniture, either in olive green or black (there's no wood anywhere on this rifle), which makes it exceptionally weather resistant. Older shooters too often think of plastic in a firearm as cheap and fragile, but such is not the case. With modern high-technology materials, such as the Nylon 66 used in Remington's rimfire rifle, it's possible to build stronger, more reliable products than with a traditional wooden stock.

The standard sighting arrangement for the AUG is simply a 1.5-power optical sight fitted to the carrying handle. No iron sights are fitted. A low-power scope like this one allows shooters to keep both eyes open (with advantages as discussed in the previous section on Springfield's Scout rifle).

The triggerguard is unusually large, allowing easy access to shooters with gloved hands. This is an important consideration in Europe, where cold weather is the norm much of the year. An enlarged triggerguard also eliminates the need for a specialized "winter trigger," the kind used with older service rifles—the M1 Garand/M14 and Kar. 98k, for example, which can become still another small part to get lost when needed. The magazine catch, located behind the magazine well, is also serrated and oversized for easy operation with gloved hands.

Despite the AUG's unusual features and characteristics, its manual safety should be familiar to most readers. It's simply a push-button located behind the trigger which, when pushed from left to right, makes the rifle safe. Pushing it the other way releases the firing mechanism and readies the rifle for firing.

The selective-fire AUG has no selector switch per se. A shooter who desires single shots need only apply light pressure on the trigger. Applying firmer pressure will produce automatic fire. This system of fire selection is actually quite controversial because, under the stress of combat, it often leads to firing an excessive number of rounds. On the other hand, this system of using the trigger pull as a fire selector does eliminate unwanted controls, such as a separate fire selector switch (as used on the M2 Carbine), a multiple-position safety (as used on the FN FAL, M16 and others), or even an additional trigger (as found in older Beretta submachine guns). Not having to cope with these controls help make the AUG easy to learn and handle. As with other selective-fire

The Steyr AUG is surprisingly controllable even on fully-automatic fire. With minor modifications it quickly and easily adapts to left-handed use as shown here (photo courtesy of Steyr GmbH).

weapons, fire discipline is a function of training. Soldiers who have been inadequately trained tend to overdo it, which is why most armed forces around the world need to budget a great deal of money for live-fire training in order to develop skilled shooters. Firing an AUG requires a strong hand on the pistol grip, with the support hand on a forward handgrip that also serves as a handle for removing the barrel. Easy barrel removal is desirable in any rifle intended for combat use, especially one that doubles as a squad support weapon or light machine gun. Fully-automatic fire can get a barrel very hot in a hurry! Another highly desirable feature on a rifle intended for combat use is a flash suppressor attached to the front of the barrel.

Steyr also offers a variety of trigger groups in its AUG series, including the option of an open-bolt operation to promote barrel cooling or a closed-bolt operation (to promote accuracy), plus a semi-automatic/3-shot burst mode or one that allows fully-automatic firing. These features help make the AUG an extraordinarily versatile weapon that is adaptable to most combat fire missions. While Steyr has built several variations of the AUG, all use the same frame (hence the "Universal" part of the AUG designation). The smallest variant is the 9mm Parabellum caliber submachine gun, the AUG Para variant, with its 16.5-inch barrel (reducing overall length to 26.2 inches). With such a barrel, the 9mm Parabellum round can develop impressive velocities, hence better ballistic flight paths than the same bullet fired from a short-barreled pistol or traditional submachine gun. The .223 caliber AUG-*Polizei* (Police), or AUG-P, features a shorter barrel than the standard AUG and comes in a choice of semiautomatic-only or selective-fire modes. The AUG's light machine gun version—the .223 caliber AUG HBAR—has a thicker, heavier 24-inch barrel with integral bipod. This variant ordinarily uses 42-round magazine for a higher rate of fire than the standard rifle version (whose 30-round magazines work fine, too).

The AUG S.A., like the standard rifle, also has a 20-inch barrel but is limited to semiautomatic fire only. Intended mostly for private sale, this is the type most commonly found in the U.S., although it remains quite rare, thanks to an executive order signed in 1989 banning its importation into America except for official police use.

The AUG is a delight to handle, being both well-balanced and easy to shoot. Even on fully-automatic fire setting, this rifle is controllable and, when fired in short bursts, capable of good accuracy. In semiautomatic fire, it's one of the most accurate .223 caliber rifles ever made, including such competitors as Colt and Ruger. In the more than 20 years since it first came into use, the AUG has established an excellent service record. Accurate, portable and utterly reliable, it ranks among the finest .223 caliber rifles ever built.

STEYR AUG

	AUG
Overall Length	31.1 inches
Barrel Length	20.0 inches
Weight	7.9 pounds
Years Produced	1977-present
Caliber & Capacity	.223 (5.56x45mm) – AUG, AUG HBAR and AUG S.A. only/30 or 42 rounds 9x19mm (9mm Parabellum) – AUG Para only/25 or 32 rounds

Winchester Model 63

Thanks to the joint efforts of the U.S. Repeating Arms Company (or USRAC, which is the current licensee for Winchester firearms) and the Miroku Company of Japan, the status of the Model 63 has changed from that of an out-of-production classic model to that of a model currently in production. Miroku has been building the revived Model 63 in Japan since 1997, while USRAC has provided licensing and technical assistance to Miroku. It has also handled advertising and sales in the United States.

The Model 63 is actually a descendant of Winchester's first semiautomatic rimfire rifle design, the Model 1903. Designed by Thomas Crossley Johnson, an up-and-coming young firearms engineer at a time when John M. Browning was at the height of his own brilliant career, Winchester's Model 1903 provided ample proof of Johnson's genius as well. Because Browning had worked with Winchester for 15 years and had given them many designs, much of Johnson's ingenuity was in figuring out ways to circumvent the many patents credited to Browning. Johnson succeeded admirably in creating an original design that offered both efficiency and beauty.

Unfortunately, Winchester's decision to chamber the Model 1903 for the company's own .22 Winchester rimfire cartridge (similar in performance and size to the .22 Long Rifle but not interchangeable with it) definitely hurt sales and frustrated consumers. Winchester finally discontinued the Model '03 in 1932 after a production run of about 126,000 units. It then introduced the Model 63, chambering the popular .22 Long Rifle cartridge. It was Winchester's first semiautomatic

The Winchester Model 63's long-barreled look is the result of a change made in 1936, when the barrel length was increased by three inches, from 20 to 23 inches, improving the rifle's balance and handling.

rifle made to handle that round. Manufactured from 1933 to 1958, the Model 63 became an important part of Winchester's product line, with total production reaching an estimated 174,692. Today, original Model 63s are a collector's item, especially in the shorter 20-inch barrel configuration (discontinued in 1936).

In 1997, the Model 63 was introduced in its revived form, following the lines of the original version, but with a few subtle changes inside and out made primarily for the sake of manufacturing convenience. Hence, few interchangeable parts exist between the old and new Model 63s. The new version, however, has retained all the old Model 73's excellent handling and charm. Incidentally, Miroku's high standards of rifle manufacture have not generally received the admiration they should. Having worked with Charles Daly, FN and Browning for many years, as well as developing a number of firearms on its own, Miroku has

The Winchester Model 63 includes a takedown feature, which enables shooters to disassemble the rifle into two pieces for cleaning and storage. Disassembly begins by unloading the magazine, then opening the breech to unload the firing chamber.

By loosening the large knurled screw at the end of the receiver, the Winchester Model 63 is divided into two pieces as shown. Note how much longer the barrel/forearm is compared with the receiver/buttstock assembly.

In testing for accuracy, the Winchester Model 63 turned in an amazing record. Point of aim was the exact center of the target—and that's where the rifle placed its bullets.

become adept at manufacturing quality firearms designs. Those who have handled or fired a Miroku-made rifle are well aware of that fact.

Like most semiautomatic rifles chambered for the .22 Long Rifle cartridge, the Model 63 employs a simple blowback mechanism. The weight of the breech is enough to hold the action shut until the bullet has left the barrel, after which the automatic reloading sequence can resume. Like many other .22 caliber self-loading rifles, the Model 63 loads from a tubular magazine (capacity: 10 rounds) located in the buttstock. The rifle's most recognizable feature is its operating sleeve. It serves as a charging handle with which to cycle the bolt before firing the first shot. It can also be used to hold the bolt open. The operating sleeve is located where tubular magazines often appear in other rifles, but the access port for the Model 62's tubular magazine is readily apparent in the buttstock—exactly the same as the classic Auto-22. The Model 63 also has a takedown mechanism, which means the shooter can divide the rifle into two parts for easy carrying and storage. A large, knurled knob at the rear of the receiver allows the shooter to separate the rear assembly (trigger and buttstock) from the front position (barrel, forend and action) of the rifle. Unlike the Auto-22, in which each half is roughly the same length, the disassembled barrel/forend and action of the Model 63 is considerably longer than the rear portion.

Handling the man-sized Model 63 has always been a pleasure, especially with the longer 23-inch barrel (standard since 1936). Shooters who are accustomed to the bolt handle protruding from the receiver's right side may take a while to get used to the Model 63's bolt handle that protrudes from the receiver's right side. This can be overcome with practice; moreover, the gun's profile is sleeker because of this arrangement. The test Model 63 was fast on target and extremely accurate for a .22. The sights-—a bead front and an open-notch adjustable rear—are appropriate for the period during which Winchester first introduced the rifle, and they are certainly adequate today at the 50-yard ranges at which shooters and gunwriters traditionally sight-in and test .22LR caliber rifles. For those who prefer a scope, the rifle comes with a grooved receiver top.

I found this rifle's accuracy absolutely outstanding: 3-shot benchrested groups fired from 50 yards grouped as small as 0.60 inches using several different brands of ammunition. Even the largest groups printed 1.4 inches or less, making the Model 63 one of the most accurate .22 caliber rifle tested for this book. Its accuracy was all the more gratifying since most rifles that disassemble into two halves are generally less accurate than rifles that don't. Nevertheless, the Model 63 easily outshot all competing rimfire rifles.

Miroku makes the Model 63 in three variants. The Grade I rifle is a relatively plain model, but the materials and workmanship are excellent. In its original form, it featured a grayed steel receiver with subdued engraving and an uncheckered walnut stock. Current Model 63 Grade I variants have high-polish blued receivers without engraving and smooth walnut stocks that are still devoid of checkering. Miroku also makes the Model 63 in a High Grade variant, featuring a stock made from select walnut with added checkering on the pistol grip and forend. Elaborate game scenes with gold

In testing, the Winchester Model 63 displayed remarkable consistency from one ammunition brand to the next. Self-loading rifles chambered for the .22 Long Rifle rimfire round rarely do this.

Although the revived modern Winchester Model 63 did its best work with standard .22 Long Rifle ammunition, it did not especially like the hyper-velocity CCI "Stinger" round. But even this group is almost perfectly centered on the target. Despite being the worst 50-yard target shot made with the test rifle, this 1.4-inch effort is still tighter and better placed on the target than could be done with most rifles.

accents are engraved on the flat-sided receiver. While the styling of the Model 63 looks dated, many old-timers desire it for nostalgia's sake, just as the Remington Nylon 66 still appeals to many (including the author) as an emblem of long-gone youth. Performance-wise, the Model 63 more than holds its own against any of the more modern .22 caliber semiautomatic rifles. I welcome the return of this classic rifle design to full production and predict it will gather a whole new generation of admirers like myself.

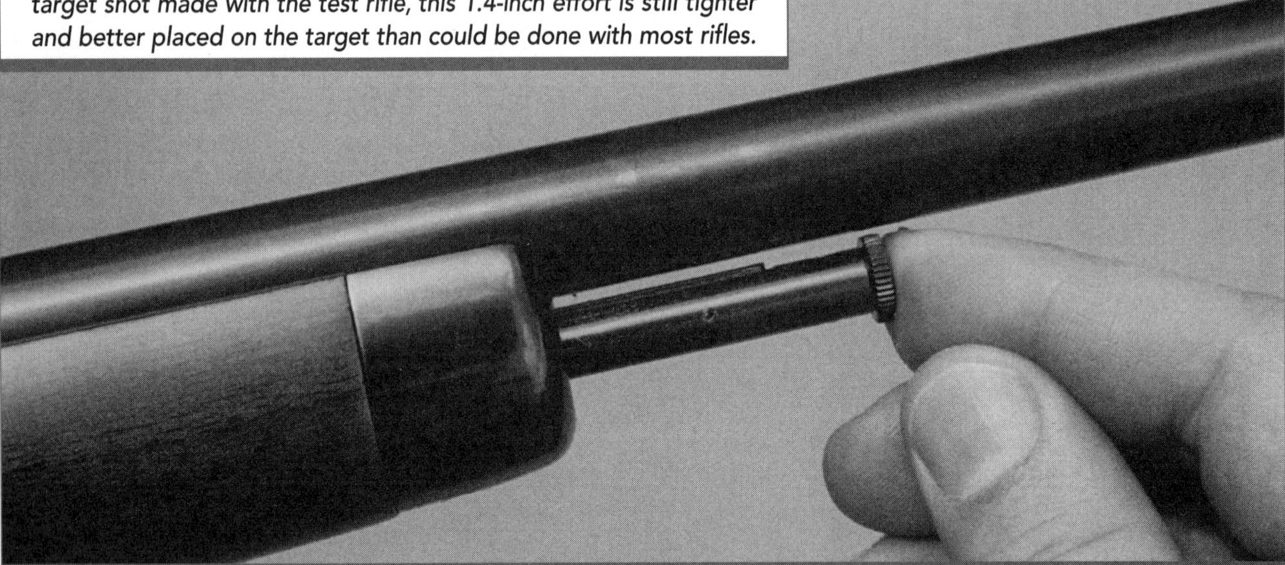

The Winchester Model 63 has a cocking sleeve or plunger located in the forearm underneath the barrel. Winchester used this device to avoid infringing on a patent held by John Browning.

WINCHESTER MODEL 63

	MODEL 63
Overall Length	39.1 inches
Barrel Length	23.0 inches
Weight	6.3 pounds
Years Produced	see text
Caliber/Capacity	.22 Long Rifle/10 rounds

Zastava (Yugoslav) Model 90

When Yugoslavia introduced its AKM rifle variant in 1970 as the M70, it became (and remains) that country's service rifle. In semiautomatic form only, it was exported for several years into the United States. When the U.S. government banned the importation of the Model 90, Mitchell Arms was left with a warehouse full of them. Forced to make some changes, the importer replaced the fixed teakwood stock and separate pistol grip of the original M70 with a plastic, fake woodgrain, thumbhole-style stock. The blonde-colored plastic "woodgrain" buttstock, complete with unnecessary rubber recoil pad, doesn't come close to matching the much darker wooden handguard made from high-quality teak. Additionally, the magazine's capacity was reduced from 20 rounds to 5 by pinning the follower. And finally, the M-70 markings were crudely obliterated and replaced by "M-90."

The basic mechanism has remained, though, and the Yugoslav AKM is still regarded as one of the most accurate variants ever, thanks in large measure to an unusually heavy receiver

The Model 70 Kalashnikov rifle has appeared in both fixed- and folding-stock versions. The one shown is a commercial version modified with a pistol grip and muzzle brake based on the Soviet AK-74.

With the folding stock secreted underneath the receiver, the Zastava Model 70 is less than 28 inches long.

The Zastava Model 70's folding stock is a bit too short for the average-sized adult male shooter. It forces him to scrunch up at the shoulder when firing.

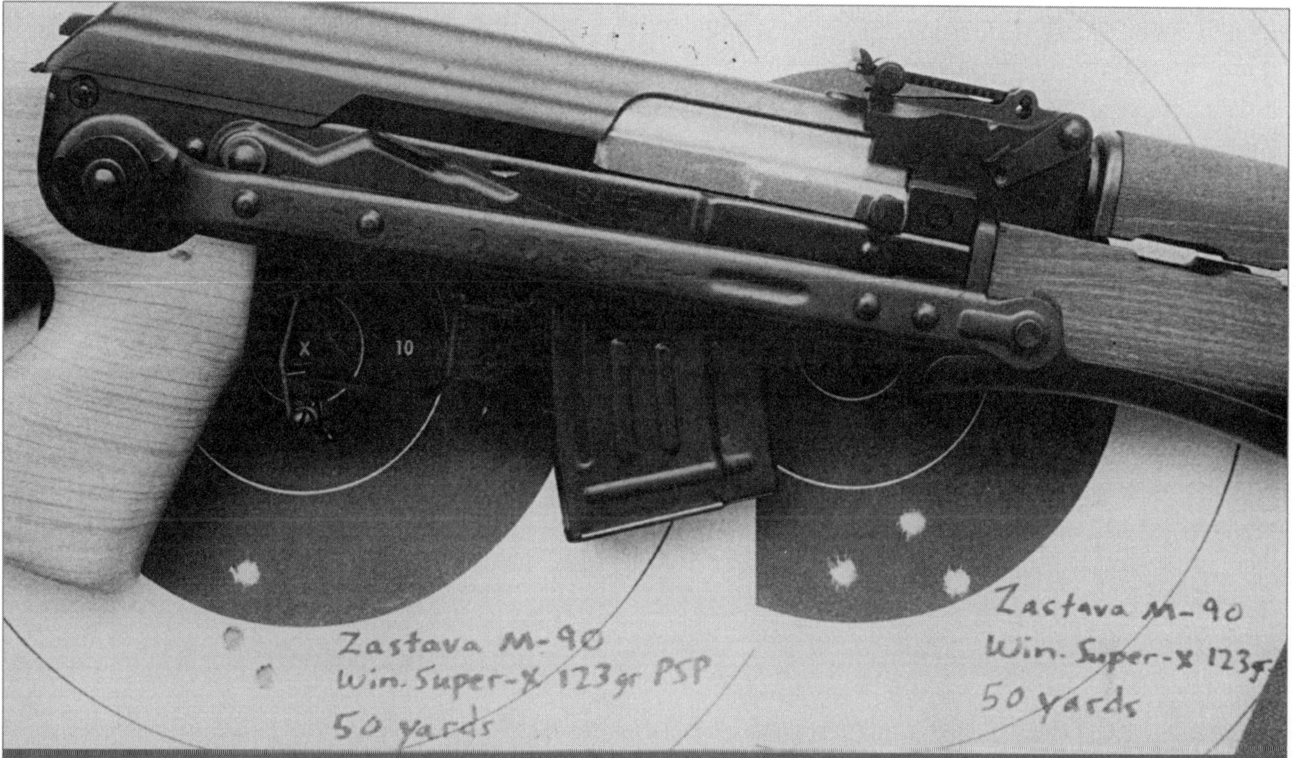

The Zastava Model 90 is highly accurate for an AK-type rifle. These 50-yard offhand groups are centered close to point of aim in the six-o'clock hold.

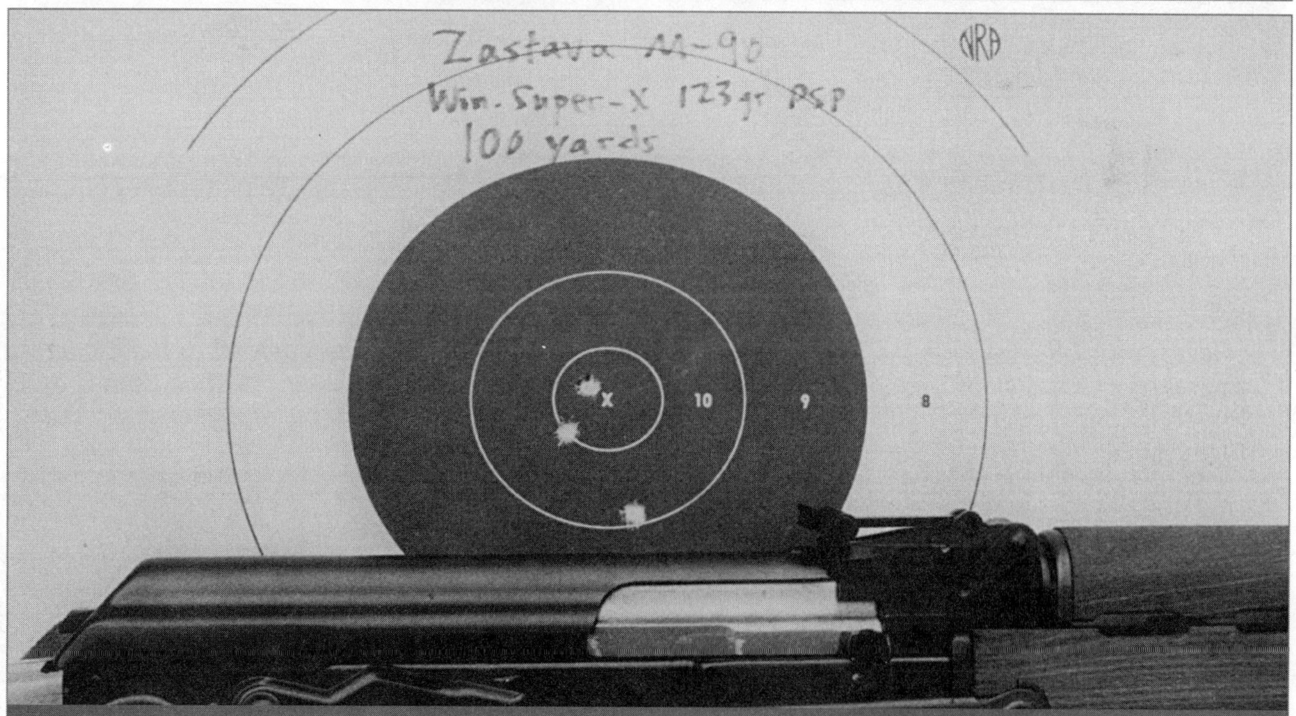

This well-centered target was shot with the Zastava Model 90 from a 100-yard benchrest position using top-quality U.S. commercial ammunition. It measures only 1.7 inches.

cover made of thicker sheet steel than usual. This increases the rigidity of the action—always helpful to accuracy—while increasing the overall weight of the rifle. From a seated benchrest at 100 yards I have fired 3-shot target groups measuring as little as 1.7 inches across with a Yugoslav M-90 using top-quality ammunition of recent U.S. manufacture. Other groups fired under comparable conditions using inferior Chinese-made ammunition usually added an inch or more to the pattern. These test results are considerably better than other AK variants. For shooters who are serious about improving accuracy, the M-90 probably remains the best AK variant ever made, despite its rather unsightly appearance.

Folding-stock AK-type assault rifles like the Zastava Model 70 (top) might be regarded as the modern equivalent of the famous "Tommy Gun" (bottom). The advantage of the AK over the Thompson is the AK's rifle cartridge which lends much better striking power, range and bullet penetration than Thompson's .45 ACP pistol round.

YUGOSLAV M-90 ("ZASTAVA")

	M-90
Overall Length	36.5 inches
Barrel Length	16.0 inches
Weight	9.5 pounds
Years Produced	see text
Caliber/Capacity	7.61x39mm/5 rounds

Appendices:

I. Integral (Iron Sights)

II. Scoping A Rifle

I. Integral (Iron Sights)

If a rifle has sights attached to it, these usually take the form of a front sight mounted near the muzzle and a rear sight mounted around the breech (either on the barrel ahead of the receiver or further back, close to the shooter). These attached, integral sights are sometimes called "iron sights."

Front sights often take the form of a thin blade in the shape of an inverted V, sometimes placed on top of a ramp. This is called a "barleycorn" sight. Its trailing edge (the portion facing the shooter's eye) may be smooth or with serrations meant to suppress reflections that might distract the shooter. Another type of front sight often fitted to rifles is a simple vertical post. While less precise than a barleycorn, it is sturdier and less likely to malfunction when struck by a blow to the rifle. For added protection, these sights often are protected by a rounded "hood" or by raised protective "ears" on either side. Still another front sight is the bead type, popular on older target rifles but used on some modern types, notably those built by Remington. The bead is often made of metal in a contrasting color, sometimes silver, or

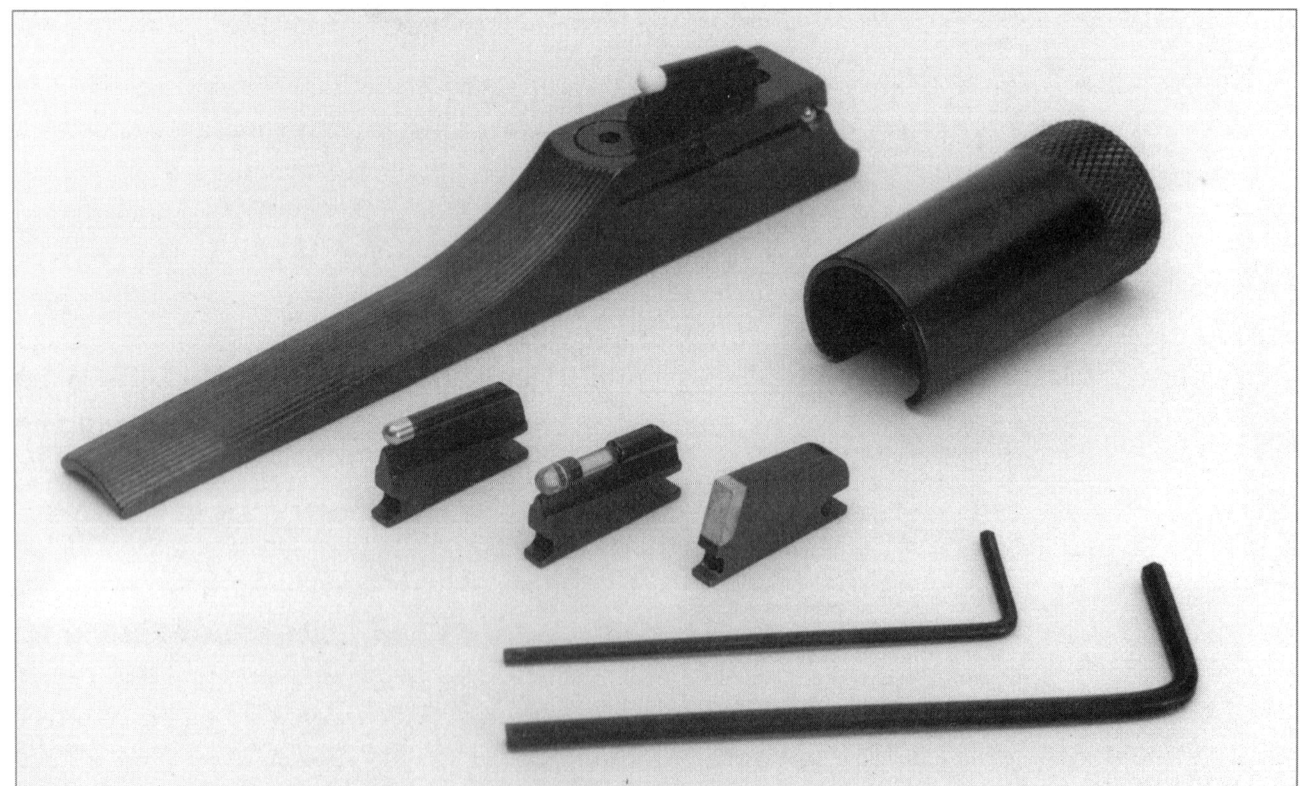

One option for shooters who wish to retrofit iron sights onto a new rifle is to obtain a universal ramp front sight from New England Custom Gun Service (Plainfield, NH).

The rear sight often allow shooters to adjust for changes in windage or elevation caused by their use of different types of ammunition. Sliding the rear sight of this Remington Model Seven further up the ramp will cause the rifle to shoot higher.

painted white or some other bright color to attract the shooter's eye.

Rear sights take several forms. A nonadjustable open notch, similar to the rear sight of a pistol is the simplest form. The notch can take either a V-shape or a U-shape. Even rifles fitted for telescopic sights have an open-notch rear sight fitted, often in folding form so it can be pushed forward and out of the way once a telescopic sight is in use. Because rifles can fire accurately at ranges of several hundred yards or more—far beyond what the typical handgun can do—iron-sighted rifles are generally available with more advanced rear sights. The more sophisticated, open-notch rear sights contain provisions for making adjustments in elevation. In its simplest form, this adjustable rear sight invokes a "leaf and elevator" configuration, by which the shooter raises the rear sight using a series of steps as the range increases. The higher the shooter raises the rear sight, the greater distance at which the rifle is sighted in. Leaf and elevator sights are especially popular on U.S.-made rifles, often appearing on .22 caliber rifles and lever-action carbines. An even more involved type of adjustable, open-notch rear sight is the tangent sight, which was especially popular on military rifles of the early 1900s. The leaf sight slides along a ramp to adjust for various distances, in some cases out to several thousand yards. For close-range work, many of these tangent-sighted rifles include a "battle sight" setting at the base of the ramp.

Another type of rear sight often fitted to rifles is the aperture or "peep" sight. Placed far back on the breech, close to the shooter's eye, this type is popular on military rifles and, to a lesser extent, on rifles intended for sporting use. The greatest advantage of a peep sight over an open rear sight is that the shooter can simply peer through the narrow aperture and concentrate on the front sight

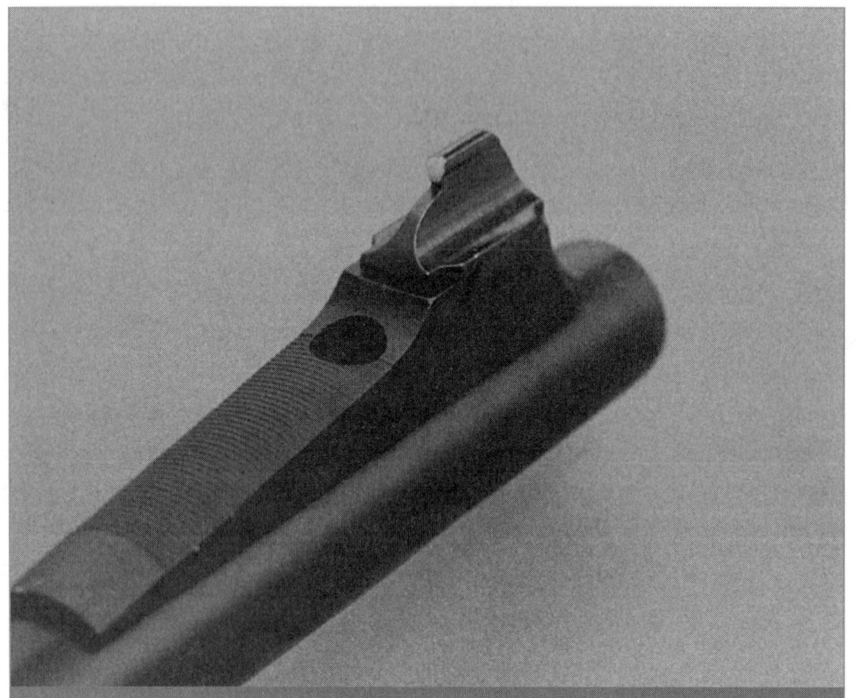

To help guide the shooter's eye to the target many commercial rifles have a dot or bead of some kind on the trailing edge of the front sight. Shown here is the front sight of a Remington Model Seven.

lateral ("windage") and elevation adjustments. In most cases involving iron sights, windage and elevation adjustments are made from the rear sight. Here's the simple rule of thumb: if the rifle is off the mark, the rear sight should be moved in whichever direction the shooter desires. If the rifle is shooting low and to the right, instead of up and to the left, then the rear sight must be adjusted accordingly. When adjusting the *front* sight of a rifle (where such adjustments are possible) then the front sight should be moved *opposite* the direction in which the shooter wishes his shots to fall.

and target. With the open sight, the shooter must focus on three things at once—the rear sight notch, its alignment with the front sight, and the target. It's physically impossible to focus on all three at once, especially for older shooters whose eyes can't change focus as rapidly as they once did. While the aperture rear sight offers less precision, it's probably a better choice for middle-aged to elderly shooters; moreover, it tends to be sturdier than other types of forward-mounted open notch rear sights.

Because of the distances involved, iron sights fitted to rifles generally have a provision whereby shooters can make azimuth or

Military rifle sights include protective "ears," or even a complete hood, around the front sight to help prevent damage, as shown in this photo mounted on a FAL 7.62x51mm rifle.

II. Scoping A Rifle

A telescopic sight or scope offers rifle shooters several advantages over iron sights as well as some disadvantages. Because a telescopic sight magnifies the target image, it ensures more accurate shooting out to greater ranges than iron sights can offer. A telescopic sight also collects more light than a shooter's eye can, enabling him to shoot longer before dawn and into the twilight darkness than shooters with iron sights.

Among the disadvantages of telescopic sights over iron sights is their inherent lack of sturdiness. That's why many military organizations restrict scopes to specialized troops, such as snipers, in the belief that the arduous duty most combat soldiers undergo can quickly put

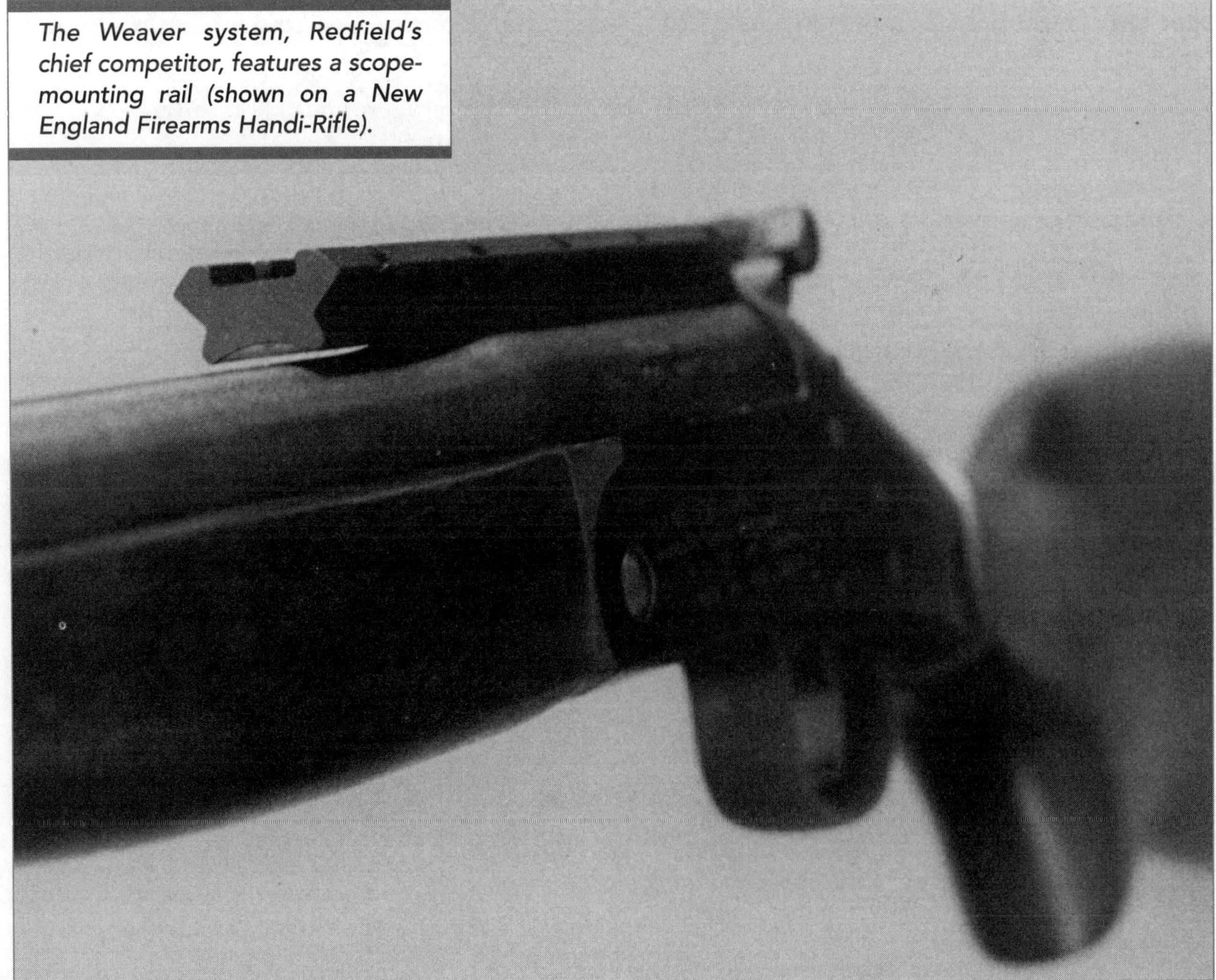

The Weaver system, Redfield's chief competitor, features a scope-mounting rail (shown on a New England Firearms Handi-Rifle).

most scopes out of commission. Telescopic sights also tend to encourage shooters to fixate on the target. With scopes that magnify well beyond the naked eye (generally anything greater than 2.5x), the shooter must close the weak eye to concentrate on the image provided by the scope. This greatly restricts the shooter's field of view, forcing him to concentrate solely on the target instead of what is around it or behind it. This narrow field of view and target fixation can not only create serious problems for soldiers, it can easily become vital factors in a hunt as well. One solution is to include both iron sights and a compatible scope-mounting system on all rifles (with the possible exception of long-range varminters). Regrettably, it's difficult to mount a scope on many types of rifles, especially modern ones that have no iron sights at all, forcing shooters to mount a scope. Having a rifle with no sights at all is really not an option for shooters who plan to hit anything.

After placing the scope onto the bottom rings of the scope mount, tighten the top rings using the tool provided.

Once both rings of a Redfield scope-mounting system have been turned into position, remove the top of each ring prior to placing the scope on the rifle.

Installing a telescopic sight is fairly involved, but each step is not all that difficult to learn.

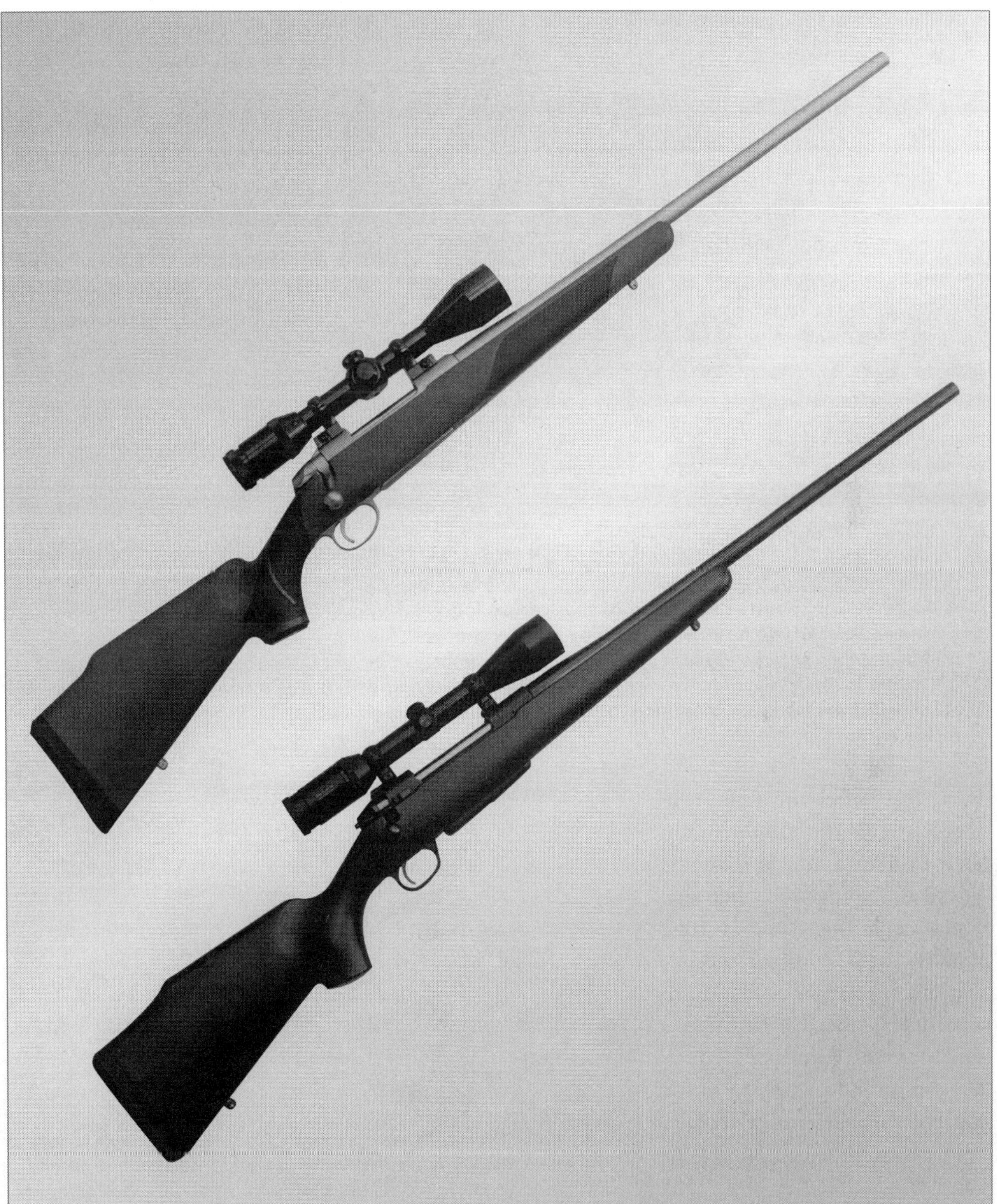

The rifle/scope combination on the left is a SAKO Model 75 with Swarovski Optik scope, while the one on the right is a SAKO Model TRG-S with a "Buck" scope made by Millett.

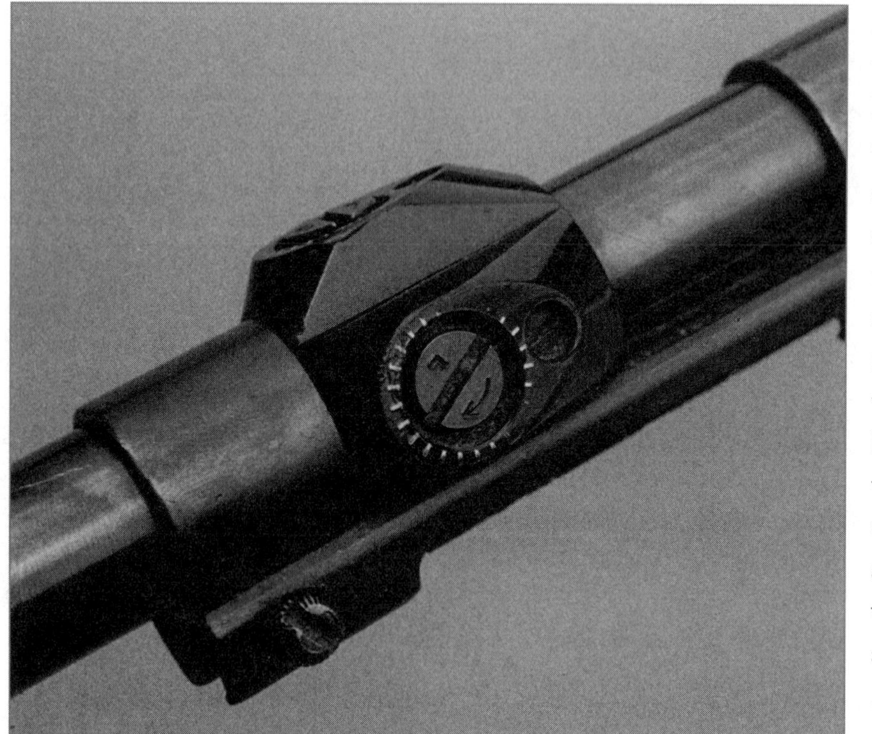

A tip-off mount consists of two clamps that can be loosened by screws and placed into position in matching receiver grooves. The clamps are then secured in place by tightening the clamps. A tip-off mount is especially effective with rifles having relatively little recoil, which explains why rifles firing the rimfire .22 Long Rifle cartridge are so popular.

First, let's select the right telescopic sight/rifle combination, then we'll learn how to make the physical connection between a telescopic sight and a rifle. Finally, we'll consider various way a scope can be sighted in to a particular rifle. The first step is to choose the right scope. Much depends on how you plan to use a particular rifle. For example, a Scout Rifle intended mostly for short-range shooting calls for a low-powered scope (2.5x or less); but a rifle used primarily for long-range varmint shooting requires a scope that can go up to 9 or 10 power, or even more. It's also important to consider the physical dimensions of a rifle and a scope. With a Scout Rifle, a long eye relief will enable you to load the rifle through the top of the open action. Long eye relief is also the order of the day when firing high-powered, hard-kicking cartridges. You don't want a scope smacking you in the eye every time you fire a shot. A compact scope probably won't work well with a long action rifle made to fire the .30-'06 or one of the magnum

Scopes containing adjustments for elevation (corrections up and down) and windage (corrections left and right) must be "sighted in" once they're placed on a rifle. Note the elevation correction control for a Tasco 4-power scope mounted on a Remington Nylon 66 rifle in .22LR caliber.

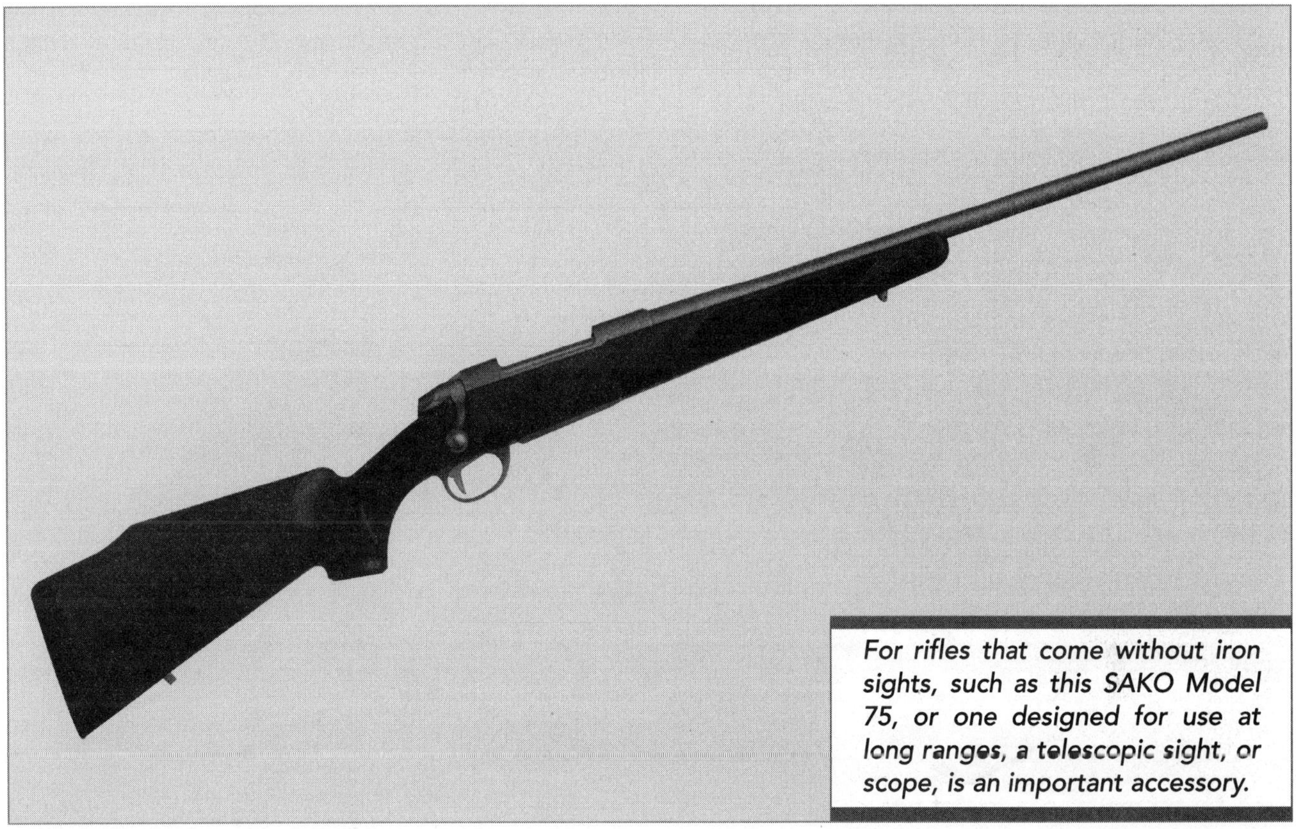

For rifles that come without iron sights, such as this SAKO Model 75, or one designed for use at long ranges, a telescopic sight, or scope, is an important accessory.

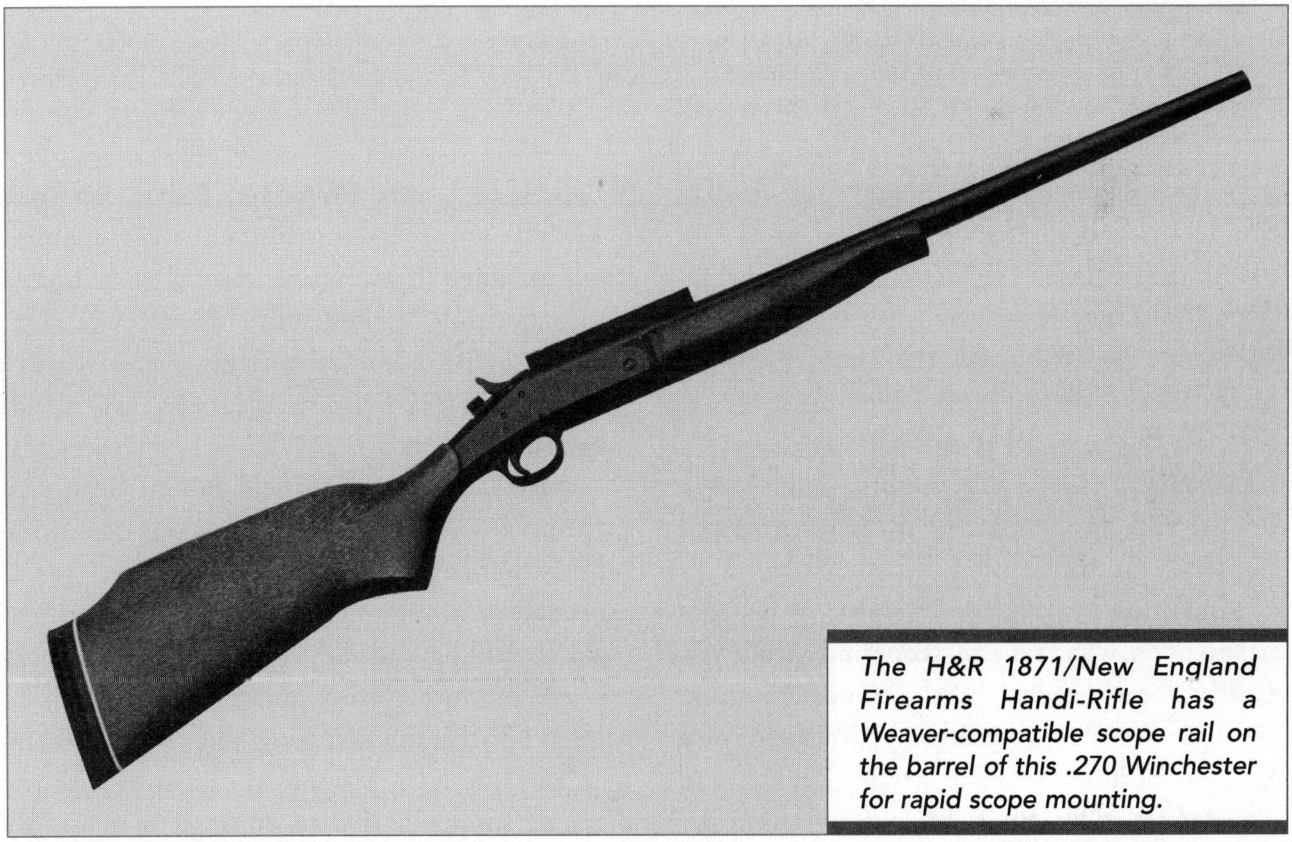

The H&R 1871/New England Firearms Handi-Rifle has a Weaver-compatible scope rail on the barrel of this .270 Winchester for rapid scope mounting.

Receivers on rimfire rifles frequently are grooved on top to accommodate a "tip-off" mount. This Remington Model 597 .22 WMR rifle not only includes a grooved receiver top, it is also drilled and tapped for conventional scope mounts.

cartridges. The scope may be too short to span the action and line up properly. The size of the objective lens is a factor too. An overly-large objective lens may dictate mounting the scope so high that the shooter cannot place his cheek against the stock and still see through the scope. The point is: Stick with a tried-and-true scope/rifle combination; or, if in doubt, seek the assistance of an experienced hunter or gunsmith.

Attaching a telescopic sight to a rifle depends on what type of scope mounting system has been selected. The two most common systems are those made by Redfield and Weaver. Both systems are strong, durable and well-tested. The Redfield system—used by Bausch & Lomb, Browning, Burris, Leupold, Millett and other manufacturers—features a dovetailed front scope mount that rotates into position, locking onto the receiver. This system enjoys an advantage over Weaver's scope primarily because of its fast, easy windage adjustments.

Installation of a Redfield mount begins by cleaning and degreasing the scope-mounting holes that have been drilled into the receiver. If no holes exist, a gunsmith should be consulted about drilling and tapping them. Next, set the scope mounting bases on the receiver, lining them up with the matching holes on the receiver, and fasten the bases to the receiver with the screws supplied. If they don't seem to fit, try another screw. Once the bases have been screwed into the receiver, assemble the front scope ring. This can be easily done by placing the upper and lower halves of the ring around a wooden dowel of the proper width (usually 1 inch or 30mm, depending on the scope size); then, using the dowel, rotate the front scope ring into its matching dovetail in the scope mount. Warning: Even though the telescopic sight seems to fit the scope ring, *don't use the scope itself to turn the front ring onto (or off) a Redfield-style scope mount.* Using a scope as a tool this way can ruin it in no time. A scope often costs as much as a rifle, so it makes more sense to use an inexpensive wooden dowel as a tightening tool.

With the front scope ring in place, attach the rear ring to the base by loosening the windage adjustment screws on either side. Once you're able to place the scope ring between them, re-tighten the windage adjustment screws evenly on each side. Now, remove the top of the front ring and place the scope on top of the front and rear lower ring halves. Check to see if the scope and rings are in proper alignment so that the scope tube lies flat and parallel to the rings. Place the top ring halves over the scope tube and tighten them evenly (using the small screws provided).

The Weaver system—used by B-Square, Burris, Tasco and several others—has an advantage over the Redfield system because its scope,

The Steyr SBS comes with its own proprietary scope-mounting system. It works easily and allows the shooter to scope his rifle in a minimal amount of time.

Always turn a Redfield-type scope mount into position with the aid of a wooden dowel (as shown above and below). Never use the scope itself.

rings and all can be removed from the rifle in a matter of seconds simply by unscrewing the rings from the base. On the other hand, the Weaver system has no capability for windage adjustments beyond the scope's own internal mechanism. Ordinarily, this would be no problem. When boresighting the rifle [see below] the scope itself will compensate for any windage adjustments that may be necessary. But Murphy's Law being what it is, you may discover one day that the rifle you bought for that once-in-a lifetime African safari isn't compatible with your telescopic sight and mounting system. You'll wish then that you had gotten a Redfield-compatible mount instead. The one-piece Weaver mount is attached by screwing it into holes drilled in the receiver. Next, scope rings are attached to the mount by tightening the clamp-type attachments on either side of the rings until they are firmly positioned (a coin can be used in the field for quick scope changes if necessary, but it's a good idea to have a screwdriver of the correct size to do this). Tighten slowly, a little at a time, alternating sides until the clamps are snug and the bottom halves of the rings are well seated. Finally, set the sight into the bottom halves of the scope rings, with the top halves placed onto the bottom halves, and screw then together.

At least one scope-mounting system—the Pos-Align rings from Burris—work with either the Redfield or Weaver system. There are also several proprietary systems used by different rifle companies that differ in minor respects from either the Redfield or the Weaver system. For most shooters, these differences will be a matter of minor or academic concern only; but if you own or work with many different types of rifles (as I did in writing this book), the differences can become an annoyance. For those who've built a large rifle collection serious thought should be given to this matter of scope mountings and compatibility before each purchase. But if your intention is to mount a scope and simply leave that combination together on a more or less permanent basis, then any differences in scope-mounting systems shouldn't offer any difficulties.

From a standpoint of which telescopic sight you select, it really makes no difference whether you select a Redfield or a Weaver-type scope mounting system. The important factor is whether your scope rings are the same diameter as the scope tube. Maddeningly, these diameters do differ. Some are one-inch (25mm) in diameter or smaller, some are 30mm in diameter, and some are in between.

Sighting in a telescopic sight determines when the scope and the rifle bore—i.e., the path the bullet takes once it leaves the barrel—are in line with one another. If the scope lined up without misalignment when it was first mounted, chances are it's already close to proper scope/bore alignment. While there are specialized tools available for boresighting a rifle, there is a simple technique that requires no special tools beyond the rifle and scope combination itself. Boresight the rifle by taking it to the firing range with the scope attached as detailed above. Remove the bolt. Set up the rifle on a secure benchrest. Look down-range, *through the bore*, at a target 100 yards in the distance. Without moving the rifle, look through the telescopic sight, adjusting the windage and elevation screws until the cross hairs are centered at the exact same spot observed through the bore. The rifle is now boresighted with that scope at that particular distance. If for some reason the scope's internal windage and elevation adjustments prove inadequate, there's a problem with the scope mount. Recheck the mounts and bases for tightness and proper alignment. If they are still too far out of alignment, you may need to add shims, or even take off some metal, before the mounts and bases are properly aligned. At that point, I'd advise checking with a gunsmith before trying anything drastic.

If you prefer a more high-tech approach to sighting in with a scope, there's a special boresighting device called a collimator. Most companies specializing in scopes and mounts sell devices of this kind. The most impressive boresighting aid, however, is a laser sold by B Square. Obviously, it's going to cost more than the simple, no-tools method described above, but for certain applications—the hunt of a lifetime, say—the investment may well be worthwhile.

The Steyr SBS scope-mounting system allows quick removal and installation of the scope.

Index

C

D

E

F

G

H

I

J